The Constitution of Capital

Also by Riccardo Bellofiore

MARXIAN ECONOMICS: A Reappraisal (2 vols)

The Constitution of Capital

Essays on Volume I of Marx's *Capital*

Edited by

Riccardo Bellofiore
Department of Economics
University of Bergamo, Italy

and

Nicola Taylor
Department of Economics
Murdoch University, Australia

First published 2004 by
PALGRAVE MACMILLAN
Houndmills, Basingstoke, Hampshire RG21 6XS and
175 Fifth Avenue, New York, N.Y. 10010
Companies and representatives throughout the world

PALGRAVE MACMILLAN is the global academic imprint of the Palgrave
Macmillan division of St. Martin's Press, LLC and of Palgrave Macmillan Ltd.
Macmillan® is a registered trademark in the United States, United Kingdom
and other countries. Palgrave is a registered trademark in the European
Union and other countries.

ISBN 1–4039–0798–6

This book is printed on paper suitable for recycling and made from fully
managed and sustained forest sources.

A catalogue record for this book is available from the British Library.

Library of Congress Cataloging-in-Publication Data
International Symposium on Marxian Theory (12th : 2002 : Università di Bergamo)
    The constitution of capital : essays on volume I of Marx's Capital / edited
by Riccardo Bellofiore and Nicola Taylor.
        p.   cm.
    Revised versions of contributions first presented at the 12th International
Symposium on Marxian Theory (ISMT) held at the University of Bergamo
in July 2002.
    "Intended as a companion to : The circulation of capital: essays on volume II
of Marx's 'Capital', edited by Christopher Arthur & Geert Reuten, Macmillan
1998, and The culmination of capital : essays on volume III of Marx's 'Capital',
edited by Martha Campbell & Geert Reuten, Palgrave Macmillan 2002"--P¨
    Includes bibliographical references and index.
    ISBN 1–4039–0798–6
    1. Marx, Karl, 1818–1883. Kapital—Congresses.   2. Capital—Congresses.
    3. Marxian economics—Congresses.   I. Bellofiore, R. (Riccardo)   II. Taylor,
Nicola, 1961–   III. Title.
    HB501.M371575 2002
    335.4′1—dc21   2003053614

10   9   8   7   6   5   4   3   2   1
13   12   11   10   09   08   07   06   05   04

Printed and bound in Great Britain by
Antony Rowe Ltd, Chippenham and Eastbourne

Contents

Preface

The essays in this collection on *The Constitution of Capital* address specific themes in Volume I of Marx's opus. Although they are arranged in an order that conforms to the structure of *Capital*, Volume I, they can be read independently. The essays make use of the most recent scholarship on Marx's work and are intended for specialists in the field as well as graduate students in the history of economic thought, political economy and philosophy.

As the title suggests, the collection is also intended as a companion to *The Circulation of Capital: Essays on Volume II of Marx's 'Capital'*, edited by Christopher Arthur and Geert Reuten, Macmillan 1998, and *The Culmination of Capital: Essays on Volume III of Marx's 'Capital'*, edited by Martha Campbell and Geert Reuten, Palgrave Macmillan 2002.

Together, these collections are the result of intensive research in the field of Marxian theory undertaken by the participants in the *International Symposium on Marxian Theory* (ISMT), a week-long working conference held annually since 1991. These meetings have stimulated the publication of many individual papers and a number of collective books in addition to the ones already mentioned. These include two books on Marx's method: *Marx's Method in 'Capital'*, edited by Fred Moseley, Humanities Press 1993, and *New Investigations of Marx's Method*, edited by Fred Moseley and Martha Campbell, Humanities Press 1997.

The essays contained in the current collection were first discussed at the 12th ISMT held at the University of Bergamo, in July 2002. This and the further cross-refereeing of the revised versions ensure the quality and coherence of the collection. We are most grateful to the Department of Economics of the University of Bergamo, which sponsored the conference, and to Amanda Watkins of Palgrave for her patient and continuing support. We also thank two anonymous referees for their stimulating comments.

Riccardo Bellofiore
Nicola Taylor

Notes on the Contributors

Christopher J. Arthur, formerly of the University of Sussex, has published in numerous journals and books. He is the author of: *The New Dialectic and Marx's 'Capital'* (2002) and *Dialectics of Labour: Marx and his Relation to Hegel* (1986). He edited and introduced: *The German Ideology* (1970; revised 1974); *Law and Marxism* (third imprint, 1989); *Engels Today: A Centenary Appreciation* (1996); and (with Geert Reuten) *The Circulation of Capital: Essays on Volume II of Marx's 'Capital'* (1998). He has also published (abridged, with an introduction) *Marx's 'Capital': A Student Edition* (1992).

Riccardo Bellofiore is Professor of Economics at the University of Bergamo, Italy. He wrote a book on the Italian Marxist scholar Claudio Napoleoni (1991), and edited a collection on Piero Sraffa (1986) – both in Italian. He acted as guest editor of a special issue of the *International Journal of Political Economy* on 'Marxian Theory: The Italian Debate' (1997). He also edited: *Marxian Economics: A Reappraisal* (1998); *Global Money, Capital Restructuring and the Changing Patterns of Labour* (1999); (with Mario Baldassarri) 'Classical and Marxian Political Economy: A Debate on Claudio Napoleoni's Views', a special issue of the *Rivista di Politica Economica* (1999); and (with Piero Ferri) two volumes on Hyman Minsky's economics – *Financial Keynesianism and Market Instability* and *Financial Fragility and Investment in the Capitalist Economy* (2001).

Martha Campbell is Assistant Professor of Economics at Potsdam College, State University of New York. She received her PhD in Economics from the New School for Social Research in 1991. She has edited (with Fred Moseley) *New Investigations of Marx's Method* (1997) and (with Geert Reuten) *The Culmination of Capital: Essays on Volume III of Marx's 'Capital'* (2002).

Fred Moseley is Professor of Economics at Mount Holyoke College (Massachusetts, USA). He received a BS in Mathematics from Stanford University in 1968 and a PhD in Economics from the University of Massachusetts in 1980. He was the Book Review Editor of the *Review of Radical Political Economics* from 1986 to 1995. He organized the ISMT in

1991, and edited its first two books, *Marx's Method in Capital: A Reexamination* and (with Martha Campbell) *New Investigations of Marx's Method.* His other books include *The Falling Rate of Profit in the Postwar United States Economy* (1991).

Patrick Murray is Professor of Philosophy at Creighton University, Omaha, Nebraska. He received his PhD in Philosophy of Science from St Louis University in 1979. He is the author of *Marx's Theory of Scientific Knowledge* (1988) and editor of *Reflections on Commercial Life: An Anthology of Classical Texts from Plato to the Present* (1996). His writings on Marx, Hegel, critical theory, modern philosophy and the philosophy of social science have appeared in numerous scholarly books and journals.

Geert Reuten is Associate Professor of Economics at the University of Amsterdam, teaching Methodology and History of Economics. He specializes in Marx's work, in Marxian political economy of capitalism and in systematic dialectics. With Michael Williams he wrote *Value-Form and the State: The Tendencies of Accumulation and the Determination of Economic Policy in Capitalist Society* (1989); he edited (with Christopher Arthur) *The Circulation of Capital: Essays on Volume II of Marx's 'Capital'* (1998) and (with Martha Campbell) *The Culmination of Capital: Essays on Volume III of Marx's 'Capital'* (2002).

Tony Smith is Professor of Philosophy and Political Science at Iowa State University. He received his PhD from the State University of New York at Stony Brook after graduate studies at the universities of Tübingen and Munich. He is the author of four books: *The Logic of Marx's 'Capital': Replies to Hegelian Criticisms* (1990), *The Role of Ethics in Social Theory* (1991), *Dialectical Social Theory and Its Critics: From Hegel to Analytical Marxism and Postmodernism* (1993), and *Technology and Capital in the Age of Lean Production: A Marxian Critique of the 'New Economy'* (2000).

Nicola Taylor graduated with Honours in Economic Theory and Policy from Murdoch University, Perth, Western Australia, where she is currently reading for her doctoral dissertation. Her interests are in Marx's thought, economic theories of money and systematic dialectics. She is a new member of the International Symposium on Marxian Theory and has contributed papers to two of the group's conferences.

1
Marx's *Capital I*, the Constitution of Capital: General Introduction

Nicola Taylor and Riccardo Bellofiore

The main aim of Marx's *Das Kapital: Kritik der Politischen Ökonomie* is to understand the conditions that make possible the existence and growth of capital on the basis of the exploitation of labour. Marx treated capital's 'formation' and reproduction in three volumes detailing the production of capital (Volume I), the circulation of capital (Volume II) and the unity of the 'the process as a whole' (Volume III). Of the three volumes, Marx published only the first as *Capital*, Volume I (1867). Selections from the second and third volumes were edited and sometimes interpolated by Engels who published them after Marx's death as Volume II (1885) and Volume III (1894).

That Marx's *Capital* remained an *unfinished* project springing from a *very long* writing and revision process creates enormous difficulties of interpretation which are too easily forgotten. The decades between the 1930s and the 1970s saw the first scholarly publications of some of Marx's preparation drafts for *Capital* as a whole and also for his preceding book, *Zur Kritik der Politischen Ökonomie* (1859), which was the first published attempt to treat 'commodity' and 'money' prior to *Capital I*. Most important among these publications were a new critical edition of the *Theorien über den Mehrwert* in the 1950s and 1960s (the first after

Kautsky's unscholarly edition, 1905–10[1]), the *Grundrisse der Kritik der Politischen Ökonomie* (which appeared in the 1930s and early 1940s in USSR, and in the 1950s in an edition also available in the West), the *Resultate des Unmittelbaren Produktionprozesses* (also known as *Chapter VI unpublished*, which again appeared simultaneously in German and Russian in the USSR in the 1930s and had a wider distribution after the Second World War), and a complete version of the *Ökonomische Manuskripte 1861–3*. Then, in the last two decades of the twentieth century, a new historical and critical edition of Marx's and Engels's writings in the original language, the *Marx-Engels-Gesamtausgabe* (the so-called MEGA[2]), began the task of publishing – for the first time – the complete *Manuskripte 1863–7*, and more generally all the available materials for Volume II and Volume III of *Capital*. These publications have led – and together with new materials still to be published must continue to lead – to a fundamental reappraisal of received opinion on Marx's method and theory. In the meantime, new approaches to the traditional debates about Marx's *oeuvre* have produced an abundant secondary literature, often putting forward novel answers to old questions. As a result, the twenty-first-century reader of *Capital* faces a difficult question. How are we to understand this great work in the light of its complex internal history, and in the light of the many and often conflicting attempts to reread and develop the categories of *Capital*, in particular the categories of its first volume?

The essays collected in this book contribute to a long-overdue reappraisal of this question by bringing the most recent knowledge and textual analysis to bear on core issues at the cutting edge of Marxian scholarship. Although these essays are complementary in that they follow the sequence of Marx's presentation, no attempt has been made to provide a comprehensive treatment of *Capital I*. Instead, three philosophers and five economists (none of whom consider this academic 'division of labour' within knowledge fruitful, especially when applied to the study of a full-fledged social scientist like Marx) have tackled specific themes that they consider essential to a twenty-first-century reevaluation – and/or heuristic development – of Marx's work.

1. The more rigorous version of *Theories of Surplus-value* came out first in Russian in 1954, then in the original German in 1956. The three volumes appeared again in 1965, 1967 and 1968 in the MEW by Dietz Verlag in Berlin, and in the MEGA[2] as part of the *Economic Manuscripts 1861–3*. For details of the MEW and the first and second MEGA see section 1 of this introduction.

This introduction provides an outline of the architectonic of *Capital* as a whole, beginning in the next section with an outline of the various manuscripts and editions, tracing the intricate publication history of Marx's economic work. This is followed by a general short overview of the parts of *Capital I* in relation to the other volumes, then a very brief discussion of some contemporary interpretations and reconstructions – namely, the ones that the editors consider most relevant in connecting the essays in this book with current debates on Marx. Finally, we present a preview of the essays.

1. The making of *Capital*

As with every great thinker, the scope for interpretation and reconstruction of Marx's system is enormous: the more so since his 'critique of economic categories' remained unfinished. In his lifetime Marx published, in fact, only a few works contributing to this project. However, its prehistory goes back to 1847, to the *Misère de la Philosophie* and *Lohnarbeit und Kapital* (although the text of this series of speeches was published by Engels after Marx's death they had already appeared as articles in the *Neue Rheinische Zeitung* of 1849), and even before these. Then we have the long preparation of two books, *A Contribution to a Critique of Political Economy* (1859) and *Capital*, Volume I, which came out in two German editions and a French edition edited by Marx himself (first German edition, 1867; second German edition, 1873; French edition, 1872–5). The text of another lecture, *Value, Price and Profit*, written by Marx in 1865, was published posthumously by Eleanor Marx in 1898. He continued to work on Volume II and also on Volume III of *Capital* until his death, apparently unconvinced that he had found a form suitable for final publication.[2] One of his last writings on economic issues was *Randglossen zu Adolph Wagners 'Lehrbuch des Politischen Ökonomie'* in 1880.

In our view, the fact that Marx did not publish the whole of *Capital* and died before its completion, together with the fact that this work was only a part of his overall theoretical project, presents a challenge to

---

2. In addition, a 27-year time lag between the first publications of Volume I and Volume III meant that *Capital I* was treated in the early literature as a work in itself, creating many difficulties that persist today. Just as important were the long time lags between the German publications of the three volumes and their translation and publication into English: 19 years for Volume I, 22 years for Volume II and 15 years for Volume III. On these and other issues see Reuten (2003).

historiography and textual analysis.[3] This is especially true within the English-speaking world.[4] The two main English editions of *Capital I* (1887 and 1976) were translated from the posthumous third German edition (1883) and the fourth German edition (1890), both edited not by Marx (who died in 1883) but by Engels – a third translation was provided by Eden and Cedar Paul in 1930 from the fourth German edition. Marx himself referred to three 'Books', corresponding to the current volumes. While Book I appeared on its own in 1867 as 'Volume I', it

3. Marx made many 'plans' between 1857 and 1866, while he was writing *Capital*. A list of these plans would include: one in the 1857–8 Introduction to the *Grundrisse* (1973: 108); two in the body of the *Grundrisse* (1973: 264, 275); two in letters to Lassalle (22 February and 11 March 1858, in 'Letters on *Capital*' (1983: 51, 56)); one in a letter to Engels (2 April 1858, *ibid.*: 57); one in the *Economic Manuscripts 1861–3* (in MEGA^2 II, 2: 3ff.); one as an Index written either in 1859 or 1861 for the *Grundrisse* (in MEGA^2 II, 2: 256ff.); one in a letter to Kugelmann 13 October 1866 and in *Letters on Capital*, 1983: 99). In the MEGA^2 the roman number indicates the 'Abteilung' (section), and the arabic number the 'Band' (volume), which may be composed of many 'Teile' (parts).
4. The immaturity of Marxist research in this language can be measured by the fact that most of the new primary and secondary literature coming out from MEGA^2 is almost unknown. We found no books in English to compare with the following three, which were most useful for this introduction: Alessandro Mazzone (2002, with many papers specifically devoted to MEGA^2; in particular, those by Roberto Fineschi (2002a, 2002b), by Rolf Hecker (2002) and by Hubman *et al.* (2002), to whom we owe much of our information); Roberto Fineschi (2001), who gives an insightful systematic dialectical rereading of the whole of Marx's *Capital* taking into account the new material in MEGA^2; Gérard Jorland (1995), whose first part is a long, detailed and almost complete survey of the debates on Marx as an economist from the 1880s up to the 1960s, omitting only writings in Russian and Japanese. Another testimony to the poor state of contemporary Marxian theory everywhere, but especially in the English-speaking world, is that after Rosdolsky's (1968) classic book almost nothing is known of the following debates on Marx's method in Germany. The observation is true both of the 'first wave' of the debate which began in the 1960s and 1970s before MEGA^2 (including, among others, Hans Georg Backhaus, 1969, 1992, 1997; Helmut Reichelt, 1972, 1995; Walter Tuchscherer, 1968; Vitali Vygodskij, 1967; and Schmidt, 1969), and of the 'second wave' which began in the 1980s (especially, Wolfang Jahn *et al.*, Manfred Müller, Winfried Schwarz, and again Vitali Vygodskij: see these and other works cited in Fineschi, 2002b). No informed discussion – either about the 'form' of value in relation to the 'substance' of value or about Marx having abandoned the category of capital 'in general' – can be pursued very far without taking these works into account (on this Fineschi, 2001 and its bibliography is again very useful).

seems that Marx at that time intended to publish both subsequent books (Books II and III) together in a single volume.[5]

To construct *Capital*, Volume II, Engels had to work on Marx's 'manuscripts' I–VIII, written between 1865 and 1880–1.[6] 'Manuscript' I, of 1865, he wrote, was such that nothing could be utilized, while 'Manuscripts' III and IV, of 1867–8, had versions ready to be printed out of Part One and the first chapter of Part Two, and these were partly included in his editing. 'Manuscript' II (1868–70) was the only draft more or less completed by Marx, who wrote that it should be taken as a basis for constructing the final manuscript, and it too finished in the printed version. Engels's own 1884–5 draft for this version also selected from 'Manuscripts' V–VI (1877), VII (1877–8), VIII (1880–1), plus other fragments and notebooks (1877–8).[7] This means that most of *Capital*, Volume II (1885), was composed by Marx more than ten years after most of the draft for Book III (1865), which was subsequently edited and published by Engels as *Capital*, Volume III (1894). Marx was working up until 1880–1 on a draft for Volume II and drafts for Volume III of *Capital* also date from 1871–9.[8] So, it seems crystal-clear that the last two volumes would not have appeared in their current form if edited by the author himself. Following the publication of Marx's original manuscripts in the MEGA[2], it is also clear that Engels's editing of important passages changed Marx's manuscripts, and may have sometimes distorted their meanings.[9] As Fineschi (2001) rightly suggests, this story leads to two crucial conclusions which cannot be evaded: Marx's *Capital* is, as we have already said, *unfinished business*; and with respect to Volumes II and III, what has been read is *not* Marx but Engels's interpretation of Marx.

5. See Arthur and Reuten (1998).
6. Though Engels labelled them as 'Manuscripts', Marx simply numbered them, writing on some of them 'Notebooks'. According to Rolf Hecker (in Mazzone, 2002), Engels made an attribution error by dating the last manuscript as 1878.
7. The complexity of the 'making' of *Capital*, Volume II, as well as Volume III, is demonstrated also by the fact that the drafts constructed by Engels will be published in MEGA[2] as independent volumes, together with the German first editions of 1885 and 1894.
8. These materials for Volume III have yet to be published in the MEGA[2]. Their titles are: Formulas and calculations relevant to the relation between rate of surplus-value and rate of profit, Rate of surplus-value and rate of profit considered from a mathematical point of view, Differential rent and interest merely as ground rent, On the rate of profit, Rate of profit and turnover of capital, Interest.
9. For an informative discussion of Engels as an interpreter and editor see Arthur (1996).

An editorial decision of particular importance to *Capital I* was a change made by Engels in the subtitle for the first English edition in 1887. Marx had subtitled the book *The Production Process of Capital*, which implies that the volume is about the 'formation' or 'constitution' (in production *and* circulation) of capital as a *specific social relation*, not merely a *technical* process of producing capitalist commodities. In the first English edition, however, the subtitle of Volume I is *The Process of Capitalist Production*. One unfortunate result of this editorial decision (and other unacknowledged changes) has been to obscure the structural relationship between the books, parts and chapters of *Capital* or at very least to render ambiguous the relation between production and circulation, at the same time opening the way to an ahistorical reading of crucial categories – such as 'abstract' labour or 'valorization' – within the capitalist labour process. Indeed, Volumes I and II of *Capital* have often been misread as books about separate, distinct processes of commodity production (Volume I) and commodity exchange (Volume II) between which relations of independence and dependence must be applied before arriving at *The Process of Capitalist Production as a Whole* (the subtitle that Engels then imposed on Volume III). Yet, Marx himself clearly signalled, in his own title for Book III, that the subject matter throughout has to do with the interrelated and fundamentally inseparable *Shapes of the Whole Process* of producing, circulating and distributing *capital*.[10]

In fact not only the books *taken together* but also *each* book *per se* constitutes the whole subject matter: not the production and circulation of commodities *divorced* and analysed as *isolated* phases, but the production and circulation of capital taken *together*, but at *different layers of abstraction*. In Marx's conception of the 'unity' of capital, *both* the production and the exchange of commodities are incorporated

10. The implications of Engels's editorial decisions for Volumes II and III are discussed in greater detail in the 'General Introductions' by Arthur and Reuten to the essay collections that form a companion to the current collection: Arthur and Reuten (1998) and Campbell and Reuten (2002). These authors note that Engels justified his Volume III subtitle by inserting sentences into the opening chapter without acknowledging the change (see Reuten's 'Introduction', in Campbell and Reuten, 2002: 5, n. 12, n. 13). Arthur (2001) also notes that Volume 35 of the English MECW (50 volumes), which reproduces the well-known Moore and Aveling translation of *Capital*, Volume I, does not always include the advertised additions Engels made to the fourth edition, notably those taken from the French edition. Arthur lists several cases where this occurs: so 'this Volume 35 is neither the original 1887 text, nor a properly updated one'.

within the circulation of capital analysed in Book II: the conditions for the origin, growth and reproduction of capital having been *previously* explained in Book I, where circulation had *already* to be taken into account in order to make sense of the production process. Marx's own unique conception of capital as a *continuous movement of value self-valorization* going on through production *and* exchange, via the *form-determination* of labour as an 'internal other', then properly grounds his study of revolutions in the whole social capital (Book III).

The unfinished business of the publication of Marx's three 'books' creates difficulties with respect to the methodology and substance of *Capital* as a whole, and these must be considered in any reading of the work. Yet, too often, the three volumes of *Capital* are treated as a complete and, so to speak, final work. This is partly because the lessons of the long 'making' of *Capital* have been slow to emerge, especially in the English-speaking world, and partly due to the complicated history of the publication of Marx's and Engels's Complete Works in the original languages in which they were written.

Beginning in 1927, a first attempt to publish a Complete Works was made at the Moscow Marx–Engels Institute by David B. Rjazanov (who had already worked on the publication of *Gesammelte Schriften*, a collection of 'selected writings' by Marx and Engels). Rjazanov was editor until 1931, then was imprisoned and replaced by Vladimir V. Adoratskij; he died in 1938 in Stalin's purge. This first Marx and Engels *Historisch-kritische Gesamtausgabe* (the first MEGA) should have included 42 volumes, divided into three sections: writings other than *Capital*, *Capital* and related material, the epistolary. Nine volumes were published under Rjazanov's editing, four volumes by Adoratskij. Until Hitler's seizure of power they were published in Frankfurt (1927), Berlin (1929–32) and Wien–Berlin (1932), with the collaboration of German institutes. It was in this MEGA (in 1932) that the *Ökonomisch-Philosophische Manuskripte 1844* (MEGA I, 2) written in Paris and *Die Deutsche Ideologie* (MEGA I, 5) were published, for the first time. The *Grundrisse* notebooks (written in 1857–8) were published in 1939–41 but not within the MEGA, which ceased in 1935 – not even a third of the way to completion. The publication was, however, related and it followed the same criteria.[11] These notebooks were not translated in English until 1973, although they had

11. In the USSR, the *Grundrisse* notebooks were published by the Marx–Engels–Lenin Institute in Moscow. They were printed again by Dietz Verlag in Berlin in 1953. The *Einleitung* 1857–8 was already known, because Kautsky published it: *Neue Zeit*, XXI, 1 (1903).

been republished twenty years before in Germany. Another important piece of the puzzle, the *Resultate des Unmittelbaren Produktionprozesses* written between 1863 and 1866, and originally intended by Marx as a final chapter or part for *Capital I*, was also published in German (and Russian) in 1933, but had little influence on English-speaking Marxism until its inclusion as an Appendix to the second English edition of *Capital I* (1976: 949–1084).[12]

The gestation period of the second MEGA was very long, extending back to the 1950s. Initial resistance in the Soviet communist party was overcome during the 1960s, only after involving the East German communist party and related institutes. In the meantime, another collection of selected writings based on scientific criteria was under way, the Marx and Engels *Werke* (MEW), completed and published by Dietz Verlag in Berlin, East Germany, in 39 volumes between 1953 and 1968 (plus two unnumbered volumes; later two other volumes were added, 40 and 42 in 1983 and 1985). The MEW was the standard edition for scholars for a long time – a period in which the need was felt to return to the production of a complete scientific edition of the same high scholarly standards as the first MEGA. This new MEGA is by convention symbolised as MEGA². MEGA² began through collaboration between the Institute for Marxism–Leninism in Moscow and Berlin, with the help of the *Instituut voor sociale geschidenis* in Amsterdam which held the originals of many papers. The first volume was printed as a 'proof' to be subjected to critical scrutiny in 1972. Then, the regular volumes commenced publication in 1975, by Dietz Verlag in Berlin. The original project was to publish 100 volumes, each one with a companion volume of critical apparatus, in four sections: I. Writings, Articles, Drafts other than *Capital*; II. *Capital* and preparatory material; III. Epistolary; IV. *Extracts, Notes, Marginalia*. The project soon had to be revised into a 165-volume enterprise (without the *Marginalia*, 133 volumes in 142 books: all with a companion book).

It is to these crucial developments that we owe the publication, between 1976 and 1982, of the whole of the *Economic Manuscripts of 1861–3* (of which the *Theories of Surplus-value* were only a part) in six

---

12. The *Results* were published in USSR in the Marx–Engels Archives again for the Marx–Engels–Lenin Institute. This was for a long time the only version in the original language. It was reprinted as such in the West by Verlag Neue Kritik, in Frankfurt a. M. in 1969 and prior to that in Eastern Germany in 1962. Independently, there have been translations in French (in 1967 by Maximilien Rubel) and in Italian (in 1969 by Bruno Maffi).

volumes, as MEGA² II, 3. They were made available in English, in the 1980s.[13] The MEGA² ceased in 1989, beginning again in 1992. Then we had the publication of the *Ökonomische Manuskripte 1863–67* in 1988 and in 1992 (but printed in 1993). The original German manuscripts of the third volume of *Capital*, as well as the first Manuscript for Volume II, were part of these, and they are now available in German. The project, after the events of 1989–91, had to be redefined (and had to find new funding). It is now edited by a new Internationale Marx-Engels-Stiftung located in Amsterdam, with academic support. MEGA² continued to be printed in Berlin by Dietz Verlag for some years, but now the publisher is Akademie Verlag. By 1992, 41 volumes were in print. By 2002, eight new volumes had appeared. The projected volumes have been reduced to 114 (again, each one with its own companion). The cuts affect, marginally in terms of quality (though hugely in terms of quantity), sections III and IV. Sections I and II should be completed for 2010, and III–IV for 2020.

The *Economic Manuscripts of 1863–7* will be completed in three volumes (MEGA² II, 4.1 and II, 4.2 are already published; II, 4.3 has yet to be published). None of them have yet been translated into English (nor for that matter into other languages with the possible exception of Japanese). In the volumes published since the 1990s, much new and important material can be found. Just to give a few examples, in the last few years volumes have been published documenting the beginning of Marx's study of political economy in Paris, Manchester and Brussels between 1843 and 1847 (IV, 2–4), notebooks of economic quotes taken by Marx from Babbage and Ure in the 1840s (IV, 3), and especially, in the critical edition of the second German edition of *Capital I* (II, 6), 'Ergänzungen und Veränderungen zum ersten Band des "Kapitals" (Dezember 1871–Januar 1872)': an important manuscript written by Marx between 1871 and 1872, in preparation for the French and second German editions, essential for a better assessment of the relationship between 'form' and 'substance' of value, and which again is not available in English.[14] The other seven manuscripts for Volume II (MEGA² II, 11), and some preparatory materials for Volume III (of the late 1870s) have still to be published, together with Engels's manuscripts for Volume II (MEGA² II, 12) and with the

13. The *Grundrisse* notebooks were published as MEGA² II, 1 and *A Contribution to the Critique of Political Economy* as MEGA² II, 2.
14. A translation in Italian will soon be published, under the editing of Roberto Fineschi who also adds an enlightening introduction.

final printed versions of 1885 (MEGA² II, 13) and 1894 (MEGA² II, 15). Engels's manuscripts for Volume III (MEGA² II, 14) should be published in October, 2003. Again, to be published in Section IV of MEGA² are almost half of the London notebooks documenting Marx's economic studies between 1850 and 1853: the 1857–8 notebooks on economic crisis, the 1868–9 notebooks on world market and crisis, the 1877–9 notebooks on banking and finance and other writings on political economy. This confirms yet again that Marx remains a 'novel' object for inquiry.

The same *Capital I* – considered in all of its drafts and editions – still contains surprises. Even the first (MEGA² II, 5) and second (MEGA² II, 6) German editions differ in some important respects. Probably the most relevant, though not the only one, is that the first edition contains a very dissimilar first chapter, to which Marx added an appendix on the controversial concept of value-form; this latter was dropped from later editions and its subject matter was partially incorporated into a rewritten first chapter. Marx himself declared that the 1872–5 French edition (the last one that he edited: MEGA² II, 7) had an independent scientific value and should be read even by those familiar with the second German edition. So, the new historical and critical edition of the *Marx and Engels Complete Works* will surely shed more light on the meaning and relevance of Marx's intentions. And these will have to be considered by the future secondary literature.

The essays in the current collection – although not specifically intended as contributions to a philological inquiry – take into account (wherever necessary) the stratification of Marx's argument. Moreover, where difficulties in influential English translations are identified (in relation to the second German or French editions) these are discussed and if possible rectified (see, for example, the chapters by Bellofiore and Reuten). Although the 1976 English edition of *Capital I* is the core text for most of the essays, some of the authors make extensive references not only to Marx's other published works but also to his manuscripts – especially the *Grundrisse* and the *Results* – and to the important appendix on *The Value Form*, written by Marx for the first German edition of *Capital I* and translated into English only in 1978.[15]

15. In 1976 the first chapter and the Appendix from the first edition, together with the *Results* and the *Marginal Notes on Wagner*, were made available in a less rigorous translation by Albert Dragstedt (1976). To our knowledge, this translation of the first chapter from the first German edition is the only one available in English.

2. The logic of *Capital*: the parts of *Capital I*

Given the complex history of *Capital* any reconstruction of the logical relation of the volumes of the existing tautology is bound to be contested. Neither will we try to do this in these few pages, except to say that all of the contributors to the current collection agree that Marx began in Volume I with abstract and simple categories then proceeded over the course of the three volumes to develop ever more concrete and complex categories. The authors also agree that this element of Marx's method is indebted to Hegel's systematic dialectics. While agreeing on the general nature of the conceptual development of *Capital*, the essays nevertheless exhibit – either implicitly or explicitly – differences among the authors concerning both the nature of Marx's dialectics and the extent to which the earlier categories in Volume I are superseded or modified by later categories.[16] In the following, we will present a (very personal) outline of the skeleton of *Capital* and the relation between its parts.[17]

16. At issue here is the difficult problem of how to interpret Marx's debt to Hegel. A major impetus for an inquiry into the question came from the 1953 and 1973 publications of the *Grundrisse* – which contains important comments on method – and subsequent studies of the Hegel–Marx connection (see Burns and Fraser, 2000). Early attempts to interpret *Capital* as a 'Hegelian' work were Banaji (1979) and Murray (1988). Smith (1990) gives a more detailed account of the systematic structure of *Capital I*, and Arthur (1998a, 2000, 2003) and the papers collected in Albritton and Simoulidis (2003) provide further invaluable analyses of the Marx–Hegel relation and the logic of *Capital* as a whole. For general accounts of the systematic dialectical method and its relevance see Arthur (1998b), Reuten (1998a) and Smith (1993, 1999); for criticism of Marx's application of the method see Backhaus (1969) and Reuten (1993, 1998b); for systematic dialectical reconstructions of *Capital*, see Reuten and Williams (1989) and Eldred *et al.* (1982, 1983). For debate on the systematic dialectical interpretation of *Capital*, see the essays in Moseley (1993) and Moseley and Campbell (1997).
17. Because the essays collected here refer mainly to the English editions, our description of the parts and chapters of Volume I follows the layout of these editions. Differences with the German editions (edited by Marx himself) are summarized in a footnote to the 1976 English edition (p. 110):

	German	English
Chapters	1–3	1–3
	4	4–6
	5–23	7–25
	24	26–32
	25	33
Parts	One–Six	One–Six
	Seven	Seven–Eight

We neither express, necessarily, the view of our co-authors nor make explicit references to disagreements among us; these are left to the reader to disentangle. This volume, like the other efforts of the International Symposium on Marxian Theory (ISMT), is the outcome of an ongoing debate and dialogue between *different* viewpoints.

In our view, the role of Marx's dialectics is to grasp a *structured totality* where each element depends on its relation to other elements and the whole. Since the totality of these relationships cannot be presented immediately the first difficulty is *where to begin*. Marx begins, in Part One, with the 'commodity' and its inner dialectical opposition between use-value and value, and then posits the 'value-form' as the peculiar modality through which this contradiction is exhibited. From here *all that is presupposed – all* of the relations of capital as a whole – is progressively *posited*. So, although value presupposes capital it begins as an empty concept, in the sense that the complex determinations and relationships that constitute capital have yet to be analysed and presented. In other words, all of the concepts in the first parts of Volume I require further *particularization* and *concretion*. The process of particularization and concretion can be most easily understood as a *double movement* that structures, on the one hand, the relation between the parts of Volume I (particularization) and, on the other hand, the relation between particular parts of all three volumes (concretion).[18]

The parts of *Capital I* are connected by a movement from *universality* to *particularity* to the *internal* (systemic) *determinations* that link these different elements into a *unity*: capital. In the first two parts of Volume I the universality of capital is initially *constituted* by the development of 'value-forms', commodity, money and capital. 'Value' is presented as a self-moving substance or *the* subject going through a process of self-valorization: *capital as value in process, as money in process*. Especially important in this theoretical journey is the transformation of money into capital, which brings about a conceptual transition from the *simple circulation* of commodities, C–M–C, where money mediates the exchange of useful objects (Volume I, Part One), to the *general formula for capital*, M–C–M′, where money becomes an end in itself (Volume I, Part Two; Volume II, Part One). This form is the most abstract–simple form of 'valorization', a process whereby an initial amount of money generates a *quantitative* difference with itself (a surplus-value) which is posited as a monetary increment (the amount by which M′ exceeds M).

18. Arthur (2002) provides a sophisticated explanation of this scheme and Reuten (2003) an interpretation.

The middle part of Volume I answers the question not only *how does capital work?* but also (and foremost) *where does it come from?* Here Marx considers 'not only how capital produces, but how capital is itself produced' and therewith sets the scene for his analysis of exploitation as a *necessary* condition for the existence of capital as valorization form. An increase in money is possible *only* thanks to capital's incorporation within itself of labour-power, and includes a brief introduction to the value of labour-power, the wage. So, Marx arrives by the end of Volume I, Part Two, at an expression of capital valorization: a movement going from an initial exchange of money for commodities (means of production and labour-power), through a production process, to the final exchange of newly produced commodities for money. Part Three then shows that to ground its self-valorization, capital must integrate (and transform) production, which implies the exploitation of living labour which is pumped out from workers over and above the necessary labour required to reproduce labour-power. Capitalists must buy workers' labour-power through the advance of variable capital in money, and then face their potential resistance (or counter-productivity) in the capitalist labour process. With this 'social constraint', they decide the level and structure of employment, techniques and the composition of output in a *monetary* and *competitive* economy grounded in the generalized production and exchange of commodities for profit.

Thus, the middle parts of Volume I – Chapter 10 in Part Three and Chapters 13 to 15 in Part Four, more than 270 pages, almost a third of the book – deal with this *fundamental yet necessary* antagonism between wage-workers and capitalists, through an inquiry which encompasses exchange (in what is now called the 'labour-market') *and* production. Particularization of capital into constant and variable capital (both monetary expenditures and their elements) constitutes the opposed poles of this 'unity in difference'. Crucially, living labour allows a *transfer* of the value exhibited by the elements of constant capital to a new product and at the same time *generates* a new 'value added', which for Marx is *nothing but* the monetary expression of the 'socially necessary labour time' extracted from workers. This new value must contain in itself a surplus-value over and above the value of labour-power: the 'source' of the former is given, for Marx, by workers' 'surplus' labour, over and above the 'necessary' labour for historical and moral 'subsistence' – because of capital compulsion. The ratio between surplus-value and variable capital Marx calls the 'rate of surplus-value' and it is dependent on the 'degree of exploitation of labour-power by capital'.

The rest of the middle part deals with methods of production and organizational techniques for increasing the rate of surplus-value. In his *genetic* account, Marx differentiates the effects of an *absolute* prolongation of the working day giving scope for a higher surplus-value with given techniques and with a given value of labour-power from the effects of technical and organizational innovations, and thereby of advances in productive-power such as advances in industries producing the consumption basket or producing means of production, that *relatively* lower the value of labour-power, giving scope for an higher surplus-value even with a given length of the working day and a given labour 'effort'. This is the distinction between absolute and relative surplus-value (Parts Four and Five), which leads into his class analysis of wage determination (Part Six).[19]

The final parts of Volume I consider capital reproduction. The category of 'accumulation' signifies that the result of productive activity is indeed the perpetuation of capital's own self-valorizing movement (Part Seven). The 'reconversion' of surplus-value into capital Marx calls 'accumulation of capital'. A *spiral* of accumulation is essential to the abstract concept of capital since, without it, capital merely collapses into money in its simple function as a means of circulating commodities (Part One). Money as capital must be *continuously* thrown into circulation: both the original money advances and their increment. Given capital's *ceaseless* and *unbounded* drive to accumulate, and given the tendency towards a higher organic composition of capital, the dynamics of exploitation culminate systematically in: (i) concentration of capital, and (ii) a reserve army of the unemployed through the expulsion of living labour. Prior to Part Seven, Marx almost always framed his argument with references to 'individual' capitals; now he introduces *direct* references to 'total' capital *as such* and to the social reproduction of the *whole capital* in an *essential* way.

At this point, Marx can show: (i) that what was originally assumed – the availability of labour-power, and the initial advances of constant and variable capital – is the *outcome* posited by the capitalist process; (ii) that among the 'equal' producers and owners of 'commodities' introduced at the outset in simple commodity circulation we now see the necessary emergence of very 'unequal' subjects in a *class* society, the working class (which has only labour-power to sell) and the capitalist class (which is the owner of money, means of production and commodities);

---

19. In *Capital I* Marx considers a higher intensity of labour as a means for the extraction of relative surplus-value.

(iii) that capital therefore not only produces and realizes a surplus-value, but also and mainly *produces capital* on an *enlarged* scale, so that; (iv) reproduction is the *reproduction of the class relation and exploitation.* Capital accumulation is capitalist 'macro' social reproduction which has to be shown to be realized through individual 'micro' and competitive behaviour. The *systemic* unity of the concept of capital is therewith demonstrated by a method that amounts to a *positing of the presuppositions.*

The final Part Eight contains eight short chapters on so-called primitive accumulation, and provides a historical account of the conditions of the capital–labour relation: the separation of workers from means of production and alternative sources of subsistence. This serves to stress Marx's fundamental point that capitalism is a mutable mode of production with foundations in a unique, historically specific class structure, based on the buying and selling of labour-power.[20]

Volume I of *Capital* is about the *process* of producing and reproducing a particular class society; it is about the *capital–labour relation* through which capitalist social relations of exploitation and accumulation are produced and reproduced. Volumes II and III have to do with the ever more complex *concretion* of this relation. In understanding the methodology of concretion, it is very important to distinguish the *process of circulation of capital* from the simple circulation (exchange) of commodities. In Volume I (Part Two) the simple circuit of capital involves a movement through *two* moments of exchange between which lies the necessary moment of production: the 'initial' exchange consisting in the purchase and sale of labour-power and means of production, and the 'final' exchange consisting in the metamorphoses of commodities into money. In Volume II (Part One) this is made more concrete through

---

20. However, as Arthur (2002) and Smith (1990: 133–5) have pointed out, Part Eight is a historical digression into primitive accumulation coupled with an attempt to set out the historical course of capital. This seems somewhat out of step with the systematic dialectical progression of categories in Volume I. In fact, Part Eight is a result of Engels's editing for the English edition of 1887 – but (as again Arthur has shown) this arrangement of the text descends from Marx's French edition. In the original German editions, a single chapter on 'primitive accumulation' was included by Marx in Part Seven. To make Part Eight, Engels, following Marx's suggestions, broke up the single chapter into several chapters. This, along with Marx's own omission of a 'transitional' chapter (the *Results*, now published as an Appendix to the 1976 English edition), allowed Engels (in his Preface to the 1887 English edition) to suggest that Volume I may be read as a complete work (see Murray, Chapter 9, and Reuten, Chapter 5 in this volume).

the metamorphoses of capital through the *intertwining* of circuits of money-capital, productive-capital and commodity-capital. Part Two is then devoted to the turnover of capital. Part Three is a *very abstract* demonstration of the *conditions of possibility* for a 'balanced growth' path independent from consumption demand. Marx stresses that these conditions are *very* unlikely to be met in reality. His 'schemes' for simple reproduction and for reproduction on an enlarged scale should *not* therefore be mistaken for an inquiry into 'concrete' capitalist dynamics.

A further concretion occurs in Volume III, which deals specifically with the concepts of profit and the profit rate (Part One), capital's continuity measure: (i) in relation to *synchronic* (inter-branch, or 'static') competition and the consequent tendency towards the establishment of a *general* rate of profit across industries, and (ii) in relation to *diachronic* (intra-branch, or 'dynamic') competition between capitals for surplus profit and the opposing tendency towards a *diversification* of the rate of profit within industries (Part Two).[21] In fact, the latter kind of competition already appeared in Volume I (Part Four, Chapter 12) when relative surplus-value production was discussed. So, when discussing the 'generality' of capital at the very high level of abstraction pertaining to Volume I, Marx had *already* found it necessary to introduce, in some way, a reference to the existence of 'many capitals': that is, to (the second kind of) competition. In this same Part Two of Volume III, devoted to the (in)famous 'transformation of profit into average profit', Marx also begins to relax two *major assumptions* maintained through Volume I and Volume II and the beginning of Volume III. Both come under the common heading that 'commodities are supposed to be sold at their values'. This means: (i) that prices are *proportional* to (the monetary expressions of) labour-values; and (ii) that all of the commodity output is *sold*. Removing these assumptions, Marx introduces new categories: 'prices of production' and 'market values/market prices'.

It must be noted that relaxing the second assumption necessarily produces a divorce of the category of 'social' value (Volume I, Part Four, Chapter 12) from any mere technical averaging of productive conditions. Value is now (Volume III, Part Two, Chapter 10) dependent

---

21. The distinction between these two kinds of competition in Marx goes back at least to Henryk Grossmann; it is at the heart of the confrontation between Marx and Schumpeter discussed in Bellofiore (1985). For a critical discussion of neo-Schumpeterian perspectives versus Marx see chapter 8 by Tony Smith, in this volume.

also on *ordinary demand* – that is, in some way it is determined *at the intersection* between production and circulation, a position implicit from the first three parts of *Capital*, Volume I. We have here an 'enlarged' notion of socially necessary labour time, which has to take into account the *possibility* that the use-value produced in a sector may show itself *not* to be a use-value *for others*. Circulation *may* therefore affect even the *magnitude* of value.[22] The idea of a crisis springing from a deficiency of commodity demand can therefore be found in these pages. Part Three of Volume III is devoted to another crisis theory, the law of the tendential fall in the rate of profit. The two theories do not necessarily conflict, since both originate from the capitalist drive to expel living labour from production. For some commentators, it is from these parts (say, after Chapter 10 of Part One in Volume III) that the more concrete study of 'competition' – that is, of *how* the immanent laws of capitalist production and reproduction *assert* themselves – begins. Therewith, Marx abandons inquiry at the level of 'capital in general'.[23]

Linked to the 'cycle of money-capital' introduced in Volume II are the notions of 'credit' and 'finance' as they are developed in Volume III (Parts Four and Five). Here, one very important implication of further concretion may be that the original M within the abstract circuit of money-capital (Volume I, Part Two) should be concretely determined by its social function as *finance to production*, a radical reformulation of the concept of money initially determined by its functions in the abstract-simple form of commodity circulation, which was conceived by Marx within a *theory of money as a commodity* (Volume I, Part One).

What this brief outline suggests is that the architectonic of *Capital* is *complex*, both with respect to the *structure of each volume* and with respect to the *levels of abstraction* that obtain *between the particular parts*

22. A point, of course, which was already there from the start: that is, from Marx's first chapter in *Capital*, Volume I – though Marx sterilized the effects of this quite early in the development of the argument, but as the result of a temporary assumption to be removed later. For one of the authors of this chapter all this does not contrast with the thesis that value and surplus-value 'ideally' originate (and 'latently' *already* exist) within production as a *moment* of the capitalist circuit, then *eventually* 'come into being' in exchange on the commodity market. It does not contrast then with Marx talking of labour time as the 'immanent' measure for value and money as its only 'necessary form' of manifestation. For an alternative view, see Taylor's Chapter 4, summarized later in this chapter (section 4, below).

23. Here again, the reference is to the German debate quoted in n. 4 and to Fineschi (2001).

of different volumes.[24] In general, the different parts of Volume I set out the *most abstract-simple determinations of the core concept of capital.* However, these 'value' concepts are *necessarily inadequate* in the sense that all require further concretion and mediation (particularization) to show how the *fundamental* and *unchanging* extraction of living labour 'materialized' in the value output *manifests itself* in capitalism. Value 'magnitudes', *always* expressed as money prices, cannot then be assumed as quantitatively fixed 'givens'.

Indeed, Marx's levels of abstraction make sense only as a conceptual progression, so that *any* fixing of concepts is inconsistent with his methodology. That Marx himself published only the first volume, however, obviously deepens the sense in which *Capital* remains an unfinished project.

3. Some debates, interpretations and reconstructions of *Capital I*

As a body of scholarly research, Marxian political economy has evolved out of controversies surrounding Marx's published works and manuscripts – to the limited extent they were known, or very often to the more limited extent they were published in the language of the commentators. Of course, a full discussion of these controversies – and the many heuristic developments arising from them – would constitute a book in itself. In this short section we can provide but a brief, general (and again, very personal) sketch of some old and new issues and concerns.

The discussion on Marx until the early 1960s focused mainly upon two controversies: (i) value theory as a theory of 'equilibrium' relative prices, the so-called 'great contradiction' between Volume I and Volume III (Böhm-Bawerk's criticism, Hilferding's reply and the so-called 'transformation problem', redefined after Dmitriev and Bortkiewicz as a simultaneous equation solution which led to Seton's disaggregated solution in 1956–7); (ii) the controversy on crisis theory, with the debate on the necessity (or not) of economic collapse revolving around the 'schemes of reproduction' in Volume II (here, key points were the polar opposition between Tugan-Baranowsky's 'harmonicist' perspective and Rosa Luxemburg's 'underconsumptionist' approach, with Lenin and Bukharin insisting instead on a 'disproportionality' view; the tendential fall in

24. For further discussion of this point the reader is directed to the companion volumes to the current collection, especially the 'General Introduction' in Arthur and Reuten (1998) and Campbell and Reuten (2002); see also Arthur (2002) and Reuten (2003).

the rate of profits as a secular tendency was put forward as an alternative collapse theory).

A key development in the past four decades has been the new emphasis on capitalism as a unique, historically specific *social form*.[25] Prior to the mid-1960s, the social character of Marx's value concept was underplayed (though, in a sense, this notion was exactly the core of Hilferding's essay). Value theory was read as if 'abstract labour' was a *mental generalization*, and its 'substance' reduced to a *material–technical* dimension, mere physiological expenditure of labour. Reproduction theory rested upon too simple an opposition between 'equilibrium' (identified with *balanced growth*) and 'disequilibrium' (identified with *collapse*). Many different strands of thought evolved from this 'material–technical' and 'equilibrium' interpretation of Marx. We refer, mainly, to *traditional Marxism* and to *neo-Ricardian* 'embodied' labour theories.[26] Neo-Ricardians ended by (rightly) criticizing traditional Marxism. Crucially, they were

25. 'Form' in capitalism – that is, its *differentia specifica* – shapes 'matter' into its own adequate 'content'. Some writers therefore consider that all entities in capitalism have a *material* and *natural* shape (such as the physical body of the commodity) as well as a *social* and *capitalist* value-form (such as the character of the 'commodity' as a *cell form* of abstract capitalist wealth). This implies a need to distinguish between 'general' (trans-historical) and 'determinate' (capitalist) categories (Murray, 1988). It also means that the 'naturalist' label which Marco Lippi attributed to Marx's position is ill-conceived. Forerunners of the new reading of Marx were, in Italy, Lucio Colletti (1968, and the last chapter of his 1969) and Claudio Napoleoni (1972, translated into German, Spanish and Portuguese but not into English, and 1973). At this time, other contributors to the debate on 'social form' and 'value-form' were Rosdolsky, Alfred Schmidt, Hans Jurgen Krahl, Backhaus and Reichelt. In France, criticism of traditional Marxism and neo-Ricardianism spread in the early 1970s through a heterodox Marxist line inspired by Michel Aglietta, Carlo Benetti and Jean Cartelier, who later renounced important tenets of their original positions and Marxism altogether. In the English-speaking literature the debate began late with the book edited by Diane Elson (1979) which contained, among others, essays by Arthur and Banaji who inspired the turn to a new systematic dialectical interpretation and, later, value-form theoretic interpretations, criticisms and reconstructions of Marx, notably Reuten and Williams (1989) and Eldred *et al.* (1982, 1985). On these and related issues, see the survey in Bellofiore (1989), the special issue edited by Baldassarri and Bellofiore (1999), the conflicting views of Bellofiore (1999) and Reuten (1999), and a debate between Murray (2001a, 2001b) and Reuten (2001) in *Historical Materialism*.
26. The leading figures of traditional Marxism, dominant from the 1940s to the 1960s, were Paul Sweezy (1946), Maurice Dobb (1940) and Ronald Meek (1956). Within the neo-Ricardian approach, the most relevant interpreters were Ian Steedman (1977) and Pierangelo Garegnani (1981).

able to demonstrate a *redundancy* of labour-values 'data' in the determination of prices of production. Their point seemed to be confirmed by Sraffa's *Production of Commodities by Means of Commodities* – where the economic system has a surplus and the real wage as a 'given' is dissolved into means of subsistence – which looked almost identical to Seton's, only without the methods of production accounted for in labour units (these were substituted by the physical measure of use-values). The two lines were however united, in the sense that both were convinced of a fundamental *identity* between Ricardo's and Marx's categories of 'value', so that the abstract labour of the latter was read as nothing but the 'difficulty of production' of the former.[27] Though different in many ways, the same reduction of Marx to a minor (or even major) but more radical left Ricardian is common to many neoclassical interpreters, from the most critical (Paul Samuelson) to the better disposed (Michio Morishima).

27. No quick and easy criticism is intended. Dobb, Meek and Sweezy were *giants* of Marxism, engaged in a continuing dialogue with the *high theory* of their time. Indeed, the relationship between Schumpeter and Sweezy, like that between Dobb and Sraffa, has *no analogue in the Marxian camp today*. Sweezy showed his stature as an intellectual by making a (partial) self-criticism against his treatment of the transformation problem in his critique of Steedman in *The Value Controversy*. We do not intend to offer a criticism of neo-Ricardian conclusions within their *own* perspective, except to note that their *interpretation* (and hence their *reconstruction* of Marx) is based on false premises that lead them to construct a *caricature*. Nothing could be more foreign to *Capital* – a work based on the idea that capitalism is an *essentially monetary* economy driven by *structurally unstable dynamics* – than the idea that prices may be derived from a given structure of the economy, described in terms of physical data and the basket of consumption goods, abstracting both from exchange and demand, and then calling them 'centres of gravity'. As for Sraffa, the issue is altogether different and cannot be easily identified with his followers. It must be stressed, since it is too easily forgotten, that the Italian economist was one of the few *great monetary economists* of his century (it suffices to recall his work of the 1920s and 1930s). He *disliked* Bortkiewicz's reading of Marx, as his notes of 1942 testify. As one can see from the subtitle, his 1960 book was meant *mainly* as a *criticism* of mainstream economics based on general equilibrium rather than as a positive, constructive new paradigm. He was hostile to axiomatic approaches. His attitude to Marxism was *against determinism* and in favour of 'conventionalism' in income distribution. And his Sections 10 and 12 read together look like a *covert* support of the 'labour theory of value': not in the sense of traditional Marxism but of (elements of) the 'New Interpretation' (a point which is confirmed by some of his papers in the Cambridge archives). On this, see Bellofiore (2001).

Thus, the 'form' of value and the 'abstraction' of labour were mis-interpreted, as respectively a money 'veil' and a 'generalization' made by the researcher. Yet in the opening chapter of *Capital*, Marx himself pointed out against the Classical Political Economists that the form of value is entirely emptied of content if the substance of value is simply collapsed into labour *as such*, without any consideration of the *capitalist form* of production *and* circulation, and hence without any considera-tion of the essential role of *money*.[28] Yet, for more than a century, most Marxists all but ignored aspects of *Capital* that clearly distance Marx's monetary (labour) theory of value[29] from Ricardo's 'difficulty of produc-tion' perspective where the labour 'embodied' is an instance of *concrete* labour, equal only in as much as it is reduced to a *physiological* dimen-sion.[30] On the contrary, Marx's 'abstraction' of labour in *Capital* is the

28. See the essays by Arthur (Chapter 2) and Taylor (Chapter 4) in this collection. A notable exception to the neglect of money in Marxian theory has been the pioneering work of Suzanne de Brunhoff in the early 1960s, to which many French and Belgian authors, as well as a couple of contributors to this volume, are indebted. As we have said, the editors are both convinced that the role of money within the critique of political economy should be *strengthened* relative to Marx's own position: with more stress going on *initial* finance to firms from the banking system as *ante*-validation of labour within circulation (labour-*power*, and hence the wage-form) and within production (labour, and hence the social form of its organization and of techniques).

29. Bellofiore (1989) was probably the first to coin the label 'monetary labour theory of value', in the title of his paper.

30. Early exceptions to the general neglect of 'social form' were Hilferding and Petry, who anticipated an influential (and original) development of the concept in the work of Isaac I. Rubin, who rightly noted that: 'It is not possible to recon-cile a physiological concept of abstract labour with the historical character of the value that it creates' (Rubin, 1928: 135). If the category of value is a social category that has meaning and relevance *only* for the capitalist mode of production, *then* the category of abstract labour producing it must also be understood as a historically specific or *social form* of labour. Rubin clearly wanted to *integrate* labour as the substance of value with labour as the form of value to have value in the full sense of the word: the determination of value refers thereby to the *unity* of content (i.e. labour) and social form of value. In a 1927 lecture, he wrote: 'labour is [the] only substance of value, but does not yet represent value . . . in order to obtain value in the full sense of the word we have to add something to labour as the substance of value, namely the social form of value. Only then do we obtain the concept of value in the sense in which it is found in Marx's work' (1927: 127). More controversially, Rubin went on to draw conclusions about the relationship between form and content in Marx and Hegel: 'content does not represent something which form attaches to from the outside, rather the content itself in its development gives birth to this form, which was contained within this content in con-cealed form. The form arises necessarily from the content itself' (*ibid*.: 136).

result of a *real* process going on in commodity-exchange and before it (though latently) *already* in production, and amounts to a 'real hypo-statization'. Thus, for Marx, what is expended during work is, at the same time, *not only* concrete labour *but also* abstract labour 'in motion' – that is, living labour manipulated by capital so that its objectification amounts 'ideally' to a (greater) amount of money (than the one anticipated in variable capital). This metamorphosis of objectified labour into money, as the 'universal' equivalent, is *necessary* in order that the heterogeneous labours expended in production (and employed by 'dissociated' producers) show eventually that they are actually proportions of homogeneous 'social' labour: both relative to average techniques *and* social needs.

We cannot here go into the epistemological, textual and analytical reasons for rejecting a material–technical interpretation of Marx's value theory, except to say that this reading is coherent not only with the way the debate on Marx was conducted at the turn of the nineteenth century – namely, with the discussions on the transformation problem and on crisis theory – *but also* with a reading of Marx in terms of a pure *analytical* (rather than *dialectical*) logic. A good example of the former is Engels's *logical–historical* misinterpretation of *Capital*.[31] According to Engels, Marx begins by describing a pre-capitalist, or immature capitalist, stage of 'simple commodity production' in which value attains its 'classical form'; then goes on to describe full-blown capitalist production as a 'secondary' derivative from value production. Read in this way, value theory is easily mistaken for a 'natural law' which applies 'universally' up until the time when it is modified 'by the onset of the capitalist form of production' (Engels, 1894a: 103; 1984b: 1037). Developments along these lines tend to foist onto Marx a procedure of

---

So, 'when we take not the finished form [value as a determined social form] as starting point, but the content itself (i.e., labour) from which the form (value) must necessarily arise ... we have to include in the concept of labour the social form of its organization in commodity production, i.e. recognize abstract universal labour as the content of value' (*ibid.*: 137). The meaning of abstract labour (in the last instance, as *activity* within production) and value (as *result* coming into being in commodity circulation) is a thousand miles from any material–technical reductionism; Rubin's message is precisely that abstract labour is 'latently' present *already* in production before final exchange (see also Bellofiore and Finelli, 1998. For an objection to Rubin's interpretation of Marx see Taylor, ch. 4, fn. 19).

31. Reasons for rejecting a logical–historical reading of Marx are discussed at length in Part I of Volume I of Bellofiore (1998), in Arthur's (2003) essays and by Reuten (1998a).

successive 'approximations' where the volumes of *Capital* must be interpreted as a series of analytic models, each bringing about a more complex approximation to capitalist reality than the last. The initial (labour) value model of simple commodity production is later modified by capitalist prices. Because this idea transmigrated (albeit in a richer form) into the work of Dobb and Sweezy, it was easy for neoclassical and neo-Ricardian critics to show how the two stages collapse into one, so that value (identified with labour-value) simply disappears. Money has no essential role to play in this determination: it appears merely as a 'veil' over the 'real' value economy, to be introduced later after the 'core' has been analysed. To be sure, the bell rang against this interpretation of Marx with the Dmitriev–Bortkiewicz–Winternitz–Seton solution, and even before: Böhm-Bawerk's criticism against material–technical labour as the substance of value was criticism enough.

The alternative view, emerging in the last decades of the twentieth century, is that Marx's crucial categories cannot be interpreted within the framework of some 'natural law' of labour allocation or price determination, in 'equilibrium'. This is because the value-form involves a central social relationship, the capital–labour relation, together with the dissociated nature of capitalist society. Of course, it is not a question of denying the role of 'material', or 'technical', or even 'natural' aspects of Marx's value theory in order to validate its social nature. Rather it is a question of which aspect plays the *dominant* role in shaping the *dynamics* of social reproduction. In asking this question, the relationship between the production of capital *and* the circulation of capital comes immediately to the fore because the socialization of labour is brought about *eventually* and *necessarily* through *money*. The sole purpose of a purchase of labour-power is production for profit, so money advanced at the start of a capital circuit also *ante*-validates labour. So, value theory cannot be limited to the determination of equilibrium prices and profit but, more importantly, it aims to explain the *conditions for the existence and functioning of a decentralized economy in which markets and money interact with production to ensure social cohesion*, and where *the capitalist labour process is a contested terrain continuously transformed through entrepreneurial innovations*. For this reason the analysis of the *valorization process* (money begetting money) cannot be separated from the methods of production and organization of labour which form the 'central' core of this process. Indeed it is the *interaction* of the two processes – 'money in motion' and 'labour in motion' – that make the capitalist form of production for profit what it essentially is. Regarding production proper, what counts is the *capitalist* labour process: how the sphere of production is *form-determined*, in a *class* (and therefore *conflict*) perspective. Here, innovation (and hence *diachronic* competition, defining the methods of production) and demand (through the influence of *social need* on the magnitude of value) *matters* in price determination.[32]

The authors represented in the current collection broadly adhere to some version of a 'social' interpretation of the concept of value, albeit in different ways and to varying degrees – the perspective presented in this introduction is simply one among the many, and – as we have anticipated – it is not representative of the thought of each and every participant in the ISMT. However, *all* of the authors *reject the heritage of the logical–historical method* imposed on *Capital* by Engels *and the economic reductionism* of traditional Marxism and its neo-Ricardian offshoots. All of the authors insist on *the centrality of money* for a correct understanding of Marxian value theory. The collection also differs from other collections on Marx in that *the connection between content and method is often made explicit* both in the authors' interpretations of Marx's value theory and in their heuristic developments of particular elements of it.

For some authors criticism of Marx's work focuses mainly (but not exclusively) on the *methodological* aspects of his *systematic dialectical* method in relation to *Hegel's logic*, and its implications for reading *Capital* and/or reconstructing its content. For others the emphasis is more on the vindication of Marx's *economic* theory of *exploitation* within a coherent reconstruction of the *monetary* aspects of his abstract labour theory of value. The map of differences is for the reader to discover, within the moving 'whole' of a collective enterprise where difference and dialogue are an essential means for self-clarification and mutual progress.

4. Outline of the essays

In Chapter 2, Christopher Arthur takes Section 3 of the first chapter of *Capital I* as the starting point for considering why the value of commodities cannot be fully expressed without money. Since this section on the forms of value is structured by a sequence of commodity relations, it is interpreted here through Russell's theory of relations, which analyses the relation of equality as reflexive, symmetrical and transitive. But in the value-form the 'sense' of each relation proceeds *from* one

---

32. On the way that concepts are 'defined' and 'subsumed' within a social constellation see Murray, Chapter 9 in this volume.

term *to* the other, where the first is active and the second passive. This suggests that value expressions must not be represented by an '=' sign, as in Marx's formulas, but rather as a relation where one commodity 'expresses its value in the use-value of' another. Arthur's analysis supports Marx's distinction between the 'relative' and 'equivalent' expressions of value which leads in *Capital I* to money as the necessary and universal equivalent form of all commodities and, at the same time, he points beyond the text to some novel implications of the price-form.

Martha Campbell's Chapter 3 contrasts Marx's position with the institutionalist view of economic relations in terms of habit to explore Marx's claim that, within capitalist economic relations, people are not subjects but merely personifications of economic roles. Chapter 2 of Volume I of *Capital* highlights the difference between them. Here Marx argues that money cannot be conventional, as the institutionalist approach maintains, because the creation of money by commodity owners is inconsistent with their atomistic character as exchangers. Marx's treatment of money illustrates the unique and peculiar way that, he contends, capitalist economic relations are constituted. Although social in origin, they are not socially created in the same way as institutions in other contexts. Instead they are objective, meaning that they must assume a material shape, as value must be embodied in money, they exist as relations among objects, and ultimately they harness human capabilities to the non-human purpose of expanding value, that is, to capital. Objectivity in this sense is distinctive of capitalism, according to Marx, but is missing from institutionalist thought.

In Chapter 4, Nicola Taylor explains then reconstructs Marx's concept of value-form over Parts One and Two of Volume I. On the basis of Marx's text, she argues that too early an introduction of the concept of abstract labour (and its pre-given measurement in socially necessary labour time) diverts attention from the main issue tackled by Marx at the start of *Capital*: namely, the development of the value-form. In particular, Marx's controversial attempt to link value-form to labour through a money commodity prevents an adequate conceptualization of how the value-form – ultimately the capital form – shapes the content of all entities and processes in capitalism, *including labour and its measurement*. This key point is made by Marx in his opening chapter, but then obscured because he introduces labour (in Part One) before the introduction of the capital form (in Part Two); as a result his monetary theory of value seems at times to involve a Ricardian move from content to form of appearance. Once the capital form is shown to determine its content, however, money alone validates the labour privately allocated and expended in production processes. Moreover, *the magnitude of value emerges in the capital circuit* not as a dimension in the simultaneous comparison of commodities, according to some equivalent property and merely mediated by money, but as a *monetary dimension* to do with the comparison of money-capital with itself at two different points in time. Taylor explores the implications of a systematic dialectic that moves from value *form* to value *content*. She argues that *value as process* (in the capital circuit) is inextricably linked with the *social use-value* of labour and commodities (independently measured in money and influenced by determinants of demand in labour and commodity markets). Thus, abstract labour has no measure other than money and value magnitudes cannot be determined by quantities of socially necessary labour time in production alone.

In Chapter 5, Geert Reuten takes up Parts Three to Five of Volume I, which contain Marx's account of the production of surplus-value. His analysis shows that Marx's formulas convey theoretical results rather than explanatory processes and mechanisms. In Reuten's view, this lack of 'heuristic' inspiration in Marx's formalization becomes an obstacle to the conceptual progress of the book, particularly after Part Four where Marx introduces the key concepts of 'productive force' (in modern jargon: technique of production) and 'intensity of labour', therewith leaving behind any simple explanation of value in terms of labour time. However, the conceptual limitation imposed by the absence of key concepts can be overcome by way of an elementary and immanent reconstruction of Marx's formalizations. Reuten's reconstruction recasts the rate of surplus-value by including *all* of Marx's main explanatory variables: extensity of labour, wages, productive force and intensity of labour. By making explicit what is already implicit in Marx's text, the reconstruction also makes explicit an important implication for the measurement of labour: that is, 'labour' entities (including the intensity of labour) cannot be directly measured independently of the monetary 'value' entities and total labour time (labour extensity), which are measured directly.

Fred Moseley's Chapter 6 presents a different outlook. According to Moseley, the standard interpretation of Marx's *Capital* is that Volume I is about the determination of the values of individual commodities, where value is defined as the labour times required to produce commodities. His paper argues that this standard interpretation is wrong, in two important respects. First, Volume I is about the determination of prices or money magnitudes. The necessity of money is derived in the very first chapter of Volume I. Marx's theory assumes that prices or money magnitudes are determined by labour-time magnitudes. In other words, money magnitudes are the *explanandi* – the variables to be explained – and labour-time magnitudes are the *explanans* – the variables in terms of which the money magnitudes are explained. The main money magnitude explained in Volume I is surplus-value, or delta M, the increment of money that emerges as a result of the circulation of capital, which is introduced in Chapter 4 and then explained in Chapter 7. Second, Volume I is about the determination of prices and surplus-value at the aggregate level, i.e. for the economy as a whole. Volume I is about the total class relation between the working class as a whole and the capitalist class as a whole. The most important aspect of this general class relation is the total surplus-value produced by the working class as a whole for the capitalist class as a whole, which is the main question to which Volume I is devoted. Volume I is not about the prices of individual commodities, which are determined in Volume III at a lower level of abstraction. In the determination of individual prices in Volume III, the total surplus-value that is determined in Volume I is taken as given (that is, as already determined).

From a very different perspective, Riccardo Bellofiore's Chapter 7 also argues for a macro-social, class and monetary reading of *Capital I*. Bellofiore first puts forward an *interpretation* of Marx's original argument in favour of the monetary nature of value and on the determination of the wage, making explicit some problems in it; he then proposes a *reconstruction* to overcome these problems by deepening the monetary and macroeconomic aspects of the labour theory of value; finally, he confronts Moseley's reading. Crucially, Bellofiore thinks that Marx grounds the reference of value to abstract labour in a theory of money *as a commodity* in Part One of Volume I, when production has not yet been introduced and the problem of its financing cannot be posed. This theory, in stronger or weaker versions, is maintained throughout the three volumes. Bellofiore argues that jettisoning this theory in favour of a view on the nature of money indebted to the theory of monetary circuit, as he proposes, may in fact *strengthen* Marx's monetary *labour* theory of value. Indeed, it is *only* because the banking *system* finances the firm sector with money created *ex nihilo* that 'labour in motion' can be treated as 'latently' abstract (ante-validation), that living is homogenized in production, and that its immediate result is 'ideal' money – *not only* because, as in Marx, abstract labour is *eventually* 'exhibited' in money as the universal equivalent (final validation). Bellofiore's *reconstruction* converges with Moseley's view on the capitalist process as a sequence of monetary phases based on the priority and autonomy of macroeconomic logic, but he does not think this logic was *explicitly* adopted by Marx in Volume I as a whole. Against Moseley, he presents quotes showing that Marx assumed the wage to be given at the subsistence level *for the working class*. It is the result of the *unconscious* decisions *of the capitalist class as a whole*, which are realized by the *conscious* behaviour of *individual* capitals in *competition*, together with class conflict: a 'macrofoundation of microeconomics'. Bellofiore objects to Moseley's 'macro' approach as mere aggregation where money is a mere 'veil' over values. Thus, in Bellofiore's view, Moseley's is not a true macro-monetary reading of Marx's *Capital*. This essay is followed by a reply by Moseley and a rejoinder by Bellofiore.

In Chapter 8, Tony Smith reviews contemporary neo-Schumpeterian perspectives which have incorporated many of Marx's insights regarding technology, including the endogenous nature of technological change in capitalism, the tendency for technology and science to become increasingly intertwined, the importance of 'learning by doing', and the significance of social institutions. This does not imply that the account of technology in Volume I of *Capital* is solely of historical interest. He argues that three theses set Marx's account apart from competing perspectives: (i) technological change in capitalism is subsumed under the valorization imperative; (ii) technological change in capitalism is essentially tied to the systematic reproduction of the capital/wage-labour relation; and (iii) technological advances in capitalism point to world historical possibilities beyond this mode of production. His chapter reconstructs Marx's arguments for these claims and assesses their contemporary relevance.

Murray's Chapter 9 brings the issue of 'social form' centre stage. He argues that Marx's concepts of formal and real subsumption (spelled out in the unfinished *Results of the Immediate Production Process*, intended to be the transition from Volume I to Volume II of *Capital*) deserve far more attention than they have received. By forcing the question 'formal and real subsumption *under what?*' these concepts point to the seminal idea of Marx's critique of political economy, namely, *specific social forms*. Marx employs the concepts of formal and real subsumption of production under capital to discriminate ways in which the power of capital, understood as specific social form, transforms pre-capitalist modes of production *socially and technically*. Real subsumption involves the social *and technical* transformation of production to better suit the end of accumulating surplus-value. This has many important consequences; for example, a revolution against capital cannot be confined to 'expropriating the expropriators', a strategy aimed at formal subsumption. In Volume I of *Capital*, Marx employs the distinction between *absolute* and *relative* surplus-value rather than the corresponding one between formal and real subsumption. Roughly speaking, the central third of Volume I is devoted to the topics of the production of absolute and relative surplus-value, that is, to formal and real subsumption, respectively. Because it forces the issue of capital as a specific social form, thinking in terms of formal and real subsumption works against a Ricardian reading of *Capital*, which focuses solely on the quantitative side of surplus-value, ignoring the qualitative. Only by appreciating the significance of specific social form can we see the gulf that separates Marx's theory of value from the classical (Ricardian) labour theory of value. Thus, in Murray's view, *Marx's value theory is nothing but a theory of the specific social form of labour and its products under capitalism*; whereas Ricardian value theory is oblivious to the whole problematic of specific social form.

Reuten's Chapter 10 also makes explicit the link between theoretical content and methodology in understanding *Capital*. For an appraisal of Marx's 'general law of capitalist accumulation' in Part Seven of Volume I, he argues, it is crucial to take into account its level of abstraction. In Volume I Marx considers accumulation 'merely as moment of the immediate process of production' and so restricts his analysis to what he calls 'the inner mechanism' of capital accumulation (these 'inner' determinations are *not* more important than 'outer' determinations; indeed, the former have no existence without the latter; and the outer determinations may modify the actualization of the inner determinations). According to Reuten, Marx's warnings about this have been deemphasized in the English translations of the work. The terrain of 'the general law' is the impact of capital accumulation on the working class. Its core is an acceleration triple of growing capital accumulation, increasing productive forces of labour and an increasing technical composition of capital – presented in three phases. In unfolding the dynamic interaction of this triple, Marx introduces the cyclical development of accumulation, though merely as an empirical reference. Reuten considers that, in Volume I, Marx does not – and methodologically could not – develop a theory of the cycle and, *a fortiori*, does not develop a labour-shortage theory of the cycle.

Although all of the essays can be read as individual contributions to particular themes, the many agreements and differences among the authors produce complementary and fruitful treatments of the logic, and therefore subject matter, of Volume I of *Capital*. An obvious example is the four very different treatments of commodity money in the systematic dialectical reconstruction of Marx's value-form analysis (Arthur's

Chapter 2 and Taylor's Chapter 4) and in the textual interpretation of
Marx's monetary macroeconomics (Moseley's Chapter 6 and Bellofiore's
Chapter 7). Yet a fundamental point of agreement emerges from these
diverse perspectives; namely that all four authors – indeed all of the
contributors – identify money as the essential key to understanding
and/or reconstructing Marx's value theory as he presented and developed
it in Volume I.

References

For Marx's 1859 publication and for the three volumes of *Capital* (1867, 1885
and 1894) the first date and details of publication are cited, followed by the
dates and details of English translations. For Marx's manuscripts, here we list
only the volumes for Abteilung II on *Capital* and preparatory material; all
other references to the relevant volumes of MEW and MEGA^2 appear in the
text of section 1 of this Introduction.

Albritton, Robert and John Simoulidis (eds) (2003), *New Dialectics and Political
Economy* (Basingstoke/New York: Palgrave Macmillan).
Arthur, Christopher J. (1996), Engels as interpreter of Marx's economics, in
Christopher J. Arthur (ed.), *Engels Today: A Centenary Appreciation* (Basingstoke:
Macmillan – now Palgrave Macmillan): 173–209.
— (1998a), The fluidity of capital and the logic of the concept, in Christopher
J. Arthur and Geert Reuten (eds) (1998): 95–128.
— (1998b), Systematic dialectic, *Science & Society*, 62/3: 447–59.
— (2000), From the critique of Hegel to the critique of capital, in T. Burns and
I. Fraser (eds): 105–30.
— (2001), On Marx–Engels Collected Works Volume 35, *Studies in Marxism*, 8: 191.
— (2002), Capital in general and Marx's *Capital*, in Martha Campbell and Geert
Reuten (eds): 42–64.
— (2003), *The New Dialectic and Marx's 'Capital'* (Leiden/Boston/Köln: Brill).
Arthur, Christopher J. and Geert Reuten (eds) (1998), *The Circulation of
Capital: Essays on Volume II of Marx's 'Capital'* (London/New York: Palgrave
Macmillan).
Backhaus, Hans-Georg (1969), Zur Dialektik der Wertform, in Alfred Schmidt
(hsg.), *Beiträge zur marxistischen Erkenntnistheorie* (Frankfurt); English translation
by M. Eldred and M. Roth (1980), 'On the dialectics of the value-form', *Thesis
Eleven*, 1/1: 99–120.
— (1992), Between philosophy and science: Marxian social economy as critical
theory, in Werner Bonefeld, Richard Gunn and Kosmas Psychopedis (eds),
Open Marxism 1 (London: Pluto Press): 54–92.
— (1997), *Dialektik der Wertform* (Freiburg: ça ira).
Baldassarri, Mario and Riccardo Bellofiore (eds) (1999), Classical and Marxian
political economy: a debate on Claudio Napoleoni's views, special isssue of
Rivista di Politica Economica, 4–5 (April–May).
Banaji, Janius (1979), From the commodity to capital: Hegel's dialectic in Marx's
Capital, in Diane Elson (ed.): 14–45.
Bellofiore, Riccardo (1985), Marx after Schumpeter, *Capital and Class*, 24: 60–74.

— (1989), A monetary labour theory of value, *Review of Radical Political Economics*, 21 (1–2): 1–25.

— (ed.) (1998), *Marxian Economics: A Reappraisal*, Volumes I and II (London/ New York: Macmillan/S Martin's Press).

— (1999), The value of labour value. The Italian debate on Marx: 1968–1976, *Rivista di Politica Economica*, 4–5: 31–70.

— (2001), Monetary analyses in Sraffa's writings: a comment on Panico, in Terenzio Cozzi and Roberto Marchionatti (eds), *Piero Sraffa: A Centenary Estimate* (London: Routledge): 362–76.

Bellofiore, Riccardo and Roberto Finelli (1998), Capital, labour and time: the Marxian monetary labour theory of value as a theory of exploitation, in Riccardo Bellofiore (ed.) (1998): 48–74.

Burns, Tony and Ian Frazer (eds) (2000), *The Hegel–Marx Connection* (London/ New York: Macmillan).

Campbell, Martha and Geert Reuten (eds) (2002), *The Culmination of Capital: Essays on Volume III of Marx's 'Capital'* (Basingstoke/New York: Palgrave Macmillan).

Colletti, Lucio (1968), Bernstein e il marxismo della Seconda Internazionale, in Lucio Colletti, *Ideologia e società* (Roma–Bari: Laterza, 1969). Translated in *From Rousseau to Lenin: Studies in Ideology and Society* (London: New Left Books, 1972): 45–108.

— (1969), *Il Marxismo e Hegel* (Roma–Bari: Laterza). Translated as *Marxism and Hegel* (London: New Left Books, 1973).

Dobb, Maurice (1940), *Political Economy and Capitalism* (London: Routledge).

Dragstedt, Albert (ed.) (1976), *Value. Studies by Karl Marx* (London: New Park).

Eldred, Michael, Hanlon, Marnie, Kleiber, Lucia and Mike Roth (1982), Reconstructing value-form analysis 1: the analysis of commodities and money, *Thesis Eleven*, 4: 170–88.

— (1983), 'Reconstructing value-form analysis 2: the analysis of the capital – wagelabour relation and capitalist production', *Thesis Eleven*, 7: 87–111.

Elson, Diane (ed.) (1979), *Value: the Representation of Labour in Capitalism* (London: CSE Books).

Engels, Friedrich (1894a), 'Preface' to *Capital*, Volume III (trans. D. Fernbach) (Harmondsworth: Penguin, 1981): 91–111.

— (1894b), 'Supplement and addendum' to *Capital*, Volume 3 (trans. D. Fernbach) (Harmondsworth: Penguin, 1981): 1027–47.

Fineschi, Roberto (2001), *Ripartire da Marx. Processo storico ed economia politica nella teoria del 'capitale'* (Napoli: La Città del Sole).

— (2002a), Per la storia della MEGA, in Mazzone (ed.) (2002): 37–48.

— (2002b), MEGA²: dalla filologia all'interpretazione critica. Un resoconto sul dibattito tedesco sulla teoria del valore negli anni 1970–80, in Mazzone (ed.) (2002): 81–108.

Garegnani, Pierangelo (1981), *Marx e gli economisti classici. Valore e distribuzione nelle teorie del sovrappiù* (Torino: Einaudi).

Hecker, Rolf (2002), La seconda sezione della MEGA² verso il completamento, in Mazzone (ed.) (2002): 49–67.

Hubman, Gerald, Herfried Münkler and Manfred Neuhaus (2002), La MEGA²: riorganizzazione e continuazione, in Mazzone (ed.) (2002): 25–36.

Jorland, Gérard (1995), *Les paradoxes du capital* (Paris: Editions Odile Jacob).

Lippi, Marco (1980), *Value and Naturalism in Marx* (London: New Left Books).

Marx, Karl (1857–58) *Ökonomische Manuskripte 1857/58* (Berlin: Dietz Verlag, 1976 and 1981) (MEGA², II, 1, Teils 1 and 2). Translated into English as the *Grundrisse* (Harmondsworth: Penguin, 1973).

— (1859), *Zur Kritik der politischen Ökonomie*, in Karl Marx: *Ökonomische Manuskripte und Schriften, 1858–1861* (Berlin: Dietz Verlag, 1980) (MEGA², II, 2). Also in MEW 13 (Berlin: Dietz Verlag, 1974). English edition by Maurice Dobb and translation by S.W. Ryazanskaya (1971), *A Contribution to the Critique of Political Economy* (London: Lawrence & Wishart).

— (1861–63), *Zur Kritik der politischen Ökonomie (Manuskript 1861–1863)* (Berlin: Dietz Verlag, 1976–1977–1978–1979–1980–1982 (MEGA², II, 3, Teil 1 to 6).

— (1863–67), *Ökonomische Manuskripte 1863–1867* (Berlin: Dietz Verlag, 1988–1992 (MEGA², II, 4, Teil 1 and 2; Teil 3 yet to be published).

— (1868–70/1877–80) *Karl Marx: Manuskripte zum zweiten Band des 'Kapital'* (MEGA², II, 11), yet to be published.

— (1867–1894) *Karl Marx/Friedrich Engels: Manuskripte und Bearbeitungsmanuskripte zum dritten Band des 'Kapital'* (MEGA², II, 14), yet to be published.

— (1867), *Das Kapital, Kritik der politischen Ökonomie, Erster Band, Der Produktionsprozeβ des Kapitals* (Hamburg, now, Berlin: Dietz Verlag, 1983) (MEGA², II, 5). For the translation of the first chapter and the appendix on the value-form from this first edition see Dragstedt (ed.) (1976). The Appendix is also available in a translation by Michael Roth and Wal Suchting published in *Capital & Class*, 4 (Spring 1978): 130–50, now collected in Simon Mohun (ed.), *Debates in Value Theory* (London: Macmillan, 1994): pp. 9–34.

— (1872), *Das Kapital. Kritik der politischen Ökonomie. Erster Band* (Hamburg, now Berlin: Dietz Verlag, 1987) (MEGA², II, 6).

— (1872–75), *Le Capital* (Paris, now Berlin: Dietz Verlag, 1989) (MEGA², II, 7).

— (1883), *Das Kapital. Kritik der politischen Ökonomie. Erster Band* (Hamburg, now Berlin: Dietz Verlag, 1989) (MEGA², II, 8). First English translation from third German edition by S. Moore and E. Aveling (1887), *Capital, A Critical Analysis of Capitalist Production, Volume I*, reproduced and updated in conformity with the fourth edition in London: Lawrence & Wishart, 1974 (also Berlin: Dietz Verlag, 1990) (MEGA², II, 9).

— (1884–5), *Friedrich Engels: Bearbeitungsmanuskript zum zweiten Band des 'Kapital'* (MEGA², II, 12), yet to be published.

— (1885) (ed. F. Engels), *Das Kapital. Kritik der politischen Ökonomie. Zweiter Band. Der Zirkulationsprozess des Kapitals.* Herausgegeben von Friedrich Engels. (Hamburg) (MEGA², II, 13, yet to be published). In MEW 24 (Berlin: Dietz Verlag). First English translation by Ernest Untermann (1907), *Capital, A Critique of Political Economy, Vol. II, The Process of Circulation of Capital*, reproduced by Lawrence & Wishart, 1974; second English translation by David Fernbach (1978), *Capital, A Critique of Political Economy, Vol II* (Harmondsworth: Penguin).

— (1890) *Das Kapital. Kritik der politischen Ökonomie. Erster Band* (Hamburg, now Berlin: Dietz Verlag, 1991) (MEGA², II, 10). Also in MEW 23 (Berlin: Dietz Verlag). English translations from fourth German edition by Eden and Cedar Paul (1930), *Capital. Volume I* (London: Everyman's Library (J.M. Dent & Sons)); and Ben Fowkes (1976), *Capital, A Critique of Political Economy, Volume One* (Harmondsworth: Penguin).

— (1894) (ed. F. Engels), *Das Kapital. Kritik der politischen Ökonomie. Dritter Band. Der Gesamtprozeβ der kapitalistischen Produktion* Herausgegeben von Friedrich

Engels (Hamburg) (MEGA², II, 15), yet to be published). Also in MEW 25 (Berlin: Dietz Verlag). First English translation by Ernest Untermann (1909), *Capital, A Critique of Political Economy, Volume III, The Process of Capitalist Production as a Whole*, reproduced by Lawrence & Wishart, 1974; second English translation by David Fernbach (1981), *Capital, A Critique of Political Economy, Volume III*, (Harmondsworth: Penguin).

Marx, Karl and Friedrich Engels (1927–35), *Historisch-kritische Gesamtausgabe. Werke, Schriften, Briefe* (MEGA), various publishers.

— (1956–89), *Werke* (MEW) (Berlin: Dietz Verlag).

— (1975–...) *Gesamtausgabe* (MEGA² (Berlin: Dietz Verlag and Akademie Verlag)).

— (1983), *Letters on Capital* (London: New Park).

Mazzone, Alessandro (ed.) (2002), *MEGA²: Marx ritrovato* (Roma: Mediaprint, Laboratorio per la Critica Sociale).

Meek, Ronald L. (1956), *Studies in the Labour Theory of Value* (London: Lawrence & Wishart). Second enlarged edition 1973.

Moseley, Fred (ed.) (1993), *Marx's Method in 'Capital': A Reexamination* (Atlantic Highlands, NJ: Humanities Press).

— Martha Campbell (eds) (1997), *New Investigations of Marx's Method* (Atlantic Highlands, NJ: Humanities Press).

Murray, Patrick (1988), *Marx's Theory of Scientific Knowledge* (Atlantic Highlands, NJ: Humanities Press).

— (2001a) Marx's 'truly social' labour theory of value: abstract labour in Marxian value theory, Part I, *Historical Materialism*, 6: 27–66.

— (2001b) Marx's 'truly social' labour theory of value: abstract labour in Marxian value theory, Part II, *Historical Materialism*, 7: 99–136.

Napoleoni, Claudio (1972), *Lezioni sul capitolo sesto inedito di Marx* (Torino, Boringhieri).

— (1973), *Smith, Ricardo, Marx*, 2nd revised edn (Torino: Boringhieri) (Eng. translation, Oxford: Blackwell, 1975).

Reichelt, Helmut (1972), *Zur logischen Struktur des Kapitalbegriffs bei Karl Marx* (Frankfurt: Europäische Verlagsanstalt).

— (1995) Why did Marx conceal his dialectical method?, in Werner Bonefeld, Richard Gunn, John Holloway and Kosmas Psychopedis (eds), *Open Marxism 3* (London: Pluto Press): 40–83.

Reuten, Geert (1993), The difficult labour of a theory of social value; metaphors and systematic dialectics at the beginning of Marx's 'Capital', in F. Moseley (ed.) (1993): 89–113.

— (1998a), Dialectical method, in J. Davis, W. Hands and U. Mäki (eds), *The Handbook of Economic Methodology* (Cheltenham: Edward Elgar): 103–7.

— (1998b), The status of Marx's reproduction schemes: conventional or dialectical logic, in Christopher Arthur and Geert Reuten (eds, 1998): 187–229.

— (1999), The Source versus Measure Obstacle in Value Theory, *Rivista di Politica Economica*, 4–5: 87–116.

— (2001), The interconnection of systematic dialectics and historical materialism, *Historical Materialism*, 7: 137–66.

— (2003), Karl Marx: his work and the major changes in its interpretation, in W. Samuels, J. Biddle and J. Davis (eds), *The Blackwell Companion to the History of Economic Thought* (Oxford: Blackwell): 148–66.

Reuten, Geert and Michael Williams (1989), *Value-Form and the State: The Tendencies of Accumulation and the Determination of Economic Policy in Capitalist Society* (London and New York: Routledge).

Rosdolsky, Roman (1968), *Zur Entstehungsgeschicte der Marxschen 'Kapital'* (Frankfurt: Europäische Verlagsanstalt). English translation by Pete Burgess (1977), *The Making of Marx's 'Capital'* (London: Pluto).

Rubin, Isaac I. (1927), Abstract labour and value in Marx's system (lecture, June 1927), *Capital and Class* (1978), 5: 107–39.

— (1928), *Essays on Marx's Theory of Value*, 3rd edn (Detroit: Black & Red, 1972).

Schmidt, Alfred (ed.) (1969), *Beiträge zur marxistischen Erkenntnistheorie* (Frankfurt: Suhrkamp).

Smith, Tony (1990), *The Logic of Marx's Capital: Replies to Hegelian Criticisms* (Albany, NY: State University of New York Press).

— (1993) *Dialectical Social Theory and its Critics: From Hegel to Analytical Marxism and Postmodernism* (Albany, NY: State University of New York Press).

— (1999), The relevance of systematic dialectics to Marxian thought: a reply to Rosenthal, *Historical Materialism*, 4: 215–40.

Sraffa, Piero (1960), *Produzione di merci a mezzo di merci* (Torino: Einaudi). In English, *Production of Commodities by Means of Commodities* (Cambridge: Cambridge University Press).

Steedman, Ian (1977), *Marx After Sraffa* (London: New Left Books).

Steedman, Ian *et al.* (1981), *The Value Controversy* (London: Verso).

Sweezy, Paul (1942), *The Theory of Capitalist Development* (New York: Oxford University Press).

Tuchscherer, Walter (1968), *Bevor 'Das Kapital' entstand* (Berlin: Akademie Verlag).

Vygodskij, Vitali (1967), *Geschichte einer grossen Entdeckung* (Berlin: Verlag Die Wirschaft). Soviet original edition, 1965.

2
Money and the Form of Value

Christopher J. Arthur

In the Preface to the first edition of *Capital*, Marx drew attention to the fact that the chapter on the commodity, and, more especially, the section on the form of value, is the most difficult (89–90).[1] Yet this section is, Marx told Engels, 'decisive' for the whole book.[2] In this chapter he felt compelled to 'popularize' the presentation of certain topics. But the intrinsic difficulty of the section on the form of value prevented this, not because it is complex; rather 'the value-form, whose fully developed shape is the money-form, is very simple and bare of content'[3] (90). The trouble is that it pertains to the most abstract issues of all in 'the analysis of economic forms', including the nature of *money*.

The difficulty, not merely of an adequate presentation, but of the problem itself, is reflected in the fact that Marx wrote up this section no fewer than four times. First came the version published in *Contribution to a Critique of Political Economy* (1859); then the version in Chapter 1 of the first edition of *Capital* (1867) was supplemented at the last minute by a special appendix; finally the material was rewritten again for the second edition (1873), a rewriting that is more than a mere conflation of the double presentation in the first.

1. Page numbers in the text are to the B. Fowkes translation of *Capital, Volume I*, 1976.
2. 22 June 1867; Marx and Engels, *Letters on 'Capital'*, 1983: 105.
3. '*Inhaltlos*', mistranslated by Fowkes as 'slight in content': cf. *Das Kapital: Erster Band*, Karl Marx and Friedrich Engels *Werke*, Band 23, 1962: 12.

1. Preliminaries

Before addressing the topic of Chapter 1, Section 3, some preliminary points must be made.

1.1 Two senses of 'Wertform'

Our difficulties in comprehending the focus of Marx's investigation start in the Preface where he gives two apparently different characterizations of 'the economic cell-form', namely 'the commodity-form of the product of labour, or the value-form of the commodity' (90). The 'or' here is clearly not an 'or' of alterity but an 'or' of identity. Yet it is not obvious that there *is* an identity, since the term 'commodity' has changed sides. On one account the topic is the product of labour and the interesting thing about it here is that it takes the social form of a commodity (in addition to its natural form). On the other account the topic is the commodity and the interesting thing about it is its value-form 'whose fully-developed shape is the money-form'. Marx connects these two topics when he says that what makes the product a commodity is its value-form; thus to develop the nature of the commodity is to develop the value-form (154).[4] Nonetheless there is a definite ambiguity in Marx's term '*Wertform*'.[5] Sometimes this is used as a specification of *form*; this occurs wherever the value-form of a commodity is contrasted with its natural form. But sometimes it is used as a specification of value; this occurs in two contexts, when value-form is contrasted with plain value, or value substance, or value magnitude, and, most interestingly for the present discussion, when it is plural: the *forms of value* listed (on 174) as commodity, money, capital, and the transitional forms developed in Section 3. It follows from the double specification implicit in '*Wertform*' that there are *two* possible errors, both committed by classical political economy: first, the naturalization of bourgeois production and hence a failure to address how the product of labour acquires a value-form (173–4); second, the failure to connect money to the value-form systematically as Marx does in Section 3 (n. 34 on p. 174[6]).

4. Marx, 1976, *Capital, Volume I*, has a mistranslation; 154, lines 4–5: for 'form of value' read 'commodity-form'; cf. *Das Kapital: Werke*, Band 23: 76.
5. This has already been pointed out by G. Reuten: 'The difficult labour of a theory of social value; metaphors and systematic dialectics at the beginning of Marx's *Capital*' (in Fred Moseley (ed.), *Marx's Method in 'Capital': A Reexamination*, 1993): 100–1.
6. Study of the first edition reveals this footnote was originally placed where it is obviously natural, namely as a final touch to what became Section 3 on the form of value: *Das Kapital Erster Band 1867*: Karl Marx and Friedrich Engels *Gesamtausgabe* (MEGA), Abteilung II, Band 5, 1983, n. 24 on pp. 43–4.

It is characteristic of a dialectically organized totality that what may be treated as form at one level may, at a higher level of abstraction, be content (for example, in Hegel's *Logic*, logical form as such is the *content* evolved by thought). So, here, it is appropriate to distinguish '*value-form*' as a reference to *value as the form* taken by the product of labour in the context of capitalist commodity production, and the '*value-form*' when the content is the *dialectic of the forms of value* addressed in Section 3 of Chapter 1.

1.2 The relation between Chapter 1 and Chapter 2

There can be no doubt that the topics of Marx's first two chapters, *and their order*, were very deliberately chosen by Marx: first 'the commodity'; and only then 'exchange'.[7] In this light it is quite extraordinary how many accounts of the form of value offend against this separation by discussion of the motives of exchangers at the more abstract level. Marx quite consciously postponed such considerations until he had already analysed the nature of what it was they exchanged, the commodity as a unity of use-value and value.

A very important point about the nature of money is involved here also. To put the point negatively, there is no trace of any discussion of barter in Chapter 1.[8] *Marx does not derive money as a device to overcome the limitations of barter*. He derives money as the form necessary to constitute value objectively.

To derive the dialectic of the forms of value from the motives of exchangers seriously distorts Marx's method. In *Capital* it is Chapter 2

---

7. One of the few to have grasped this is Mario Robles-Baez: 'On Marx's dialectic of the genesis of the money form', 1997. A complete collapse of the value-form into the exchange system, and hence of Chapter 1 into Chapter 2, is characteristic of the interpretation advanced by C. Benetti and J. Cartelier, for example. Robles-Baez refutes a paper by Benetti; here we use Cartelier: 'Marx's theory of value, exchange and surplus value: a suggested reformulation', *Cambridge Journal of Economics*, 1991, as our reference point throughout. Cartelier says Marx's discussion of the value-form is intended 'to bring out the conditions of effective exchange relations' (259). But Marx says nothing about that in Chapter 1, Section 3: the point of the section is to arrive at an adequate expression of value. This presupposes that there *is* a problem about effective exchange between dissociated producers; and the predication of money as the actual universal equivalent does indeed solve that problem; but the dialectic of the value-form itself keeps that issue latent.
8. As Marx notes, the abstraction he employs in discussing the simple form is '*x* commodity *A* = *y* commodity *B*', which is *not* that of 'direct exchange of products' which has the form '*x* use-value *A* = *y* use-value *B*' (*Capital I*: 181).

that studies the activities of *exchangers*, and their intersecting motives; this is within the context set by the objectivity of the value-form developed through analysis of the exchange relations established between *commodities* in Chapter 1. The only occasion for uncertainty here is on the question of money. There is an interesting textual story to tell about this. It took Marx four tries before he got it right! In the 1859 *Contribution* ... there is no separate chapter on exchange, although one could mark a place in the text where this transition occurs in the first chapter on 'the commodity';[9] but the development of the form of value occurs on both sides of this divide. When *Capital* presented the same material again in 1867 the division is clearly made; and what is notable now is that money it is not treated at all in 'Chapter' (here 'Section') 1! But in the appendix on 'The form of value', thrown in at the last minute, it is added! Somewhat embarrassedly, perhaps, Marx wrote to Engels this had been done 'only for continuity'.[10] However, by the second edition Marx had definitely decided to put the money *form* into Chapter 1.

In sum, Chapter 1 as a whole is not studying the process *of* exchange, neither is it about proposals *for* exchange, it is asking what it is to *be* a commodity; and to be a commodity involves *all* the determinations of Chapter 1, including those of Section 3 on its *form*, in which it is shown that an adequate expression of the value of commodities requires the existence of money.

1.3 Tools of analysis

Below I shall bring to bear on Marx's discussion the theory of relations expounded by Bertrand Russell.[11] Russell symbolizes 'x has the relation R to y' as 'xRy'. Russell holds that aRb is a different relation from bRa, even where it implies it; this is because it is characteristic of a relation of two terms that it proceeds *from* one *to* the other, it has a '*sense*'. On his intensional view of relations two relations may have the same extension (cover the same values of a and b) without being identical. Indeed he holds that every relation has a *converse*, i.e. that there is a relation R^* such that aRb is equivalent to bR^*a for all values of a and b. Equally important is Russell's further point that with certain relations – notably

---

9. Marx, *A Contribution to the Critique of Political Economy*, Marx and Engels *Collected Works* (MECW), Volume 29, 1987: 282, last para.
10. 27 June 1867; *Letters on 'Capital'*: 108.
11. The following is drawn from Russell's *Principles of Mathematics*, sections 28, 94, 95, 151, 152, 157, 209, 210.

that of 'equality' – the converse is the *same* as the original relation; such relations are called *symmetrical*. For an example of Russell's terms, consider the marriage of Jean and Joe. 'Jean is the wife of Joe' implies the converse, 'Joe is the husband of Jean', but there is no symmetry since it is wrong to say 'Joe is the wife of Jean'. Of course 'spouse of' is symmetrical, and of course the 'sense' of the relations could be side-stepped by saying 'Joe and Jean are spouses'.

Equality has the property of being reflexive, symmetrical and transitive (RST), i.e. 'a term which has the relation at all has it to itself; if A has the relation to B, B has it to A; if A has it to B, and B to C, A has it to C'. Thus: '$a = a$' (R); 'if $a = b$, then $b = a$' (S); and 'if $a = b$, and $b = c$, then $a = c$' (T). Russell's 'principle of abstraction' states that such relations 'are always constituted by possession of a common property', or 'identity of content', a 'third term' to which both sides of the original relation have one and the same relation, here the same magnitude.

Thus far Russell: however, I wish to add something. An important consideration in Marx's text is the connection between aRb and bRa. Of course if R is symmetrical, because bRa is the converse of aRb, this is no problem; but I am going to argue that the expression of value (where $R = $'has a value expressed in the use-value of') is not really a symmetrical relation. Accordingly I coin the term *reversed relation* or simply *reverse* to refer to bRa where aRb and bRa both hold, but are not derivable from each other as converses. This is the case whenever a reciprocal relation is disaggregated into two similar, *complementary*, yet *different*, relations. For example, if we shake hands, I shake your hand and you shake mine even though 'shake' is not a symmetrical relation. Or, if a marriage ceremony involves exchange of rings, 'Joe gives a ring to Jean' and 'Jean gives a ring to Joe' even though 'gives to' is not symmetrical. Notice that the 'converse' of the first relation is 'Jean received a ring from Joe'; this is *not* the same relation as the original; thus the apparent symmetry in such cases is not a result of aRb and bRa being the converse of each other. They are parallel in form, but are *different* relations. Unfortunately the Fowkes translation of *Capital* puts 'converse' for these relations, but, since this is not Russell's sense of converse, below I shall amend in this light the translation of '*Rückbeziehung*' to 'reversed relation'. The Moore and Aveling translation puts 'opposite', which I use occasionally.

2. The argument of *Capital*

Marx begins by analysing the commodity into use-value and exchange-value. 'Use-value' is identified with the *body* of the commodity, with its 'natural form'; at the very same time commodities are socially imputed as 'bearers' of 'exchange-value' (126). How can exchange be more than a matter of the transfer from hand to hand of use-values, incommensurable as such? Marx gives the following argument designed to show that commodities may be predicated with a value in virtue of which they are (in the right physical proportions) equivalents. In relations of exchange a given commodity, which exchanges against many others, therewith acquires a range of exchange-values. Every valid exchange-value 'cannot be anything other than the mode of expression, the "form of appearance", of a content distinguishable from it' (127). This certainly seems to license a claim that every such exchange-value is 'equivalent' to every other. But Marx goes further. He argues that these exchange-values are 'equal', are of 'identical magnitude'. Moreover the exchange relation 'can always be represented by an equation', and the significance of this is that it shows 'a common element' must be present on both sides of the equation 'which in itself is neither the one nor the other' (127). This 'common factor' is 'value' (128).

Although Marx immediately goes on to correlate such 'value' with the labour expended in the production of a commodity, this is a separate step in his argument. Marx later made this very clear in his notes 'On Wagner': 'Exchange-values ... represent something *common to them* [commodities] which "is wholly independent of their use-values", namely *"value"* ... Thus I do not say "the common social substance of exchange-value" is "labour", and since I deal with the *form of value*, i.e. the development of exchange-value, at some length in a separate section, it would be curious if I were to reduce this "form" to a "common social substance", labour.'[12]

Marx's identification of value with objectified labour has proved a hugely controversial matter, into which I do not intend to enter. What concerns me here is the validity of the prior inference from exchange-relations to value. To reach Marx's conclusion quite restrictive premises have to be invoked. As we saw in Russell's theory of relations, the inference that a relation is one of equality (which then licenses the further inference to a common property) may be made when the relation in question is reflexive, symmetrical and transitive. The difficulty in Marx's case is that '*A* exchanges against *B*' is not necessarily transitive since owners of *A* and *C* may know nothing of their mutual relation to *B*. However, an exchange system may be considered ideally RST if it is assumed no possibility of arbitrage exists (something that in fact requires money). But there is a further difficulty. Even if it is acceptable to speak

12. Marx, 'On Wagner', MECW, Vol. 24, 1989: 533–4.

of the commodities as having value which appears as exchange-value, there remains the problem whether this is simply a way of referring in abbreviated form to these relations, or whether, as Marx seems to say in some places, these relations must express something *intrinsic* to the commodities, that value has a material ground in the commodities prior to exchange. This is a problem, I believe, because commodity exchange is not a naturally given system expressing the natural properties of commodities; it is a socially imposed form of existence of goods, a social practice which may create a false impression of reflecting such a pre-given content. (If there were such a given value content then money would be a mere numeraire, whereas we shall see below that it is *necessary* that it exist, in order to posit the actuality of value.)

Moreover, the identification of value with labour does not help us here because Marx very properly draws attention to the distinction between concrete and abstract labour; considering the commodity as a value means disregarding the concrete labours of the producers and treating it as a representation of labour 'in the abstract', he says (128). But this determination of labour is itself a purely social one. The magnitude of value makes reference to the complex notion of socially necessary labour time; but even the qualitative problem of ascertaining the meaningfulness of the concept of 'abstract labour' simply mirrors the problem already noted about the validity of the reduction of exchange-value to value.

Marx recognizes that, if the presentation is about our external reflection on them, *we* analytically reduce commodities to values, but fail as yet to show how *they* express their own value. That is why Section 3 is necessary to complement the analytical grounding, effected 'externally' earlier. For such commodity-values, which 'merely existed as our abstraction', now 'must appear as their own mutual relation' in order to remove the suspicion that such a mental abstraction has no truth.[13] And the same goes for the labour content: 'Only particular commodities, particular use values embodying the labour of private individuals, confront one another in the exchange process. Universal labour time itself is an abstraction which, as such, does not exist for commodities.' However, it is not merely 'our abstraction' if it is seen that there is a real abstraction carried through in the process of exchange: 'The different kinds of individual labour, represented in these particular use values, in fact become labour in general, and in this way social labour, only by

13. Marx, *Contribution* . . . MECW, Vol. 29: 285.

actually being exchanged . . . Universal social labour is consequently not a ready-made prerequisite but an emerging result.'[14]

Marx is evidently concerned that value, and abstract labour, are mere abstractions unless an adequate form of expression of such a presupposed essence is developed; ultimately money is derived to meet this requirement. But whence come these abstractions in the first place? Here it seems to me Marx gives two answers, which are perhaps compatible. Frequently (as we have just seen, and shall see again below) the abstraction results from his own analysis; it is a *theoretical* reduction of exchange-values to value. But he is also able to argue that the abstraction is more than a move in theory, it results from the way in which exchange itself objectively treats commodities as abstractions of themselves, in that all the various natural properties they have are set aside and only their character as exchangeables is left. Social practice declares that a commodity as a value does 'not contain an atom of use-value' (128). The same goes for abstract labour: in the words of the French edition of *Capital*: 'only exchange produces this reduction [of concrete to abstract], by bringing the products of the most diverse kinds of labour into relation with each other on an equal footing'.[15]

The important thing to notice is that in both cases the commodity is the matter of an 'external reflection' upon it, whether its reduction from a perceptible use-value to a shell for a posited value essence results from theoretical, or material, practice. This value is not yet *presented* as such by the commodities themselves. The task Marx has to undertake is to show how the commodities themselves reflect value into themselves through the development of their value relations. The section on the form of value traces the representation of value itself, from less adequate to more adequate forms. Thus the development of the forms of value is not looking at the expressions of *a given essence*; rather its object is just as much to *form this essence*, by so shaping the commodity manifold as to *posit* this presupposition. The variety of the exchange equivalents, of Section 1, while apparently expressive of a presumed essence, do not give it the required unitary form. It follows that the section on the *form* of value, where exchange-value as the 'necessary mode of expression, or form of appearance, of value' (128) is investigated, is an essential complement to the first two sections, for, unless an adequate *social form* of value can be developed, value itself has not yet been properly grounded. Moreover, it is the systemic constitution of

14. Marx, *Contribution* . . . MECW, Vol. 29: 286.
15. *Le Capital, Paris 1872–75*, MEGA II, Band 7, 1989: 55.

the value essence that grounds the systemic determination of its magnitude on socially necessary labour time.

In his introductory remarks to the section, Marx also gives advance notice that he will (in the course of this study of the social reality of the commodity) 'show the origin' of the money-form, 'a task never even attempted by bourgeois economics' (139). This argument will show value gains an *adequate form* only in and through money.

3. The forms of value

The context of this discussion is set when Marx (rather too late in the exposition, in truth) says: 'When, at the beginning of this chapter, we said in the customary manner that a commodity is both a use-value and an exchange-value, this was strictly speaking wrong. A commodity is a use-value or object of utility, and a "value". It appears as the two-fold thing it really is as soon as its value possesses its own particular form of manifestation, which is distinct from its [the commodity's] natural form' (152).

The question to be addressed, then, is: *how* is 'the value of a commodity *expressed'*; *how* does it 'acquire a *form of appearance of its own?*'[16] Only if it *is* adequately expressed does value become *posited* as the 'opposite' of use-value. Marx observes that value contains 'not an atom of matter' and has a 'purely social' reality (138–9). If it is 'purely social', then looking for the value essence *within* an isolated commodity is clearly futile; we must go *outward* from it to its developing relations. Certainly value cannot be present in the commodity as such: 'we may twist and turn a single commodity as we wish; it remains impossible to grasp it as a thing possessing value ... [Value] can only appear in the social relation between commodity and commodity' (138–9).

It will be important in what follows to distinguish carefully between the *relations* of commodities, and the *expression of value* of commodities. The latter is derived from, and manifested in, certain relations, but is not the same thing as them. Marx certainly explains the possible expressions of value by reference to the development of commodity relations, but he does not always make clear that two different concepts are involved. It is probably this conflation which introduces incoherence into his exposition when he provides propositional functions to articulate the

---

16. Marx, 'The Value-Form', in *Debates in Value Theory*, edited by S. Mohun, 1994: 11. Throughout this section I shall draw also on this text which appeared as an appendix to the first edition of *Capital*.

forms of value. These propositions, we shall show, are not consistent with the commentary that follows them.

Let us begin with 'the simple form of value'. This is how it is given at the head of the discussion: *The simple, isolated, or accidental form of value* is:

x commodity $A = y$ commodity B, or: x commodity A is worth y commodity B (139).

(And his examples substitute '20 yards of linen' and '1 coat'.)

Now what sense can be made of the '=' in the first version? As it stands the proposition makes no sense because A and B are incommensurable use-values. To make any sense of it requires expanding the '=' to 'equal in value'. Indeed it is tempting on such a view to read here 'The value of A = the value of B'. But this reading of the simple form of value is refuted by Marx himself when he develops his commentary, we shall see. The alternative proposition 'A is worth B' is better because it establishes that what is at issue is the attempt to find an adequate form of expression for the value of A, and that B plays the role of A's equivalent. However the proposition still allows the following misreading: 'A is worth the value of B, or what B is worth'. If we now turn to Marx's own commentary we find the above propositions are flatly contradicted. Marx stresses that in expressing the value of A in its equivalent B, *B appears as a use-value, not a value*. 'Hence, in the value-relation, in which the coat is the equivalent of the linen, the form of the coat counts as the form of value. The value of the commodity linen is therefore expressed by the physical body of the commodity coat, the value of one by the use-value of the other' (143).

If this is so, the original two versions of the simple form should be scrapped and replaced with the following propositions, reflecting Marx's discussion of it.

Form I[17] *The simple form of value*:

'z **of commodity** A **expresses its value in** y **of the use-value** B'; or more concisely: '**The value of** zA *is* yB'.

---

17. I follow the numbering I–IV, used in the first edition, rather than the A–D of the second; and I shall go beyond Marx in exploring the price-form; see V and VI below.

The first commodity is said to be in 'the relative form of value', the second commodity fulfils the function of its equivalent, 'it is in the equivalent form' (139). Marx spells out the polarity as follows: 'It is not the latter commodity whose value is being expressed. It only provides the material in which the value of the first commodity is expressed' (140).[18]

Marx expressly denies that the simple form of value is reflexive: 'I cannot express the value of linen in linen. 20 yards of linen = 20 yards of linen is not an expression of value' (140). It is also not symmetrical; considering the expressions '20 yards of linen are worth one coat' and 'one coat is worth 20 yards of linen', Marx comments: 'Here *both*, linen and coat, are *at the same time* in relative value-form and in equivalent form. But, *nota bene*, for two different persons and *in two different expressions of value*, which simply occur *at the same time*.'[19]

While '*z* commodity *A* = *y* commodity *B*' is on the face of it reflexive and symmetrical,[20] the proposition I here propose is not. 'The use-value of *B* is expressed in the value of *A*' is evident nonsense; while the converse relation 'The use-value of *B* expresses the value of *A*' is clearly not the same relation as '*expresses in*'. (The reversed expression is treated below.) Only the reformulation of the simple form I have suggested gives meaning to the sharp distinction Marx draws between the 'poles' of the value-expression, because the relation 'expresses in' implies a *distinction* between what expresses itself and what it is expressed in. This polarity powers the dialectic of the section on the forms of value and is the 'germ' of money. The simple form of value 'is, so to speak, the cell-form or, as Hegel would say, the *in itself of money*'.[21] The condition of existence of the 'inner opposition' of use-value and value (developed in Section 1) is that it be *externalized* in the *form* of value, '*represented by*

18. Cartelier (1991) writes, 'Marx puts forth the concept of the *relative form of value* and that of the *equivalent* form denoting, respectively, the commodity the private agent produces and supplies for the market and the commodity she or he wishes to bring back from the market' (258). But Marx says nothing about taking commodities to market in his definitions.
19. Marx, 'The Value-Form,' in *Debates in Value Theory*, edited by S. Mohun, 1994: 13. Cf. *Capital I*, p. 140.
20. In formal logic, that is; but there is an informal logic of mathematics in which $x = f(y)$ is not taken as reflexive and symmetrical because it is understood x is the variable whose value is to be determined and y determines it. Possibly Marx had this at the back of his mind. But, note, in the form of value, A, unlike x, is the *active* party that determines itself to B.
21. Marx, *Das Kapital, Erster Band 1867*, MEGA II 5: 28n.

an *external opposition*, i.e. the *relation* of *two* commodities'.[22] What is required is to show that the 'essence' of *A* is value; but such value cannot appear *in A* because as an isolated commodity it is merely use-value, so it must appear in something *other* than the use-value *A*, namely the use-value *B*. Paradoxically the claim that *A* is a value requires *A* to *exclude* this value from itself and posit it in *B*. Even if *B* is itself a value (as at this stage it is) *its* value-expression is as it were stifled at birth so that the use-value *B* figures as the actualization of *A*'s value. In the first edition of *Capital* a lot of attention is paid to this polarity of the value-form.

> It is relatively easy to distinguish the value of the commodity from its use-value... These abstract opposites fall apart... It is different with the *value-form* which exists only in the relation of commodity to commodity... Instead of falling apart, the opposing determinations of the commodity are reflected against one another... The commodity is right from the start a *dual* thing, use-value *and* value, product of useful labour *and* abstract coagulate of labour. In order to manifest itself as what it is, it must therefore *double* its form... Now since the natural form of a commodity is the exact opposite of its value-form, it has to turn *another* natural form – the *natural form of another commodity* – into its value-form.[23]

Marx again takes the opportunity to stress the difference between 'our analysis' and the concrete logic of the value expression: 'If I say: *As a commodity* linen is use-value *and* exchange-value, this is my [N.B.] judgment about the *nature* of the commodity gained by analysis.' As opposed to this, in the expression of value 'the linen itself says it'.[24]

Marx further develops the polarity by arguing that because 'the first commodity plays an active role, the second a passive one', it is impossible for the same commodity to play both roles at the same time (139). 'The same commodity cannot simultaneously appear in both forms in

---

22. Marx, 'The Value-Form' in *Debates in Value Theory*, edited by S. Mohun, 1994: 23.
23. Marx, 'The Commodity, Chapter One, Volume One of the first edition of *Capital*' in *Value: Studies by Karl Marx*, trans. A. Dragstedt, 1976: 21–2; translation of last word corrected; cf. Marx, *Das Kapital Erster Band 1867*, MEGA II 5: 31–2.
24. Marx, 'The Value-Form' in *Debates in Value Theory*, edited by S. Mohun, 1994: 24.

the same expression of value. These forms rather *exclude* each other as polar opposites' (140). (When Marx stresses that relative and equivalent forms are 'opposed extremes' (140) this is only obscured by using '=' in the expression of value, which implies identity without opposition.)

Marx then moves to consider the *reversed* expression (in his terms 'y commodity $B = x$ commodity A'), in our terms, 'yB expresses its value in the use-value zA'. It is important to consider whether the reverse expression is the *same* as the first. Using '=' it is of course thus symmetrical. But, as we have seen, Marx contradicts this implication of '=', and so he does here, strongly emphasizing that *a different expression* of value is evolved (140). Marx is quite correct. Although 'yB expresses its value in the use-value zA' looks similar to 'zA expresses its value in the use-value yB' it is a different case because it is not derivable from the latter as its converse. (Rather, the converse is 'The use-value yB expresses the value of zA'.) In the Appendix to the first edition Marx says the reversed expression has the same content but a different *form* of value. The two expressions are in fact 'opposed' ones because the commodities have exchanged roles.[25]

An abstract, purely formal, external standpoint of analysis, 'our' analysis, can 'bear in mind', so to speak, at the same time *both* opposite value expressions: that of A in B and that of B in A. But *concretely* they exclude each other because once we have 'A expresses its value in B' we cannot have the reversed expression, because in the same universe of value a commodity cannot play both roles. This is brought out clearly by comparing with the original expression the converse of the reversed expression. This gives us the following antithesis: 'A expresses its value in the use-value B' and 'A – as use-value – expresses the value of B'. In the first, A is playing the active role and seeking its equivalent in B; but, in the second, A is playing the passive role of serving as such an equivalent. Both are certainly *potential* roles that A may be given, but they are exclusive of one another *in the same value space*.[26]

The consideration that the simple form of value has a complementary reversed expression also leads Marx to consider the analytical option of abstracting from this relatedness altogether. In the first edition: '[If we say] 20 yards of linen *and* 1 coat *are equivalents*, or *both are values of*

25. Marx, 'The Value-Form' in *Debates in Value Theory*, edited by S. Mohun, 1994: 13.
26. Benetti and Cartelier refuse to believe Marx could mean to 'exclude' the reversed expression; they take the two expressions as complementary, with disastrous results as we shall see below.

equal magnitude', then 'we do not express *the value* of either of the two commodities in *the use-value* of the other. *Neither* of the two commodities is hence set up *in equivalent form*. *Equivalent* means here only *something equal in magnitude*, both things having been silently reduced in our heads to the abstraction *value.'*[27] (Yet this reduction was just what Marx did in Section 1: implicitly therefore this statement is a comment on the inadequacy of that section, an inadequacy to be corrected in this section.) In the second edition: 'If we say that, as values, commodities are simply congealed quantities of human labour, *our* analysis reduces them, it is true, to the level of *abstract* value, but does not give them a form of value distinct from their natural form. It is otherwise in the value-relation of one commodity to another. The first commodity's value character emerges here through its own relation to the second commodity.' (141–2; emphasis added).

As before, Marx contrasts 'our' analytical reduction to an abstraction with the real relating of commodities. To say '*A* and *B* are equal in value' loses precisely the concrete specificity of the polarity that constitutes the value relation. Only through the real relations of the commodities themselves can this analytically imposed abstraction become objectively concretized.

The same point applies to the *labour* represented in the first commodity: 'In order to retain linen as a merely corporeal expression of human labour one has to abstract from all that which makes it to be really a thing. Any objectivity of human labour which is itself abstract (i.e., without any additional qualities and content) is necessarily an abstract objectivity – a *thing of thought.'*[28] The product under this description has merely a 'phantom-like objectivity' (128). But the equivalent form of value *posits* this objectivity of abstract human labour. 'It is only the expression of equivalence between different sorts of commodities which brings to view the specific character of value-creating labour, by actually reducing the different kinds of commodity to their common quality of being human labour in general' (142).

This is a form of self-analysis:

Everything our analysis of the value of commodities previously told us is repeated by the linen itself, as soon as it enters into association with another commodity, the coat. Only it reveals its thoughts in

27. Marx, 'The Value-Form' in *Debates in Value Theory*, edited by S. Mohun, 1994: 16–17.
28. Marx, 'The Commodity, Chapter One . . . of the first edition of *Capital*': 19–20.

a language with which it alone is familiar, the language of commodities. In order to tell us that labour creates its own value in its abstract quality of being human labour, it says the coat, in so far as it counts as its equal, i.e. is value, consists of the same labour as it does itself. In order to inform us that its sublime objectivity as a value differs from its stiff and starchy existence as a body, it says that value has the appearance of a coat (143–4).

To sum up: the exchange relation of *A* and *B* allows two opposite expressions of value to be inferred, that of *A* in the use-value *B*, and that of *B* in the use-value *A*. Marx correctly argues these are *different* expressions, and are not symmetrical, although they spring from the same objective relation. Marx also argues correctly that nothing is gained by abstracting from the 'sense' of these two expressions so as to reduce *A* and *B* to 'equivalents'. This would be 'our abstraction'. What has to be addressed is how the development of the real relations of the commodities allows that 'abstraction' to gain explicit expression, to become concrete.

Next Marx moves to another important topic: 'the peculiarities of the equivalent form'. The background, let us remind ourselves, is that: 'By means of the value-relation the natural form of commodity *B* becomes the value-form of commodity *A*' (144). Marx derives from this three 'peculiarities'.

The first peculiarity which strikes us when we reflect on the equivalent form is this, that use-value becomes the form of appearance of its opposite, value... Since a commodity cannot be related to itself as equivalent, and therefore cannot make its own physical shape into the expression of its own value, it must be related to another commodity as equivalent, and therefore must make the physical shape of another commodity into its own value-form (148).

If commodities had value in isolation such an equivalent would be merely a numeraire. But since value 'is something purely social' (149), it is not a matter of finding a numeraire but of positing this presupposition.

The second peculiarity is that in the equivalent form 'concrete labour becomes the form of manifestation of its opposite, abstract human labour' (150). With regard to this second peculiarity we find that Marx presents an interesting aspect of it, namely that there is here an *inversion* of abstract and concrete. In the Appendix he says: 'This *inversion* [*Verkehrung*] . . . characterises the expression of value.'[29] The same idea reappears in compressed form in the second edition:

> In the value expression of the commodity matters are topsy-turvy [*verdreht*]. In order to express the fact that, for instance, weaving creates the value of the linen through its general property of being human labour rather than in its concrete form as weaving, we contrast it with the concrete labour which produces the equivalent of the linen, namely, tailoring. Tailoring is now seen as the tangible form of realization of abstract human labour (150[30]).

The third 'peculiarity' is that 'private labour becomes the form of its opposite, namely labour in its directly social form' (151). I have here corrected the translation which puts 'takes the form'.[31] To get it right requires an understanding of the role played by the equivalent form. The problem is this: how can commodities achieve social recognition, if immediately a commodity is a use-value produced privately by concrete labours? The answer is that in the form of value the equivalent is posited as the opposite of what it is immediately, its own shape becomes the form of the required universal determinants, its use-value stands for value, its concrete labour stands for abstract labour, and its private labour stands for sociality of labour. All three cases of peculiarity are parallel, and the translation should reflect this.

In fact all three cases involve the inversion Marx explicitly stresses only in the second peculiarity. Here, we see that the commodity in equivalent form appears as a use-value (whence the product of private concrete labours) but 'in and for itself', essentially, it is value (and hence represents abstract social labour). If the constitutive context of

29. Marx, 'The Value-Form' in *Debates in Value Theory*, edited by S. Mohun, 1994: 19.

30. Translation amended; cf. *Das Kapital: Erster Band, Werke*, Band 23: pp. 72–3.

31. This mistranslation was discovered by Cyril Smith: 'Hegel, economics, and Marx's *Capital*', 1996: 245–6. Curiously all three translations of *Capital* (B. Fowkes; S. Moore and E. Aveling; E. and C. Paul) make this mistake, but both translations of the same sentence in the first edition Appendix (M. Roth and W. Suchting; A. Dragstedt) get it right.

this 'inverted world' is ignored then the natural form of the equivalent appears fetishistically as a site of inherent value.[32]

Now we come to an important passage in which Marx explains the logic of his transition from the simple form. This is necessary because of its 'insufficiency' (154). It is worth dwelling on this. It is all too easy to read an argument like Marx's as a sequence of deductions in which a well-founded premise has its implication drawn out. But here, in Section 3, the movement is the reverse. The simple form is quite *insufficient* to establish an adequate expression of value, value is *not* well-founded as yet; hence the necessity to pass to a more complex value-form and to test its capacity to do better at expressing value.[33]

The 'deficiency' (Moore's translation) of the simple form is that in it a commodity is related only to one other, which means that value has not achieved the universality of its expression implied by the assumption made in Section 1 that underlying the web of exchange relations is some force that regulates them, that the many exchange-values a commodity may have yet exist in a unity. Moreover there is nothing special about the value equivalent *B* that would grant it a role as a privileged interlocutor with *A*. One could just as well have taken *A*'s relation to *C*, or to *D*, under review.

In this way Marx develops the simple form to a more comprehensive value-form: 'the total or expanded form of value' (154). Unfortunately, as always, Marx's formula employs the '=' sign. If we replace this with our improved formula then we have:

Form II *The expanded form of value*

$$z \text{ of commodity } A \text{ expresses its value in: } \left\{ \begin{array}{l} y \text{ of commodity } B \\ \text{or } x \text{ of commodity } C \\ \text{or } w \text{ of commodity } D \\ \text{or so on and so forth} \end{array} \right.$$

At first sight it seems Marx has solved his problem because he says this form demonstrates that 'the value of the linen remains unaltered in magnitude, whether expressed in coats, coffee, or iron, or in innumerable other commodities' (156). But this is not at all plain since all these commodity-equivalents are incommensurable. Notice also that the

32. This is listed as a 'fourth peculiarity' in the first edition: Marx, 'The Value-Form' in *Debates in Value Theory*, edited by S. Mohun, 1994: 21.
33. The method used is explained in my 'Systematic dialectic', 1998 and 2002.

connector here, significantly, is 'or', not 'and' (when reversed in the general form it will be 'and').[34]

Why in the expansion of the simple form does Marx arrive at the connector 'or' to link the various equivalents? In Section 1 these were clearly considered as a whole when Marx deduced from these many equivalents that a commodity has the inner essence of value. But when Marx expands the simple form it cannot result in such a heterogeneous bundle of use-values because the parameters of the problem under consideration demand that the form be unitary. Hence *B*, *C*, *D*, and so on are *alternative* 'units' of value logically implicit in commodity relations. These are *alternative* ways to express *A* as a value. So the problem of an adequate unitary expression of value, and its magnitude, remains to be solved. This is then precisely what Marx says when he again discovers 'defects' in the expanded form (156). These are:

1. The series of *relative* expressions of value is necessarily incomplete; and it is a motley mosaic of alternative expressions each inconsistent with the others (as is signified by the 'or').
2. All the putative particular *equivalent* forms are only limited expressions of value, none of which can exclude all the others. (Marx puts 'each of them excludes all the others', but my way of putting the point is preferable. This is because Marx has already noticed the exclusionary character of this form of value under the first point, about the alternative relative expressions. Here, where what is at issue is the adequacy of the *equivalent* form of value, we are considering something which must be adequate to the unity of essence, that is, must be *singular*; the 'defect' is that there are many such candidates. So *A*'s 'choice' of equivalent is underdetermined; none of the candidates can exert a special force of attraction.)
3. Each commodity that may be placed on the left has a different set of relative value expressions; hence they are not able to achieve a *unitary* expression of value.

Once again, no adequate expression of value has been found. Marx solves the difficulty posed by these defects in the expanded form by *reversing it* so as to present next 'The general form of value' (157). Discarding, as before, Marx's use of ' = ', we have:

34. Robles-Baez (1997) points this out (p. 53). He stresses that this point refutes the Benetti/Cartelier interpretation of the expanded form which reads the 'or' as if it were an 'and'.

Form III *The general form of value*

$$
\left.\begin{array}{l}
y \text{ of commodity } B \\
\text{and } x \text{ of commodity } C \\
\text{and } w \text{ of commodity } D \\
\text{and so on and so forth}
\end{array}\right\}
\begin{array}{l}
\text{each express their value in } z \text{ of} \\
\text{commodity } A
\end{array}
$$

It is important to notice that this is a *new* form of value, not merely a restatement of the expanded form.[35] It is the reverse of the expanded form, but it is *not symmetrical* with it because it is not its converse (which is '*B*, or *C*, or *D*, etc. express the value of *A*'). This, in turn, is because the polarity of the expression has a definite *sense*. Before, it was *A* that endeavoured to express *its value* in the use-values of the other commodities: now the other commodities each express *their value* in the use-value *A*. *A* has completely changed in form from the active role in the expression to the passive role.

The superiority of the general form over the previous forms is that 'the commodities now present their values to us, (1) in a simple form, because in a single commodity; (2) in a unified form because in the same commodity each time' (157). A homogeneous dimension of value has been found. Only because of this can it be the case that 'By this form, commodities are, *for the first time, really* brought into relation with each other as values, or permitted to appear *to each other* as exchange-values' (158; my emphases, aimed at bringing out the fact that 'our abstraction' of Section 1 is beginning to gain a foothold in the *logic of the concrete*).

But the establishment of the value dimension 'can only arise as the joint contribution of the whole world of commodities' (159) by excluding from themselves a single commodity to be posited as the universal

35. Cartelier (1991) presents a figure labelled 'Expanded form of value (and its reversal)' (259). This 'form' is identical with its reversal only because it is completely *symmetrical*. Cartelier therewith offends against a basic principle; all forms of value are *by definition* asymmetrical. The commodities on the left have their value expressed; those on the right express it. Cartelier's diagram, therefore, *could not be any form of value*. On inspection, it turns out to be a representation of a multilateral set of exchange relations. Having misread Marx, changing all his 'or's to 'and's, hence transforming exclusionary forms into complementary ones, it is not surprising Cartelier gives a diagram having nothing to do with Marx's expanded form, nor, *a fortiori*, with his general form. Benetti's version of this same claim, that a reversal of the expanded form generates the expanded form again, is comprehensively refuted by Robles-Baez (1997): 47–60.

equivalent. Formally every commodity may 'aspire' to the status of universal equivalent, but since the *active* role in positing a value expression is played by the commodity in *relative* form it is up to the *generality* of commodities so to posit their universal equivalent. The commodity that achieves this status does so, not because of its own efforts, but by being excluded by them. Having chosen one there would be absolutely no reason to select another, still less for all to be selected.

The commodity excluded from the rest so as to serve as their universal equivalent now has a most peculiar status. As a use-value it is an individual commodity, but at the same time it is posited as the universal commodity. Marx stresses the strangeness of this: 'It is as if alongside and external to lions, tigers, rabbits, and all other actual animals, which form when grouped together the various kinds . . . of the animal kingdom, there existed also in addition *the animal*, the individual incarnation of the entire animal kingdom.'[36]

Gold is *the* commodity, not just an instance of the type. This may seem a dizzying exercise in metaphysics; but the practical proof that this dialectic of presupposition and posit has generated a new objectivity is that the universal equivalent now has an entirely new, objectively perceptible, social use-value. It is *immediately exchangeable* in a way other commodities are not. 'Its own natural form is the form assumed in common by the values of all commodities; it is therefore directly exchangeable with all other commodities' (159).

The dialectic of the value-form has now generated an important result. In the simple form the notion of the peculiar role played by the equivalent was already implicit, but in that case nothing new happened when the opposite expression was considered. 'Here it is still difficult to keep hold of the polar antagonism' (160). But now we see the expanded form and the general form are opposite expressions too, but they are massively different in their practical implications. 'Here we can no longer reverse the equation . . . without altering its whole character' (160). The singularity of the universal equivalent *makes* commodities socially commensurable in a homogeneous value space for the first time.

Let us now consider the transition to money. Marx identifies the defect of Form III in two sentences: 'The universal equivalent form is a form of value in general. It can therefore be assumed by any commodity' (162). Yet there cannot be more than one universal equivalent; therefore some principle of selection must exclude all but one possibility.

36. Marx, 'The Commodity, Chapter One . . . of the first edition of *Capital*': 27.

Logically there is nothing to distinguish them. But the problem is solved when 'social custom' excludes all but one commodity, say gold (162).

However it is necessary to expand upon Marx's presentation so that its logic is clear. We saw that Marx admitted as a defect of the expanded form that numerous such expressions may be constituted, starting from every available commodity. When reversed, these alternatives give alternative universal equivalents, which of course logically exclude one another. Although these many universes of value are all possible, they are not compossible; yet we have not given adequate grounds for granting one of them actuality.

In the first edition of *Capital* Marx explicitly recognized the point. He asks himself how his chosen example, linen, reached the position of universal equivalent: 'what was the way in which linen was metamorphosed into the universal equivalent, actually?' Of course it was simply 'our analysis' that chose linen as *our* example. So, if 'what holds for linen holds for every commodity', then, Marx deduces, many simple and expanded forms are equally possible.[37] Thus he gives in the first edition a list of the multiple expanded forms of different commodities:

Form IV:

20 yards of linen = one coat *or* = u coffee *or* = v tea *or* = x iron *or* y wheat *or* = etc.
One coat = 20 yards of linen *or* = u coffee *or* = v tea *or* = x iron *or* y wheat *or* = etc.
u coffee = 20 yards of linen *or* = one coat *or* = v tea *or* = x iron *or* y wheat *or* = etc.
v tea = etc.[38]

He comments as follows: 'But each of these equations *reflexively* yields coat, coffee, tea, etc. as [potential] universal equivalents.' This means, he correctly notes, that 'from our present standpoint the universal equivalent has not yet by any means crystallised'.[39] But the discussion

37. Marx, 'The Commodity, Chapter One ... of the first edition of *Capital*': 33.
38. Marx, 'The Commodity, Chapter One ... of the first edition of *Capital*': 33. Robles-Baez (1997) cites this, and he comments that the series of *separate* expressions should be treated as implicitly *disjunctive* (p. 54).
39. Marx, 'The Commodity, Chapter One ... of the first edition of *Capital*': 33, translation amended; cf. Marx, *Das Kapital Erster Band 1867*, MEGA II 5: 42.

now stalls *without* a transition to the money-form. He notes this means the analysis of the commodity forms is now 'contradictory';[40] only at the end of the chapter does he promise to resolve such contradictions in the chapter following, on exchange.

The Appendix to the first edition is an improvement on the first chapter in that the original version of 'Form IV' disappears (without notice) and is replaced by the argument that although 'as such' the universal equivalent form 'can pertain to *any* commodity . . . a commodity never *actually* [*wirklich*] functions as a general equivalent except insofar as its exclusion and hence its equivalent form is a result of an *objective social process*'.[41] Hence the content of 'Form IV' is here replaced by 'the money-form' and the transition to it is made simply through noting that 'the universal equivalent *socially* becomes the *money-commodity* or functions *as money*'.[42] It links back to the simple form, having been developed from it by a 'series of metamorphoses' which it 'must run through in order to win its finished shape'.[43] However, it is important that the selection of gold retroactively denies any other commodity the opportunity to 'run through' to money. The logic of the concrete requires that there be only one universal equivalent if value is to be determinate rather than a still indeterminate potential. Once it *is* so determined we cannot concretely go back and redetermine it.

Contrary to Marx's insinuation (162–3), the transition to money is thus not at all an easy one. The steps in the argument are as follows: (1) formally *any* commodity *could* serve as universal equivalent; (2) really *only one* commodity *can* serve as universal equivalent (at least at the same time); (3) necessarily, to ground value one *must* be selected. This is logically required but must be practically undertaken. Unless one, and *only* one, *is* socially selected the universal equivalent form is not actual. 'In other words it has a directly social form because, and in so far as, no other commodity is in this situation' (161). Money makes it so.

The money-form is *the* form of value, its most adequate expression. The first chapter of the second edition has it as follows (162; as before, Marx's ' = ' sign has been replaced):

40. Marx, 'The Commodity, Chapter One . . . of the first edition of *Capital*': 34.
41. Marx, 'The Value-Form' in *Debates in Value Theory*, edited by S. Mohun, 1994: 31, translation amended.
42. Marx, 'The Value-Form' in *Debates in Value Theory*, edited by S. Mohun, 1994: pp. 31–2.
43. Marx, 'The Value-Form' in *Debates in Value Theory*, edited by S. Mohun, 1994: 33.

Form IV *The money form of value*

20 yards of linen
1 coat
40 lb of coffee   all express their value in 2 ounces of gold
10 lb of tea
half a ton of iron
and so on

Following Marx, we have given examples of commodities, rather than variables *A*, *B*, *C* and so on because it is important to the money-form that a *specific* commodity *is* the universal equivalent, and in being so excluded itself excludes all other specific commodities from its place.

But there is here a non-logical premise, namely that gold has been specifically selected for this role. However, Marx's 'logical' argument demonstrates *what money is*. This is already known when in Chapter 2 Marx moves to see how generalized exchange is articulated by money. There Marx says the key thing about money is that without it products 'do not confront each other as commodities, but as use-values only', *not values* (180). 'Our analysis of the commodity' showed this, 'but only the action of society can turn a particular commodity into the universal equivalent' (180). However, this is lost sight of. 'What appears to happen is not that a particular commodity becomes money because all other commodities express their values in it, but, on the contrary, that all other commodities universally express their values in a particular commodity because it is money. The movement through which this process has been mediated vanishes in its own result, leaving no trace behind' (187).

Marx briefly notes that implicit in the money-form is price, since each commodity now has its value specified in gold coin (163). However, I believe there is much more to say about this. We can start from Marx's observation that, since gold is money itself, it has no price (189). But has it value? Here Marx's answer is defective. He says the same thing as he did with the universal equivalent when he stated that its value is given in the expanded form already treated earlier (Form II) (161). He says again: 'The expanded relative expression of value, the endless series of equations, has now become the specific relative form of value of the money commodity ... We have only to read the quotations of a price-list backwards, to find the magnitude of the value of money expressed in all sorts of commodities' (189). In effect he goes back behind money to the bare *commodity* status of gold, losing the peculiar status of immediate exchangeability it has *as money*.

But this overlooks two very interesting circumstances. First of all, the whole point of the simple form, and the expanded form, was to allow a commodity to express its value in another use-value because it could not express its value in its *own* natural body. But money *does* express value in its own use-value because money fixes the peculiarities of the equivalent form which we discussed earlier, namely that its use-value counts as value. It has no need to express its value in some other commodity because as value-for-itself it does not need an expression of value-in-itself as do the other commodities. Money shows it is *value-for-itself* in being immediately exchangeable. The universal equivalent, originally posited to serve passively as the representation of value, now becomes active as money, attracting the other commodities to solicit it *as* their expression of value. As already value, what money expresses in its relations with other commodities is its *purchasing power*.

Second, if the money-form is reversed, it does not return us to the expanded form, just because gold now has the special property of expressing price. We get, I suggest, a new expression of value:

Form V *The price-equivalent form*

$$
\text{a unit of gold is the price of:} \left\{ \begin{array}{l} z \text{ of } A \\ \text{and } y \text{ of } B \\ \text{and } x \text{ of } C \\ \text{and } w \text{ of } D \\ \text{and so on} \end{array} \right.
$$

There are two important points about this price-form that make it very different from Form II, the expanded form. In the latter, as we had occasion to stress, the commodities on the right were *alternatives* to each other (signified by Marx's use of the connector '*or*'). As a result the commodity on the left could not express its value adequately because it got lost in this endlessness. Now, however, the price-form allows money to *comprehend* this infinity under its own form-determination as the value universal that specifies itself in all commodities (thus we have the connector '*and*'). Since gold is already socially validated as the incarnation of value, it has no need whatsoever to express its value through its equivalents. Rather it demonstrates that it is value incarnate through granting other commodities social recognition as values.

From this follows another result of central importance. In this form *the commodities are now explicitly posited as equivalents* – not just of gold, but – *of each other*, through the mediation of money. This is because 'the price of z of A=the price of y of B' *is* reflexive, symmetrical and transitive. This is the culmination of the whole 'dialectic' of the forms of value. The presupposition (carried forward from Section 1) that the commodities are equivalents is now explicitly posited in the price form, rather than remaining immanent in their abstract identity.

It was mentioned earlier that Marx says money has no price. This is because there is no possibility of reversing the price-equivalent form of value: it would be idiotic to say that commodities A, B, C, D etc. form prices of the money-commodity. The illusion that money has a price is based on the fallacy that all value equivalents can function as prices of each other. But the whole point of price is that it is conceptually unitary, enabling value to emerge as a homogeneous universal dimension of commodities; hence the singleness of money and its office. Only money is *immediately* exchangeable. This is for the reason Marx gives:

> Like the relative form of value in general, price expresses the value of a commodity (for instance a ton of iron) by asserting that a given quantity of the equivalent (for instance 2 ounces of gold) is directly exchangeable with iron. But it by no means asserts the [reverse], that iron is directly exchangeable with gold...If the owner of the iron were to go to the owner of some other earthly commodity, and were to refer him to the price of iron as proof that it was already money [he would get a dusty answer] (197–8).

If the price-equivalent form is transformed into its converse, another interesting result emerges. The price-relative form allows all commodities separately to register their new socially unified status as values in specific relative prices:

Form VI *The price-relative form*

1 unit of A:	is priced at	z of money
1 unit of B:	is priced at	y of money
1 unit of C:	is priced at	x of money
1 unit of D:	is priced at	w of money, etc.

The units of A, B, C, etc. are of course incommensurable physical magnitudes. But the money units on the right are not merely by definition commensurable, such that the *relative* worth of commodities may be compared, they are *additive*. A heterogeneous bundle of commodities may be treated as a homogeneous amount of value. What *they* are worth together may be stated as a singular amount. This means that value is now objectively posited as the *substance* of commodities, reducing their use-value shape to its shell.

With value as a substance Marx can properly speak, in a later chapter, of C–M–C as a 'metamorphosis', the way a substance, here value, changes shapes. Every commodity is now exchangeable with every other through the *mediation* of money. So we see now that in virtue of ideally serving as common expression of value, money serves materially as commutator of values.

4. Conclusion

What has been shown is that efforts to find a way for value explicitly to posit itself in objective form fail in a pure commodity-exchange system, even if reflexive, symmetrical and transitive, because it exhibits only an immanence of value within such exchange relations. Only with money is a new exchange relation the basis of a peculiar expression of value in which it serves as the universal equivalent of all other commodities.

It is crucial to understand that, when 'the value of zA is yB', A is the active force and B the passive expression of A's search to find something which is and is not A, so that it can distinguish within its forms between use-value and value. This means that the alternative 'The value of yB is zA' is not merely the reverse of (i.e. not the converse), but is materially opposed to, 'The value of zA is yB', in that in this case B is the active force that says 'The value of yB is zA'. Both opposed expressions are abstractly possible; but once one commodity has taken the active role it cannot coherently be put as passive equivalent at the same time, because value needs a simple unitary way of expressing itself through-out the whole value space; in effect A and B would then be unstable disruptive forces in this field until one is fixed in relative and one in equivalent form.

The simple form is defective because A's choice of B is arbitrary; it could equally well have chosen the alternative C, or D, etc. They are alternatives because the need for an identical expression is already presupposed by the analytical identity reached in Section 1. If all these alternatives are listed we have Marx's expanded form, that is, 'The value of zA is yB, or xC, or wD, etc.' The defect is the lack of unitary expression. This we have in the reverse relation 'The values of yB, and xC, and wD, and nN etc. are each A'. This is in effect a list of simple expressions which do not exclude each other here (the fact that B expresses its value in *A* does not exclude *C* so doing) so the connector is '*and*' not '*or*'. This we might call 'a' general form of value; but it is not yet *the* universal equivalent form, even though in the second edition Marx says it is only a small step to reach money. The problem with the positing of *A* as an equivalent of all others is that *A* is passive. The active role is therefore played by the other commodities which each stand in the relative form of a list of simples. But by the same logic that led us to expand the simple form of *A*, all these others, for example 'The value of *yB* is *zA*', cannot be sure that *A* *is* their adequate expression since there is the potential alternative that 'The value of *yB* is *xC*' etc. There is no reason for *B* to be attracted only to *A* rather than any other potential equivalent. Just as *A* in the first case, it has alternatives. So one could follow with *B* the same route as with *A* such that *B* ends up as in a 'general' form.

Implicit then in the set of exchange relations are a manifold of potential value expressions. There are many potential points of origin such that we have multiple expanded forms (similar to Marx's first edition Form IV): 'The value of *zA* is *yB*, or *xC*, or *wD*, etc.' *or* 'The value of *yB* is *zA*, or *xC*, or *wD*, etc.' *or* 'The value of *xC* is *zA*, or *yB*, or *wD*, etc.' *or* etc. Since in each of these expressions 'The value of *A* is *B*' is matched by an expression 'The value of *B* is *A*' in another, they are exclusive of one another. A commodity is once in relative position and in the rest is a particular equivalent.

Likewise the multiple 'general' forms: 'The value of *yB* and *xC* and *wD* etc. is *zA*,' *or* 'The value of *zA* and *xC* and *wD* etc. is *yB*', *or* 'The value of *zA* and *yB* and *wD* etc. is *xC*', *or* etc., involve putting a commodity in equivalent form once but relative form in all others. All these general forms are potential ways to actualize value. But, once again, these forms exclude one another. The two lists of alternatives together comprise the complete set of potential value expression. But it is not determined which commodity will actually serve as the universal equivalent form of value.

Value achieves unitary objective actuality only if one of the potential universal equivalents is selected to serve as money. But only social practice can elevate one commodity above the others. The singularity of gold brings a condensation of one possible universe of value to a focus and creates a homogeneous value space (leaving other potential spaces unactual).

In spite of its infelicitous expression, which I have endeavoured to correct, Chapter 1, Section 3, is a brilliant exercise of dialectical thinking on Marx's part, which locates money within the commodity world while leading beyond it.[44] He shows that money is no mere veil of 'essential value relations' but is itself essential to the system of capitalist commodity production. In sum, what was important, he says, was 'to prove that the value-*form* arises out of the value-*concept'*.[45]

References

Arthur, Christopher J. (1998), Systematic dialectic, *Science & Society*, 62/3: 447–59; revised version in Christopher J. Arthur, (2002), *The New Dialectic and Marx's 'Capital'* (Leiden: Brill Academic Publishers).

Cartelier, Jean (1991), Marx's theory of value, exchange and surplus value: a suggested reformulation, *Cambridge Journal of Economics*, 15/3 (September): 257–69.

Marx, Karl (1962), *Das Kapital: Erster Band*, Karl Marx and Friedrich Engels *Werke*, Band 23 (Berlin: Dietz Verlag).

— (1976), *Capital, Volume I* (trans. B. Fowkes), (Harmondsworth: Penguin).

— (1976), 'The Commodity, Chapter One, Volume One of the first edition of *Capital'*, in *Value: Studies by Karl Marx* (trans. A. Dragstedt) (London: New Park): pp. 1–40.

— (1983), *Das Kapital Erster Band 1867*, Karl Marx and Friedrich Engels *Gesamtausgabe* (MEGA), Abteilung II, Band 5 (Berlin: Dietz Verlag).

— (1987), *A Contribution to the Critique of Political Economy*, in Karl Marx, and Frederick Engels, *Collected Works*, Volume 29 (London: Lawrence & Wishart).

— (1989), 'On Wagner' in Karl Marx, and Frederick Engels, *Collected Works*, Volume 24 (London: Lawrence & Wishart).

— (1989), *Le Capital 1872–75*, Karl Marx and Friedrich Engels, *Gesamtausgabe* (MEGA) Abteilung II, Band 7 (Berlin: Dietz Verlag).

— (1994), 'The Value-Form', in *Debates in Value Theory*, edited by S. Mohun (London/New York: Macmillan/St Martin's Press).

— and Frederick Engels (1983), *Letters on 'Capital'* (trans. A. Drummond) (London: New Park Publications).

Reuten, Geert (1993), The difficult labour of a theory of social value: metaphors and systematic dialectics at the beginning of Marx's *Capital*, in Fred Moseley (ed.), *Marx's Method in 'Capital': A Reexamination* (Atlantic Highlands, NJ: Humanities Press): 89–113.

Robles-Baez, Mario (1997), On Marx's Dialectic of the Genesis of the Money Form, *International Journal of Political Economy*, 27/3 (Fall): 35–64.

Russell, Bertrand (1972), *The Principles of Mathematics* (London: George Allen & Unwin).

Smith, Cyril (1996), Hegel, Economics, and Marx's *Capital*, in (eds) T. Brotherstone and G. Pilling *History, Economic History and the Future of Marxism* (London: Porcupine Press).

44. To avoid misunderstanding: staying close to Marx, I am arguing that a commodity money is adequate to the purpose of Chapter 1, namely to give an objective expression of the value of commodities; but I believe the concept of value could be further developed such that a commodity-base for money could be made redundant.

45. Marx, 'The Commodity, Chapter One ... of the first edition of *Capital'*: 34.

3
The Objectivity of Value versus the Idea of Habitual Action

Martha Campbell

Marx warns in the Preface to *Capital* that he will deal with individuals 'only in so far as they are ... the bearers of particular class relations and interests'.[1] Veblen challenges Marx precisely on this score, maintaining that class interest does not provide 'a competent' explanation of economic institutions and their transformation over time.[2] In reviving this challenge more recently, Hodgson explains that the defect Veblen found in Marx's analysis is that 'it failed to connect the actor with the specific structures and institutions, and failed to explain thereby human motivation and action'.[3] Hodgson, like Veblen, proposes that this crucial link is established when economic activity is conceived in terms of habit. This chapter contrasts these two ways of explaining economic activity, with the aim of discovering how Marx would answer Veblen.

Veblen's challenge is taken up, first, because he makes a reasonable point. On the one hand, the idea of habitual action allows for the social and the historically varied nature of economic activity. On the other hand, Marx's position is definitely peculiar: he speaks of capitalist production in terms of 'natural laws ... with iron necessity', of individuals as 'creature[s]' of their economic relations, and, in contrast to them, of value as a 'subject' or agent.[4] In reality, however, only people act and

1. Marx, 1867: 92.
2. Veblen, 1919: 314.
3. Hodgson, 1999a: 133.
4. Marx, 1867: 91, 92, 255.

they do so to realize purposes of their own. What meaning can there be in conceiving the combined outcome of their actions as the actions of a separate, non-human subject? As against these considerations, however, Marx cannot be unaware of the alternative Veblen proposes; it belongs, broadly speaking, to the Aristotelian tradition. This suggests that Marx knows full well how peculiar his argument is and that he means by it to draw attention to a peculiarity of capitalism.

I will argue that this is the case: the aspect of Marx's theory that Veblen saw as a fault is the expression of Marx's case that value is 'objective'. This chapter focuses on one aspect of value's objectivity: that value is an abstraction that must take on a material embodiment. Hodgson's critique of Marx is considered here to bring out the difference between value objectivity and habit. This will locate Marx's theory relative to institutionalist thinking. In addition, it focuses on a characteristic that, for Marx, distinguishes capitalism from all other modes of production.

1. Hodgson's critique of non-institutionalist economics

The primary target of Hodgson's criticism is the neoclassical concept of rational economic man: the atomistic, optimizing individual taken as given. The issue is so central for Hodgson that he proposes to define institutionalism by the rejection of this concept and the replacement of it with 'the idea that the individual is socially and institutionally constituted'.[5] Hodgson's critique of analytical Marxism, both for employing the concept of the 'rational agent' and for interpreting Marx in terms of it, makes clear that Hodgson rejects this reading of Marx.[6] Further, Hodgson recognizes and agrees with Marx that self-interested individuality is in reality associated with the dominance of capitalist institutions.[7] Nevertheless, Hodgson sees the same fundamental flaw in neoclassical and Marxian theory. This, as already noted, is the failure 'to connect the actor with ... specific structures and institutions', which leaves a 'conceptual gap' between 'actor and social structure'.[8]

---

5. Hodgson, 2000: 327. Although it is a constant theme, Hodgson's most extensive critique of methodological individualism is in Hodgson, 1988.
6. On Roemer, see Hodgson, 1991: 78–89; on Elster, see Hodgson, 1999a: 277, n. 13.
7. See Hodgson, 1991: 86. Hodgson's precise words are important: 'Although *the individual is never truly isolated and self-interested*, elements of the idea of "rational economic man" do correspond to real shifts in the economy and society' (emphasis added). See also 1999b: 230.
8. See Hodgson, 1999a: 133, 144. In the earlier passage, Hodgson is summarizing Veblen's critique of Marx. Hodgson evidently agrees with it and extends it both to neoclassical and Austrian theory.

The gap appears in Marx's theory by his attribution of self-interested action to classes, meaning his claims that workers struggle for shorter hours and higher wages and capitalists for higher profits. Hodgson maintains that these are 'little else than the principles of maximization also common to neoclassical theory'.[9] As in neoclassical theory, one view is mistakenly attributed to all economic actors (in Marx's case to all members of one class). The problem according to Hodgson is that in reality 'human agents [do not] gravitate to a single view of the truth' (meaning of the actions that would be in their self-interest); rather 'consciousness... is made up of deeply rooted habits of thought and based on culturally given concepts'.[10] Even if Marx does not take the self-interested individual as given, his theory is inadequate because (like neoclassical theory) he does not explain 'the historical origin of such calculative behavior and the mode of its cultural transmission'.[11] On one score, Hodgson conceives Marx and neoclassical theory to have taken equally wrong but opposite paths: neoclassical theory claims, but fails, to be completely universal whereas Marx tries, but fails, to be completely historically specific.[12] Adequate explanations must combine transhistorical and historically specific features. Murray has argued persuasively that this is just what Marx does.[13] The issue here, however, is not whether the charge is true but its connection for Hodgson to the concept of the rational individual. Because Marx paid insufficient attention to the definition and uses of transhistorical categories, Hodgson contends, 'we might stumble on the abstract concepts – such as scarcity and utility – pertaining to neoclassical theory'.[14]

Although Hodgson focuses on optimizing rationality, he intends his critique of this notion to illustrate a more general error. In general terms, this error is the appeal to any single, putatively fundamental principle. Hodgson argues instead that influences are in fact varied, that

---

9. Hodgson, 1999a: 131. Although Hodgson does not say this in his own voice, he cites two very striking 'observations': Parsons's claim that 'Marx's historical materialism... is... fundamentally a version of utilitarianism' and C. Wright Mills's claim that 'Marx's view of class consciousness is... as utilitarian and rationalist as anything out of Jeremy Bentham' (*ibid.*: 277, n. 14).
10. Hodgson, 1999a: 132, see also 136.
11. *Ibid.*: 131. Hodgson (1991: 87) points to Weber as a model. Unlike Marx, Weber appeals to *many different* factors: the Protestant ethic, the separation of production from the household and kinship, the emergence of the state and of other institutions based on 'rational–legal' routines.
12. See Hodgson, 1999a: 141–2, and 1999b: 230–1.
13. See Murray, 1988.
14. Hodgson, 1999a: 124.

causation must be conceived to be 'cumulative', or that variety is 'functionally necessary for economic systems'. Hodgson calls this the 'impurity principle'.[15] On its basis, for example, Hodgson argues that the individual is never 'truly isolated and self-interested' (1991: 86), that economic relations cannot be exclusively contractual (1988: 168–9, 211), and that actually existing capitalism is never purified of non-capitalist elements (1999a: 124) – as he states: 'the market has ineradicable social and collectivist aspects' (1988: 178). He also rejects the idea that profit maximization describes the behaviour of firms (1988: 137–9) and *any general theory* of price. From Hodgson's perspective, the utility and labour theories of value are equally untenable, likewise the metaphor of centres of gravitation, whether the centre is the classical concept of 'natural price', Marx's prices of production or the neoclassical notion of equilibrium price.[16] Although Hodgson often tempers his criticisms of Marx, he regards Marxian and neoclassical theory to be the same in all the foregoing respects.

Hodgson's alternative to both Marx and the neoclassicals is that society is irreducibly particular. This means that prices are 'social conventions' or market 'norms' (1999a: 145). Their character as such reflects the fact that they are 'the outcome of a process in historical time' (1988: 184). Hodgson maintains moreover that prices *must* be conventional if they are to be regarded as legitimate, if they are to serve the informational function required of them, and if uncertainty is to be reduced sufficiently for markets to work.[17] On the question of the firm as profit-maximizing, Hodgson again identifies the Marxian with the neoclassical position (in this case represented by Milton Friedman) and against both argues that:

Expectations and estimates are necessarily imperfect. Also they are always culturally and historically conditioned. 'Maximizing profits'

15. Hodgson, 1999a: 139, 1998: 302, and 1999a: 146.
16. On utility and labour theories of value see 1999a: 145; on centres of gravitation see 1988: 186–7, 207. Hodgson claims that 'the labour theory of value is untenable' (1991: 25) and also that it hinders rather than helps in 'the stripping away of' the 'masks and misconceptions' inherent in the appearances of the capitalist system. It is clear, however, that he associates any labour theory of value with 'the concept of embodied labour' (1991: 75). I agree that this concept sheds little light on capitalism but maintain also that it is Ricardo's rather than Marx's theory of value.
17. On historical time see Hodgson, 1988: 187; on legitimacy *ibid.*: 186; on the conditions required for markets to work, *ibid.*: 184. Overall, Hodgson maintains that 'the market . . . generates and promulgates (variable) norms and conventions to deal with uncertainty' (*ibid.*: 206).

leads us to no single or obvious value... Institutions and culture vary from firm to firm and from country to country. The objectives of firms are culturally and institutionally specific (1999a: 137–8).

Last, as opposed both to neoclassical individualism and Marx's 'objective, structural powers', Hodgson argues that causation is both top-down as well as bottom-up: 'individuals create and change institutions, just as institutions mold and constrain individuals'.[18] In Veblen's words:

> The growth and mutations of the institutional fabric are an outcome of the conduct of the individual members of the group, since it is out of the experience of the individuals, through the habituation of the individuals, that institutions arise; and it is in this same experience that these institutions act to direct and define the aims and end of conduct.[19]

Hodgson's criticism of the way Marx presents agency and action is posed in terms of Marx's claims about the self-interested action of classes. In *Capital*, however, Marx's approach to these questions is established well before he comes to the central relationship between wage labour and capital. He first speaks of individuals as 'personifications of economic relations' in connection with their relation as exchangers. As this is the simplest version of this claim, it is the place to look to come to terms with his explanation of economic action in capitalism.

2. The exchange process in *Capital*

The first time we encounter real people in *Capital*, and so can consider their actions and intentions, is in Chapter 2 on the exchange process.

18. Hodgson, 2000: 326. Hodgson also criticizes Marx's case that capitalism will be replaced by socialism on the grounds that it involves an erroneous teleology (see 1998: 302–5). While this point will not be addressed here, it is noteworthy that for Hodgson the problem with this argument is again the absence of variety. Like the neoclassical notion of equilibrium to which Hodgson compares it, it posits a single outcome. Agreeing with Veblen, Hodgson maintains instead that 'multiple futures are possible' (1999a: 139).
19. Cited by Hodgson, 2000: 326, from Veblen's essay on 'The limitations of marginal utility'.

As distinct from exchange-value, which is just the relation of commodities to each other, this process is the actual activity or performance of exchange. It transforms the properties the commodity is supposed to have from ideal into realized use-value and value.[20] As neither the action of exchanging nor the appraisal of use-value can occur without human beings, they must be brought in at this point. Their introduction brings out starkly that Chapter 1 of *Capital* is not about society in any normal sense but exclusively and literally about the society of commodities.[21] Its concluding section on the fetishism is devoted to the reason for this: that, in capitalism, the process of 'social metabolism', as Marx calls it, does in fact involve 'social relations between things' rather than among people.[22] The absence of people before Chapter 2 is not just a literary flourish but expresses Marx's point that in capitalism the realization of human purposes serves as the means for the realization of the objective property of products or value.

In keeping with this, when social relations in the normal sense are introduced in Chapter 2, their characteristics are derived from the characteristics of commodities, that is, as preconditions for the

20. This point emerges more clearly in Marx's presentation of the exchange process in the *Contribution*, in which he emphasizes that these characteristics of the commodity become (*werden*), act or take effect (*betätigt*), are in process (*prozessierende*) and that 'the *exchange process* of commodities is the *real* relation that exists between them' (Marx, 1859: 282). As Arthur notes (this volume), the key difference between Marx's presentation of the exchange process in *Capital* and the other versions in the *Contribution* and the *Grundrisse* is the clear separation Marx makes in *Capital* between exchange-value, which pertains only to commodities, and the exchange process. As the presentation in *Capital* is very condensed, the other two versions will be used to expand on its meaning.

21. Marx speaks of the commodity as 'a citizen of the commodity world' (1867: 155), of money as 'the joint contribution of the whole world of commodities' (*ibid.*: 159), of commodities 'making' one commodity the material embodiment of their value (*ibid.*: 160). In Chapter 2 he refers back to the exposition of money in Chapter 1 as demonstrating that the 'social action of commodities' sets money apart (*ibid.*: 180). It is true that human need and labour are discussed in Chapter 1 but this is only because and to the extent that these are required to explain the commodity's characteristics, use-value and value. The commodity and its relations are the subject of Chapter 1.

22. Marx, 1867: 198, 170. By 'metabolism' (*Stoffwechsel*), Marx means the interaction of human beings with nature through which needs are satisfied. This encompasses all relations of production, or the entire system of relations for producing and satisfying needs, which in capitalism includes the exchange process.

commodity-form. As Marx argues, objects cannot be commodities unless they are exchanged. To be exchanged rather than transferred in some other way – such as seized or given as gifts – members of society must relate to each other as private owners. Marx's reference, and so response, to Hegel's explanation of property is implicit in his echo of Hegel's argument in the *Philosophy of Right*. In a fuller exposition along these lines in the *Grundrisse*, Marx spells out how the relation of exchange gives the parties to it the qualities of equality – because as owners they are formally the same – and freedom – because each acts in accordance with self-interest.[23] The argument employs the same line of reasoning as Marx's case in Chapter 1 of *Capital* that, within and by the exchange of commodities, labour counts as equal human labour.

For Hegel, the significant aspect of the exchange relation is the 'relation of will to will' embodied in contract. As he says, this relation is the 'true and proper ground in which freedom is existent'.[24] It follows that contract is a component of the social system that makes freedom real. For Marx, the system to which contract belongs achieves a different result. As he states, the 'content' of the relation of wills is 'determined by the economic relation'. The 'content' Marx means is value, but at this point in *Capital* he has yet to show why value is the content of the exchange process. Beginning in Part II of *Capital*, Marx will spell out the preconditions for value to exist as a recognizable and established property of commodities (as it is presented in Part I). The conclusion he will reach is that the existence of value in this sense is guaranteed only on the basis of capitalist production: because only

23. Marx, 1939: 241–7. Marx's argument in this passage recalls the sections on property and contract in the *Philosophy of Right*. He plays devil's advocate showing how simple circulation can foster 'apologetics' for capitalist relations (*ibid.*: 240). To do this he adopts the apologists' premise (which he exposes as false at the end of the passage, *ibid.*: 247–50) that developed simple circulation stands on its own, independently of the capital relation. This premise is responsible for an important difference in language from *Capital*. Because of it, Marx declares that the 'content' of the exchange relation falls 'entirely outside economics'; by content, he means the use-values of the objects exchanged and the needs of the exchangers (see 1939: 241, 242). If simple circulation is not severed from the capital relation, it is a moment in the circuit of capital and, accordingly, its content is value. Thus 'content' means value in *Capital* (and in other passages in the *Grundrisse*).
24. Hegel, 1821: 57.

capitalist production must continually restore commodities to circulation, the visible commodity world is the effect of capital.[25] Since the goal of capitalist production is to increase value, the dependence of circulation on capital means that all aspects of circulation – including the relation of wills in contract – are aspects of the process of value creation.

Marx's answer to Hegel, then, is that private property and contract are integral parts of the system that makes value, rather than freedom, real. It follows that the exchangers themselves, as elements of this system, are instrumental in the expansion of value, rather than agents (subjects in their own right). This is conveyed by Marx's description of them as 'bearers of economic relations' (they are on a par with the use-values, described as the 'material bearers of exchange value' in Chapter 1).[26] That the relation of contract is part of the system of value implies also that contract need not be 'part of a developed legal system'. The argument, later in *Capital*, that capitalist production creates fully developed commodity circulation, means that circulation is not the creation of the legal system. In fact, the legal system will turn out to be inadequate to the task: since the law regarding private property cannot even differentiate the capital relation from exchange pure and simple, it can hardly specify the conditions required for the existence of

---

25. In other words, capitalist production is the sufficient condition for developed circulation. This argument is based on the straightforward idea that if value is to be existent it must be reproduced, and for it to be reproduced on the social scale that we find in modern society, it must be the goal, not just of trade and money lending, but of production. This is the point of Marx's statement: '*Circulation ... does not carry within itself the principle of self-renewal. The moments of the latter are presupposed to it*, not posited by it. Commodities constantly have to be thrown into it anew from the outside, like fuel into a fire. Otherwise it flickers out in indifference' (1939: 254–5). Only if production is capitalist does it necessarily and continuously throw off commodities. For interpretations of *Capital* along these lines see Banaji (1979), Campbell (1993), Arthur (1993 and 1997: 12–21). Since Marx has yet to argue that developed circulation presupposes capitalist production, he points instead to the senselessness of Proudhon's attempt to retain the relations of simple circulation but discard the coexisting relation of capital to wage labour (Marx, 1867: 178, n. 2, see also Marx, 1939: 248).

26. Marx, 1867: 179 and 126. In the earlier passage, Marx says 'exchange value' because he has yet to distinguish this from value; with his later revision that 'a commodity is a use-value ... and a "value"', the claim becomes that use-values are material bearers of value (*ibid.*: 152).

commodity circulation.[27] Last, the idea that law is the basis of circulation provides no way of explaining why social relations would exist as relations among things.

To return to the argument of Chapter 2, if, so far, the characteristics of owners are merely implied by the commodity, the feature that does belong exclusively to human beings and is introduced with their consideration is their capacity to appreciate whether a commodity is useful (as Marx puts it, their 'sense of the concrete physical body' of commodities by their 'own five and more senses').[28] In the absence of this capacity, use-value can only be ideal or intended (the ideal character of use-value in Chapter 1 of *Capital*, then, is one of the signs of its abstraction from people). The same is true of value, since it presupposes use-value. Like the contract relation, owners' views about the usefulness of commodities are already implicit in the commodity-form. The exposition of these views yields the contradiction between use-value and value, but in a different version than appeared in Chapter 1.

That commodities are by nature exchanged means that owners regard their own commodities as values, which means both as useless to themselves and as unconditionally equal to anyone else's commodity. On the other hand, they scrutinize commodities owned by others as use-values, with the result that they regard another commodity as equal to their own only if it has the physical characteristics required to satisfy their specific, individual needs.[29] Since this is true for all owners, every

---

27. The idea that property and so circulation is founded on law and its enforcement implies both that the social aspect of the economy is legal and that production itself is not social. It is the basis both of Mill's dichotomy between distribution (including property) as social and production as natural, which Marx criticizes in the Introduction to the *Grundrisse*, and of Rodbertus's distinction between social concepts as 'historico-legal' and economic concepts as 'logical' (meaning natural), which Marx criticizes in his 'Notes on Adolph Wagner' (see Marx, 1879–80: 205–7, 211). These are examples of what Hodgson calls the 'add-social-context-and-stir' method. His (1999a: 145) argument against it, that 'institutions are not merely constraints bearing upon a pre-existing and 'non-institutional' economy ... because the economy is not pre-given without institutions and culture' has precisely the same meaning as Marx's (1939: 87) characterization of production as the 'appropriation of nature on the part of an individual within and through a specific form of society'.
28. Marx, 1867: 179.
29. In a situation where there is no money, 'a commodity is an equivalent for those who do not possess it, although only insofar as it has use value for them' (Marx, 1867: 182).

commodity is simultaneously regarded as equivalent regardless of its material characteristics, and the opposite, equivalent subject to its having definite material characteristics. Posed in terms of the owners rather than the objects, the contradiction between the use-value and value of the commodity is transformed into the more familiar contradiction between the 'exclusively individual and exclusively social' character of exchange.[30] Commodity owners are inextricably tied together in a 'system of all-around material dependence' since they must both buy and sell to satisfy their needs.[31] At the same time, because they are indifferent to each other's needs in their exclusive concern with their own, their interdependence involves no community, but is a relationship of mutual 'isolation and foreignness'.[32] As with the versions of the same contradiction presented in Chapter 1, some *thing* must embody the social and general side of this opposition, or must possess the peculiarities of the equivalent form, for this contradiction to exist in reality.

In the absence of such an embodiment, value exists only as an abstraction or idea. (As Marx says in the *Contribution*, exchange-value 'has merely existed as our abstraction or, if one prefers, as the abstraction of the individual commodity owner, who ... has it on his conscience as exchange value'.[33]) In the exchange process, each owner's view of his or her own commodity as unconditionally equivalent to any other would give rise to as many claims to equivalence as there are different kinds of commodities. Since each of these would exclude every other, there would be no quality of equivalence. All claims to equivalence would collapse, leaving the owners just with use-values in all their material

---

30. Marx, 1867: 180.
31. Describing the interdependence inherent in exchange in the *Grundrisse*, Marx states: 'exchange value ... already in itself implies compulsion over the individual, since his immediate product is not a product for him, but only *becomes* such in the social process, and since it *must* take on this general but nevertheless external form; and that the individual has an existence only as a producer of exchange value, hence ... that he is ... entirely determined by society' (1939: 247–8). Neoclassical theory lacks this aspect of exchange and so, also, the contradiction that Marx emphasizes.
32. Marx, 1867: 182. Here again, Marx's fuller discussion in the *Grundrisse* makes the too brief statement in *Capital* comprehensible: the relationship of exchangers is characterized by self-seeking (each serves 'as means, in order to posit the self as end in itself') and mutual indifference ('reciprocity is a necessary fact ... but ... is irrelevant to each of the two subjects in exchange and ... interests him only in so far as it satisfies his interest ... without reference to that of the other') so that the common interest is not of a 'higher order' but just 'the generality of self-seeking interests'(1939: 244–5).
33. Marx, 1859: 285.

variety.[34] The owners cannot create the quality of equivalence by their collective intention since then exchange would not be an 'exclusively individual' process. Directly collective action, in other words, violates one of the definitive features of the exchange process.[35]

Things must therefore be the other way around: the abstraction from specific use-values – or, in positive terms, the quality of equivalence – must already have a separate embodiment in order for commodity owners to regard their property as possessing value (and for the owners themselves to have the contradictory characteristics of all-sided dependency and reciprocal isolation and foreignness). In other words, instead of being an abstraction that commodity owners (or 'we') make, value must be an abstraction that commodity owners confront as given (it is 'prosaically real and by no means imaginary', imaginary here meaning something 'thought'; 1959: 289). Once this abstraction exists as money, human actions and intentions may be formulated in terms of it; each one's commodity is potential value for them, and they regard it as such, because money is already present.[36] They do not think of value and

34. This reproduces the expanded value-form in another version. Each commodity is a 'particular equivalent' because its owner regards it as value. Among the defects of the expanded value-form, however, is that its equivalent form is inadequate because 'the only equivalent forms which exist are limited ones, and each of them excludes all the others' (Marx, 1867: 156–7).
35. It is also true, as will emerge later, that if commodity owners were not 'exclusively individual' – if there were community – there would be no reason for social wealth to exist as qualitative equivalence – as abstract – or as a thing.
36. Marx's claim is that, in money, value becomes a real abstraction. As Arthur explains, this means that 'pure forms . . . are objectively present in a realm other than thought' (Arthur, 1993: 86). Arthur emphasizes that it is essential to Marx's theory that value is not just an idea but must be incarnated; this, he maintains, is 'why Marx's theory of money is so different from both Ricardian and neoclassical conventionalisms' (*ibid*.: 80). One of the ways this appears in *Capital* is by the distinction Marx draws between value being the result of 'our analysis' and its being expressed in commodity relations themselves by the universal equivalent (see 1867: 141, 143, 158; in the *Contribution*, Marx emphasizes that with the universal equivalent, value transcends the character it has in the expanded form as 'our abstraction' or as 'theoretical' – meaning the result of the way commodities are 'regarded'; 1859: 285, 287). It appears also in Marx's repeated emphasis on the materiality value acquires in the money commodity (by Chapter 2, 'we are acquainted with only one function of money, namely, to serve . . . as the material in which the magnitudes of . . . values are socially expressed' (1867: 184); 'the material of gold ranks only as the materialization of value' (*ibid*.: 199)) and in his reference to money as value's body (*Wertkörper*) (*ibid*.: 143). (As Marx uses the term 'embodied' to refer to the relation of value to money, this is how the

settle on some thing to represent it; instead, their actions are based on value's existence as money. As Marx puts it, the commodity owners have 'already acted before thinking' (1867: 180). At the very least, then, his claim that money is set apart by the 'social action of all other commodities' refers to this order of determination: that the actions of commodity owners presuppose money but it is not the product of their thought (or, as we will see, of their convention). As will emerge shortly, this is part and parcel of what value is.

For the moment, Marx's claim poses a question about how money comes into being: since the established (as opposed to sporadic) existence of commodities presupposes money, how could commodities exist before money, so as to set it apart by their 'social action'? Marx's answer is that money results from a historical process, in which each of the components of value, as it exists fully fledged in capitalism, comes into being one at a time. In Marx's stylized history, each stage forms the basis for the next; but also, each stage introduces only those devices that are necessary to handle the obstacles to exchange as it exists at that particular point (at each stage, 'the problem and the means for its solution arise simultaneously' (1867: 182)). In its main outlines: first, well before the majority of needs are satisfied through exchange, the regularization of exchange promotes production intended for exchange and this, in turn, causes exchange ratios to become normalized, or non-accidental. Second, one object comes to be set apart to stand for qualitative equivalence only once the variety of goods exchanged requires a separate expression of what is common to them. Last, the process is completed when the role of embodying equivalence is permanently affixed to something whose physical properties match those of value (in Marx's language, when one commodity 'crystallizes' into the money-form (1867: 187)). Although the social use-value of embodying value, which derives from gold's relation to all ordinary commodities, and the

---

concept of embodiment figures in his theory.) The upshot is that Marx presents value as being just as externally present as use-value, calling this value's objectivity (the parallel is particularly striking in his statement: 'The product of labour is an object of utility [*Gebrauchgegenstand*]' in all societies but only one society 'presents the labour expended in the production of a useful article as an "objective" [*gegenständlich*] property of that article' (*ibid.*: 153–4)). The point is disguised somewhat because Marx's distinction between *objective* (which does not entail the idea of embodiment) and *gegenständlich* (which does) does not carry over into English (an instance of the former is the 'objective fixedness and general social validity' which the uniform relative form of value attains, and so forth; *ibid.*: 162).

ordinary use-value, which derives from gold's physical properties, have nothing to do with each other, in gold, value acquires an appropriate body.[37]

The solution this offers to the puzzle of how money originates from commodities is that commodities and money develop together, as counterparts of each other: the commodity, or relative form side of the relation, never evolves past the money, or equivalent form side. Money is given to modern society from the past (which is why commodity owners just confront it). As is true for every earlier stage, however, it acquires a new character in the new context. The generalization of the commodity-form – in other words, of production for sale – makes money into a universal equivalent in the truest sense. Since capital produces only commodities, this is money's role in capitalism.[38]

Besides explaining how money comes into being, this history ties money to commodities. This same link is revealed in a different way in Section 3 of Chapter 1, by the explanation of the relative and equivalent forms as 'the two poles of the value form'.[39] Marx returns to this connection again and again both because the conception of value depends on it and because it is disguised. His reason for insisting that commodities create money is to forestall the alternative view: that value

---

37. The whole of this story may exemplify what Engels has in mind when he asserts that 'the law of value prevailed for a period of some five to seven millennia' (Marx, 1894: 1037). Marx, however, says nothing about value prevailing in any context but capitalism and his argument that capitalist production is required for value to be a normal property of goods explains why it would not. Instead it is noteworthy, first, that all the characteristics described singly in the historical account – production for exchange, the normalization of prices, the embodiment of qualitative equivalence – are aspects of fully constituted value. Second, the history of value's emergence is reconstructed in hindsight from value in its finished form. This is a case of human anatomy containing 'the key to the anatomy of the ape' (Marx, 1939: 105); the finished form indicates what to pick out from the past. Because it is constructed backwards, the account is not teleological. That is, there is no suggestion that history leads inevitably to capitalism; instead, since capitalism does in fact exist, the elements of value can be recognized in different, historically earlier configurations of the relationship between commodities and money.
38. Marx maintains that the commodity-form becomes universal only once labour becomes wage labour (1867: 274, n. 4). Hence also, this is when value comes to exist 'in its purity and generality' (1939: 252).
39. Marx, 1867: 160. Marx classifies this relationship as a 'determination of reflection' and illustrates it by the relationship of king and subjects (*ibid*.: 149, also 143).

originates from money, which in turn implies that, in themselves, commodities and money are unrelated. This view seems more reasonable than Marx's (it is, as we will see, more prevalent) because it is suggested by the way money appears. Once the role of equivalent settles on one thing (gold), the equivalent has no apparent connection to its counterpart, the relative form. This split is unavoidable. That is, value must be a 'real abstraction', or exist as a separate thing, because the qualitative equivalence of commodities takes the place of direct community; but precisely because money is set apart from ordinary commodities, it seems completely unconnected to and unlike them. This being the case, however, money cannot appear as the embodiment of a property it shares with commodities; as a result, the homogeneity and unity of the commodity world (in other words, value) is completely hidden. Marx suggests that even when money is metallic money, it is unrecognizable as a commodity: 'the memory of use value . . . has become entirely extinguished in this incarnation of pure exchange value' (1939: 239–40). The disguise can only be more complete the more money becomes unlike commodities, as bank or paper money.[40]

Also contributing to money's disguise is that intention plays no part in forming its relation to commodities. This is brought out by the example of weighing sugar with pieces of iron, which Marx uses to illustrate how an equivalent works. Marx presents this example entirely in terms of intention: '*we* take various pieces of iron' as a standard, '*we* put' the sugar in relation to them, 'when *we throw* both of them into the scales, *we see* . . . that . . . as weight they are the same'.[41] By contrast, money develops in response to the exigencies of exchange, not in order to perform the role it acquires in capitalism (so far, this is to supersede the particularity of commodities as use-values and tie mutually indifferent individuals into a unity, but ultimately it is to create value). Accordingly, Marx's description of value contrasts strikingly with his description of weight: people 'do not bring the products of their labour into relation with each other as values because they see these objects merely as the material integuments of homogeneous

---

40. See Marx, 1867: 161, n. 26: 'It is by no means self-evident that the form of direct and universal exchangeability is an antagonistic form, as inseparable from its opposite, the form of non-direct exchangeability, as the positivity of one pole of a magnet is from the negativity of the other pole.' The rift is more pronounced with paper money, Marx maintains, because paper as means of circulation ('coin') can be a symbol of gold as universal equivalent, but also just because paper is not a commodity.

41. *Ibid.*: 148–9, emphasis added.

human labour'; instead, they equate labour by equating products 'without being aware of it'.[42] Of course, we can devise ways of measuring weight only because we experience it independently of measuring it. Because value is both social and unintended, there is no way of detecting it apart from money. This makes its existence difficult to detect even in its expression. The relation of commodities to money, in other words, does not show that as values they are the same, in the way that sugar and iron appear the same as weight when they are in a scale. Further, no one uses money as a universal equivalent, as this function relates to the economic system as a whole, not to the purposes of any individual member of society (in Marx's words: 'it is not at all apparent on its face that its character of being money is merely the result of social processes... This is all the more difficult since its immediate use value for the living individual stands in no relation whatever to this role'[43]).

As a final irony, value's character as an abstraction that must be embodied is even expunged from Marx's argument. When he states that the 'physical object, gold or silver in its crude state becomes... the direct incarnation of human labor' his point is that the abstraction, human labour, has a physical embodiment (it is not, as it is often interpreted, that the labour hours spent in gold production are immediately social).[44] If we lose sight of the concept of a real abstraction, which is one of the major points of Chapters 1 and 2, we lose sight also of Marx's point that value belongs to commodities. It is not our property, but theirs; if it were ours, it would not have to take on material embodiment. The symbol and conventional theories of money conceive value to be ours.

3. Time chit, symbolic and conventional money

One of the ways of conceptually detaching money from its relation to commodities is by the time chit proposal. The idea that the amount of social labour a commodity contains could be stipulated involves the supposition that the interconnection among labour activities does not need to be established indirectly by the relation of commodities to money; that 'universal social labor' is not an 'emerging result' of exchange

---

42. *Ibid.*: 166–7.
43. Marx, 1939: 239.
44. Marx, 1867: 187. As is apparent in context, the statement presupposes that the universal equivalent form has already been tied to gold or silver.

but 'a ready-made prerequisite'.[45] The idea that commodities would retain their value character without their value being determined only in their exchange is self-contradictory: it supposes that we have both abdicated our connection to others (and our responsibility for the values that define social wealth) and yet still control them. While the time chit idea is hardly mainstream, it offers insight into more prevalent notions of money.

A more usual way of severing the material and polar relationship between money and commodities is to say that money is a symbol.[46] This locates the origin of value in our ideas or customs, or makes value 'our abstraction' (as Marx puts it, the value character of commodities is regarded as 'the arbitrary product of human reflection', where arbitrary means external to the commodity world or to the nature of commodities (1867: 186)). It means that 'we' arrive at the idea of wealth in general, either tacitly by our customs or as a principle, and collectively make this abstraction tangible by treating some object as its representative. Money is then conventional; like private property it is thought to be constituted by recognition. In this conception, money is the embodiment society has assigned to value, and in turn the value character of ordinary commodities stems from their relation to money. This is the inversion Marx argues against repeatedly:

> What appears to happen is not that a particular commodity becomes money because all other commodities express their values in it, but, on the contrary, that all other commodities universally express their values in a particular commodity because it is money (1867: 187).

To say that money is value (the inversion of Marx's view) means that value is not inherently 'objective' (in Ricardo's terms, value is not

---

45. Marx, 1859: 286. It does not matter that the time chitters intend exchange-value to express the amount of labour time actually spent; this amount is just as arbitrary as any other. For Marx, the 'metallic form' of money is the contrast notion to money conceived as 'posited by society' as labour money. Because of this he states: 'the illusion that metallic money allegedly falsifies exchange value arises out of total ignorance of its nature' (1939: 240) (this being the *Grundrisse*, he means value rather than exchange-value).

46. Marx, 1867: 185; 1859: 289.

intrinsic); in other words, that value is not the property of commodities but a property we attribute to them.[47]

Marx expresses his alternative to the idea of money as a symbol by saying that money is instead a 'social relation of production'.[48] Again, the point this makes is that 'the social determinations of labour' necessarily exist as 'material characteristics', in the sense that these are properties of commodities and money (after all, as Marx notes, 'the properties of a thing do not arise from its relations to other things, they are, on the contrary merely activated by such relations' (1867: 149)). Because value is, in this sense, their characteristic and social relation, it is the 'social action of commodities' rather than our action that sets money apart. Commodity owners, of course, recognize the same single object as money. But Marx distinguishes 'our' part in the formation of money from 'theirs' (commodities'). Theirs consists of the embodiment of the quality of equivalence, involving polarity, all-inclusiveness, unity and closure (the characteristics spelled out in Forms A to C of Chapter 1, Section 3). Ours consists of the association of that embodiment with a particular object, which Marx attributes to custom rather than to the action of commodities (the transition from Form C to D).[49] The symbol idea of money reduces all to custom.

47. In another reference to the inversion, Marx states that 'the thing in which the magnitude of value of another thing is represented appears to have the equivalent form independently of this relation, as a social property inherent in its nature' (1867: 187). The social property refers to the symbol, which is obviously not natural but is considered 'inherent' in money in the sense that it is not thought to arise from the commodity world (see also 1867: 149 and 1939: 239). The idea of symbol or conventional money means that there is no distinction between exchange-value and value (from this stand-point, therefore, the concept of 'intrinsic' value is a misconception). The example of the second point that Marx uses throughout Chapters 1 and 2 of *Capital I* is Bailey's argument against Ricardo (see, for example, 1867: 155, n. 25). The symbol idea itself, however, is widely held (Marx notes a host of examples of it, including Hegel, *ibid.*: 185, n. 11) and appears to be the most prevalent alternative to the concept of money as mechanism, i.e., as a means of increasing the efficiency of exchange (see 1859: 191).

48. Marx, 1867: 176 and 1859: 289. It should be emphasized that Marx's relations of production include the exchange process. See his argument that circulation is a moment of production and that this is one of the distinctive features of capitalism (1939: 252–3).

49. This is one of a number of places where, Marx indicates, a variable must be fixed (at least at any given moment) but is not determined by value; therefore a determination by custom is necessary. In this case, since custom determines which object value's embodiment is associated with, that object

In this way, like the time chit proposal (but without that proposal's reference to labour), the symbol idea supposes that the social inter-connection of production does not have to be established through the relation between things (or 'objectively'). This leaves two possibilities. One is that there *is* no interconnection, at least within the economic domain. This is the neoclassical idea of the atomistic individual as given. It corresponds to the idea of money as a machine that increases the efficiency of exchange since 'society' is just the aggregate of given individuals. The other is that there are, contrary to all appearances, only direct connections among the units of economic activity, firms (or 'capitals'). This is the institutionalist position, at least as it is represented by Hodgson. In contrast to both, in a statement that would appear absurdly self-contradictory except for the argument that leads up to it, Marx maintains that once money becomes the 'incarnation of all human labor' people are 'related to each other ... in a purely atomistic way' (1867: 187). Atomism, in other words, is a social relation that combines the contradictory aspects of the 'exclusively individual' and the 'exclusively social'.

4. Human needs and capabilities

Before reconsidering Hodgson's critique, one point that was made in passing needs to be elaborated. As noted above, Marx identifies human purposes with the use-value side of the commodity: the senses that appraise the usefulness of commodities are the human compon-ent of the exchange process. He will do the same when he comes to production (the labour process): the human component is the purpose that is realized in the materials and that guides the way they must be

---

can change: it can be gold, paper with no connection to gold, electronic transfers. These are all objects in the sense of external things. The differ-ence among them is irrelevant to the argument from Form A to Form C of Chapter 1, Section 3, which contains the 'fundamental changes' in the exposition of the money-form (Marx, 1867: 162). The more developed forms of money do make the equivalent form more difficult to understand: it is harder to see how money could arise from the social action of commod-ities if money itself is not a commodity; in other words, it is harder to see how money is not a symbol. As the case of gold illustrates, the objects that serve as the embodiment of value, although not specified by value, are not accidental. Marx implies in *Capital II* and *III* that money evolves into bank money under the pressure of valorization, that therefore bank money is the money of capitalism (see Campbell, 1998 and 2002).

transformed.[50] As evidence of the diversity of human needs and capabilities, Marx points to the division of labour (which appears as a way of reducing costs, rather than of improving the quality of use-value, only from the perspective of capitalism (see Marx, 1867: 486)). Marx emphasizes that this diversity is completely different from the abstract and uniform character of value (in complete indifference to human senses, as a value, the commodity is a 'leveller...always willing to exchange not only soul but body, with each and every other commodity' (*ibid.*: 179)). In addition, value exists in abstraction from all particularity by being set apart, as money, from all the various goods that actually satisfy needs. Because the social character of wealth exists independently, however, the relation of all particular goods (and by extension, activities, members of society) to it is precarious. A commodity's value is its place relative to the total social product, but this is entirely 'haphazard and spontaneous' and knowable only after the fact, when any mistakes in anticipated value are 'corrected objectively in the market'.[51] These differences (value's abstractness and objectivity) between value and the needs and capabilities of human beings show value's character as 'alien'. This is borne out by Hodgson's 'impurity' principle, the irreducible particularity of social life. As I will argue, the applicability of this principle to all societies except capitalism brings out the strangeness of value.[52] One of Marx's ways of alerting us to value's inhumanness is by quoting Aristotle's famous argument that the

> sandal...may be worn and is also exchangeable. Both are uses of the sandal, for even he who exchanges the sandal for the money or the food he is in need of, makes use of the sandal as a sandal. But not in its natural way. For it has not been made for the sake of being exchanged
> (Marx, 1867: 179, n. 3).

50. See Marx, 1867: 284. Marx states: 'the purpose ... determines the mode of activity with the rigidity of a natural law and he [man] must subordinate his will to it'. This might seem to suggest that in production we are at the mercy of natural laws. It is true that laws of nature must be observed in order to achieve what we want, but nature is thereby used as a means for the sake of a human end. It is the reverse with capital where the satisfaction of human needs is made the means for the end of creating value.

51. Marx, 1867: 202, 201. To clarify, human purposes always relate to a social whole, but in other societies people know 'their place' or what they are supposed to do.

52. Even in capitalism, value applies only in the limited sphere of the economy. By its influence on our ideas, it intrudes on other areas of interaction. These other areas, such as the family, are based on other bonds (see Murray, 2000).

In other words, products are made to satisfy needs. When products are used to acquire other products that satisfy needs (when money is used as a medium of exchange), they are still used for this intended purpose. In capitalism, the sandal is made for the sake of exchange, and the creation of use-values is (from capital's standpoint) an unfortunate and tedious requirement that capital must submit to in order to create more value. Human purposes – the satisfaction of needs and development of capabilities – are harnessed to the production of something inhuman.[53] Human needs are met and human capabilities developed only to the extent required for value creation. Because human purposes are means to something external to and unlike them, human beings are 'bearers' or 'personifications' of the economic relations through which value is created.

5. Reconsidering Hodgson's institutionalism

How then does Marx's theory compare with Hodgson's institutionalism and what reply can it give to Hodgson's critique? As Hodgson recognizes, Marx's argument includes elements that are normally considered 'institutions'; the examples here have been property and money. If Marx's argument were pursued further, other examples would emerge. Marx indicates that the theory of value presupposes certain norms: the character of simple average labour, the ordinary standard of living (the worker's 'so-called necessary requirements' or 'customary means of life'), the length of the working day.[54] These must all be given at any place and time; value relations incorporate them, but cannot determine them. The incorporation of these 'cultural' and historical factors is exactly what Hodgson is advocating. It would seem then that Marx would not disagree with Hodgson's claim that economic life is 'always culturally and historically conditioned'.[55]

In part also, Hodgson's criticisms seem to arise from the fact that he is thinking at a more concrete level than Marx, but this in itself begins to bring out a real difference. That is, it could be argued that the absence of variety, especially in *Capital I*, results from the fact that Marx sets

---

53. Marx (1867: 254) claims that the capitalist makes valorization 'his subjective purpose', but this means that the capitalist is merely an actor on behalf of value. The capitalist's non-humanity is revealed by his unconcern with needs.
54. See Marx, 1867: 135, 275, 382, 344. As Hodgson notices (1991: 13), the 'moral' aspect of the wage is similar to the idea that the wage bargain involves an 'implicit contract'.
55. Hodgson, 1999a: 137, quoted above.

aside the characteristics that differentiate individual capitals because he is not concerned with their interdependence or interaction. The argument in *Capital III*, although still more abstract than Hodgson's discussions of the firm, requires that capitals be diverse.[56] Marx's idea of a 'normal' technique, however, is not a 'norm' in Hodgson's sense. Rather, it is a weighted average. This is the result of price being the mode of social evaluation of products – the fact that the total product of one industry 'counts as one single article of commerce' – together with perpetual technological change.[57] Both are implications of the principle of value. Thus, while Marx incorporates institutional features, even at the most abstract level of his theory, Hodgson's approach completely denies the singleness and uniformity of Marx's value.

To take another example, Marx's history of the development of money, although very brief, seems to exemplify Hodgson's conception of institutional change (it seems to be exactly the kind of explanation Veblen advocates in the description quoted earlier). Money develops by stages without any overarching purpose; it develops out of practices rather than by 'agreement between individuals'.[58] For Marx, however, this meandering process of institutional evolution comes to an end once the original accumulation puts capitalist production in place. From then on, institutions and technology change, but this change is driven by the single purpose of generating more value.[59]

The true difference to which both paths lead is that, for Marx, atomism exists in reality; it is not a figment of the neoclassical imagination. Likewise, the abstract character of value – its singleness and qualitative sameness – is real. Further, Marx's argument makes these characteristics out to be unique to capitalism and to constitute its difference from earlier

---

56. See, for example, Reuten, 1991.
57. Marx, 1867: 202. In defence of Marx, Sherman (1998: 55) argues that 'Marx examined at great length ... the process by which new technology spawns variety'. In reply Hodgson (1998: 301) argues that while 'Marx acknowledged some growth of complexity and variety in economic systems' he did not do so 'at great length'; moreover 'the equalization of the rate of profit would lead to some degree of standardization of technology'. Both miss the point that technological change in Marx comes from the pressure to create more value; value is 'pure', and in modes of production uniquely so.
58. Hodgson, 1988: 166.
59. On technological change see Smith (2002 and Chapter 8 in this volume); an example of institutional change within capitalism is the development of the credit system (see Campbell, 2002). That capitalism is driven by valorization does not imply that the reign of value never ends; on the contrary, its historical character suggests that it will.

societies. Both require money in its uniquely capitalist role. As argued in connection with Marx's presentation of the exchange process, the abstraction value, or the qualitative equivalence of commodities, cannot exist unless it has an embodiment in money. In addition, because, as value, social interdependence is abstract and embodied as money, atomism is the way people relate to each other.

It follows, then, that Marx would agree with Hodgson that all modes of production prior to capitalism are characterized by the irreducible particularity implied by the ideas of habit, custom or culture. He agrees, further, that such features not only do, but must figure in capitalist production. He parts company with Hodgson in maintaining that value, in being abstract and objective, is qualitatively different from these other features, that it dominates capitalist production and is unique to capitalism. As argued earlier, Marx's first, most abstract, explanation of money offers one example of his conception of the relation between custom and value in capitalism: custom must dictate which object serves as money; but, although custom plays a necessary role, it has no bearing on what is 'fundamental' about money in capitalism, the universal equivalent form.[60] From the perspective of Marx's theory, then, by extending the impurity principle to capitalism and rejecting all theories of value, Hodgson's institutionalism misses the feature that distinguishes capitalism.[61] This difference between Hodgson and Marx may be illustrated by the difference in their concepts of money.

Hodgson, like Keynes, conceives of money as a convention and as a 'means of overcoming uncertainty'.[62] This position is consistent with the idea that the existence of money has consequences that presuppose money and that would not exist without it. For example, Hodgson cites Mitchell's argument that money has 'changed human mentality and nature'; as Mitchell states, 'the money economy ... makes us all react in

---

60. See Marx, 1867: 162–3.
61. For example, because Hodgson sees the theory of value as 'untenable' he proposes to save Marx's explanation of exploitation by presenting it in terms of use-value (1991: 66–77). This means though that he eliminates the characteristic that distinguishes capitalist from other forms of economic exploitation. Tony Smith (Chapter 8, this volume) makes a similar point regarding neo-Schumpeterian thought, namely, that its shortcomings come from the lack of an adequate concept of capital.
62. Hodgson, 1988: 166. Hodgson's view may not be precisely the same as Keynes's but they are the same for my purposes because money is conventional and exists because there is a need, which money satisfies, to cope with uncertainty.

standard ways to the standard stimuli it offers'.[63] Similarly, Hodgson rightly criticizes the argument that money exists because it reduces transactions costs on the grounds that the transactions themselves, and so higher-cost transactions, wouldn't exist if money didn't.[64] These points are perfectly consistent with Marx's argument (although, since he does not emphasize them, they are evidently not his key point).

The disagreement comes over the reason for the existence of money. According to Marx, there must be a representative of the socially valid character of wealth in addition to and apart from the goods that actually satisfy needs because interdependence is indirect and unintended rather than collective. This is the aspect that is unique to Marx and missing from the idea of money as conventional. For the latter, there is not atomism but collectivity in the recognition of money as the adequate form of social wealth. Further, in the conventional view, money exists, not to bridge the contradiction inherent in atomistic social relations, but because people want it, since owning it enables them to avoid uncertainty. It is undeniable that for the individual in capitalism owning money avoids the uncertainties associated with owning physical means of production (and using them to produce for sale). The uncertainty that money overcomes (and the only uncertainty it overcomes) is that there can be no assurance that goods themselves will prove to be socially valid wealth. But this uncertainty would not exist if social production were not organized around value, that is, if money did not have its uniquely capitalist role. Hence the idea that money is required to cope with uncertainty is problematic: it proposes that money is devised to solve a problem that would not exist if money did not exist as it does in capitalism, as a universal equivalent. To state the same point in another way, if collective recognition could constitute a representative of social wealth, there would be no need for such a representative. Collective recognition could just determine which particular goods constitute wealth without having the social

63. Hodgson, 2000: 324. Similarly, Murray (1997: 54–6) argues that the neoclassical idea of utility is an illusory concept of use-value engendered by money. Murray, however, bases his case on Marx's argument, rather than institutionalism. As this illustrates, it is unlikely, as Hodgson alleges, that Marx's theory would lead us to think in terms of neoclassical abstractions.

64. The transactions costs argument, Hodgson argues, makes the false assumption 'that there are arrangements outside the conventional money-based markets for which transacting involves higher costs' (1988: 297, n. 5). This illustrates the difference between conception of money as mechanism and as conventional.

character of wealth exist in the abstract, separate from these particular goods themselves.

6. Conclusion

Like Marx, institutionalism recognizes the irreducibly social and historically determinate character of economic activity. Because of this, the comparison between Marx and institutionalist explanation brings out what is, for Marx, the extraordinary feature of economic activity in capitalism: that it claims to create wealth pure and simple and is organized by this purpose. As a result, capitalism presents wealth as if it were something qualitatively single (uniform) that supersedes and encompasses all particular instantiations (as manifested in the relationship between all commodities and money). Because this uniformity is specifically capitalist, capitalism has a 'principled' character absent from all other modes of production. In contrast to the varied and material goods that actually satisfy needs, value – the capitalist illusion of wealth – is insubstantial ('phantom-like' or 'ghostly', as Marx calls it (1867: 128)). Because value exists apart from all particular goods, their relation to it is accidental. For this reason, capitalism is indifferent to all particularity, of goods, activities and individuals. Finally, because value is qualitatively uniform, it is purely quantitative and therefore infinite. Because human beings are harnessed to the creation of something endless that is indifferent to their needs, they are not the subjects of their economic life. Neoclassical theory misconceives the consequences of these characteristics as transhistorical and disassociated from the institutions of capitalism. Institutionalism errs in denying that these consequences are real.

On the positive side, that objectivity is unique to value means that other relations, even in capitalism, are entirely different from it. They are of the kind described by institutionalism. Finally, that capitalism is historical means that value's reign is temporary.

References

Arthur, Christopher J. (1993), Hegel's *Logic* and Marx's *Capital*, in Fred Moseley (ed.) (1993).

— (1997), Against the logical–historical method: dialectical derivation versus linear logic, in F. Moseley and M. Campbell (eds) (1997).

Arthur, Christopher J. and Geert Reuten (eds) (1998), *Money in the Circulation of Capital: Essays on Volume II of Marx's 'Capital'* (London/New York: Macmillan/St Martin's Press).

Banaji, Jairus (1979), From the commodity to capital: Hegel's dialectic in Marx's *Capital*, in Diane Elson (ed.) *Value: The Representation of Labour in Capitalism* (London: CSE Books, 1979).

Campbell, Martha (1993) 'The commodity as "characteristic form", in *Economics as Wordly Philosophy: Essays in Honor of Robert Heilbroner*, R. Blackwell, J. Chatha and E.J. Nell (eds.) (Basingstoke: Palgrave Macmillan).
— (1998), Money in the circulation of capital, in C.J. Arthur, and G. Reuten (eds) (1998).
— (2002), The credit system, in M. Campbell and G. Reuten (eds) (2002).
— and Geert Reuten (eds) (2002), *The Culmination of Capital: Essays on Volume III of Marx's 'Capital'* (Basingstoke/New York: Palgrave Macmillan).
Hegel, G.W.F. (1821), *Philosophy of Right* (trans. T.M. Knox) (London/Oxford/New York: Oxford University Press, 1967).
Hodgson, Geoffrey M. (1988), *Economics and Institutions: A Manifesto for Modern Institutional Economics* (Cambridge: Polity Press).
— (1991), *After Marx and Sraffa* (London: Macmillan – new Palgrave Macmillan).
— (1998), A reply to Howard Sherman, *Review of Social Economy*, LVI/3 (Fall): 295–306.
— (1999a), *Economics and Utopia: Why the Learning Economy is not the End of History* (London/New York: Routledge).
— (1999b), *Evolution and Institutions: On Evolutionary Economics and the Evolution of Economics* (Cheltenham/Northampton: Edward Elgar).
— (2000), What is the essence of institutional economics?, *Journal of Economic Issues*, XXXIV 12: 317–29.
Marx, Karl (1859), *A Contribution to the Critique of Political Economy*, Karl Marx and Frederick Engels, *Collected Works*, Vol. 29 (London: Lawrence & Wishart, 1987).
— (1867), *Capital, Volume I* (trans. B. Fowkes) (Harmondsworth: Penguin, 1976).
— (1879–80), Notes on Adolph Wagner, in Terrell Carver (trans. and ed.) *Karl Marx: Texts on Method* (Oxford: Basil Blackwell, 1975).
— (1894), *Capital, Vol. III* (trans. D. Fernbach) (Harmondsworth: Penguin, 1981).
— (1939), *Grundrisse* (trans. M. Nicolaus) (Harmondsworth: Penguin, 1973).
Moseley, Fred (ed.) (1993), *Marx's Method in Capital* (Atlantic Highlands, NJ: Humanities Press).
— and Martha Campbell (eds) (1997), *New Investigations of Marx's Method* (Atlantic Highlands, NJ: Humanities Press).
Murray, Patrick (1988), *Marx's Theory of Scientific Knowledge* (Atlantic Highlands, NJ: Humanities Press).
— (1997), Redoubled empiricism: the place of social form and formal causality in Marxian theory, in F. Moseley and M. Campbell (eds) (1997).
— (2000), Marx's 'truly social' labour theory of value: Part II, How is labour that is under the sway of capital *actually* abstract?, *Historical Materialism*, 7 (Winter): 99–136.
Reuten, Geert (1991), Accumulation of capital and the foundation of the tendency of the rate of profit to fall, *Cambridge Journal of Economics*, 15/1: 79–93.
Sherman, Howard J. (1998), Critique of the critique: analysis of Hodgson on Marx on evolution, *Review of Social Economy*, LVI/1 (Spring): 47–58.
Smith, Tony (2002), Surplus profits from innovation: a missing level in *Capital III*?, in M. Campbell and G. Reuten (eds) (2002).
Veblen, Thorstein (1919), *The Place of Science in Modern Civilization* (New Brunswick, NJ/London: Transaction Publishers, 1990).

4
Reconstructing Marx on Money and the Measurement of Value

Nicola Taylor[1]

A contentious feature of Marx's *Capital* is his treatment of money, especially in relation to the logic of circulation. On the one hand, Marx conceives of money as a 'body of value', an immediate embodiment of (abstract) universal labour. If time is the measure of labour, then the 'real' (non-monetary) measure of value is the time socially necessary to produce the money commodity: gold. Yet, there is also in *Capital* the outline of an elementary 'form theory', wherein monetary abstraction does not arise substantially in production but in the practical relation of commodity exchange, itself a means of *associating* previously *dissociated* commodities and labour.[2] Now, money is a necessary condition for the existence of the (capitalist) value-form of exchange; it constitutes the value dimension wherein heterogeneous use-values (commodities) are validated as *social values* and the heterogeneous labours that produced them are validated as *social labour*.

1. I thank Christopher Arthur, Riccardo Bellofiore, Martha Campbell, Fred Moseley, Patrick Murray, Geert Reuten and Tony Smith for their erudite comments on various drafts of this chapter, and also Michael Eldred for his critical and stimulating interventions on the final draft. I am, of course, responsible for any errors remaining.
2. Reuten and Williams (1989: 56–9) use the term 'dissociation' to distinguish the micro-organization of labour in independent production units (dissociated labour) from the monetary macro-organization of labour in capitalist markets (associated labour), so the value-form is initially determined as a *universal means of association*.

These two options for the theory of money are related to two very different conceptions of Marx's method. In distinguishing between these conceptions the main issue is whether form arises out of content or content out of form.[3] Those who argue for the logical priority of content tend to stress Marx's explanation of how surplus value comes about, or is determined, by labour time in production. Along this track commodity money acts as a veil over real production relations in a theory of exploitation where the homogenization of labour takes place prior to exchange (see Moseley, Chapter 6). Those who attribute logical priority to form tend to stress the way in which real entities and processes – labour and production – are themselves shaped, or determined, by the monetary value-form in such a way that they acquire dual aspects of measurement in time and money (Arthur, 2002c, 156–8, and Reuten, Chapter 5). This second track implies the inseparability of production and exchange which are taken for interdependent moments within a unity, and this 'implies a method of exposition which engages the value-form first' before introducing the question of how value magnitudes are determined (Arthur, *ibid.*: 157). Hence it makes little sense to talk about the *content of value* before full development of the *forms of circulation* up to the capital-form.

The current chapter follows the second path to examine its implications, both for reading and for reconstructing Volume I. The first two sections identify some problems in Marx's own concept of money in relation to the measurement of value and labour. The next three sections systematically reconstruct Marx's theory of value-forms up to the capital-form, without recourse either to embodied labour or commodity money. A final section briefly sets out some of the conclusions of the reformulation

3. It is not a question of separating form and content (indeed the two are inseparable!) but a question of logical priority. In the English literature, a major impetus for an inquiry into Marx's logic came from the 1973 translation of Marx's *Grundrisse* notebooks (1857–8 drafts for *Capital I* which contained important comments on method), the publication in English in the 1970s of Isaac Rubin's (1927) lectures and (1928) essays, the German debate (especially the 1969 writings of Backhaus, translated into English in 1980) and subsequent studies of the Hegel-Marx connection (see Burns and Fraser, 2000). Early Anglo-American attempts to interpret *Capital* as a 'Hegelian' work with a movement from form to content were Banaji (1979) Arthur (1986) and Murray (1988). Smith (1990) gives a more detailed account of the systematic structure of *Capital I*, while Arthur (1998, 2000, 2002a) and the essays in Albritton and Simoulidis (eds, 2003) provide further invaluable analyses of the logic of *Capital* as a whole. For general accounts of Hegel's systematic dialectical method and its relevance for the interpretation and reconstruction of Marx's *Capital* see Eldred and Hanlon (1981), Eldred, Hanlon, Kleiber and Roth (1982, 1983), Reuten (1998), Reuten and Williams (1989) and Smith (1999). For debate and some criticisms of these Hegelian interpretations, see the essays in Moseley (ed. 1993) and Moseley and Campbell (eds 1997).

in relation to the interconnection between money, labour and time in capitalist society. Marx's own understanding of this relation is then reconsidered. On the one hand Marx himself showed that, as the capital form develops, the absence of any quantitative link between labour time and the magnitude of value must emerge as a core feature of the capitalist phenomenon to be explained. On the other hand the analysis of Volume I must be considered deficient, to the extent that Marx remained mired throughout this first book in a Ricardian problematic where labour time ultimately determines value magnitudes.

1. Value-form and the Ricardian legacy

As pointed out by Levine (1983), the main idea behind the Ricardian theory of *value* is that a set of production conditions underlies the logical structure of exchange relations. Analysis of value in the sphere of production requires that money be excluded as a *determinant* of commodity exchange and this gives rise to a logical problem: how to theorize and measure value relations between commodities without reference to money, while at the same time explaining the necessity for money?

In Marx's view, the best representatives of the classical school (Smith and Ricardo) failed to solve the 'riddle of money' because they failed to appreciate the indirect sociality of labour in capitalism. Indirect sociality derives from the fact that economic activity is *dissociated*: (i) labour-power (a capacity of workers) and means of production (belonging to capitalists) are separated through private property relations and must be reunited in order for production to take place, (ii) production and consumption are separated in place and time implying market mediation, and (iii) useful objects are produced not for the immediate satisfaction of the producer's own needs, but solely for the purpose of monetary profit (in Marx's words, the motive for production is 'valorization').

Indirect sociality in a dissociated system has a number of implications for classical labour theories of value. To begin with, labour time is not synonymous with value (as Ricardo would have it) because the labour expended on producing commodities proves to be social only *ex post* when products of labour are successfully exchanged. According to Marx, this amounts to a clear distinction between 'private labour' allocated in advance of production and 'private labour that has proven to be social' after production, such that the latter alone constitutes a quantitative dimension underpinning the exchange of commodities *as values*. The errors of the classical system arise, then, from an inadequate understanding of the way in which the character of labour (and its measurement) is shaped by social organization:

Political economy has indeed analysed value and its magnitude, how-ever incompletely, and has uncovered the content concealed within these forms. But it has never once asked the question why this con-tent has assumed that particular form, that is to say, why labour is expressed in value, and why the measurement of labour by its duration is expressed in the magnitude of the value of the product.

(Marx, 1976a: 173–4[4])

The criticism expressed by Marx is quite straightforward: the classical political economists did not ask *why labour and the measurement of labour must take on a value-form*. He goes on to say that the reason the 'best representatives' of the classical school overlooked this fundamen-tal question was because they failed to see the historical 'specificity' of the 'value-form of the product of labour and consequently of the com-modity-form together with its further developments, the money form, the capital form, etc.' (*ibid.*: 174, n. 34). This would seem to imply that the categories commodity, money, value and labour can be grasped only through an analysis of their character *as determined by* the social relation itself. At the same time, however, Marx wants to prove the proposition that labour time 'exclusively determines the magnitude of the value of any article', placing value and labour in a definite causal relation (*ibid.*: 129).

Marx's attempt to overcome classical naturalism and systematically unite money (value-form) and labour time (value substance) is expressed with unusual clarity in his 1867 *Appendix* to the first German edition of *Capital*.[5] There he also introduces the notion of an 'equivalent form' of the commodity serving as value measure in distinction from the 'relative form' of the commodity whose value is measured. Through a compari-son of these forms of value, Marx links the concrete (private) labour expended in production with the abstract (social) labour that comes into being in an exchange of commodities; the nexus for the unity of the two is the material 'body' of a commodity serving as 'equivalent value-form'.

4. *Das Kapital* was first published in German in 1867. The first English transla-tion by S. Moore and E. Aveling (1887) used the third German edition, edited by Engels. A later English translation by B. Fowkes (1976) used the fourth German edition and contains useful notes on Engels's editing. Page numbers cited here refer to the B. Fowkes translation.
5. An English translation of 'Die Wertform' by Michael Roth and Wal Suchting (1978) first appeared as 'The Value Form', *Capital and Class*, 4 (Spring): 130–50.

The argument goes as follows (Marx, 1994: 17–22; all italics are in the original citations unless otherwise stated):

- First, quality and quantity are united in the equivalent form of a commodity, while in the relative form these elements fall apart. In the relative form, use-value expresses an inherent quality of the commodity while value expresses an *alien* quantitative relation to the whole world of exchangeable objects. In the equivalent form, however, the use-value of the commodity *is* its function as a value measure. In the same way that a heavy body used to measure the weights of other heavy bodies takes on in addition to intrinsic heaviness 'the form of appearance of heaviness' so too 'the *natural form* of the commodity becomes the *value-form*' (17).
- Second, concrete labour and abstract labour are united in the equivalent form while the relative form immediately represents only a quantity of concrete labour. Because the commodity measuring value immediately represents the concrete labour worked up in it as an '*embodiment of undifferentiated human labour*' an inversion takes place: the 'sensibly-concrete' or differentiated labour embodied in the relative form of the commodity *counts* as homogeneous human labour (as value substance) only in the act of bringing it into a relation with the 'abstractly-general' equivalent form of the commodity (18).
- Third, direct exchangeability implies that in the body of the equivalent commodity '*private labour becomes the form of its opposite, labour in immediately social form*' (19). In contrast, the private labour embodied in the relative commodity becomes social labour only when it is expressed as a proportion of the labour embodied in the equivalent commodity. The result is 'reification': the equivalent form has become the *sole means for measuring the social usefulness* of labour; hence the social relationship between private producers appears as an external relationship between the objects that they independently produce: 'as a *value relation or social relation of these things*'. Thus, commodities seem to have '*properties pertaining to them by nature*' and the equality of particular labours appears self-evident '*as a value property* of the products of labour' (22).
- Fourth, reification is quite obvious in the relative form because the value of a commodity finds objective expression only in exchange for a commodity serving as equivalent value measure; value is therefore 'something completely distinct from [the relative commodity's] own sensible existence'. In contrast, the equivalent form obscures the phenomenon of reification by expressing private concrete labour as

immediately social abstract labour, the substance of value. Hence, '*within our practical interrelations*' the property of being value is not external to the value measure, but intrinsic to it (23).

The *Appendix* establishes a link between value and labour through a 'body of value', the commodity serving as 'equivalent form' or 'value-form'. The unity of concrete (private) labour and abstract (social) labour in the body of the equivalent commodity is repeated again in the first chapter of Volume I of *Capital*. Commodities in their immediate existence contain only a quantity of concrete labour which expresses no inherent value: 'We may twist and turn a single commodity as we wish; it remains impossible to grasp it as a thing possessing value' (Marx, 1976a: 138). Commodities, *in themselves*, are not values because value has a *purely social* existence pertaining to the need to establish exchange relations, with a quantitative dimension. Again, Marx repeats his assertion that value is fully objectified only in an exchange with an equivalent commodity, that is, when diverse labours are equalized and expressed as proportions of 'abstract human labour': 'From this it follows self-evidently that it [value] can only appear *in the social relation* between commodity and commodity, (*ibid.*: 139; italics added).

A solution to the classical riddle of money follows directly from Marx's critique and reformulation of Ricardian value theory. In this solution, the labour time contained in a money commodity – 'a general equivalent form of value' – is the true measure of the *social value* of the labour time contained in all other commodities. Commodity money (gold) measures value because: (i) it shares in common with other commodities an amount of embodied concrete labour (measured in time), and (ii) it is distinguished from other commodities by the fact that it is immediately exchangeable, hence the concrete labour worked up in the material 'body' of gold is immediately abstract labour (measured as socially necessary labour time), the social substance of value. Yet, when Marx comes in Chapter 3 of *Capital* to discuss the function of money as a measure of value he seems to deny that this is so:

It is not money that renders the commodities commensurable. Quite the contrary. Because all commodities, as values, are objectified human labour, and therefore in themselves commensurable, their values can be communally measured in one and the same specific commodity, and this commodity can be converted into the common measure of their values, that is into money. Money as a measure of value is the necessary form of appearance of the measure of value which is immanent in commodities, namely labour time.

(Marx, 1976a: 188)

The first sentence of the above citation signals a clear retreat from the purpose of the *Appendix*, which aimed to show that *money alone* renders commodities commensurable because *money alone* embodies concrete labour in a form that is immediately abstract 'objectified human labour'. According to the *Appendix*, value arises '*only in the act* of bringing it [a commodity] into a relation with the "abstractly-general" equivalent form of the commodity' (Marx, 1994: 18; *italics added*). Now, on the contrary, commodities seem to be constituted as values (objectified labour) solely by virtue of the fact that they require labour time for their production: 'all commodities, as values, are objectified human labour, and therefore in themselves commensurable'. How can this be? How can value be both alien to the commodity (as argued in the *Appendix*) and intrinsic to it (as argued in *Capital I*)?

In part, the key to resolving the ambiguity is to see that for Marx the commodity in isolation *never* expresses itself *as value* – even where Marx does not say so explicitly. Hence the reference in the above passage to 'commodities, as values' already refers implicitly to *commodities in the act of an exchange with a money commodity*, and as such 'all commodities as values' are indeed objectified human labour. But even with this caveat, uncertainty remains as to the role of money in constituting commodities as values. In the *Appendix*, money and value cannot be separated: money *does* render commodities commensurable *because* it renders abstract and comparable what is commensurable in them: namely, the abstract (social) labour that comes into being when concrete (private) inherently incommensurable labour is expressed as a proportion of the labour time embodied in the money commodity. If the quantitative movement of the money commodity is determined like that of any other commodity by the amount of labour time necessary for its production, then the money commodity immediately expresses what is common to the measure and the measured: a quantity of *socially validated* labour time. Commodity money is therefore the only immediate expression of value and the only true measure of *the social value of the labour time expended on all other commodities*.

The conclusion of the *Appendix* conforms well to Hegel's (1985: section 139)[6] unity of ground and existence, in that value cannot exist

---

6. Hegel's *Enzyklopädie* was first published in 1817.

separately from money: 'appearance shows nothing that is not in the essence, and in the essence there is nothing but what is manifested'. By contrast, the passage from *Capital I* seems to retreat to a Ricardian conception of reification where labour rather than the value-form is the 'essence' to be understood, explained and defined 'in contrast to the form of appearance, in a formal, logical way as the universal, typical and principle' (Backhaus, 1980: 101;[7] also Reuten, 1993). But, if the labour time embodied in *all* commodities is the true measure of value, then the 'objective form' into which socially equalized 'human labour' necessarily 'coagulates' must also be interpreted as a physiological labour embodiment (either in the body of a particular commodity, or universally in the money commodity) that takes place independently of any monetary abstraction in exchange. Money is no longer the 'body of value' that renders commodities commensurable; on the contrary, it is but a phenomenal 'form of appearance' of value, imposed from without upon the 'true' measure of value in labour time.

Which is it to be? Either money has the *intrinsic* 'property of being value' (*Appendix*), or money is merely a *form of appearance* of a value that is already immanent in all commodities as a quantity of labour time (*Capital I*). One cannot have it both ways. That Marx does try to have it both ways produces a number of difficulties. Most immediate of these is the question of how an 'immanent measure' of value in labour time is to be theorized if the labour expended in a private production process actually produces no value until it is rendered abstract through a quantitative relation with money. The next section briefly outlines Marx's concepts of value substance (abstract labour) and value measurement (socially necessary labour time), focusing on the problems of abstraction therein.

2. Labour time and the problem of abstraction

The first abstraction that appears in *Capital* is not, in fact, labour but *capitalist wealth* in its elementary cell form: the commodity. But, having suggested the determinate character of the commodity as a capitalist form of wealth, Marx immediately suspends the presupposition and instead generalizes commodities as 'use-values for others, social use-values' (Marx, 1976a: 131). It is in this context of generalized commodity exchanges that 'value' is first introduced as a term for the relation of equivalence between commodities, 'the common factor in the exchange relation' (*ibid.*: 128).

---

7. Backhaus's *Zur Dialektik der Wertform* was first published in 1969.

Marx follows this with well-known propositions about the 'substance' and 'magnitude' of value. As to 'substance' he suggests that the only property remaining in a commodity once its useful properties are discarded is that of being a product of labour, so that 'congealed quantities of homogeneous human labour' give the exchange relation its 'phantom-like objectivity' (*ibid.*: 128). In order that qualities of labour should be considered 'equal human labour' abstraction must also be made from qualities of labour to arrive at 'human labour-power expended without regard to the form of its expenditure'; in aggregate this 'human labour-power' constitutes society's total labour capacity, the 'total labour-power of society' (*ibid.*: 128–9). To effect the aggregation, however, diverse (inherently incommensurable) skills must be treated as units of 'homogeneous' labour-power, where each unit is 'the same as any other, to the extent that it has the character of a socially average unit of labour-power and acts as such' (*ibid.*: 129). Given this simplification, a pre-market measurement of the magnitude of value comes to depend on some average quantity of abstract labour required to produce a commodity with a given level of technology and skill (*ibid.*: 129).

What all of this implies about the exchange abstraction is that quantities of privately performed labour are socially equalized across individual production processes, such that the 'individual commodity counts here only as an average sample of its kind' (*ibid.*: 130). The determinant of the '*congealed labour time*' represented in the exchange-value of a commodity is, then, the productivity of labour: the greater the productivity of a particular unit of labour the less is the commodity's social value (and vice versa). The determinants of labour productivity are, in turn, 'the workers' average degree of skill, the level of development of science and its technological application, the social organization of the process of production, the extent and effectiveness of the means of production, and the conditions found in the natural environment' (*ibid.*: 130). Marx concludes that: 'What exclusively determines the magnitude of value of any article is therefore the amount of labour socially necessary, or the labour time socially necessary for its production' (*ibid.*: 129).

But is this really what the practical relation of commodity exchange achieves? Do the technical conditions of production provide a proper ground for the qualification 'socially necessary', given the dissociation of production and consumption? Objections arise on a number of levels, the first and most crucial to do with Marx's inadequate justification for choosing abstract labour as the common substance of value over the alternative candidate: abstract usefulness or utility. Abstract usefulness is, in fact, recognized by Marx when he defines the commodity as a 'use-value for others', which *has no value unless it is sold*. Value and 'social use-value' or 'utility' are therefore interrelated concepts, as Marx realized and Engels emphasized when he inserted sentences in parentheses into Marx's text in the fourth German edition of Volume I of *Capital*:

> He who satisfies his own need with the product of his own labour admittedly creates use-values but not commodities. In order to produce the latter he must not only produce use-values but use-values for others, social use-values. (And not merely for others... In order to become a commodity, the product must be transferred to the other person, for whom it serves as a use-value, through the medium of exchange.) Finally, nothing can be a value without being an object of utility. *If the thing is useless, so is the labour contained in it; the labour does not count as labour, and therefore creates no value.*
>
> (Marx, 1976a: 131; italics added)

If the thing is useless, the labour embodied in it creates no value; but to be useful the thing must be transferred. With Engels's amendment, the value-form of commodity exchange depicts a mode of *social synthesis* where usefulness holds everything together. Not only does the labour time spent in production count as a social average for the production of particular commodities under given conditions, but the quantity of commodities produced must also correspond to a demand for these commodities; if not, labour is useless and no value is created. Of course it is not *use-value* (the particularity of commodities) but *universal or abstract usefulness* (a dimension of all commodities as 'social use-values') that remains implicit along with *abstract labour* in the 'jelly' of the exchange relation. With this caveat, Böhm-Bawerk's well-known criticism remains relevant: a simple reversion of the sequence of Marx's investigation leads to abstract usefulness rather than abstract labour as the sought-after commonality in the constitution of value.

The full complexity of the problem is not, however, captured by Böhm-Bawerk. What his criticism overlooks is Marx's own constitution of the commodity as a very peculiar product, a value-form which immediately posits an exchange structure that shapes relations not only between producers (between types of labour) but also between users and things. Fundamentally, the usefulness of labour is inseparable from the usefulness of commodities. Hence, labour time is from the outset 'socially necessary' in a double sense: (i) in the technical sense described by Marx, and also (ii) in the social sense that use-values created by capital *must find willing buyers* in order that the labour expended on them create value.[8] That Marx posits, but then neglects, the shaping of the use-value sphere by the value-form is a key criticism developed over the rest of this chapter. It is a criticism that extends, moreover, to the shaping of the labour process (hence concrete labour) by the capital form, a point developed in section 6, below.

The difficulties are in fact evident from the first pages of *Capital*, Volume I. There core categories (use-value and value, concrete labour and abstract labour) make a first appearance not as oppositions brought into being by the value-form, but as simple postulates arrived at via: (i) a *mental generalization* of abstract labour from the particularities of concrete labour and of value from the particularities of use-value, coupled with (ii) an analytic *reduction* of heterogeneous skills to 'simple labour-power', with the latter notion justified purely by analytic convenience: 'we shall henceforth view every form of labour-power directly as simple labour-power; by this we shall simply be saving ourselves the trouble of making the reduction' (Marx, 1976a: 135). As a result, Marx's presentation exhibits precisely those flaws observed by Hegel (1985: 177) in his *Logic*: namely, that in scientific thinking 'Various grounds may be alleged for the same sum of fact' without demonstrating any inner connection to the phenomenon to be explained. To establish value as the 'inner connection' between capitalist phenomena Marx must show *why* the articulation of production and exchange within a dissociated system requires the value-form of association, and also show *how* the value-form succeeds in equalizing and measuring inherently heterogeneous labours, skills and products. Rather than take this route from value-form to the determination of value substance and value measure, the early pages of Volume I embark upon the classical question of *what is formed* behind a system of *generalized commodity exchanges*.

8. Isaac Rubin was the first to reject a purely technical account of value theory as inconsistent with Marx's concept of 'social value'. He rightly suggests that: 'It is not possible to reconcile a physiological concept of abstract labour with the historical character of the value which it creates. The physiological expenditure of energy as such is the same for all epochs and, one might say, this energy created value in all epochs. We arrive at the crudest interpretation of the theory of value, one which sharply contradicts Marx's theory' (1972: 135; translated from the third Russian edition (1928) *Ocherki po teorii stoimosti Marksa*).

In consequence Marx's project is burdened from the start with an axiomatic assumption of value content *extraneous* to its form of appearance.

These criticisms of Marx's approach to analytic abstraction illuminate twin facets of a single core problem: the indeterminate character of abstract labour and socially necessary labour time as *pre-monetary* categories. In this regard, the solution provided by commodity money turns out to be no solution at all. Even if the Hegelian unity of money and value (in the *Appendix*) is adopted in preference to the Ricardian separation of money and value (in the third chapter of *Capital*), the argument for *money as value-form* or 'body of value' still depends upon a labour-embodied theory of value, which in turn appears supported only by analytic abstractions and simplifying assumptions.

3. Value-form: from commodity-form to money-form

Fortunately, a different logic exists alongside the Ricardian logic of the first two sections of the opening chapter of *Capital* (Arthur, 2002b; Murray, 1993; Smith, 1990). Space allows but an outline of this alternative logic, restricted in the following pages to establishing some reasons for engaging the value-form of exchange prior to any discussion of the content and measure of value. The key sources in Volume I of *Capital* are: (i) the derivation of money in Part One (ch. 1, section 3, 138–63), and (ii) the transformation of money into capital in Part Two (chs 4–6, 247–80).

To begin with, the concept of 'value-form' requires a clear restatement. Fundamentally, *value-form* is an abstract-simple concept of association that presupposes an economic structure where wage labour is organized in independent production units, and where commodity exchanges establish market relations among autonomous producers and consumers. In a word, the value-form presupposes *capitalism* as the social form that grants to the concepts of money, value and labour their meaning.[9] Two implications follow. First, the concept of value (as a determination of the value-form) is inapplicable outside of the structure that it presupposes; there can be no trans historical 'law' of value. Second, the concept of

9. In his 1857–8 *Grundrisse* notebooks, Marx (1973: 107) explicitly comments on the determinate character of economic categories: 'It would therefore be unfeasible and wrong to let the economic categories follow one another in the same sequence as that in which they were historically decisive. Their sequence is determined, rather, by their relation to one another in modern bourgeois society.' The *Grundrisse* was first published in German in 1953, although limited selections appeared in 1939 and 1941. It was not published in English until 1973.

value has at best a *provisional* existence; its actuality is precisely what must be determined by thinking through the immanent interconnections among the categories to which it applies (Reuten and Williams, 1989: 10). The way to do this is through categorical progression, where axioms are eschewed and more complex–concrete categories develop out of the *inadequacies* of the simple–abstract concepts originally posited (Arthur, 2002b; Smith, 1990).

Where should reconstruction along these lines begin? Marx began with the commodity, but behind the definition of the commodity as 'use-value for others' there lies a principle of *dissociation* from which the 'value-form' is immediately derived *as means of association* (Arthur, 2002b: 87; Reuten and Williams, 1989: 56; Smith, 1990: 96). From this viewpoint, Marx's derivation of money (ch. 1, section 3) describes a first determination of the *value-form of exchange*, from which the 'money-form' emerges out of the 'commodity-form' as a necessary and immanent condition for the existence of value relations:

- *x commodity A = y commodity B.* In this simple or accidental form of value, a definite quantity of commodity *A* exchanges for a definite quantity of commodity *B* bringing them into a relation of equivalence. Value is posited as a term expressing the equality of two commodities, such that the exchange-value of *A* is captured in the use-value of *B*.
- *x commodity A = u commodity B* or *= v commodity C and so on.* In this total or expanded form of value, structural determination becomes more complex because each single exchange is located within a system of such exchanges. Value is further determined as a principle of homogeneity or unity that obtains universally in a world of commodity exchanges.
- *u commodity A and v commodity B and w commodity C all exchange for x commodity N.* In this general form of value, one commodity emerges against which all other $n-1$ different commodities exchange. The categories of use-value and value are *united* in this n^{th} commodity, a 'body of value' which has the intrinsic use-value of representing the exchange-values of all other commodities.
- *u commodity A and v commodity B and w commodity C all exchange for a sum of money.* In this transition from the general form to the money-form, use-value (quality) and value (quantity) are reconstituted as an *opposition* of particularity (commodity) and universality (money). As pure quantity, money now faces the whole world of pure qualities, or commodities; it is an autonomous measure vested with the abstract

capacity to equate, ideally, all heterogeneous commodities on the market as proportions of abstract social wealth: *as values*.

This reconstruction of Marx's derivation of money differs from the text of *Capital* in three important ways. First, value is not derived by way of an abstraction from the useful properties of commodities. On the contrary, categories of use-value and value are derived *together* from the value-form of exchange as a dialectical opposition, so that each has meaning only in a relation with the other. In this relation, value (money) and use-value (commodity) are intertwined modes of being of the exchange relation.[10] In the simplest expression of these modes of being, value (quantity) cannot fully express itself because the equation contains only two particular (and therefore inherently incommensurable) qualities, or use-values: *A* simply exchanges for *B* and a reciprocal need is met. As a category of the value-form, value is nevertheless implicit from the outset in the operation of gathering commodities together and positing them as *social use-values*. Moreover, it is in striving to overcome the inadequacies of the elementary (commodity) forms of value that the objectivity of value begins to emerge not as a property of particular commodities but as a social power to validate the usefulness of commodities and, in doing so, unite them generically as proportions of abstract social wealth (Arthur, 2002c; Levine, 1983).

A second difference with Marx concerns the *essential* character of money. In the above reconstruction, the universality of money derives from its social *function* in relating each use-value to all other use-values as portions of abstract social wealth (Williams, 1992, 1998). Money is therefore *necessary* not because it unites concrete labour and abstract labour in a 'body of value' (which takes us only as far as the general form) but because money itself constitutes the value dimension as a 'unity in difference' where money as an 'ideal signification' of abstract social wealth becomes 'the only adequate form of existence of exchange-value in the face of all the other commodities, here playing the role of use-values pure and simple' (Marx, 1976a: 227). In the value-form of the exchange relation, quantity and quality emerge as

10. Reuten and Williams (1989: 13, 28) describe the opposition of universality and particularity as 'the basic form of internal opposition or contradiction' which 'refers to the interdependence of opposed concepts – the unity of opposites; it concerns the distinction between the moments in a single concept'. Compare the unity of the exchange relation constituted by the dialectical opposition of use-value (quality) and value (quantity) with Marx's analytic derivation of value from use-value.

opposite but interconnected poles; value objectified as pure quantity in an 'endless series of equations', proves to be 'a socially given fact in the shape of the prices of the commodities' (*ibid.*: 189). If this important point is obscured in Marx's own exposition, it is mainly because he depicts the money-form as itself a commodity-form (gold). Hence the general form as Marx describes it is not fundamentally different from the money-form, except in the very weak sense that gold emerges by social convention as a universally valid monetary measure.[11] Why a valid measure of value must *necessarily* be a commodity, Marx is unable to say (except by repeated reference to the labour value argument).[12]

A final and crucial difference with Marx is that the derivation of money from the *value-form of exchange* requires no reference to *value substance* (for which a further development of the value-form up to the capital-form is needed). Rather, the commodity-form and the money-form emerge together out of the value-form, and each requires the other. Commodities (particularity) require money (universality) in order that they exist as 'use-values for others'; conversely, money exists because it confirms the sociality of each commodity by relating its particular use-value to all other use-values and, in so doing, confirms each one as socially useful (hence a contributor to abstract social wealth). What is *common* to the commodity-form and to the money-form is not

11. Marx (1976a: 204) provides only historical (contingent) justifications for his transition from the 'general-form' (where any commodity may be an equivalent form of value) to the 'general equivalent form' (where only one commodity is the equivalent): 'Gold, as we saw, became ideal money, or a measure of value, because all commodities measured their values in it, and thus made it the imaginary opposite of their natural shape as objects of utility, hence the shape of their value'. And again: 'I assume that gold is the money commodity, for the sake of simplicity' (*ibid.*, 188).

12. In Chapter 3 of *Capital*, Volume I, Marx comes closest to abandoning commodity money to the extent that he fully recognizes that money functioning as means for purchasing (hence circulating) commodities need have no material (gold) content, but merely has to be ratified as legal tender by the state (1976a: 194). In fact, Marx retains an argument for commodity money only at the cost of losing logical congruence between the *concept of money* and the full determination of money by its *social functions*. This is most clear in his dichotomization of the functions of money as 'measure of value' and 'means of circulation' where only the first function conforms to the proposition that money is a commodity. For the view that Marx does not, after all, have a theory of commodity money see Campbell (1997) and Williams (2000).

therefore a *substance* but the social *relation* which grants to these concepts their intelligibility.

Ultimately, money is necessary not because it allows a hypothetical link between labour and value but because 'it is absolutely necessary that value, as opposed to the multifarious objects of the world of commodities, should develop into this form, a material and non-mental one, but also a simple social form' (Marx, 1976a: 195). Removing the false notion of 'material' money from this sentence does nothing to alter its meaning, since Marx's reference to necessity in any case relates to the way in which the dialectic of value-forms captures an objective relation between dissociated social structures. In isolation, each commodity is but a particular use-value, albeit potentially a social use-value. Only in exchange does the commodity express its sociality, its social usefulness, its universal relation to the whole world of commodities: 'In the form of *money*, all properties of the commodity as exchange-value appear as an object distinct from it, as a form of social existence separated from the natural existence of the commodity' (Marx, 1973: 145). A reconstruction of money as pure quantity grounds Marx's own distinction between the social world of value and the natural properties of commodities in a way that the general form of value – precisely because it is a particular (material) commodity – cannot.

That *money is pure quantity* is exactly what one must conclude from the dialectic of value-forms. What one cannot conclude is that labour constitutes the content of social value, or that this substance is what money indirectly measures in exchange. This is because the abstract universal concept of value, as it appears in the simple form of circulation *C–M–C* (commodity–money–commodity) remains completely ungrounded on any material production basis. Although quantity is present, no 'law' of magnitude is expressed here. To deal with questions of substance and magnitude, Marx must introduce (in Part Two of Volume I) a very different form of circulation *M–C–M* (money–commodity–money) which 'from the point of view of its function, already is capital' (1976a: 248). With the introduction of a monetary form of circulation, the crucial transformation of money into capital begins.

4. Value-form: from money-form to capital-form

The core achievement of Part One of *Capital* is Marx's analysis of value-form, from which the commodity-form and money-form are subsequently derived. The achievement of Part Two is to set in motion a further transformation that takes value theory beyond the concepts of the 'simple form' of circulation, *C–M–C*, examined in Part One. A more complex determination of the value-form, *M–C–M*, is necessitated by an inadequacy: namely that the simple form abstracts from money 'as an end in itself'. Marx develops the distinction between the two forms of circulation as the focal point of Chapter 4:

> The simple circulation of commodities – selling in order to buy – is a means to a final goal which lies outside circulation, namely the appropriation of use-values, the satisfaction of needs. As against this, the circulation of money as capital is an end in itself, for the valorization of value takes place only within this constantly renewed movement. The movement of capital is therefore limitless.
>
> (Marx, 1976a: 253)

Marx explains: the 'possessor of money' as the 'conscious bearer [*Träger*] of this movement' of money is a capitalist; 'the valorization of value' is his 'subjective purpose, and it is only in so far as the appropriation of ever more wealth in the abstract is the sole driving force behind his operations that he functions as a capitalist' (1976a: 254). What is important here is that the immediate aim of the capitalist is neither the production of use-values nor the profit on a single transaction, but 'the unceasing movement of profit-making', and this can be achieved only 'by means of throwing his money again and again into circulation' (*ibid.*: 254–5). Money functions as capital only when it is *perpetually* thrown into circulation, and it is in this sense that the movement of capital is inherently limitless.[13]

What does '*limitlessness*' in the concept of capital mean for the further determination of the value-form? The first point to note is that the *C*s and the *M*s have changed position. In the simple form of commodity circulation, *C–M–C*, money 'does nothing but mediate the exchange of commodities', vanishing altogether in 'the final result of the movement'; but, in the monetary form, *M–C–M*, money gives to value a particular shape: 'above all an independent form by means of which its identity with itself may be asserted. Only in the shape of money does it [value] possess this form' (1976a: 255) and assert its identity with itself. Here the concept of the *magnitude of value* makes a first appearance as something immanent not in commodities but in a *monetary* comparison of

---

13. Williams (2000) argues that hoarding gold withdraws money from circulation. When money functions as capital, then, *a retreat to gold* in times of crisis is not a confirmation of the necessity of commodity money (as Marx thought) but an asset purchase, *a retreat from money as capital.*

value with value over time. The second point to note is that the two *M*s are qualitatively the same, unlike the *C*s exchanged in the simple form of circulation. The immediate implication is that the capital form of circulation is intelligible only if it is viewed as a process driven by the requirement for quantitative expansion, *M–C–M'* (where *M'* is a greater sum of money than that originally advanced in *M*). Hence, the simple valorization form, *M–C–M'*, describes a 'general-formula for capital' or 'the form in which it [capital] appears directly in the sphere of circulation' (*ibid.*: 257).

With the valorization form, Marx arrives at an important point in the development of the concept of value. In *M–C–M'*, money *initiates* – rather than merely *mediates* – a drive towards the limitless expansion of abstract wealth. Once money has become an 'end in itself' the dimension of value magnitude is constituted *independently* as a comparison of money with itself at two different points in time. Hence the concept of magnitude acquires, in addition to its monetary form, *a temporal dimension*. As a temporal phenomenon, value is posited as the *subject* of a movement through time:

In simple circulation, the value of commodities attained at the most a form independent of their use-values, i.e. the form of money. But now, in the circulation M–C–M, value suddenly presents itself as a self-moving substance which passes through a process, and for which commodities and money are both mere forms. But there is more to come: instead of simply representing the relations of commodities, it now enters into a private relationship with itself, as it were. It differentiates itself as original value from itself as surplus value . . .
(Marx, 1976a, 256)

When value enters into 'a private relationship with itself', it becomes capital; with this the concepts of money *and* commodity are together transformed. No longer do they enter into an exchange relation at opposite poles but, instead, 'money and the commodity function only as different modes of existence of value itself, the money as its general [universal] mode of existence, the commodity as its particular or, so to speak, disguised mode' (1976a: 255). It is a fundamental development. No longer are we dealing with the unity of quantity and quality in the simple value-form of the exchange relation, instead we are dealing with the *unity of value as subject* wherein: 'capital is money, capital is commodities' (*ibid.*). Indeed, it is only through alternating moments of 'fixity' in these *universal* and *particular* moments that value 'preserves and expands itself', so becoming 'value in process, money in process, and, as such, capital' (1976a: 255–6).

As capital, money itself becomes the *subjective* object of desire of economic actors (capitalists), so that the augmentation of value (of money-capital) becomes the core characteristic of capital as a valorization form. Money is moreover the only form in which the *objective* difference between original value, *M*, and surplus-value (the difference between *M'* and *M*) can be measured – hence money is the sole autonomous measure of the success of capital as a valorization form. The relation of these subjective and objective determinations of capital become extremely important in the next stage of the argument, as it leads Marx into two related but different questions: (i) the classical question of the source of value and (ii) the question of the determinants of the magnitude of value.

5. The source and measure of value

Introducing the first problematic, Marx faces the picture of capital as 'limitless expansion' with an apparent contradiction (Part Two, Chapter 5). If the valorization form M–C–M' has to do only with circulation and if circulation is a realm where equivalent relations obtain then how is it possible to explain the larger sum of money that results? Even if 'cheating' takes place, the loss of value to one of the partners in an exchange is exactly equal in amount to the gain of the other partner so that, in aggregate, it is impossible to conceive of an increase in wealth arising out of the process of circulation alone: 'However much we twist and turn, the final conclusion remains the same...Circulation, or the exchange of commodities, creates no value' (Marx, 1976a: 266).

To explain how an increase in value arises under the capital form, Marx proposes (Chapter 6) that one must begin by asking what happens in the *time interval* between the moments, *M–C* and *C–M'*. What happens is the production of commodities. Marx argues that production is a *necessary* process whereby commodities come into being. Hence, the circuit of money capital is more concretely described as a process wherein value transforms itself via *successive movements through exchange and production*: M–C–P–C'–M' (where the two *C*s are different commodities and *P* is production). Marx, in fact, does not fully describe capitalism in this way until Volume II (Part One); nevertheless, his analysis of the 'sale and purchase of labour-power' (in Chapter 6 of Volume I) sets the scene for his description of the capital circuit. Fundamentally, production implies the existence of a variety of potentials, of which labour is but one. Is it then possible to demonstrate that labour is the sole source of value?[14]

In approaching this classical problem in Volume I, Marx proposes that the value of labour-power (the commodity purchased by money-capital prior to production) and the value of the commodity produced by labour (in production) are *potentially* of 'two different magnitudes', and this 'difference was what the capitalist had in mind when he was purchasing the labour-power'.[15] The idea that labour-power is a com-modity (with a value and a use-value) then becomes the cornerstone of Marx's Part Three analysis of production where the identification of the *source of value* in labour and the objectification of the 'immanent' (labour time) *measurement of value* in money seamlessly merge together. This is because a comparison can be made between the labour time embodied in the gold paid to workers in wages prior to production and the labour time embodied in the gold received by capitalists on the commodity market after production. Alternatively, commodity money can be abandoned and the real wage paid to workers equated with the labour time socially necessary to reproduce the subsistence bundle that capitalists will supply to workers at the end of the capital circuit. In either case, the result is a theory of exploitation connecting wages and profits with the division of the working day into definite proportions of 'necessary' labour (contained in the gold or subsistence bundle/wage) and 'surplus' labour (contained in capital/profit goods).

One objection to this line of argument has already been noted in section 2 of this chapter: namely that the concept of 'socially necessary labour time' is merely asserted as a simplifying assumption, with no attempt made to show how different (inherently incommensurable) skills can be compared prior to market evaluation. The same criticism now extends to Marx's notion of the value of labour-power, which requires an additional *ad hoc* assumption – namely that labour-power is a *commodity* with a value that equates to the socially necessary labour time embodied in gold or the subsistence bundle. The assumption is

---

14. At the abstract–simple level of abstraction proper to the value-forms, labour is merely *posited* as the source of value, a *possibility* that requires a far more concrete–complex analysis beyond the scope of the current chapter (and also beyond Part Two of *Capital*).

15. Marx (1976a: 300–1) writes: 'What was really decisive for him [the capitalist] was the specific use-value which this commodity [labour-power] possesses of being a source not only of value, but of more value than it has itself. This is the specific service the capitalist expects from labour-power, and in this trans-action he acts in accordance with the eternal laws of commodity exchange.'

difficult to sustain, because the commodity is further determined in Marx's Part Two analysis of the capital circuit as a product produced with wage-labour. As human capacities are clearly not produced in capitalist factories by wage-labour as marketable commodities for purposes of profit, it is difficult to see how labour-power qualifies as a commodity, or how it is governed by the same principles of equivalence (eternal laws) that govern other commodity exchanges. On the contrary, a lack of equivalence is implicit in the wage bargain which makes explicit the legal right of capitalists as purchasers of labour-power to direct the transformation of a potential to labour into actual labour in a production process under their control. If Marx misses these subtleties it is because he (wrongly) treats both money (Part One) and labour-power (Part Two) as commodities, for the sole purpose of excluding *a priori* unequal exchange as an explanation for surplus-value.

In fact, the determination of wage rates (the value of labour-power) is a complex matter that has to do not only with labour *productivity* (as it determines the value of gold or the value of the consumption bundle) but with capital's *demand* for labour-power. The first clue to the complexity of the demand for labour-power lies in the 'subjective' intention identified by Marx himself: that is, capitalists' *expectations* that profits will result from a transformation of potential labour (labour-power) into actual labour (activity). But, validation of production decisions requires more than the unleashing of the potential of labour-power in productive activity. It requires *also* that new commodities find *willing purchasers* on capitalist markets. So logically, and really, what capitalists have in mind when they express (in labour markets) a demand for labour-power are not magnitudes of labour time as Marx proposed, but the prices of labour-power for each day that it is employed in relation to the *expected* prices of the objects that labour will produce. The 'limitlessness' of capital is therefore contradicted not only by the *inherent uncertainty* of the transformation of labour-power into labour, but also by the capacity of capital to shape 'limitless' desires (new preferences) and to set prices (in commodity markets).

Along with productivity, the *social structure of the market* faced by any particular capital is therefore one of the crucial determinants of the size (or magnitude) of value. This is so because the magnitude of value comes into being only in the capital circuit as a monetary comparison of M' with M, measured *after* production and *after* exchange. Two things are important in this conception of the magnitude of value, irrespective of whether or not it can be demonstrated that labour is the source of that value. First, the measure of the magnitude of value cannot be conflated with the monetary validation of commodities (and labour time) in the final commodity exchange (measured in prices). While quantity is certainly present in the exchange of a commodity for money, the transformation is one of value in its particular moment into value in its universal moment, and it takes place at a single point in time. So the passage of time, the magnitude of value as a relation with itself, *M in comparison with M'*, exists here (in commodity exchange) only indirectly, by virtue of the fact that exchange is but a moment within the circuit of capital as a whole. Second, the magnitude of value cannot be measured in socially necessary labour time because the size of *M'* is dependent both on labour productivity *and* on the structure of markets. Uncertainty is at the very heart of the capital circuit, where an independent production process – involving successful transformation of the *potential* to labour (labour-power) into *actual* labour (activity) – may yet count for nothing in the success of value as capital.[16]

Inside the circuit of capital, then, success requires monetary validation in a double sense: on the one hand, validation in commodity prices of the social usefulness of commodities and, hence, of the sociality of the labour (and time) that went into producing them; on the other hand, social validation of private decisions to purchase labour power and commit resources to a production process, which requires a monetary result that does not exhaust the wage bill. Marx recognized the interconnection of these two forms of monetary validation in *Results of the Immediate Production Process*, a chapter written for (but excluded from) the first German edition of Volume I.[17] There he writes that: 'the labour *objectified* in the means of production can only be increased . . . to the extent to which it sucks in living labour and objectifies it as *money*, as *general social labour*' (Marx, 1976b: 994). Indeed, it is 'pre-eminently' the objectification of labour (activity) as money (a result), that confirms 'the *valorization process* as the authentic aim of capitalist production'.

16. This is a viewpoint shared by Reuten and Williams (1989: 70) who write: 'The argument that only labour potentially creates value-added should in no way be read to imply that value-added is in some way proportional to labour . . . It is only the validation of labour and its products in the market that determines where and how much value (-added) is actualised'. Reuten (1999) further suggests that Ricardo shunted political economy off down the wrong track when he conflated an argument for labour as the source of value with the measurement of value in labour time – unlike Smith who saw no difficulty in proposing labour as the source of value, while measuring value magnitudes in corn or wage rates.

17. The *Results* were first published in Russian and German in 1933, and are included as an Appendix to the 1976 English edition of *Capital I*.

What, then, are we to make of Marx's attempts (in the *Appendix* and the first chapters of *Capital*) to provide a pre-monetary measure of abstract labour in socially necessary labour time (determined by the productivity of labour) which, *ceteris paribus*, then determines the magnitude of value? The first step in untangling the confusions of money, labour and time is to see that private concrete labour (activity measured in time) is itself transformed in the exchange of commodities, when abstract labour emerges not as a *determinant* of the magnitude of value but a *result*: as objectified social labour (measured not in time but in money).

6. Money and the measurement of labour and value

To complete the picture, this section reconstructs Marx's labour categories by deriving the dialectical opposition of concrete and abstract labour from the value-form. That is: the unity of labour as a determination of the value-form is constituted, like the unity of value, via its transformations into moments of particularity and universality within the capital circuit.

In the capital circuit, labour and time first appear together in the wage rate which specifies how much money capitalists are willing to pay for each hour of labour activity, on the expectation: (i) that labour-power (not itself a commodity) can be transformed (in production) into marketable commodities, and (ii) that monetary returns from the sale of these commodities will exceed the wage bill.[18] Once labour-power enters the orbit of capital, monetary abstraction dominates over the private allocation of labour signifying the transition of the value-form from the sphere of exchange to capitalist production (Eldred and Hanlon, 1981: 29).

In so far as the capital form shapes production processes to the ends of profit it now fully determines its content, instantiating labour as a dual concept, where particular (concrete) labour in production is dialectically opposed to universal (abstract) labour in exchange.[19] Because

---

18. Reuten and Williams (1989) coin the term 'ideal precommensuration' to refer to capitalists' value calculations, reflected in the wage contract and the 'anticipated imputation of value in production' (Reuten, this volume, ch. 5, section 1.1).
19. One influential thinker, Isaac I. Rubin, misinterprets the implications of the shaping of production and labour by the capital-form. He attributes to Marx a peculiar reversal of Hegelian logic where: 'Form necessarily grows out of the content itself ... From this point of view, the form of value necessarily grows out of the substance of value. Therefore ... labour as the content of value does not differ from labour that creates value' (Rubin, 1972: 117–18). This is wrong, as Arthur (2002c, 2002d) points out. For Hegel *and* for Marx,

the duality of labour arises directly out of the uncertainty of dissociated production and consumption, the unity of value (as capital) and the unity of labour (as it is shaped by capital) come together in the stages of the circuit as a 'unity composed of the labour process and the process of creating value' (Marx, 1976a: 293):[20]

- Stage 1, 'ideal precommensuration'. On labour markets, an external productive capacity (labour-power) is purchased by capitalists on the expectation of future profits. Time appears as a definite period in the wage contract and value appears in its universal moment as money which potentially begets money, as capital.
- Stage 2, the transformation of labour-power into activity. In production, *money is absent* and productivity is the sole determinant of how much of a particular commodity (potential money) is produced with a particular unit of concrete labour (potentially useful/social labour). Higher productivity and the shortening of turnover time increase capital's augmentation, *ceteris paribus*, by diminishing the labour time needed to produce a commodity as well as the passage of time before the validation of labour time is effected in markets.[21] Yet, quantified labour time (mathematically amenable in so far as it can be summed in hours) is not the dimensional space within which the

---

the value-form violently imposes itself on its content, forcing both commodities and labour to take on a double character. In the case of the commodity 'there is nothing in the natural substance of goods that demands recognition in value. It is rather the other way round: this form is imposed on the objects concerned, and posits value as their *inner* substance so that, in spite of their visible heterogeneity, as *values* they are of identical substance and thereby commensurable' (Arthur, 2002d: 188, original italics). Nothing could be clearer: the content of commodities *as values* is necessarily posited by the value-form, not by any natural substance. Equally, value creating (living) labour is not – as Rubin believes – identical with the (abstract) labour that is the content of value: the former 'is presupposed *to* exchange and actualized *after* exchange but simply not present *in* exchange' while the latter comes into being only '*through* exchange . . . because it is the form of exchange that establishes the necessary social synthesis in the first place before labours expended may be commensurated in it' (Arthur 2002c: 157–8, original italics). Here, contra Rubin, there is nothing in the living labour expended in production that demands recognition in value. On the contrary, 'value is an unnatural form that clings, vampire-like, to labour and feeds off it' (*ibid.*: 157). Far from being merely the 'social form of appearance of labour' the value-form of exchange *alone* imparts to labour its peculiar (abstract) character as the content of value.
20. See also Reuten (this volume, Chapter 5).
21. *Ceteris paribus* in this context holds constant purchase and selling prices.

social usefulness of activity has its measure. On the contrary, value is 'fixed' at the end of production in its particular moment (the commodity) and labour appears only as so many hours of *potentially useful* activity (expended on producing a commodity). Only in the final exchange do commodity prices validate capital's initial alloca-tion of labour and objectify activity as a successful result (as abstract labour).

- Stage 3a, the measurement of labour and commodities in exchange. In exchange, *time is absented* through the monetary abstraction required to associate a multitude of particular labour processes and products and measure their contribution to the growth of abstract social wealth. The measurement of social labour is inseparable from the measurement of commodities since the endless series of price equations equating commodities simultaneously equates, and valid-ates as social labour, the labour time expended on producing them. Although exchange lies within the capital circuit, value as process (as capital in motion) does not exist in exchange, any more than it exists in production; rather, value is 'fixed' in each of these moments. Exchange is but *a single point in time* where value manifests in its universal moment, as money or quantity.
- Stage 3b, the measurement of value as capital *after* production and *after* exchange. When value is measured as capital it is brought into a monetary relation with itself *at two different points in time*. The com-parison of surplus-value (M') with original value (M) provides an 'actual commensuration', a social indicator of the *size* or *magnitude* of capital's success as a valorization form.

In this reconstruction of the relation of value to labour, value is the *subject* of a process to which labour is *subjugated*. As activity, concrete labour produces use-values (potentially useful objects) and, since capital is here as particularity, commodities are value in its particular moment. This does not mean that commodities *contain* value, any more than they contain hours of useful labour. No useful labour is present in production, because the labour process has yet to achieve monetary validation through the sale of its products (private labour has yet to prove itself socially useful). Labour time itself requires *ex post* validation when commodities prove themselves as *social use-values* (when consumers willingly buy them). An *ex post* validation of hours of labour time is therefore effected *only* in the monetary association of labour activities and processes (in the final exchange), where time truly disappears and the inversion effected by the value-form is complete. In other words:

in exchange, labour and time are reconstituted as a monetary relation among things, where demand (rather than productivity) impacts negatively, positively or not at all on the social valuation of commodities, labour and time.

In each transformation of value, then, *labour counts differently*. Prior to production and exchange, through ideal precommensuration, labour is brought into the orbit of capital through the exchange of labour-power for money-capital. When labour counts as activity in production (potential money) it is measured by the hours of the working day (and intensity), as stipulated in the wage contract. When labour counts as a result in exchange (actual money), the social contribution of particular activities to the production of abstract wealth is confirmed because, in money, the initial allocation of labour and subsequent expenditure of labour time are subjected to a market-driven evaluation of commodities by willing purchasers (workers purchasing means of consumption and capitalists buying means of production). So, when we consider the process of production and exchange, where the concept of value acquires a more complex articulation as *value in motion*, what is validated (measured) is not labour at all but the valorization form itself. When money *measures the magnitude of value* it functions as a measure of capital's achievement in subsuming the whole of its content (commodity, labour and time) under the *social* (monetary) imperatives of the value-form.

7. Conclusion

The main aim of this chapter has been to explain and reconstruct Marx's concept of value-form over Parts One and Two of Volume I of *Capital*. On a systematic dialectical reading of the text, the main problem is too early an introduction of the concept of abstract labour (and its pre-given measurement in socially necessary labour time); indeed, the first two sections of Marx's first chapter divert attention from the main issue tackled by Marx at the start of *Capital*: namely, the development of the value-form. In particular, Marx's controversial attempt to link value-form to labour through a money commodity prevents an adequate conceptualization of how the value-form – ultimately the capital-form – shapes the content of all entities and processes in capitalism, *including labour and its measurement*. This key point is made by Marx in his opening chapter (notably in his critique of classical political economy), but then obscured because he introduces labour (in Part One) before the introduction of the capital-form (in Part Two); as a result his theory of money seems at times to involve a

Ricardian move from labour content to its monetary form of appearance. When Marx does introduce the capital-form, however, it is clear that for him money alone validates the labour privately allocated and expended in production processes. Moreover, *the magnitude of value emerges in the capital circuit* not as a dimension in the simultaneous comparison of commodities, according to some equivalent property and merely mediated by money, but as a *monetary dimension* to do with the comparison of money-capital with itself at two different points in time. Inside the capital circuit, *value as process* is inextricably linked with the *social validation* of labour and commodities (independently measured in money and influenced by determinants of demand in labour and commodity markets). Thus, logically, abstract labour can have no measure other than money and value magnitudes cannot be determined by quantities of socially necessary labour time in production alone.

What does this appraisal mean for the future of Marx's theory of money as he presented it in Volume I of *Capital* and, perhaps more importantly, what does it mean for the future development of Marxian theories of value? With respect to the latter, the conclusion is that Marxian theories prioritizing production must be abandoned. On the one hand, capital must bring into its orbit an alien entity, a non-commodity (labour-power), and transform it into activity (actual labour) by subsuming it *in production* under the aspect of time (the working day). On the other hand, success depends upon the outcome of two *market-driven exchanges*: (i) the preliminary exchange of labour-power for wages, and (ii) the final exchange of the products of labour for money which depends, *inter alia*, on the desirability of the use-values offered for sale (which depends on the foresight of the capitalist in stimulating and catering to consumer wants). These twin dimensions constitute capital as a 'limitless' subject predominant over its own movement through moments of production and exchange that acquire intelligibility (unity) only within the circuit. Put differently, production and exchange are *interdependent* moments constituted within a social process *through which labour is itself transformed into capital*.

With respect to Marx's own theory, what is gained, and what must be abandoned? Crucially, a systematic development of Marxian theory from form to content retains Marx's core concept, value-form (which in the capital form determines its content), while at the same time moving away from his labour theory of value. This brings out three substantive differences with Marx. These are: (i) a difference in where the abstractness of abstract labour comes from: the value-form rather than abstraction from particular labour, (ii) a difference in the dimension within which value has its magnitude: the capital circuit rather than any commonality in commodities, and (iii) a difference in what money *essentially is*: neither commodity nor embodiment of (abstract) labour but the sole autonomous measure of abstract wealth, both initiating and validating private decisions over labour allocation and production under the capital-form. This implies a new direction for the theory of money: away from Marx's *value theory of money* where money is but an indirect measure of labour towards a *monetary theory of* value where the capital-form gives rise to the concept of abstract labour, therewith necessitating the social measurement of labour in money.

References

Albritton, Robert and John Simoulidis (eds, 2003) *New Dialectics and Political Economy* (Basingstoke/New York: Palgrave Macmillan).

Arthur, Christopher J. (1986), *Dialectics of Labour: Marx and his Relation to Hegel* (Oxford/New York: Basic Blackwell).

— (1998), The fluidity of capital and the logic of the concept, in Christopher J. Arthur and Geert Reuten (eds) (1998): 95–128.

— (2000), From the critique of Hegel to the critique of capital, in T. Burns and I. Fraser (eds): 105–30.

— (2002a), *The New Dialectic and Marx's Capital* (Leiden/Boston/Köln: Brill): 79–110.

— (2002b), Marx's *Capital* and Hegel's *Logic*, in C.J. Arthur (2002a): 79–110.

— (2002c), The spectre of capital, in C.J. Arthur (2002a): 153–74.

— (2002d), Hegel's theory of the value-form, in C.J. Arthur (2002a): 175–200.

Backhaus, Hans-Georg (1980), On the dialectics of the value-form (English translation by M. Eldred and M. Roth), *Thesis Eleven*, 1/1: 99–120 (original, 1969).

Banaji, Janius (1979), From the commodity to capital: Hegel's dialectic in Marx's *Capital*, in Diane Elson (ed.): 14–45.

Burns, Tony and Ian Frazer (2000), *The Hegel–Marx Connection*, (Basingstoke/New York: Palgrave Macmillan).

Campbell, Martha (1997), Marx's theory of money: a defence, in F. Moseley and M. Campbell (eds), *New Investigations of Marx's Method* (Atlantic Highlands, NJ: Humanities Press): 89–120.

Eldred, Michael and Marnie Hanlon (1981), Reconstructing value-form analysis, *Capital and Class*, 13: 24–60.

Eldred, Michael, Marnie, Hanlon, Lucia, Kleiber and Mike Roth (1982), Reconstructing value-form analysis 1: the analysis of commodities and money, *Thesis Eleven*, 4: 170–88.

— (1983), Reconstructing value-form analysis 2: the analysis of the capital–wage–labour relation and capitalist production, *Thesis Eleven*, 7: 87–111.

Hegel, Georg Wilhelm Friedrich. (1985), *Hegel's Logic* (trans. W. Wallace) (Oxford: Oxford University Press) (original, 1817).

Levine, David P. (1983), Two options for the theory of money, *Social Concept*, 1: 20–9.

Marx, Karl (1973), *Grundrisse* (trans. M. Nicolaus) (Harmondsworth: Penguin).

— (1976a), *Capital, Volume I* (trans. B. Fowkes) (Harmondsworth: Penguin) (original, 1867).

— (1976b), *Results of the Immediate Process of Production*, in *Capital, Volume I* (trans. B. Fowkes) (Harmondsworth: Penguin): 943–1084.

— (1994), The value-form (trans. M. Roth and W. Suchting), in S. Mohun (ed.), *Debates in Value Theory*, (London/New York: Macmillan/St Martin's Press): 9–34 (original, 1867).

Moseley, Fred (ed.) (1993), *Marx's Method in 'Capital': A Reexamination* (Atlantic Highlands, NJ: Humanities Press).

Moseley, Fred and Martha Campbell (eds) (1997), *New Investigations of Marx's Method* (Atlantic Highlands, NJ: Humanities Press).

Murray, Patrick (1988), *Marx's Theory of Scientific Knowledge* (Atlantic Highlands, NJ: Humanities Press).

— (1993), The necessity of money: how Hegel helped Marx surpass Ricardo's theory of value, in F. Moseley (ed.), *Marx's Method in 'Capital': A Reexamination* (Atlantic Highlands, NJ: Humanities Press) 37–61.

Reuten, Geert (1988), Value as social form, in Michael Williams (ed.), *Value, Social Form and the State* (London: Macmillan – new Palgrave Macmillan): 42–61.

— (1993), The difficult labour of a theory of social value: metaphors and systematic dialectics at the beginning of Marx's 'Capital', in Fred Moseley (ed.), *Marx's Method in 'Capital': A Reexamination* (Atlantic Highlands, NJ: Humanities Press): 89–113.

— (1998), Dialectical method, in J. Davis, W. Hands and U. Mäki (eds), *The Handbook of Economic Methodology* (Cheltenham: Edward Elgar): 103–7.

— (1999), The source versus measure obstacle in value theory, *Rivista di Politica Economica*, 4–5: 87–116.

Reuten, Geert and Michael Williams (1989), *Value-Form and the State: The Tendencies of Accumulation and the Determination of Economic Policy in Capitalist Society* (New York and London: Routledge).

Rubin, Isaac I. (1972), *Essays on Marx's Theory of Value* (trans. M. Smardzija and F. Perlman) (Detroit: Black & Red) (original, 1928).

— (1978), Abstract labour and value in Marx's system (lecture, June 1927), *Capital and Class*, 5: 107–39 (original, 1927).

Smith, Tony (1990), *The Logic of Marx's 'Capital': Replies to Hegelian Criticisms* (Albany, NY: State University of New York Press).

— (1999), The relevance of systematic dialectics to Marxian thought: a reply to Rosenthal, *Historical Materialism*, 4: 215–40.

Williams, Michael (1992), Marxists on money, value and labour-power: a response to Cartelier, *Cambridge Journal of Economics*, 16: 439–55.

— (1998), Money and labour-power: Marx after Hegel, or Smith plus Sraffa?, *Cambridge Journal of Economics*, 22: 187–98.

— (2000), 'Why Marx neither has nor needs a commodity theory of money', *Review of Political Economy*, 12/4: 435–52.

5
Productive Force and the Degree of Intensity of Labour: Marx's Concepts and Formalizations in the Middle Part of *Capital I*

Geert Reuten *

The first volume of Marx's *Capital* (1867) is subtitled 'The production process of capital'. This reveals the twofold object of the book of, first, an outline of the capitalist *form* of production – that is, in contradistinction to other modes of production – and, second, the production of capital itself – that is, its continuity. There are again two aspects to this object. The first is highlighted in the middle part of the book – Parts Three to Six – on the production of surplus-value. It sets out how the production of surplus-value (profit) is the motive force of capital, how surplus-value is actually produced and so how capital grows. The second aspect is the resulting process of accumulation of capital – treated in the end part of the book.

In this chapter I survey the middle part of *Capital I*, therein especially focusing on Marx's formalizations. As will be seen, he formalizes explanatory *results* rather than either 'explanatory *processes*' or 'mechanisms'. Absent from the formalizations are Marx's key concepts such as: productive forces, labour productivity, extensity and intensity of labour,

* I am grateful for the stimulating comments by Chris Arthur, Riccardo Bellofiore, Martha Campbell, Fred Moseley, Patrick Murray, Tony Smith and Nicola Taylor. I also thank my Amsterdam colleague Mark Blaug for his comments.

and the value of labour-power (or the wage rate). Therefore also, these formulas are deprived of heuristic inspiration.[1]

In section 2 I follow the text of this middle part and make some elementary beginnings to an immanent reconstruction of Marx's formalism. As to the content of this reconstruction I restrict myself to the key concepts mentioned in the previous paragraph. By 'immanent' reconstruction I mean that I base myself on Marx's concepts – that is qua intention: even an immanent reconstruction cannot be but interpretative. The idea of an immanent reconstruction is not to further develop the theory at hand, but to understand it better – thus my intentions are historiographic.[2]

The general conceptual terrain of the middle part of *Capital I* will briefly be surveyed in section 1 (only the first subsection goes beyond an immanent reconstruction).

Apart from 'normal' historiographic accounts of Marx's texts, the reader will find quite a bit of comparison between Marx's German text and its English translation by Ben Fowkes. Some of this comparison is critical of the translation. However, I should like to voice my high esteem for the translator. I know by experience how difficult it is to write in a foreign language. Translation, however, is a far more difficult task. It is just inevitable – especially with authors such as Marx – that the translator interprets the text. This may not be a problem so long as we have fairly standard interpretations on which the translator can rely. However, as soon as interpretations shift then the particular translation of key terms may no longer be obvious.

All page references to *Capital I* in the Fowkes translation of its fourth edition are denoted by an *F* followed by a page number. Those to the fourth German edition of *Das Kapital I* are denoted by a *G* and page number (*MEW* edition). Sometimes I also refer to the earlier English Moore and Aveling translation, as indicated by *MA* and page number. Throughout this chapter I insert quite a few footnotes. Of these, notes 3–4, 7, 13, 19, 37, 39 and 42 are introductory; the others are for the specialist.

---

1. Other formalizations of Marx, such as his reproduction schemes, have been heuristically inspiring (see Reuten, 1998). In effect, within the Marxian tradition the *Capital I* formulas have mostly been replicated instead of enriched. I make no plea for any formalism to dominate the enquiry or its presentation. Opting myself for a systematic-dialectical methodology, I believe nevertheless that, in many instances and *at one and the same* conceptual level (especially for the analysis of a dialectical 'moment'), formal treatments may provide helpful tools.
2. Of course a better understanding might, next, play a role in the further development of a theory, or even a reconstruction in the sense of a new construction.

1. The production of capital

1.1 A comment on dimensions: monetary value and labour time

I begin with a brief comment on the 'dimensions' in which Marx casts his analysis of the process of production of capital. Note first his particular level of abstraction here: his analysis deals with an average production process – in regard to the quantity and quality of both the means of production used and the labour used, and in regard to their organization.[3]

One of Marx's greatest insights, in my view, is that he comprehends the capitalist production process as a unity of labour process and of {ideal} valorization process.[4] In the opening Chapter 7 of the middle part Marx writes:

> Just as the commodity itself is a *unity of* use-value and value, so the process of production must be a *unity of labour process and process of creating value*....

---

3. In effect, he abstracts from intra-branch and inter-branch differences, including differing production periods and compositions of capital (dealt with in Volume III, Parts One and Two). He also assumes that the output produced will be sold – or at least that any discrepancy in this respect is the average one (the complications, especially in the context of accumulation of capital are dealt with in Volume II, Part Three). He assumes that there is no difference between production time and labour time – or he assumes that this difference indeed is the average one (further dealt with in Volume II, Part Two). Finally he abstracts from finance and banking – or he assumes that its functions are integrated into the average capital that he treats (explicitly dealt with in Volume III, Parts Four and Five).

   At the current level of abstraction Marx achieves, in effect, similarities to a macroeconomic treatment (the concept of macroeconomics dates only from the 1930s), without however losing the connection to microeconomic processes. I say 'similarities' – it is not macroeconomic; if that term were applicable it would be for Part Three of *Capital II* when Marx explicitly considers 'the functioning of the social capital – that is of the total capital' (Marx, 1885: 468). (For the latter interpretation as the construction of a macroeconomics, see Reuten, 1998: esp. 190–5.)

   One implication of dealing with the average production process is that 'labour' always means 'socially necessary labour', that is, (1) it is of average skill and dexterity; (2) it produces at the prevailing productive forces; (3) any supply/demand discrepancies are either abstracted from or considered to be the average ones.

4. 'Valorization', i.e. value augmentation. The interpolation of 'ideal' will be explained later on.

The production process *as a unity of labour process and process of creating value*, is a process of production of commodities; *as a unity of labour process and process of valorization*, it is a capitalist process of production, or the capitalist form of the production of commodities.

(F: 293 and 304 – amended;[5] G: 201 and 211)

Thus Marx is pointing out here the specific capitalist value-form of production. Expressed otherwise, we have a unity of a process of physical production (labour process) and a process of {ideal} value augmentation (valorization process). We have two things coinciding, as unity. As simple as this may appear in practice (it is happening all the time in capitalist enterprises), its analysis is complex especially dimensionally: we have value categories (homogeneous); time (homogeneous); heterogeneous physical inputs and outputs; and labour that can be conceived of in terms of homogeneous time, but that is itself heterogeneous.

Throughout this middle part Marx, as we will see, uses two dimensions for his analysis in general and his representations/equations in particular: a value dimension and a labour-time dimension. Without exception the value entities are expressed in *monetary* terms (£); the same applies to all numerical examples.[6] It is necessary to emphasize this since in some accounts of Marx's theory 'value' is itself taken to have a labour-time dimension. This is a wrong account of Marx's *Capital* (those same accounts often adopt the term 'labour values' – one that is never used in *Capital*). As we will see, Marx, at the level of abstraction of *Capital I*, aims to *explain* value (monetary dimension) in terms of labour time – therewith, of course, value is not discarded of its monetary dimension. (Value is the abstract counterpart of price, at the level of abstraction – *Capital I* – where the distinction between surplus-value and profit is still

5. For the first starred text Fowkes has 'unity formed of' for '*Einheit von*' ('formed of' has some connotation of separate elements); for the second starred text he has 'unity composed of the labour process and the process of creating value' for '*Einheit von Arbeitsprozeß und Wertbildungsprozeß*'. Fowkes uses better English, but it seems especially important here not to add 'the' before 'labour process' as this may suggest (as for my first amendment) that it is pre-given; Marx's view is that the character of the labour process itself is affected by it being a valorization process – thus the latter is not just added on to the first.

   Similarly, for the first starred text after the ellipsis, Fowkes has,' considered as the unity of the labour process and the process of creating value' for '*Als Einheit von Arbeitsprozeß und Wertbildungsprozeß*'; the last amendment is alike.

6. Elson (1979) pointed this out.

implicit; the distinction is also not yet relevant – Marx reaches this by presenting the average capital.)

Besides the two dimensions mentioned, Marx adopts an intuitive notion of physical labour productivity increase: increases in the number of use-values (goods) produced by a unit of labour (but he always ends up by expressing these use-values in terms of price multiplied by quantity).[7]

The main problem in understanding Marx's texts (beginning with Part One of *Capital I*) is that he proceeds, step-wise, to find an endogenous dimensional reference point (or reference points), one that is (or are) *internal to his object of enquiry*, one that is (are) key to the functioning of his object of enquiry.[8] Its core terms, in Marx's view, are the monetary dimension and the time dimension. The early parts of each of the three volumes of *Capital* theorize the interconnection of these dimensions in increasing complexity and concretion (Volume I, Parts One and Two; Volume II, Part One; Volume III, Part One) ending up with *the* measure of capital, the rate of profit over time. Thus we end up with the connection of the monetary dimension with the time dimension in general, not the particular *labour* time (of *Capital I*). However, that does not mean that labour time becomes irrelevant at the *Capital III* level of analysis, just that we reach an overarching category.

The labour and labour-time category retains relevance at any level of abstraction in three respects. First, for the grand organization of the production process (the technique adopted) and, related, the planned organization of the intensity of labour (say 'speed'). Second, for the common day-to-day organization of production on the production floor, the management of output per labourer, that is, per unit of labour time. Third, the renumeration of labour time, that is, the wage rate. With the first and third fixed for a period of time, the second determines the level of output and so profits. Earlier I wrote that Marx adopts in his analysis an 'intuitive' notion of physical labour productivity increase. At the point of production there is nothing intuitive about it.

In Marx's choice of categories and dimensions, and especially in the particular way he phrases his theory, there are undoubtedly also other

7. Without value imputation (i.e. prices), the notion of physical productivity must of course be intuitive, because different use-values cannot be added up.
8. In contradistinction to external constructs, such as – later on in history – Fisher's index numbers, or Sraffa's standard commodity (both analytical commodity baskets). These are measures or devices of the analyst; they do not actually play a role in the functioning of the object of enquiry. (Though for index numbers we have a case of reflexivity, in that after their 'invention' they may be adopted in practice – e.g. some consumer price index in wage bargaining.)

issues at stake. For one, Marx (1867) intervenes in the discourse of the Ricardian economics of his day (with its 'labour embodied' theory of value), at times radically breaking away from it (his value-form theory), at others operating within it or at least at its margins. An additional problem here is that Marx sometimes, misleadingly, speaks about values (the *explanandum*) as 'expressions' of labour (the *explanans*). (In the same vein a neoclassical economist might, also misleadingly, speak about prices as 'expressions' of utility or preferences.) Apart from the few remarks in the next paragraph, I will not comment on these aspects in the remainder of this chapter (for more see my 1993, Murray's 2000a comment on it, my 2000 reply, and Murray's 2002 rejoinder).

I take the circuit of capital {M–C...P...C'–M'}, i.e. its growth via the stages of investment (M–C), production (C–P–C') and sales (C'–M'), to be an interconnected process. From the perspective of the valorization (i.e. augmentation) of capital, the 'moments' of the circuit (M–C; C–P–C'; and C'–M') can be distinguished but not separated. Thus valorization of capital, the 'production' of capital, is the unity of this process. To stress this is in part a value-form theoretical development from Marx (i.e. with Marx beyond Marx – see e.g. Reuten and Williams, 1989 and much of the work of Christopher Arthur, Tony Smith and Patrick Murray; see also Nicola Taylor's Chapter 4 in this volume).[9] This development builds on *one* of the theoretical lines in *Capital*. On the other hand Marx often tends, so it seems, to attribute a predominance to the 'moment' of production, especially when he is discussing production. His terminology of 'production' of surplus-value and 'production' of capital (apparently in abstraction from the other moments) seems to reflect this attributed predominance. In face of the unity of this process, I consider Marx's terminology misleading. For the value-form theoretical view, more specifically, there is properly speaking no production of 'value'; we have value inputs (M–C) and the valorization result in C'–M', i.e. when commodities are validated and commensurated in the market in terms of money. In between (C–P–C') this result is *anticipated*, hence in production we merely have an 'ideal' precommensuration, or an anticipated imputation of value.[10] Hence we have no production *of* value, but physical

---

9. This does not imply that these authors agree with the particular way I briefly phrase this here.
10. Usually capitalist firms, their management and their shareholders and other financiers do not worry about this. It is especially in times of crisis that balance sheets are shown to be 'anticipations'. The notion of 'anticipation' and 'ideal precommensuration' is amplified in Reuten, 1988: 53–5 and Reuten and Williams, 1989: 66–8. See also Taylor's Chapter 4 in this volume.

production *in terms of* value. Having said this, I will for the purposes of this chapter – and apart from a few reminders in footnotes – just report Marx's own terminology in this respect.

1.2 The terrain of the middle part of 'Capital I'

In this subsection I briefly survey the general terrain of the middle part of *Capital* I (Parts Three to Six, over 400 pages), against the background of Part Two.[11,12]

Capital, writes Marx in Part Two of *Capital I*, is 'the unceasing movement of profit-making' (F: 254). We have a movement from money (M) into more money: $M \ldots M + \Delta M$. But, 'unless it takes the form of some commodity, it does not become capital' (F: 256). Marx expresses this in the formula M–C–M' (where C is the value of a commodity, or of commodities, and $M' = M + \Delta M$). This is a formula of exchange, derived from the simpler M–C–M. The latter is a strange act, namely buying (M–C) in order to sell (C–M). It is an 'inversion' of C_i–M–C_j, i.e. selling C_i in order to buy a qualitatively different C_j (F: 258). Here, money is merely a facilitator – it does not really matter. In the strange, inverted, form M–C–M, though, money is all that matters; however, it makes sense only as M–C–M', that is, when the end result is an increment (ΔM), a 'surplus-value' as Marx calls it. In M–C–M' value is

the subject of a process in which, while constantly assuming the form in turn of money and commodities, it changes its own magnitude, throws off surplus-value from itself considered as original value, and thus valorizes itself independently. For the movement in the course of which it adds surplus-value is its own movement, its valorization is therefore self-valorization (F: 255).

So capital is a movement of self-valorizing value, of throwing off surplus-value.[13] Part Two is closed off with the introduction of a particular commodity and commodity market, that of labour-power. The existence of

---

11. However, for the purposes of this chapter I abstain from a specific treatment of the relatively short Part Six on 'Wages' (Chapters 19–22, together about 35 pages). See Bellofiore's Chapter 7 in this volume.
12. The next three paragraphs of this subsection are adapted from Reuten (2003a).
13. Note that the concept of 'profit' has been 'bracketed' – until *Capital III* – and replaced by the both simpler and more abstract notion of 'surplus-value'.

this market is predicated on the workers' lack of means of production. We also have a brief introduction of the value of labour-power, i.e. the wage, which in principle should be sufficient to reproduce labour-power. How much is 'sufficient' depends on physical, historical and moral elements (F: 272–5).

In the middle part of *Capital I* (Parts Three to Six) we see 'not only how capital produces, but how capital is itself produced' (F: 280). That is, how surplus-value (ΔM) is produced – thus the (potential) expansion of capital. How can surplus-value be explained? Reconsider M–C–M'. 'The change in value of the money...cannot take place in the money itself...The change must therefore take place in the commodity'... (F: 270). Hence the key to M–C–M' lies in C. In an analysis of the production process, Marx next shows how this is the site where the value of C is turned into C'.

In the exchange M–C, capital in money-form is turned into capital in commodity-form: means of production and labour-power. Means of production bought are static elements; they have on average a fixed technical lifetime and have their value transferred to the product, whence Marx terms the part of capital laid out on it *constant capital* (F: 311–17).[14] Labour-power, or labour capacity, is exchanged against the wage; so the labourer sells his or her capacity to labour (for the time agreed by contract). A change in C can only be engendered by this *active* living element, labour. And since this capacity is in principle variable, both in time (length of the working day) and in intensity – as we will see in more detail later on – Marx terms the part of capital laid out on it *variable capital*. During production labour is 'subordinated' to capital: 'the worker works under the control of the capitalist...the product is the property of the capitalist and not that of the worker' (F: 291–2). In labour resides the potential to produce a surplus product, or, in value terms: surplus-value. Thus labour potentially generates a surplus-value beyond the wage – or, from the point of view of the capitalist, a surplus-value beyond the capital advanced. Marx calls the ratio between the amount of surplus-value and the capital laid out in wages the 'rate of surplus-value' or the 'degree of exploitation of labour-power by capital' (F: 320–7).

14. Means of production derive their value – we might add – not from the process of production in which they figure as means of production, but from the process of production in which they were produced; labour-power is not produced for sale in a capitalist process of production (Reuten, 1988 and Reuten and Williams, 1989, ch. 1, §9; see also Taylor's Chapter 4 in this volume).

Part Three is on 'The production of absolute surplus-value' (Chapters 7–11, about 150 pages). Central to it is the increase in the rate of surplus-value through extension of the working day. In my view this part serves didactic purposes, similarly to Marx's recurrent procedure of starting with 'simple reproduction' (stationary state) before setting out 'expanding reproduction'. In this case it allows Marx to introduce systematically both the concept of 'the value of labour-power' and the drive for increase in the rate of surplus-value. This didactic procedure of Marx's also has a surprise effect. How could we still have – as happened in Marx's day – an increase in the rate of surplus-value, or perhaps a constant rate, when we have a decrease of the working day?

This question is the core issue treated in Part Four on 'The production of relative surplus-value' (Chapters 12–15, some 215 pages). Both regular 'revolutions in the productive forces' and increases in the intensity of labour (each with very different effects as we will see in section 2) allow for a constant or even an increasing rate of surplus-value along with a decreasing length of the working day. Both of these are core to the capitalist mode of production.

The synthetic Part Five bears the dull but appropriate title of 'The production of absolute and relative surplus-value' (Chapters 16–18; it is a relatively short part, extending to 30 pages).

In sum, for the explanation of surplus-value (and the rate of surplus-value), Marx posits four factors: (1) the magnitude of the value of labour-power; (2) the length of the working day; (3) the productive force of labour; and (4) the intensity of labour. He deals with the first two in Part Three (see section 2.1 below) and the next two in Part Four (see sections 2.2 and 2.4). Sections 2.3 and 2.5 provide reconstructions of Marx's formal explanatory treatment.

2. Determinants of (the rate of) surplus-value

2.1 The rate of surplus-value

Part Three, 'The production of absolute surplus-value', begins with two chapters setting out the distinctions between the 'Labour process and the valorization process' (Chapter 7) and between 'Constant capital and variable capital' (Chapter 8) – briefly discussed in section 1.2 above.[15]

---

15. All chapter indications refer to the English editions of *Capital I*. The English editions break up the German fourth chapter into three (Chapters 4–6). Hence from Chapter 7 onwards, the equivalent German chapter should be counted two back.

In Chapter 9 Marx formalizes these distinctions, decomposing capital advanced (**Z**) into constant capital (c) laid out on means of production, and variable capital (v) expended on labour-power (F: 320–1).[16] The starting point for his formalization (equations M–1 to M–5 below) is a (stylized) empirical reference:

> The surplus-value generated in the production process by **Z**, the capital advanced, i.e. the valorization of the value of the capital **Z**, presents itself to us first as the amount by which the value of the product exceeds the value of its constituent elements.
>
> (F: 320 – C amended into **Z**, cf. the previous note)

Capturing this, Marx *formally* starts with a number of identities and definitions.

$$Z = c + v \qquad\qquad \text{[accounting identity] (M–1)}$$

As valorized **Z** is 'transformed' into:

$$Z' = (c + v) + s \qquad\qquad \text{[accounting identity] (M–2)}$$

where s is surplus-value. Thus in **Z–Z'** we have the abbreviated formula of the production by and of capital.

Henceforth all of Marx's equations/representations are indicated with M–. Unless made explicit otherwise, the dimension of all equations is monetary (as indeed Marx has it explicitly in terms of pounds, £; cf. also F: 327–9 where Marx, using empirical cases, derives s from business accounts.). All equations apply to a definite time period (a production period); I have refrained from adding on time subscripts as these would be uniform for all equations (up to equation 14). For each equation I indicate their analytical status in square brackets; the particular terms are mine (M–2, for example, is named 'a tautology' by Marx – F: 320).

16. Fowkes uses the symbol C for capital advanced (instead of my **Z**). This is confusing because the German M–C–M' formula is G–W–G'. In the chapter at hand Marx uses for 'capital advanced' the symbol C in German (i.e. not 'W', see G: 226ff.) – which, if it were related to the formula, would seem nearer to the (English) M than to C. This makes a difference which actually gets lost in both the translations (cf. MA: 204ff.).

Marx calls 'the new value created' (y) 'the value-product' and the output (x) 'the value of the product'.[17]

$$y \equiv v + s \qquad\qquad \text{[definition] (M–3)}$$

$$x \equiv (c + v) + s \qquad\qquad \text{[definition] (M–4)}$$

The s over v proportion is called 'the rate of surplus-value' (e).

$$e \equiv s/v \qquad\qquad \text{[definition] (M–5)}$$

As a ratio of equal dimensions $e \equiv s/v$ is of course a dimensionless number. Crucially from a theoretical point of view Marx (F: 324–6) casts the 'same' ratio (F: 326) in terms of 'surplus labour' (*SL*) and 'necessary labour' (*NL*).[18]

$$e^\star \equiv SL/NL \qquad\qquad \text{[definition] (M–6)}$$

$$e = e^\star \qquad\qquad \text{[explanatory device] (M–7)}$$

Thus he posits $e^\star$ as an explanation for e. There is a difficulty here. So far, there is nothing in itself wrong with positing the one ratio as an explanation for the other, or with positing surplus labour(-time) as an explanation for surplus-value. There is a problem, however, if the *explanans* ($e^\star$, or *SL*) cannot be measured independently of the

17. The right-hand sides of (M–3) to (M–6) are Marx's (the symbols y, x, e, and $e^\star$ are mine). Although it is not important in the context of the problematic of the current chapter, it should be noted that soon in Chapter 9 Marx abstracts from fixed capital, thus interpreting both Z and c as circulating capital (F: 321). Next, and until the second section of Chapter 15, Marx also sets $c = 0$ (F: 324). However, the context here and in Chapters 10–14 rather points at moving 'constant capital' to the background: 'In order that variable capital may perform its function, constant capital must be advanced . . . appropriate to the special technical conditions of each labour process' (F: 323).
18. 'Surplus labour' and 'necessary labour' are 'the labour expended' during 'surplus labour-time' and 'necessary labour-time' (F: 325). Thus we see Marx making the distinction of 'labour' and 'labour-time', anticipating his discussion of 'intensity of labour' in later chapters (see section 2.4 below). It seems, though, that for the time being we can treat the concepts as similar, especially for a discussion of the average capital.
   The term 'necessary labour' should be distinguished from the term 'socially necessary labour' as referred to in note 3; the similarities of these terms is 'inconvenient', as Marx remarks in a footnote (F: 325, n. 5).

explanandum (*e* or *s*). This is not uncommon in science, but it is never-theless a problem and far from a perfect situation.[19]

So far we have entities (*c*, *v*, *s*) that are, in principle, observable and measurable. However, *by themselves* (in isolation from the already known *s/v* ratio, one that can be measured) *SL* and *NL* cannot be meas-ured. Another observable and measurable entity might be the labour time of workers, e.g. ten hours a day. Given a particular length of the working day we could, analytically, divide that up into one part in which an amount of value is produced equivalent to wages (equivalent to variable capital, *v*) and call this 'necessary labour(-time)' (*NL*), and another part in which an amount of value is produced equivalent to the surplus-value (*s*) and call this 'surplus labour(-time)' (*SL*). This is in fact what Marx does (F: 329–31).[20]

Another way to think about this is that (M–6) together with (M–7) simply makes explicit the idea that at a given wage per day, an exten-sion of the working day results, in general, in an increased value-product. On this account (M–6) with (M–7) have elementary explanatory meaning.[21]

Early on in the last chapter of Part Three, Chapter 11, Marx provides a decomposition of the surplus-value in his earlier representations.[22]

19. Incidentally it may be noted that for the present-day mainstream paradigm in economics – which emerged soon after 1867 and that aimed to explain prices or demand in terms of utility, and later on in terms of preferences – a similar problem applies: the *explanans* cannot be measured independently of the *explanandum* (of course this does not make Marx's problem more comforting).
20. Possibly one could argue that in this respect Marx is near to an abductive (Pierce) or a retroductive (Lawson) proceeding. An uncompromising empiri-cist would consider it doubtful if (M–6) adds anything explanatory to (M–5). What it achieves, in effect, is to breach the idea that the wage is the equiva-lent of the labour delivered. In whatever way this may be appraised – and in reference back to the misconceived notion of 'labour values' (see section 1.1, just after note 6) – Marx endeavours to provide an explanation of surplus-value in terms of labour (time). To conceive of value itself in terms of labour (time) is to collapse the explanation – and Marx definitely does not do this.
21. Though it is either analytical or largely intuitive. Let *TL* be total labour time. Then we can rewrite (M–6) into: $e^* \equiv (TL - NL)/NL$, with *TL* in principle observable and *NL* unobservable. Now we could posit: *s* varies with *TL*, *ceteris paribus*. This may make analytical sense if the theory makes sense. However, Marx has yet to unpack a host of other factors affecting *s* (in all the rest of *Capital* at least), so that the '*ceteris paribus*' makes no empirical sense.
22. Marx in a change of notation has $S = (s/v)V$ and $S = P(a'/a)n$ where *P* is the wage rate per day ($= \underline{w}$ in my notation).

$$s = (\underline{s}/\underline{v})v \qquad\qquad \text{[definition] (M–8)}$$

$$s = \underline{w}\,(a'/a)n \qquad\qquad \text{[explanatory device] (M–9)}$$

where:

s = the mass of surplus-value;
v = variable capital;
$\underline{s}$ = surplus-value per worker per average day;
$\underline{v}$ = variable capital advanced per worker per day (hence in fact the equivalent of the wage rate per day);
$\underline{w}$ = the wage rate per day ('the value of one individual labour-power');
a' = surplus labour (surplus labour time);
a = necessary labour (necessary labour time);
a'/a = the average 'degree of exploitation';
n = the number of workers employed (i.e. measured in days);
$\underline{s}/\underline{v}$ = the average rate of exploitation per worker per day (but as this is a dimensionless ratio it may as well be applied to any other time unit).

(Hence the underlined symbols in M–8 and M–9 are in value per time dimension; a' and a in time dimension. This way we end up with the monetary value dimension for s – at least if we interpret Marx's 'the number of workers employed' for n (F: 418) as working days, which can readily be inferred from the context.)

Note that as ratios we have the equalities of

$$e \equiv s/v = \underline{s}/\underline{v} = a'/a \qquad\qquad \text{[recapitulation of explanatory device] (10)}$$

The $\underline{s}$ in the $\underline{s}/\underline{v}$ of (M–8) cannot be measured independently of s and v. Similarly the a'/a of (M–9) cannot be measured independently of s and v. (See the comment on (M–6) and (M–7) above.)

Anticipating Marx's discussion of absolute and relative surplus-value in Part Five, I add on a definition here (equations 11 or 12 are not Marx's):

$$wL \equiv v \qquad\qquad \text{[definition] (11)}$$

where w is the wage rate per hour and L the amount of *labour hours hired*. Hence we may rewrite (M–9) as

$$s = e^*(wL) \qquad \text{[explanatory device] (12)}$$

Marx writes: 'the mass of surplus-value $\{s\}$ is determined [*bestimmt*] by the product of the number of labour-powers $\{L\}$ and the degree of exploitation of each individual labour-power $\{e^*\}$...We assume throughout, not only that the value of an average labour-power $\{w\,?\}$ is constant, but that the workers employed by a capitalist are reduced to average workers' (F: 418; G: 322 – symbols in curled brackets added).

The advantage of this notation (12) is that the number of hours hired (L) – as well as their remuneration (w) – has been made explicit. It seems that in his representation (M–9) Marx tried to bring this in – unsuccessfully though, since the working day itself is a variable (cf. Marx's $\underline{w}$ and n). On the other hand, in equation (12) we seem to have lost Marx's distinction between labour-power (L) and labour (L).[23] Or at least, this is now merely implicit.[24] In this last respect, representation (12) – to be found in much of contemporary Marxian theory – is defective.[25] Later on we will retrieve Marx's labour–labour-power distinction (sections 2.3 and 2.5).

2.2 The 'productive force' of labour

Part Four of *Capital I* presents 'The production of relative surplus-value'. In its first chapter, Chapter 12, Marx introduces a key factor into his presentation: 'change in the productive force of labour'.[26] Before going into this, a note on translation is required. In the context of production we will generally need to differentiate between changes that have to do with the exertion of labour only or mainly, and changes that have to do with the interconnection of changes in the means of production, technology and the exertion of labour. It seems to me that in the German text Marx makes important differentiations in this respect. Fowkes translates the German *Produktivkraft* by 'productivity'.[27] This is

---

23. In fact Marx's $s = \underline{w}(a'/a)n$ also does not bring out the distinction between labour and labour-power (the same applies to all of Marx's equations in *Capital*) although this one does make explicit the *value* of (a day's) labour-power.
24. The reader may observe that the same happens in Sraffian types of approach.
25. And including some of my own earlier work.
26. Earlier on it was sometimes briefly anticipated.
27. Most of the time at least – e.g. F: 453, 2nd paragraph – Fowkes translates *Produktivkraft* into 'productive power' and on F: 508 it is translated into 'productive forces' (cf. G: 407). Not only do we lose terminological connections, the English text also makes connections that are absent from the German (esp. with the German term *Produktivität der Arbeit* and when Fowkes translates

unfortunate, as Marx sometimes also uses the term *Arbeitsproduktivität* (labour productivity) – this will be seen to be especially important in the context of his presentation of 'intensity' of labour, discussed in the next subsection. In all of the following texts I will amend the translation for *Produktivkraft* into 'productive force' (marked *...* – I use the same mark for any other amendments, as specified in footnotes).[28]

In Chapter 12 Marx writes:

Hitherto, in dealing with the production of surplus-value...we have assumed that the mode of production is given and invariable....The technical and social conditions of the process and consequently the mode of production itself must be revolutionized *so as to increase the productive force of labour*... (F: 431–2 – amended;[29] G: 333–4).

Introducing this by way of an example Marx writes:

increase in the *productive force* of labour...cannot be done except by an alteration in his [the labourer's] tools or in his mode of working [*Arbeitsmethode*], or both. Hence the conditions of production of his labour, i.e. his mode of production, and the labour process itself, must be revolutionized. By an increase in the *productive force* of labour, we mean an alteration in the labour process of such a kind as to shorten the labour-time socially necessary for the production of a commodity, *hence a smaller quantity of labour acquires the force* of producing a greater quantity of use-value (F: 431 – amended;[30] G: 333).

---

this into 'productivity of labour', 'productivity' being his most frequent translation for *Produktivkraft*). We have the same problem in the *Results* (translated by Livingstone). Moore and Aveling (*Capital I*) translate *Produktivkraft* into 'productiveness' (at least those instances I have checked).

Generally there are two translation options for the term *Kraft* as in *Produktivkraft*: power and force. The former is adopted in the *Grundrisse* translation (productive power) and the latter in the *The German Ideology* and the 1859 *Critique* Introduction (productive force).

28. Note that I do not claim to use better English than Fowkes.
29. For the starred text Fowkes has 'before the productivity of labour can be increased' for '*um die Produktivkraft der Arbeit zu erhöhn*'.
30. For the first and second starred text Fowkes has 'productivity' for '*Produktivkraft*'. For the third he has 'and to endow a given quantity of labour with

Productivity (it seems to me) has an imprecise meaning.[31] I am pretty sure that Marx always reserves his term *Produktivkraft* (productive force) for – as he says in this quotation – the production of a greater quantity of use-value by a smaller (or by the same) quantity of labour (and it usually goes along with price decrease). My hypothesis is that the notion of 'socially necessary labour-time' – see the quotation – is associated with this notion of productive force and that, in this context, 'productive force' must be taken as average.

In the subsequent chapters of Part Four (13–15) Marx further conceptualizes the development of productive force by way of a historical description of the development of 'tools', via manufacture, into (Chapter 15, Section 1) 'machinery and large-scale industry'. Generally Marx associates an increase in productive force with changes in the organization of the labour process (for example, related to scale and division of labour and to changes in the composition of capital).[32]

2.3 A formal and immanent reconstructive intermezzo on capitalist revolutions in the productive force of labour

It is not until Chapter 18 (i.e. the last chapter of Part Five) that Marx returns to his formulas for the rate of surplus-value, however, without improving on the previous ones – i.e. those discussed in section 2.1 above. Nevertheless, in view of the conceptual progress made by Marx so far (Chapter 11 to Chapter 15, Section 2), there is reason to do so. (Marx does not do it here, and does not return to it in similar contexts later on.)

We saw that the potential of labour for producing use-values (the potential use-value productivity) is affected by the productive force; modern economists would say the state of technology and its implementation. Thus given that state, any labour is potentially exerted at a particular productive force.

---

the power . . . ' for *'ein kleinres Quantum Arbeit also die Kraft erwirbt'*. My point for this amendment is not only the reference to shortening of the labour day, but foremost the *reversion* of the apparently active element – with Fowkes's 'endow', labour seems to be put in the passive position.

31. In both mainstream and in much of Marxian economics it loosely refers to a combination of effects of technological change and effectiveness of labour. (I will come back to this in section 2.4.)

32. The concept of the 'composition of capital', the c/v ratio, is mostly only implicit in Part Four (it is alluded to in Chapter 15 (F: 571 and 577–8). It makes a proper appearance in Part Seven. See my Chapter 10 in this volume.

A revolution in the productive force of labour can be envisaged as a change in technological trajectory (T) – think of grand technologies such as that of steam engine, electricity, petrol motor, computer. They originate in particular branches and then diffuse gradually throughout all or most of the branches in the economy. Let us simplify a trajectory (*i*) into a certain value *c* of specific means of production that could potentially be worked up by an amount of average labour (measured in time).

$$T_i \supseteq \text{«}c/L\text{»} \qquad \text{[definition of approximation] (13)}$$

Thus *c/L* stands for a certain value (£) of means of production that could be worked up by a particular amount of labour in a definite period of time. (*Analytically* we might put *L* to unity, e.g. an hour, whence we have, e.g. £10 per labour hour.) The guillemets here indicate the specificity of means of production and labour; $\supseteq$ is the sign for 'contains or equals'. Within a trajectory we have bounded variations in *c/L* ratios coming about in tranches (blocks) of diffusion (variations say of a range of 40 per cent – in the analytical example ranging from £10/hr to £14/hr, coming about, for example, in five tranches). We call any one such tranche a *state* of the technological trajectory (*ST*), or a *state* of the development of the productive forces:[33]

$$ST_{i(t)} \supseteq \text{«}c/L\text{»}_{(t)} \qquad \text{[definition] (14)}$$

The subscript (*t*) stands for that particular state of trajectory (*i*) – it also stands for a definite period in time (e.g. 1850–60) in a region (e.g. Great Britain and France).

Let us now consider production (recall that the accounting dimension of the production process is a monetary one).[34]

$$x = \text{«}c/L\text{»}_{(t)} \, L^{\beta} \qquad [\beta > 1]^{[35]}$$
$$\text{[determination; step of heuristic approximation] (15)}$$

---

33. The 40 per cent range is one in the absence of inflation or deflation of prices. Remember that c is in value terms. States of the trajectory are associated with a dissemination of the technology over a new tranche of branches in the economy.

34. In this accounting the management of firms anticipates sales and so carries out a commensuration of heterogeneous entities (means of production, labour in process) before the deed so to speak, and thus carries out 'an ideal pre-commensuration'. Cf. the last paragraph of section 1.1 above.

35. Obviously for $\beta = 1$ we would merely have a reproduction of the value of means of production, i.e. without any value added.

Hence, as before, x is the gross output in value terms (e.g. £). «c/L» is the quantity of means of production in value terms *that could, potentially, be worked up* by a quantity of labour (hours). The c is some value of means of production *at the point when workers enter the business gate* (at the point where they enter 'the hidden abode of production' – F: 280). Thus «c/L» is for example (£40 million)/(4 million potential labour hours).[36] The outer right-hand L in representation (15) is the actual labour employed (measured in hours), i.e. actual labour time. The factor β in L^β is *the actual exerting power* of labour (per hour). For the time being we take β to be a (stylized) *constant*, as attached to the productive force «c/L»$_{(t)}$.

I make a strict distinction between, first, the productive force of labour («c/L»$_t$), second, labour-power in the conventional sense (the L in «c/L»), i.e. a potential, and third, the 'actual exerting power of labour' (L^β) – this distinction is returned to in section 2.5.[37] Apart from the value of

---

36. It may be misleading to add: (£40 million)/(4 million potential labour hours) = £10 per potential labour hour, as we did in the analytical example. «c/L» is fixed plant-wise, hence the average or modal «c/L» is fixed. Underlying L is a technical matrix with in its column the number of workers simultaneously required to operate the means of production at a point in time, and with in the rows of the matrix the duration of the production process (in hours). (Of course «c/L» is only relatively 'fixed'. We may have major restructuring/reorganizations of capital – i.e. of plants or clusters of plants – which in effect introduce new states of the trajectory.)

37. I have been following so far (and will below) Marx's *Capital I* simplification (generally) of abstracting from means of production that last beyond the production period. (Including those we would simply have «K/L»$_{(t)}L^\beta$ – see Reuten, 2002.) For readers familiar with neoclassical economics, it should be noted that representation (15) may look like a particular 'production function'. However, its conceptualization (especially as to what are variables and as to how a 'technique' is defined) is different from orthodox meanings:
   - c are *specific* means of production (measured in monetary terms: prices times quantities);
   - the concept of c/L is that of a plant (or plants), and thus is incompatible with marginalist notions as including marginal productivity (see also the previous note);
   - c/L is taken to be 'almost' fixed in the short run: «c/L» (the guillemets should be warning for that); thus we are within a particular *state* of a technological trajectory – in which only moderate variations in c/L (say within a 8 per cent bound) can be profitably applied (that is macroeconomically; micro variations may be larger).
   - there is no blue book of techniques that can profitably be used – no substitution in the orthodox sense: we are on a one-way trajectory.
   (For some other differences in this respect between the neoclassical and the Marxian approach see Smith, 1997. See also his Chapter 8 in this volume for contrasts with neo-Schumpeterian views.)

labour-power (see section 2.5) we have herewith collected all of the main variables that Marx adopts in his Part Four analysis of relative surplus-value.

Before further commenting on β in the next subsection, we may proceed with a simple example (simple purely illustrative numbers). Let «c/L» = £40 m/(4 m labour hours). Let $\beta = 1.16$ (at $L = 4$ m hrs). Then, because $4^{1.16} = 5$, $x = £50$ m. Assume the average wage rate to be £1.50. From Marx's equation (M–4) and definition (11) we have the accounting identity:

$$s = x - (c + wL)$$

$$s = £50\,m - [£40\,m + (£1.50)(4\,m)] = £50\,m - (£40\,m + £6\,m) = £4\,m$$

$$x = c + wL + s = £40\,m + £6\,m + £4\,m$$

So this gets us back to Marx's type of example. In fact my statement 'let $\beta = 1.16$' is analogous to statements of his, such as 'if 1 hour's labour is exhibited in 6d', where d is a monetary unit.[38]

Indeed all of Marx's formulas are *results*. The advantage of a representation such as (15) is that we see some more of the explanatory dynamic behind those results: an explanatory dynamic that Marx sets out in his text.

As indicated, in Parts Three to Six of *Capital I* all of Marx's focus is on the rate of surplus-value. In terms of the formalization of the current subsection we have for that rate:[39]

$$e = \frac{s}{v} = \frac{\{«c/L»_{(t)}\}\{L^{\beta-1} - 1\}}{w} - 1 \qquad \text{[explanatory device] (16)}$$

---

38. E.g. F: 433. Instead of 'exhibited' Fowkes has 'embodied' for '*stellt sich dar*' (G: 335). 'Embodied' rings of course Ricardian bells (perhaps it should, perhaps not; in some contexts Marx uses the term *verkörpert*, i.e. embodied).

39. Representation (16) is derived as follows:

$$x = «c/L»_{(t)}L^{\beta}$$

$$s = x - (c + v)$$

$$s = \{«c/L»_{(t)}L^{\beta}\} - \{c + wL\}$$

$$e = \frac{s}{v} = \frac{\{«c/L»_{(t)}L^{\beta}\} - \{c + wL\}}{wL} = \frac{\{«c/L»_{(t)}L^{\beta-1} - c/L\}}{w} - 1$$

Thus at the *prevailing* productive force of labour «c/L»$_{(t)}$, the rate of surplus-value depends positively on the 'actual exerting power of labour' β and negatively on the wage rate w. So far β is a constant power. Note that it cannot be directly measured independently of surplus-value (s).[40]

According to Marx the main concomitant of revolutions in the productive forces is a decrease in the value of commodities. To the extent that these are wage goods, such revolutions allow for nominal wage decrease at any level of real wages. Thus *between states* of technological trajectories we have, *ceteris paribus* (specifically the factors affecting the subsumption of labour), the rate of surplus-value pushed up. Indeed this, for Marx, is the heart of the production of relative surplus-value. Thus we have

$$w = w^* + f(\Delta ST_{(t)}) \qquad\qquad [f' < 0] \qquad\qquad (17)$$

where w^* summarizes the labour market aspects of the general state of subsumption of labour.[41]

2.4 Degree of intensity of labour

We now proceed from the point where we left Marx's text prior to the reconstructive intermezzo of the previous subsection. Note first that Marx *up to this point* – as he reminds us early on in the section now under discussion – conceptualized increase in the production of relative surplus-value as being engendered by increase in the use-value productivity of labour. '*The same amount of labour-time adds the same value* as before to the total product, but ... is spread over more use-values. Hence the value of each single commodity falls' (F: 534; italics added).[42]

In Section 3(c) of Chapter 15, Marx presents the concept of 'intensity of labour'.[43]

---

40. Though one might devise experiments ('slow down'), or adopt indirect measures for changes in β.
41. The further determination of the state of subsumption is beyond the confines of this chapter (see Murray, 2000b and his Chapter 7 in this volume). The prevailing rate of unemployment is merely one obvious factor affecting w^*.
42. This is based on a number of assumptions that Marx repeats over and over again. Next to the three assumptions associated with the concept of 'socially necessary labour' (see note 3) it is assumed that competition results in the pushing down of prices when productivity rises spread over branches of production.
43. Here he introduces it systematically – the term was used five times before in passing: in Chapter 1 (F: 129; G: 153), Chapter 7 (F: 303; G: 210), Chapter 11 (F: 424; G: 328) and Chapter 14 (F: 460; G: 361 and F: 465; G: 365). In two

something we have already met with, namely the intensity of labour, develops into a phenomenon of decisive importance. Our analysis of absolute surplus-value dealt primarily with the extensive magnitude of labour, its duration, while *the degree of its intensity* was treated as a given factor. We now have to consider the inversion [*Umschlag*] of extensive magnitude into intensive magnitude, or magnitude of degree (F: 533 – amended;[44] G: 431).

Marx directs our attention here both by the terms 'decisive importance' and 'inversion/break' (*Umschlag*). Thus next to the magnitude of labour (*L*), Marx introduces its degree of intensity. In fact part of my reason for introducing the formalization of section 2.3 is to be able to put sharp focus on this. In terms of my representation (15) or (16) a change in the 'actual exerting power of labour', the β in L^β, is at stake. Henceforth I will call this the 'degree of intensity of labour'.[45] Marx – as he does often when introducing an important new concept – uses a number of adjectives to stress the concept. Here is a key formulation – it is also a key citation for the current chapter:

the development of *the productive force and the economization of the conditions of production* imposes on the worker an increased expenditure of labour within a time... This compression of a greater mass of labour into a given period now *counts for what it really is, namely an increase of the quantity of labour.* In addition to the measure of its 'extensive magnitude', *labour-time now acquires a measure of its *degree of density**... the same mass of value is now produced for the capitalist by, say, 3⅓ hours of surplus labour and 6⅔ hours of necessary

---

other instances Marx uses in German the term '*potenzierte Arbeit*' which both Moore and Aveling and Fowkes render into 'intensified labour' (F: 135; MA: 51; G: 59; and F: 435; MA: 302; G: 337).

44. For the starred text Fowkes has 'its intensity' for '*der Grad ihrer Intensität*'. The insertion of the German for 'inversion' is by Fowkes. It seems to me that *Umschlag* is a quite heavy term, pointing to a new moment. Other candidates for the translation would be 'break' (as in 'break in the weather') or 'turn' (as in 'turn in relationship').

45. I challenge the reader who is not convinced by my L^β representation to come up with an alternative representation for the italicized text in the next quote.

labour, as was previously produced by 4 hours of surplus labour and 8 hours of necessary labour.

(F: 534 – amended and italics added;[46] G: 432–3)

Thus we see a crucial conceptual progress (concretization) in comparison with the earlier simpler (more abstract) conception summarized at the opening of this subsection: *no longer do we have the simple parallel between value and labour-time.*[47]

Marx indicates as main factors bringing about this intensity increase an increase in the speed of the machines, and the same worker having to supervise or operate a greater quantity of machinery (F: 536). In the remainder of the section he cites reports as evidence for this process.

The issue is taken up further in the synthetic Part Five – apart from a brief passage in Chapter 16 (F: 646) mainly in its Chapter 17. Note that all along Marx's primary problematic is not so much the determination of the magnitude of value, but rather the relative magnitudes of

46. For the first starred text Fowkes has 'the development of productivity and the more economical use of the conditions of production' for '*der Entwicklung der Produktivkraft und der Ökonomisierung der Produktionsbedingungen*'. For the second he has 'intensity, or degree of density' for '*das maß ihres Verdichtungsgrads*'.

Concerning the term 'measure' a general warning – for all of *Capital* – is appropriate. The meaning of the German term '*maß*' is complicated. The relevant meaning *here* seems near to 'grade' or 'degree' – or 'measure' as in the phrase 'to considerable measure'. (For at least some explication of the term see Inwood, 1992: 240.)

47. Or 'socially necessary labour-time' (see note 3). For the purposes of the current chapter I will not quarrel with historiographers who argue that *Capital* is based on a linear logic (instead of a systematic-dialectical) and that already in the first section of Chapter 1 Marx writes: 'Socially necessary labour-time is the labour-time required to produce any use-value under the conditions of production normal for a given society and with the average degree of skill and intensity of labour prevalent in that society' (F: 129; G: 53). At that point we cannot know what he means by 'degree of intensity'; he subsequently 'blends out' the intensity issue and returns to it systematically in Chapter 15.

I just wrote 'no longer do we have the simple parallel between value and labour-time'. In fact we see breaks in this parallel (conceptual progress) here in *Capital I* and in all the volumes of *Capital* (particularly also in Parts Two and Three of *Capital II*). There is no particular dichotomy in this respect between Volumes I and III. Nevertheless, as indicated in section 1.1, labour time for Marx remains all along an important reference point for the analysis of (changes in) the capitalist production process.

surplus-value and the price of labour-power.[48] At a given average real wage rate per 'normal working day', the latter relative magnitudes depend on:

> (1) the length of the working day, or the extensive magnitude of labour, (2) the normal intensity of labour, or its intensive magnitude, whereby a given quantity of labour is expended in a given time and (3) the *productive force* of labour, whereby the same quantity of labour yields, in a given time, a greater or a smaller quantity of the product, depending on the degree of development attained by the conditions of production (F: 655 – amended;[49] G: 542).

All these three are variable, and next Marx analyses their variation in turn. I focus on the intensity of labour (Section 2 of Chapter 17).

> if the length of the working day remains constant, a day's labour of increased intensity will be incorporated *in an increased amount of value*, and, assuming no change in the value of money, in an increased amount of money…A given working day, therefore, no longer creates a constant value, but a variable one…
>
> (F: 661, italics added;[50] G: 547)

So far this repeats – though in a very clear formulation – the inversion/ break indicated above. However, in two subsequent statements Marx (I think) muddles the issue for the inattentive (preoccupied?) reader. Here is the first one.

> Whether the magnitude of the labour changes in extent or in intensity, there is always a corresponding change in the magnitude of the value created, independently of the nature of the article in which that value is *exhibited* (F: 661 – amended;[51] G: 548).

---

48. The upshot of this is, in my view, that when we have reached the introduction of the concept of profit (in Volume III), profit/wage ratios are affected by the factors mentioned in the next quote.
49. For the starred text Fowkes has 'productivity' for '*Produktivkraft*'.
50. The italicized text reads in German: '*in höherem Wertprodukt*' – literally: in an increased value-product' (*y* in equation M–3). The same for 'value' in the next sentence. The same for the *first* term 'value' in the next citation.
51. For the starred text Fowkes has 'embodied' for '*sich darstellen*'.

Although as to the letter of the text there is nothing to complain about, it might (carelessly) be read as a repetition of the conceptualization cited at the very opening of this subsection. In fact the 'magnitude of labour' has now been cut loose from labour time; labour time no longer 'corresponds' to value (at least not diachronically).

Such a (careless) reading and its implication might be reinforced by the next, and final, text of this section in Chapter 17:

> If the intensity of labour were to increase simultaneously and equally in every branch of industry, then the new and higher degree of intensity would become the normal social degree of intensity, and would therefore cease to count as an extensive magnitude (F: 661–2; G: 548).

Again, this is fair enough – as well as consistent with Marx's general approach. However, it seems to deemphasize the conceptual progress 'of decisive importance'.[52] To the extent that over time (diachronically) we have recurrent increases in the 'normal social degree of intensity', the value-producing potential of labour cannot be measured diachronically by labour time independently of the value produced.[53] (By itself this does not make the explanatory power of the theory useless; it makes it more problematical.)

As indicated, Marx returns to his formula for the rate of surplus-value in the final chapter, 18, of Part Five. It is a mystery why he, after making subtle distinctions in the previous chapters, relapses into the simple s/v result and its 'surplus-labour' over 'necessary labour' counterpart.

The intensity matter is returned to in Chapter 25 of Part Seven, 'The general law of capitalist accumulation', however without much further development (F: 788–9 and 793).[54]

---

52. Marx continues immediately after the text just quoted: 'But even so, the intensity of labour would still be different in different countries, and would modify the application of the law of value to the working days of different nations. The more intensive working day of one nation would be represented by a greater sum of money than the less intensive day of another nation' (F: 662). Systematically this international context is irrelevant here. Relevant would be to say that 'the law of value' does not apply, generally, over time (that is not diachronically).

53. Thus one hour of $SNLT_{(t)} \neq SNLT_{(t+1)}$ (where $SNLT$ is socially necessary labour time).

54. There are also a couple of related passages in the *Results* (included in Marx, 1867F: 987, 991–2, 1021, 1024–6; cf. 1034–5).

It is obvious that in terms of the reconstructive formalization of the previous subsection Marx's .new 'normal social degree of intensity' of labour would be posited in terms of changes in the degree β in L^β associated with a state of the 'productive forces' or the state of a trajectory. Of course this does not increase the explanatory power of the theory; it does focus, though, on the conceptual development (and it may help in developing it further).

2.5 Once again the value of labour-power and the wage rate

From all of the middle part of *Capital I* – indeed all of the book – it is obvious that Marx always conceives of wages, and the value of labour-power, in terms of *days* or weeks. Indeed this directs all his theorizing about absolute and relative surplus-value. Theoretically this seems as poignant as an engraved *Gestalt* (in the sense of Kuhn). On the one hand this is, understandable historically, that is, from the perspective of the practice of the second half of the nineteenth century (including struggles over the length of the working day and the working week); the perspective of if, and how well, one can live off a day's or a week's wage. On the other hand, however, this is difficult to understand given that it is Marx's aim to set out 'capital' and its development from *its* perspective, that is, immanently.

Whereas Marx's conceptualization of labour-power is fine as and when he introduces it in Part Three (absolute surplus-value), there is a problem when he moves to Part Four (relative surplus-value) and introduces shortening of the working day. The daily value of labour-power is by itself not of interest to capital, but rather the value of labour-power per hour of labour time (that is, the value of labour-power relative to the actual time of employment).

Reconsider Marx's equations (see section 2.1)

$$s = (\underline{s/v})v \tag{M–8}$$

$$s = \underline{w}(a'/a)n \tag{M–9}$$

and the added

$$wL \equiv v \tag{11}$$

$$s = e^*(wL) \tag{12}$$

Remember that the underlined symbols are in per day terms, and w and L in per hour terms. If s were measured over a year (for example), n would have to be the 'number of workers times the number of labour days in a year'. (If s were measured over one turn-over time of capital, n would have to be the 'number of workers times the number of days of turn-over time'.)[55]

Let the value of labour-power per day, $VLP\text{-}d = \underline{w}$; the length of the working day = WD (i.e. a number of hours). Recall that w = the wage per hour, and L the number of hours worked. Thus we have:

$$w \equiv \underline{w}/WD \qquad\qquad\qquad \text{[definition] (18)}$$

$$L \equiv n(WD) \qquad\qquad\qquad \text{[definition] (19)}$$

hence

$$wL = \underline{w}n \qquad\qquad\qquad \text{[implication] (20)}$$

Thus there is no problem in translating wL into Marx's terminology of 'the value of labour-power'. But what is labour-power in these 'different' frames? Labour-power is the potential to perform labour (for a day, says Marx) at some definite extensity (i.e. a number of clock hours) and intensity. What do we lose if we reduce this to intensity per hour? Nothing (note that for Marx a substitution between extensity and intensity is possible). Then we can interpret L as a number of labour-power per hour (labour potential) and L^β as labour actually exerted at some degree of intensity.

Here is the rephrase. Workers sell their labour-potential L (= labour-power) by the hour.[56] In production it is exerted *at* a prevailing productive force (*Produktivkraft*) *with* a certain degree of intensity L^β (= labour).

All this merely makes more explicit what is in Marx's text. It also makes more explicit that the only directly measurable entities are all value entities, as well as total labour time (extensity). All other 'labour' entities, including the intensity of labour (L^β) cannot be directly measured independently of the value entities and of labour extensity.

---

55. Of course, relevant for capital is the investment of (variable) capital including Sundays, so to speak.
56. Irrespective of the fact that depending on labour contracts this may go in packages (e.g. 40 hours a week).

3. Summary and conclusions

Key to the production process of capital – the subject of *Capital I* – is the production of surplus-value. The middle part of the book explains how it is produced. Marx comprehends the capitalist production process as a unity of labour process and of valorization process – this sets the frame for his analysis, including its dimensions. He starts from value entities, always in monetary dimension, and aims to explain these in terms of: (1) productive forces ('techniques of production' – this term is anachronistic); (2) extensity of labour; (3) intensity of labour; (4) the value of labour-power. The point of the 'unity' view is the interaction, the melding, of the two processes – the valorization process affects the content of the labour process and this works back again on valorization.

In line with his general method, Marx starts this middle part with an abstract and simple account – the production of absolute surplus-value. In effect this means that he treats all but factor 2, the extensity of labour, as constant. Next – under the head of the production of relative surplus-value – he brings in variations in the other three factors mentioned.

Unfortunately, when it comes to Marx's formalization of his analysis – the main subject of this chapter – he sticks *in effect* to the simple account ($e = e^*$, i.e. $s/v = SL/NL$ – section 2.1). It is not obvious that he sticks to the simple account, because once we accept $e = e^*$ as a useful explanation it remains in force after the complications have been brought in – now other variables have an effect *on* the e^* ratio. This is why I have complained that Marx formalizes results instead of explanatory processes (or mechanisms).

I have shown that it is not too difficult to 'immanently reconstruct' Marx's formalization such that all four factors are captured (see equation 16 in section 2.3). Its upshot is a reconceptualization of Marx's 'value of labour-power' into a value per unit of time, a wage rate (section 2.5). The corollary advantage of the latter concept is that it matches the perspective of capital – which fits Marx's general approach in *Capital* of presenting an immanent analysis of capital.

Comments on the secondary literature have been beyond the confines of this chapter. Some of that literature misconceives Marx in making 'him' identify value with a labour(-time) dimension (hence the collapse of any explanatory force of his theory in this respect). Perhaps Marx misleads the superficial reader with his, in effect, dimensionless ratios. However, he *always* casts value in monetary terms.

As to the explanatory force of $e = e^*$ (in either its simple or its complex representation) I indicated that the *explanans* (e^*, or surplus labour in relation to total labour) cannot be measured independently of the

144   *The Constitution of Capital*

explanandum (*e*, or surplus-value in relation to the value-product). Marx was well aware of this measurement problem – highlighted in the variability of labour intensity – as well as of course the main further inversions/breaks to come in the later volumes of *Capital* (much of which had been drafted before 1867).

References

Superscripts indicate first and other relevant editions; the last mentioned year in the bibliography is the edition cited.

Arthur, Christopher and Geert Reuten (eds) (1998), *The Circulation of Capital: Essays on Volume II of Marx's 'Capital'* (London/New York: Macmillan/St Martin's Press).
Bellofiore, Riccardo (2003), Marx and the macro-monetary foundation of micro-economics, Chapter 5 in this volume.
Elson, Diane (1979), The value theory of labour, in Elson (ed.), *Value – The Representation of Labour in Capitalism* (London: CSE Books).
Inwood, Michael (1992), *A Hegel Dictionary* (Oxford/Cambridge, Mass.: Blackwell).
Marx, Karl (1867[1] G, 1890[4]), *Das Kapital, Kritik der politischen Ökonomie, Band I, Der Produktionsprozeß des Kapitals*, MEW 23 (Berlin: Dietz Verlag, 1973).
— (1867[1] MA, 1883[3]), *Capital, A Critical analysis of capitalist production, Volume I* (trans. of the 3rd German edn. by Samuel Moore and Edward Aveling (1887[1]) (London: Lawrence & Wishart, 1974).
— (1867[1] F, 1890[4]), *Capital, A Critique of Political Economy, Volume I* (trans. of the 4th German edn by Ben Fowkes (1976[1])) (Harmondsworth: Penguin, 1976).
— (1885[1], 1893[2]), ed. F. Engels, *Das Kapital, Kritik der politischen Ökonomie, Band II, Der Zirkulationsprozeß des Kapitals*, MEW 24 (Berlin: Dietz Verlag 1972) (first Engl. trans. by Ernest Untermann (1907), second Engl. trans. by David Fernbach (1978[1])), *Capital, A Critique of Political Economy, Volume II* (Harmondsworth: Penguin, 1978).
— (1894), ed. F. Engels, *Das Kapital, Kritik der politischen Ökonomie, Band III, Der Gesamtprozeß der kapitalistischen Produktion*, MEW 25 (Berlin: Dietz Verlag, 1972) (first Engl. trans. by Ernest Untermann (1909), second Engl. trans. by David Fernbach (1981[1])), *Capital, A Critique of Political Economy, Volume III* (Harmondsworth: Penguin, 1981).
— (1933), *Results of the Immediate Process of Production*, (Engl. trans. by Rodney Livingstone), Appendix in *Capital, Volume I* (Harmondsworth: Penguin, 1976).
Moseley, Fred (ed.) (1993), *Marx's Method in 'Capital': A Reexamination* (Atlantic Highlands, NJ: Humanities Press).
Murray, Patrick (2000a), Marx's 'truly social' labour theory of value: Part I, Abstract labour in Marxian value theory, *Historical Materialism*, 6: 27–66.
— (2000b), Marx's 'truly social' labour theory of value: Part II, How is labour that is under the sway of capital *actually* abstract?, *Historical Materialism*, 7: 99–136.
— (2002), Reply to Geert Reuten, *Historical Materialism*, 10/1: 155–76.
— (2003), The social and material transformation of production by capital: formal and real subsumption in 'Capital Volume I', Chapter 7 in this volume.
Reuten, Geert (1988), Value as social form, in Michael Williams (ed.), *Value, Social Form and the State* (London: Macmillan – now Palgrave Macmillan): 42–61.

— (1993), The difficult labour of a theory of social value; metaphors and systematic dialectics at the beginning of Marx's 'Capital', in F. Moseley (ed.) (1993): 89–113.

— (1998), The status of Marx's reproduction schemes: conventional or dialectical logic?, in C. Arthur and G. Reuten (eds) (1998): 187–229.

— (2000), The interconnection of systematic dialectics and historical materialism, *Historical Materialism*, 7: 137–66.

— (2002), Marxian Macroeconomics: some key relationships, in Brian Snowdon and Howard Vane (eds), *Encyclopedia of Macroeconomics* (Aldershot: Edward Elgar): 469–80.

— (2003a), Karl Marx: his work and the major changes in its interpretation, in Warren Samuels, Jeff Biddle and John Davis (eds), *The Blackwell Companion to the History of Economic Thought* (Oxford: Blackwell): 148–66.

— (2003b), The inner mechanism of the accumulation of capital: the acceleration triple, Chapter 10 in this volume.

Reuten, Geert and Michael Williams (1989), *Value-Form and the State: The Tendencies of Accumulation and the Determination of Economic Policy in Capitalist Society* (London/New York: Routledge).

Smith, Tony (1997), The neoclassical and Marxian theories of technology: a comparison and critical assessment, *Historical Materialism*, 1: 113–33.

— (2003), Technology and history in capitalism: Marxian and neo-Schumpeterian perspectives, Chapter 8 in this volume.

Taylor, Nicola (2003), Reconstructing Marx on money and the measurement of value, Chapter 3 in this volume.

6
Money and Totality: Marx's Logic in Volume I of *Capital*

Fred Moseley

A widely accepted interpretation of Marx's theory (e.g. Morishima, 1973; Steedman, 1977) is that Volume I of *Capital* is primarily about the determination of the labour-values of individual commodities. In other words, Volume I presents mainly a *microeconomic* theory, and the main microeconomic variables determined are the *labour-values* of commodities, rather than the prices of commodities.

I have argued in previous papers (Moseley, 1993, 2000, 2002) that Volume I is primarily about the determination of the total increment of money (ΔM), or total surplus-value, produced in the capitalist economy as a whole. In other words, Volume I presents mainly a *macroeconomic* theory, and the main macroeconomic variable determined is the total money profit for the economy as a whole. I have called this a 'macro-monetary' interpretation of Marx's theory. (Others who have presented various aspects of such a 'macro-monetary' interpretation include Mattick, 1969; Yaffe, 1976; Rosdolsky, 1977; Mattick Jr, 1981; Carchedi, 1984; Foley, 1986; and Bellofiore, 1989.)

This chapter provides further detailed textual evidence to support these two main points – that Volume I presents a monetary theory and that it presents a macroeconomic theory of the total surplus-value.

1. Volume I is about money

According to a widely held interpretation of Marx's theory (e.g. Steedman, 1977; Morishima, 1973 etc.), Volume I of *Capital* is about the *labour-values* of commodities, i.e. the labour times required to produce commodities. The main variables determined in Volume I are the labour-values of individual types of commodities. The key concepts of constant capital, variable capital and surplus-value are interpreted to be defined in Volume I in terms of labour-times – as the quantities of labour-times required to produce the means of production, the means of subsistence and surplus goods, respectively. The 'value rate of profit' is defined as the ratio of the labour-value of surplus goods to the sum of the labour-values of the means of production and the means of subsistence. According to this interpretation, money and prices play no essential role in Volume I. Prices are not determined in Volume I. It is argued that money and prices are sometimes used in Volume I to illustrate labour-values or as a shorthand for labour-values, but money and prices are not themselves the subject of Volume I, or determined in Volume I. Rather, labour-values are determined in Volume I. One can write the equations which represent the theory in Volume I without introducing money at all (e.g. Steedman, 1977: Chapters 3 and 4; Morishima, 1973: Chapters 3–5). Volume I is often described as presenting the 'value system'.

I argue that this 'labour-value' interpretation of Volume I is mistaken. Volume I is not about the determination of labour-values. Rather, Volume I is about the determination of quantities of money and prices. These money magnitudes and prices are *determined by* quantities of labour-time, which are taken as given. In logical terms, money magnitudes and prices are the *explanandum*, the variables that are to be explained or determined, and quantities of labour-time are the *explanans*, the givens in terms of which the *explanandum* is explained or determined. Money magnitudes and prices in Volume I are not inessential illustrations or short-hand for labour-values, but are themselves the variables that are determined or explained in Volume I.

This section reviews some key chapters in Volume I in order to support this 'monetary' interpretation of Volume I.

1.1 Part One: Commodities and money

Volume I is about money from the very beginning (see the chapters by Arthur and Taylor in this volume). Part One of Volume I is entitled 'Commodities and *money*' (emphasis added), thus clearly indicating the importance of money. The necessity of money in a commodity-producing economy is derived in the very first chapter, in the important but usually neglected Section 3 of Chapter 1, as the 'necessary form of appearance' of the abstract labour contained in commodities. Very briefly, Marx's argument is the following. In order for each commodity to be exchangeable with all other commodities, the value of each commodity must be comparable with the value of all other commodities in some objective, socially recognizable form. Because the abstract labour which Marx assumed to determine the value of commodities is not directly observable or recognizable as such, this abstract labour must acquire an objective 'form of appearance' which renders the values of all commodities observable and mutually comparable. This necessity of a common unified form of appearance of the abstract labour contained in commodities ultimately leads to the conclusion that this form of appearance must be money. Money is not an inessential illustration for labour times. Money is the *necessary* form of appearance of labour times.

> Because all commodities, as values, are objectified human labor, and therefore in themselves commensurable, their values can be communally measured in one and the same specific commodity, and this commodity can be converted into the common measure of their values, that is into money. Money as a measure of value is the necessary form of appearance of the measure of value which is immanent in commodities, namely labor-time (Marx, 1867 (1977): 188).

For discussions of Marx's derivation of the necessity of money from the labour theory of value, see Rosdolsky (1977: Chapters 5 and 6); Weeks (1981: Chapter 6); Murray (1988: Chapter 14). Marx considered this derivation of the necessity of money from the labour theory of value to be one of the most important advances of his theory over classical economics, which had simply taken money for granted or had explained the existence of money in ad hoc fashion on the basis of the practical difficulties of barter, unrelated to its theory of value.

> Now, however, we have to perform a task never even attempted by bourgeois economics. That is, we have to show the origin of this money-form, we have to trace the development of the expression of value contained in the value-relation of commodities from its simplest, almost imperceptible outline to the dazzling money-form. When this has been done, the *mystery of money* will immediately disappear (Marx, 1867 (1977): 139; emphasis added).

We could add that no other economic theory since Marx has been able to successfully accomplish this important task – to derive the necessity of money from its basic theory of value.

At the end of Section 3 of Chapter 1, the *price* of commodities is derived as the exchange-value of all other commodities with the money commodity. At this abstract stage of the theory, it is assumed that the prices of commodities are proportional to the labour times required to produce them, with the proportionality factor being the inverse of the labour time required to produce a unit of the money commodity (e.g. gold). At a later, more concrete stage of the analysis (Part Two of Volume III), the prices of individual commodities are more fully determined, in such a way that prices are not simply proportional to the labour times required to produce them, but are also affected by the equalization of profit rates across industries. The point to emphasize here is that Chapter 1 presents an initial, abstract theory of *prices*, which are exchange-ratios with *money*. Chapter 1 does not present a theory of the determination of labour-values. Rather, the magnitudes of labour times are *presupposed*, i.e. taken as given, in Chapter 1 (and throughout *Capital*), and used to derive the prices of commodities. The relation of determination between prices (P) and labour times (L) derived in Chapter 1 can be expressed by the following simple mathematical equation:[1]

$$P = m L \tag{1}$$

where m is the money-value added per labour-hour (which is assumed to be equal to the inverse of the labour time of a unit of gold, i.e. $m = 1/L_G$; e.g. 0.5 shillings per hour). In mathematical terms, prices are the dependent variables and labour times are the independent variables. (However, it should be noted that the relation between prices and labour times in Marx's theory is different from the usual mathematical sense of dependent and independent variables, because Marx's theory derives prices as the *necessary* form of appearance of labour time. There is no such explanation of necessity in the usual meaning of dependent and independent variables.)

The short Chapter 2 ('The process of exchange') discusses the actual emergence of *money* out of the actual process of circulation. One of the main points of Chapter 2 is a critique of the 'fetishism of money',

---

1. This equation is not explicit in *Capital*, but I think it accurately expresses the logic of Marx's theory of value presented in Chapter 1.

according to which gold appears to be money because of its own intrinsic nature, rather than because of the social relations between commodities which require that all other commodities express their value in gold (Marx, 1867: 176).

Chapter 3 is entitled '*Money*, or the circulation of commodities' (emphasis added). The title indicates again that Chapter 3 is about money. More precisely, Chapter 3 is about the main functions that money performs as part of the circulation of commodities: measure of value (the objective social representation of the abstract labour contained in commodities), means of circulation (the means by which commodity owners exchange their commodities for other commodities), hoards, means of payments for debts, and 'world money' (i.e. international reserves).

Therefore, we can see that Part One of Volume I is all about money. The necessity of money is derived in Chapter 1, its actual emergence in circulation is discussed in Chapter 2, and its most important functions are derived in Chapter 3. Part One is not about the determination of 'labour-values'.

1.2 Part Two: The transformation of money into capital

Part Two introduces the all-important concept of *capital*, the central concept of Marx's theory, as the title of the book suggests. Unfortunately, this key concept is often ignored in interpretations of Marx's theory. Capital is defined in Chapter 4 ('The general formula for capital') in terms of *money*, as money that becomes more money, through the purchase and sale of commodities. The title of Part Two is 'The transformation of *money* into capital' (emphasis added). The transformation of money into capital happens as a result of the emergence of *more money* at the end of the circulation of capital. The circulation of capital is represented symbolically as $M-C-(M+\Delta M)$. In the circulation of capital, money plays an even more important role than in the simple circulation of commodities analysed in Chapter 3. Indeed money (or more precisely, more money) is the aim and purpose of the whole process. Therefore, the main purpose of Volume I is to explain where this increment of money, ΔM, comes from, and what determines its magnitude. The main purpose of Volume I is not to explain the determination of 'labour-values'.

The related key concept of *surplus-value* is also defined in Chapter 4 in terms of money, as the increment of money, ΔM, that transforms money into capital.

More *money* is finally withdrawn from circulation than was thrown into it at the beginning. The cotton originally bought for £100 is for example re-sold for £100+£10, i.e. £110. The complete form of this process is therefore M–C–M', where M'=M+∆M, i.e. the original sum plus an increment. The increment of excess over the original value I call 'surplus-value' (Marx, 1867 (1977): 251; emphasis added).

Chapter 5 ('Contradictions in the general formula') argues that one cannot explain the emergence of this increment of money as long as one's analysis is restricted to the sphere of circulation only (i.e. only the acts of buying and selling are considered, as Marx's theory in Volume I has been restricted up to this point) because, according to Marx's assumption no additional value is produced through the acts of circulation. According to Marx's theory, the acts of buying and selling only transform a given amount of value from commodities to money, or vice versa. These acts of circulation do not produce additional value. Hence, they cannot be the source of surplus-value, or ∆M.

Chapter 6 ('The purchase and sale of labor-power') identifies the key precondition that must be fulfilled if the increment of money is to emerge at the end of the circulation of capital: labour-power (the source of additional value) must be available on the market for capitalists to purchase, i.e. the majority of the population must possess no means by which they could produce for themselves and hence must sell their labour-power to capitalists in order to survive. At the end of Chapter 6 is Marx's dramatic passage from the sphere of circulation to the 'hidden abode of production', in which 'the secret of *profit-making* must at last be laid bare' (280; emphasis added). Here we can see again that 'profit-making' is the main question of Volume I. 'Profit-making' is making *money*.

1.3 Part Three: The production of surplus-value, or more money

Chapter 7 is the most important chapter in Volume I, in which Marx's theory of surplus-value, or the 'secret of profit-making', is presented. This theory is clearly presented in terms of money. The whole point of the theory is to explain where the increment of money that emerges at the end of the circulation of capital comes from and what determines its magnitude (3 shillings in Marx's example). Marx exclaimed at the conclusion of the presentation of his theory: 'The trick has at last worked. *Money* has been transformed into capital' (301; emphasis added). The 'trick' is the emergence of the 3 shillings. 'Money [is] ... transformed into capital' by the emergence of these 3 shillings.

The magnitude of surplus-value, e.g. 3 shillings, is determined, according to Marx's theory, by the excess of the working day over necessary labour, i.e. by the magnitude of surplus labour. This relation of determination between surplus-value (increment of money) and surplus labour can be expressed by the following equation:[2]

$$S = m \ (L_T - L_N) \tag{2}$$
$$S = m \ L_S$$

where L_S stands for surplus labour, L_T for total labour,[3] and L_N for necessary labour. This theory is illustrated in Chapter 7 by Marx by the following numerical example:

3 shillings = 0.5 sh./hr (6 hrs)
        = 0.5 sh./hr (12 hrs – 6 hrs)

The labour-time quantities on the right-hand side of these equations are the independent variables, which are taken as given, presupposed, and then used to determine the dependent variable, the money quantity on the left-hand side of the equations, the magnitude of surplus-value, or ΔM.

In Chapter 8, the key concepts of constant capital and variable capital are defined as the two components into which the initial money-capital that begins the circulation of capital is divided; i.e. $M = C + V$. Since capital in general is defined in terms of money, so are the components of capital, constant capital and variable capital. Constant capital is that portion of the initial money-capital that is used to purchase means of production, and variable capital is that portion of the initial money-capital that is used to purchase labour-power. Constant capital and variable capital are not defined in terms of quantities of labour time.

Chapter 9 introduces the key concept of the rate of surplus-value. The rate of surplus-value is defined in terms of a ratio of two quantities of money-capital, the ratio of the magnitude of surplus-value (ΔM) to

2. Again, this equation is not explicit in *Capital*, but I think it accurately expresses the logic of Marx's theory of surplus-value presented in Chapter 7.
3. Total labour (L_T) depends not only on the length of the working day, but also on the intensity of labour. Labour of above average intensity is equivalent, in the determination of the value produced, to a longer working day.

the magnitude of money variable capital. In Marx's main example in Chapter 9, surplus-value is equal to £90, and variable capital is equal to £90, so that the rate of surplus-value is 1.0, or 100 per cent.

Marx then went on in Chapter 9 to derive the 'degree of exploitation', which is a ratio of labour-time quantities, from the rate of surplus-value, which as we have seen is a ratio of quantities of money-capital. The 'degree of exploitation' is the ratio of surplus labour (*SL*) to necessary labour (*NL*). Necessary labour and surplus-value are derived from variable capital and surplus-value as follows. Necessary labour is derived as the number of hours required for workers to produce new value (in terms of money) which is equal to the money variable capital with which their labour-power is purchased, i.e. $NL = V/m$. Surplus labour is then the difference between the total working day and necessary labour. Derived in this way, necessary labour is proportional to variable capital and surplus-value is the same proportion to surplus-value, so that the 'degree of exploitation' (the ratio of surplus labour to necessary labour) is by definition equal to the rate of surplus-value (the ratio of surplus-value to variable capital).

It should be clear from Chapter 9 that the rate of surplus-value is defined as a ratio of money magnitudes, both from the definition of the rate of surplus-value itself and also from the derivation of the rate of exploitation from the rate of surplus-value. If the rate of surplus-value were defined in terms of labour times (as the ratio of surplus labour to necessary labour), then it would make no sense to distinguish between the rate of surplus-value and the rate of exploitation, and to derive the latter from the former, as Marx clearly does in Chapter 9.

We could go on, chapter by chapter in Volume I, and the conclusion would be the same. The key concepts of capital, constant capital, variable capital and surplus-value are all consistently defined as quantities of money. Parts Four to Six are mainly about the various means by which the magnitude of surplus-value, or the increment of money (ΔM) that emerges at the end of the circulation of capital, can be increased: by increasing the working day, by increasing the intensity of labour, or by reducing necessary labour (by means of technological change and increased productivity of labour).

Part Seven is about the 'accumulation of capital'. The accumulation of capital is defined as the reinvestment of money appropriated as surplus-value in one period as additional capital in the next period. In Marx's main example in Chapter 24, the initial capital advanced is a sum of money (£10,000) and it produces a surplus-value of £2,000. This surplus-value of £2,000 is then reinvested as additional capital by purchasing more means of production and labour-power, which produces an additional surplus-value of £400. The main point of this chapter is that the source of the £2,000 that is reinvested as additional capital is the surplus labour of workers, not the capitalist's own labour (as might be supposed of the original capital of £10,000). Thus workers are doubly exploited: not only do they produce more value than they are paid, but the money-capital with which they are paid is itself the result of the surplus labour of workers of previous periods.

Thus I conclude that Volume I is clearly all about money. The main variables which are determined in Volume I are monetary variables, especially the increment of money (ΔM) that emerges at the end of the circulation of capital. The main purpose of Volume I is to explain the origin and magnitude of this increment of money. The interpretation that Volume I is about the determination of 'labour-values' and that money is inessential completely misses the main purpose of Volume I.

2. Volume I is about the total surplus-value

We have seen above that the main question of Volume I is the origin and magnitude of surplus-value, or ΔM. Now the question is: to what level of aggregation does Marx's theory of surplus-value in Volume I apply: to the surplus-value produced by an individual capital, or by all the capitals in a single industry, or by all capitals together in capitalist production as a whole?

I argue that Volume I is about the *total surplus-value* produced in the capitalist economy as a whole. Volume I in general is about the total class relation between the working class as a whole and the capitalist class as a whole. The most important aspect of this general class relation is the total surplus-value produced by the working class as a whole for the capitalist class as a whole. That is the main question to which Volume I is devoted.

It is not always obvious in Volume I that Marx's theory of surplus-value applies to the total surplus-value produced by the working class as a whole (although I think it is obvious in other places that will be reviewed below), because the theory is often illustrated with a numerical example of an individual capital and even a single, solitary worker. However, the individual capitals in Marx's examples represent the total social capital of the capitalist class as a whole. Each individual capital is considered only as an average, representative 'aliquot part' of the total social capital, rather than as a distinct individual capital, different from other individual capitals. The individual capital is analysed in terms of what this capital has in common with all other capitals – the production of surplus-value.

One important passage that clearly states that the individual capitals in Volume I represent the total social capital is provided by a key outline of Volumes I and III towards the end of the *Manuscript of 1861–63*. This manuscript is where Marx developed for the first time his theory of the distribution of surplus-value that would later be presented in Volume III. Towards the end of this manuscript, Marx attained sufficient clarity to write outlines of Volume I and Volume III that are very close to their final form. In a detailed outline of the important Part two of Volume III, Marx noted that the conclusions of Volume I (on the determination of value and surplus-value) are still valid for the total social capital, although the prices and profits of individual capitals will differ from their values and surplus-values. In Volume I, Marx noted, individual capitals are considered as 'aliquot parts' of the total social capital, i.e. not as actual individual capitals that differ from one another.

> *For the total capital*, however, what has been explained in Chapter I [i.e. in Volume I] holds good. In capitalist production, each capital is assumed to be a unit, an aliquot part of the total capital.
>
> (Marx–Engels, 1861–63d (1991): 299; emphasis added)

In other words, the theory of surplus-value in Volume I is really about the total surplus-value produced by the total social capital. The individual capitals in Volume I represent the total social capital.[4]

The fact that Volume I is about the total class relation between the capitalist class as a whole and the working class as a whole, and thus is about the total surplus-value produced by the working class as a whole, is especially clear in several key chapters in Volume I that will be reviewed below.

---

4. Felton Shortall (1994) has emphasized this representative function of the individual capitals analysed in Volume I. Shortall argues that, in Volume I, 'the individual capital was only considered in so far as it was stripped of all particularity. It stood as the immediate representative of all capitals, as the abstract generality of capital as such. Consequently, the individual capital could be taken as a simple microcosm of the totality of social capital, its direct and immediate individual embodiment' (Shortall, 1994: 452). (See also Rosdolsky (1977: 48) and Foley (1986: 6) on the representative nature of individual capitals in Volume I.)

2.1 Part Two: The general formula for capital

As we have already seen, the question of the origin of surplus-value is first posed in Chapter 4 in terms of the 'general formula for capital'. Towards the end of Chapter 4, Marx notes that the general formula for capital applies to all types of capital – both capitals in the sphere of production (industrial capital) and capitals in the sphere of circulation (commercial capital and interest-bearing capital). In other words, Marx's question of the origin of surplus-value applies to the total surplus-value appropriated in the capitalist mode of production as a whole, not to individual amounts of surplus-value appropriated in a particular sphere, nor in a particular branch of production. The general formula for capital is just that, a *general* formula, that applies to all capitals together, and thus applies to the total social capital.

The general formula for capital is illustrated in Chapter 4 by an individual capital, a capital in the cotton industry. However, the question of the origin of surplus-value applies, not just to this single capital in the cotton industry, but rather to all capitals together, and hence to the total social capital. The individual capital in the cotton industry represents what all capitals have in common – the production of surplus-value – and thus represents the total social capital. Marx commented on the general formula for capital in a passage in Volume II as follows:

> The capitalist casts less value into circulation in the form of money than he draws out of it, because he casts in more value in the form of commodities that he has extracted in the form of commodities... *What is true for the individual capitalist, is true also for the capitalist class ... the capitalist simply personifies industrial capital ...*
>
> (Marx, 1884 (1978): 196–7; emphasis added)

As we have seen above, Chapter 5 argues that it is not possible to explain the emergence of surplus-value if the analysis is restricted solely to the sphere of circulation. This conclusion follows obviously from Marx's assumption that exchange is the exchange of equivalent values. If equivalent values are exchanged, then neither party to the exchange gains a surplus-value ('where there is equality, there can be no gain').

Marx argued further that, even if it is assumed that exchange is the exchange of non-equivalent values, one still cannot explain surplus-value on the basis of exchange alone. If there is an exchange of non-equivalent values (e.g. due to cheating), then one party to the exchange will indeed gain a surplus-value as a result of the exchange, but the other party will necessarily suffer an equal loss. The net gain for both parties is zero. Therefore, for both parties together, exchange alone cannot be a source of surplus-value. Marx then extended this argument to the total surplus-value produced by the capitalist class as a whole: although one could explain the surplus-value of individual capitals by cheating, one cannot explain the surplus-value of the capitalist class as a whole by cheating. Marx concluded: 'The *capitalist class of a country, taken as a whole*, cannot defraud itself' (266; emphasis added). This argument is a clear indication that Marx's theory is intended to explain the total surplus-value of the 'capitalist class as a whole', not the surplus-value of individual capitalists only.[5]

Chapter 6 derives the necessary condition for the appropriation of surplus-value by the capitalist class as a whole – the existence of a *class of wage-labourers* who own no means of production themselves, and therefore must sell their labour-power to capitalists in order to survive. This precondition clearly applies to the capitalist mode of production as a whole. Marx states that capital (and wage-labour) 'announces a new epoch in the process of social production' (274). Marx is not talking here about individual capitals, nor about individual industries, but rather about the capitalist mode of production in its entirety. The capitalist mode of production requires a class of property-less workers.

In Chapter 6, the theory is once again illustrated by an individual capitalist and an individual worker. But clearly the theory is not only about these two individuals. Rather, the theory is about the capitalist class as a whole and the working class as a whole. The individual capitalist

---

5. In an earlier draft of Volume I in the *Manuscript of 1861–63*, Marx elaborated on this point further:

> If we take all the capitalists of a country and the sum total of purchases and sales between them in the course of a year, for example, one capitalist may admittedly defraud the other and hence draw from circulation more value than he threw in, but this operation would not increase by one iota the sum total of the circulating value of the capital. In other words, the *class of capitalists taken as a whole* cannot enrich itself as a class, it cannot increase its *total capital*, or produce a surplus-value, by one capitalist's gaining what another loses. The sum total of capital in circulation cannot be increased by changes in the distribution of its individual components between its owners. Operations of this kind, therefore, however large a number of them one may imagine, will not produce any increase in the sum total of value, any new or surplus-value, or any gain on top of the total capital in circulation.
>
> Marx–Engels, 1861–63a (1988): 25; emphasis added

represents the capitalist class as a whole and the individual worker represents the working class as a whole.[6]

Towards the end of Chapter 6, Marx presents the transition from the sphere of circulation to the sphere of production ('the hidden abode of production'). These are the two analytical spheres into which Marx divided the capitalist mode of production as a whole. This analytical distinction between the sphere of circulation and the sphere of production is itself further evidence that Marx's theory in Volume I is about the capitalist mode of production as a whole. The transition to the sphere of production in Chapter 6 is not a transition for an individual capital only, but rather for all capitals together; in other words, it is a transition to the sphere of capitalist production as a whole.

2.2 Parts Three and Four: The determination of the total surplus-value

Chapter 7 presents Marx's basic theory of surplus-value, his answer to the most important question in a theory of capitalism: what determines the magnitude of surplus-value? Marx's answer to this question, as we have seen above, is that the magnitude of surplus-value depends on two main variables: (1) the length of the working day and (2) the necessary labour time required for workers to reproduce an equivalent to their money-wage, which in turn depends on the productivity of labour.[7]

As in previous chapters, the theory is illustrated with a numerical example of a single capital, a capital in the cotton yarn manufacturing industry. The determinants of the magnitude of surplus-value – the length of the working day and the necessary labour time – are illustrated in terms of the working day of a single worker, a spinner of yarn. However, Marx's theory is clearly not only about the surplus-value produced by this single yarn spinner, but rather is about the total surplus-value produced by the working class as a whole. The determinants of surplus-value – the total working day and the necessary labour time – are the same for all workers. The yarn spinner in Chapter 7 represents the working class as a whole.

6. Marx remarked in the *Results* manuscript, written in 1864–65: 'If we think of the whole of capital as standing on one side, i.e. the totality of the purchasers of labour-power, and if we think of the totality of the vendors of labour-power, the totality of workers on the other, then we find that the worker is compelled to sell not a commodity but his own labour-power as a commodity' (Marx, 1867 (1977): 1003; thanks to Riccardo Bellofiore for pointing out this passage to me).
7. As mentioned above in note 3, the value produced, and hence also the surplus-value produced, also depends on the intensity of labour.

This important point is made explicit in Chapter 11 ('The rate and mass of surplus-value') which provides a summary of Marx's theory of surplus-value to this point (which includes only absolute surplus-value, not yet relative surplus-value). The chapter begins with the same example of a representative individual worker as in earlier chapters, with variable capital=3 shillings and surplus-value=3 shillings. Then Marx states that if 100 workers are employed simultaneously by a given capital, then the total variable capital of all workers together will equal 300 shillings and the total surplus-value will also equal 300 shillings, i.e. $V = n V_A$ and $S = n S_A$ (where V_A and S_A are the average variable capital and the average surplus-value per worker, respectively).

Later in Chapter 11, Marx briefly applies the same method of aggregation to the economy as a whole. Marx states in an important passage:

> The labor which is set in motion by the *total capital of society may be regarded as a single working day*. If, for example, the number of workers is a million and the average working day is 10 hours, the *social working day* consists of 10 million hours. With a given length of the working day, *the mass of surplus-value can be increased only by increasing the number of workers*, i.e. by increasing the size of the working population.
>
> (Marx, 1867 (1977): 422; emphasis added)

This passage is clear evidence that the theory of surplus-value in Volume I applies to the total surplus-value produced by the working class as a whole. Marx's point here is that with a given working day (and given necessary labour), this total surplus-value can be increased only by increasing the size of the working class.

Marx made this same point in the *Grundrisse* (the first draft of Volume I), in the *Manuscript of 1861–63* (the second draft of Volume I, which has recently been published for the first time), and in *Wages, Prices, and Profit* (written in 1866, just before the publication of the first edition of Volume I). In the *Grundrisse*, Marx wrote:

> If a certain limit is given, say e.g. the worker needs only half a day in order to produce his subsistence for a whole day – and if the natural limit has been reached – then an increase of absolute labour time is possible only if more workers are employed *at the same time*, so that the real working day is simultaneously multiplied instead of only lengthened (Marx, 1857–58, 1973: 386; emphasis in the original).

Surplus time is the excess of the working day above that part of it which we call *necessary* labour time; it exists secondly as the multiplication of *simultaneous working days*, i.e. of the *labouring population* . . . A labouring population of, say, 6 million can be regarded as one working day of 6×12, i.e. 72 million hours: so that the same laws applicable here (*Ibid.*, 398–9; emphasis in the original).

And in the *Manuscript of 1861–63*, Marx wrote again:

The *amount of surplus value* evidently depends not only on the surplus labour performed by an individual worker above and beyond the necessary labour time; it depends just as much on the number of workers employed simultaneously by capital, or the number of simultaneous working days it makes use of, each of these = necessary labour time + surplus labour time . . . In other words: the amount of surplus value – its total amount – will depend on the number of labour capacities available and present in the market, hence on the magnitude of the working population and the proportion in which this population grows.
(Marx–Engels, 1861–63a (1988): 185–7; emphasis in the original)

This law only implies that with a constant productivity of labour and a given normal day, the amount of surplus value will grow with the number of workers simultaneously employed (*Ibid.*, 206).

And in *Wages, Prices, and Profit*, in which Marx explained his theory of surplus-value at a congress of the International Workingman's Party, Marx remarked: 'There will also be nothing changed if in the place of one working man you put the whole working population, twelve million working days, for example, instead of one' (Marx–Engels, 1968a: 218).

In these passages, it is clear and explicit that Marx's theory of surplus-value applies to the total surplus-value produced by the working class as a whole.

Further important evidence that Volume I is about the total surplus-value produced by the working class as a whole is provided by Chapters 10–18, which are about the two main ways to increase the amount of surplus-value produced by the working class as a whole: (1) increase the length of the working day ('absolute surplus-value') and (2) reduce the necessary labour time by technological change which increases the productivity of labour ('relative surplus-value').

Chapter 10 is about the first determinant of surplus-value – the length of the working day. This chapter is about the determination of the length of the working day *for the working class as a whole*, not the length of the working day for individual workers or groups of workers. Marx argued that the length of the working day is determined by a *class struggle* between the capitalist class as a whole and the working class as a whole. Since the amount of surplus-value produced depends in part on the length of the working day (and varies positively with the working day), capitalists will strive to lengthen the working day or at least will resist attempts by workers to reduce the working day. Workers, on the other hand, have a vested interest in reducing the length of the working day in order to provide more 'free time' for leisure, recreation etc. Therefore, the length of the working day will be determined by the class struggle between capitalists and workers, the outcome of which depends on the relative balance of forces between these two classes.

Chapter 12 begins Part Four, which is about the second way to increase surplus-value – by reducing the necessary labour time through technological change which increases the productivity of labour. Chapter 12 derives technological change as an inherent tendency (an 'immanent drive') of the capitalist mode of production from Marx's basic theory of surplus-value. Once legal limits to the length of the working day are established, the primary means by which surplus-value can be increased is through technological change which increases the productivity of labour and thereby reduces necessary labour. Marx concluded: 'Capital therefore has an immanent drive, and a constant tendency, towards increasing the productivity of labor' (Marx, 1867 (1977): 436–7). This conclusion of an inherent tendency toward technological change clearly applies to the capitalist mode of production as a whole.

Once again, the theory of relative surplus-value and technological change is illustrated by a single worker. However, this theory clearly applies, not just to a single worker, but to all workers together. The effect of technological change on the price of wage goods, and hence on necessary labour and surplus labour, is a *general* effect, which happens to all workers. Therefore, technological change will not only reduce necessary labour and increase surplus labour for the single worker in this illustration, but will do so for the working class as a whole.

Thus we can see that, by the end of Part Four of Volume I, Marx has presented his basic theory of surplus-value, which provides an explanation of the determination of the total surplus-value produced in capitalist production as a whole. According to Marx's theory, the total surplus-value depends on: (1) the average working day (L_T),[8] (2) the average necessary labour time (L_N) (these two together determine the average surplus-value produced per worker), and (3) the number of workers simultaneously in capitalist production as a whole (n). This theory can be represented by the following equation:[9]

$$S = n \left[m \left(L_T - L_N \right) \right] = n \left[m \left(L_S \right) \right] \tag{3}$$

This basic theory of the determination of the total surplus-value is not revised or modified in the later volumes of *Capital*. No new variables are later added to this basic equation of the determination of the total surplus-value. This theory is amplified by exploring further the complex determination of the key variables on the right-hand side of this equation $(L_T$ and $L_N)$. But the basic theory of surplus-value, as represented by this equation, remains the same.

2.3 Part Seven: Accumulation of the total social capital

Part Seven provides further important evidence that Volume I is about the total class relation between the capitalist class and the working class, and thus that the theory of surplus-value presented in Volume I is about the total surplus-value produced by the working class as a whole.

The main point of Chapter 23 (on 'Simple reproduction', which assumes that all the surplus-value produced in each period is consumed and none is accumulated as additional capital) is that the reproduction of the total social capital also accomplishes the reproduction of the working class as a whole, because workers spend all or most of their wages on consumer goods, and therefore must continue to sell their labour-power to capitalists.

Similarly, the main point of Chapter 24 ('Accumulation of capital') is the 'inversion' of the laws of commodity exchange (based on the exchange of equivalent values) to the law of capitalist appropriation (based on the exploitation of workers). When the class relation between capitalists and workers was first analysed in Chapter 6 of Volume I, that

8. As mentioned above, the total labour also depends on the intensity of labour.
9. Again, this equation is not explicit in *Capital*, but I think it accurately expresses the logic of Marx's theory of surplus-value presented in *Capital*.

relation appeared to be an exchange of equivalents, in the sense that capitalists paid workers the full value of their labour-power. In Chapter 7, Marx's theory revealed that the relation between capitalists and workers was instead one of exploitation of workers by capitalists in production, because workers produce more value than they are paid. In this chapter, Marx argues (as we have seen above) that workers are 'doubly exploited' in the sense that workers not only have to produce surplus-value for capitalists, they also have to produce the variable capital with which they are paid, i.e. the variable capital is itself almost entirely the result of the surplus labour of other members of the working class in previous periods. This conclusion of the double exploitation of workers obviously applies to the working class as a whole.

Finally, the main point of Chapter 25 ('The general law of capitalist accumulation') is the effects of the accumulation of the total social capital on the working class as a whole (as Marx says in the first sentence of the chapter). The main factor in this analysis is the composition of the total social capital (the ratio of constant capital to variable capital for the economy as a whole), and the tendency of this ratio to increase over time as a result of technological change. The increase in the composition of the total social capital reduces the demand for the labour-power of workers, and hence increases unemployment, or the 'industrial reserve army', of the working class as a whole. The 'general law' of capitalist accumulation is that the capitalist mode of production tends to produce both increasing wealth in the hands of capitalists and increasing misery suffered by workers.

Therefore, we can see that Part Seven is about the accumulation of the total social capital and its effects on the working class as a whole. The accumulation of the total social capital is the reinvestment of the total social surplus-value produced by the working class as a whole. The analysis of the accumulation of the total social capital in Part Seven *takes as given* the total surplus-value that is to be accumulated. Part Seven is not about the determination of the total surplus-value, but rather about the division of the total surplus-value into consumption and accumulation. Since the total surplus-value is taken as given, this total surplus-value must have been already determined in previous chapters in Volume I, which is indeed the case, as we have seen.

2.4 *Further textual evidence*

This section briefly presents further textual evidence from elsewhere in Marx's writings that Volume I is about the total surplus-value produced by the working class as a whole.

In August 1867, soon after the first edition of Volume I was finally published, Marx wrote a letter to Engels in which he stated that one of the two best points of his book was the determination of the total surplus-value prior to its division into the individual parts of profit, interest and rent.

> The best points in my book are: ... 2) the treatment of *surplus-value independently of its particular* forms as profit, interest, rent, etc. ... The treatment of the particular forms by classical economy, which always mixes them up, is a regular hash (Marx–Engels, 1968b: 180).

Five months later (in January 1868), Marx made a similar comment in another letter to Engels. This time the prior determination of the total surplus-value is described as one of the 'three fundamentally new elements' of his book:

> 1) That in contrast to *all* former political economy, which *from the very outset* treats the different fragments of surplus-value with their fixed form of rent, profit, and interest as already given, I first deal with the general form of surplus value, in which all these fragments are still undifferentiated – in solution, as it were (Marx–Engels, 1968b: 186).

Marx's theory of the division of the total surplus-value into these individual parts is presented in Volume III of *Capital* (see Moseley, 1997 and 2002 for detailed discussions of Marx's theory of the distribution of surplus-value in Volume III). This theory of the distribution of surplus-value *takes as given* the total amount of surplus-value that is to be distributed. This total amount is taken as given because it has already been determined by Marx's theory of surplus-value in Volume I, as we have seen. There are a number of passages in the important concluding Part Seven of Volume III, in which Marx explicitly states that the quantity of surplus-value that is taken as given in the theory of the distribution of surplus-value in Volume III is determined by the quantity of surplus labour, i.e. that it is determined by the theory of surplus-value presented in Volume I. A good example is the following passage:

> The *value freshly added each year by new labor* ... can be separated out and resolved into the different revenue forms of wages, profit, and

rent; *this in no way alters the limits of the value itself*, the sum of the value that is divided between these different categories. In the same way, a change in the ratio of these individual portions among themselves cannot affect their sum, *this given sum of value* . . . What is given first, therefore, is the mass of commodity values to be divided into wages, profit, and rent, the absolute limit to the sum of value portions in these commodities. Secondly, as far as the individual categories themselves are concerned, their average and governing limits are similarly given . . . We have thus an *absolute limit* for the value component that forms *surplus-value* and can be broken down into profit and ground-rent; this is *determined by the excess of the unpaid portion of the working day over its paid portion*, i.e. by the value component of the total product in which this surplus labor is realized. If we call *this surplus-value whose limits are thus determined* profit, when it is calculated on the total capital advanced, as we have already done, then this profit, considered in its absolute amount, is equal to the surplus-value, i.e. it is just as regularly determined in its limits as this is. It is the ratio between the total surplus-value and the total social capital advanced in production. If this capital is 500 . . . and the surplus-value is 100, the absolute limit to the rate of profit is 20 percent. The division of the social profit as measured by this rate among the capitals applied in the various different spheres of production produces prices of production which diverge from commodity values and which are the actual averages governing market prices. But this divergence from values *abolishes neither the determination of prices by values nor the limits imposed on profit by our laws* . . . This surcharge of 20 per cent . . . is itself determined by the surplus-value created by the total social capital, and its proportion to the value of this capital; and this is why it is 20 percent and not 10 percent or 100 percent. The transformation of values into prices of production does not abolish the limits to profit, but simply affects its distribution among the various particular capitals of which the social capital is composed . . .

(Marx, 1894 (1981): 998–1000, emphasis added;
see also 961, 984–5, 994, and 1002)

There are also several similar passages in the first draft of Volume III in the *Manuscript of 1861–63*. For example:

The equalization of the surplus-values in the different spheres of production does not affect the absolute size of this total surplus-value;

but merely alters it distribution among the different spheres of production. *The determination of this surplus-value itself, however, only
arises out of the determination of value by labor-time.* Without this, the
average profit is the average of nothing, pure fancy. And it could then
equally well be 1,000% or 10%.

(Marx–Engels, 1861–63b (1989): 416, emphasis added;
see also Marx–Engels, 1861–63c (1989): 469;
and Marx–Engels, 1861–63d (1991): 99)

Therefore, I conclude that Volume I of *Capital* is about the determination of the total surplus-value produced by the working class as a
whole and appropriated by the capitalist class as a whole. This aggregate
nature of Marx's theory of surplus-value in Volume I is not always
obvious, but is clear from this review of these key chapters in Volume I
and these other writings.

3. Implications

In this chapter, I have presented substantial textual evidence to support
the macro-monetary interpretation of Marx's theory, according to which
Volume I is mainly about money (or the determination of monetary
variables), and, more precisely, is mainly about the determination of
the total surplus-value, or the total increment of money (ΔM), that
emerges in the circulation of the total social capital. This interpretation
has important implications for the evaluation of the logical consistency
and the explanatory power of Marx's theory.

With regard to logical consistency, this macro-monetary interpretation implies that there is no logical contradiction in Marx's determination of prices of production in Part Two of Volume III. There is no
contradiction between the 'value rate of profit' in Volume I and the
'price rate of profit' in Volume III. There is only one rate of profit in
Marx's theory, the price rate of profit. The price rate of profit is derived
in Volume III from the total surplus-value which is determined in
Volume I, and is then taken as given in the determination of prices of
production in Volume III. Marx did not 'forget to transform the inputs'
of constant capital and variable capital from values to prices of production, because the same quantities of money constant capital and money
variable capital are taken as given in the determination of both values
in Volume I and prices of production in Volume III (see Moseley, 1993
and 2000 for an extensive presentation of this argument). Marx's
determination of prices of production is logically consistent. Therefore,

the very widespread reason for rejecting Marx's theory – logical inconsistency – is not justified. The further evaluation of Marx's theory should focus on its empirical explanatory power, compared to the explanatory power of other economic theories.

With regard to the explanatory power of Marx's theory, according to the macro-monetary interpretation, Marx's theory in Volume I explains a wide range of important phenomena of capitalist economies. To begin with, as discussed above, the 'necessity of money' in capitalist economies is explained in Chapter 1 on the basis of the labour theory of value. This derivation of the necessity of money is an achievement that no other economic theory, before or after Marx, has been able to accomplish. In particular, Sraffa's theory, or the Sraffian interpretation of Marx's theory, provides no explanation of the necessity of money. Money is simply taken as a given feature of capitalist economies, without an explanation of its necessity, and money plays almost no role in this theory. Similarly, neoclassical economic theory also provides no explanation of the necessity of money in capitalist economies. As expressed by Frank Hahn, one of the leading proponents of neoclassical theory: 'The most serious challenge that the existence of money poses to the theorist is this: the best developed model of the economy [i.e. neoclassical general equilibrium theory] cannot find room for it' (1983: 1).

Furthermore, Marx's theory in Volume I explains the *actual* total surplus-value produced in the real capitalist economy, not a *hypothetical* total surplus-value, that is proportional to the 'labour-values' of surplus goods, as in the Sraffian interpretation. Marx's theory in Volume I does not determine a hypothetical total surplus-value that later has to be transformed into the actual surplus-value, so that its magnitude changes, and no longer depends solely on surplus labour. Instead, Volume I determines the actual surplus-value, as proportional to surplus labour, which is then taken as given and does not change in magnitude in the later analysis of the distribution of surplus-value in Volume III (i.e. the total surplus-value is not affected by the distribution of surplus-value, or the determination of individual component parts of surplus-value).

Finally, there are a number of other important phenomena of capitalist economies that are explained on the basis of Marx's 'surplus labour' theory of surplus-value, and that cannot be explained on the basis of other economic theories of profit: inherent conflicts over the length of the working day and over the intensity of labour, inherent technological change, the tendency of the rate of profit to fall, periodic crises, etc. (see Moseley, 1995 for an extensive evaluation of the explanatory power of Marx's theory, in response to Mark Blaug's negative appraisal).

Therefore, it would appear that Marx's theory of surplus-value is both logically consistent and has greater explanatory power than either Sraffa's theory or neoclassical theory. Further research obviously needs to be done on the relative explanatory power of Marx's theory and these other theories, but this further empirical research should at least recognize and acknowledge that Marx's theory is logically consistent and that it does not contain the 'logical flaws' that are widely alleged.

References

Bellofiore, Riccardo (1989), A monetary labor theory of value, *Review of Radical Political Economy*, 21.

Carchedi, Guglielmo (1984), The logic of prices as values, *Economy and Society*, 13.

Foley, Duncan (1986), *Understanding Capital: Marx's Economic Theory* (Cambridge, Mass.: Harvard University Press).

Hahn, Frank (1983), *Money and Inflation* (Cambridge, Mass.: MIT Press).

Marx, Karl (1857–58), *Grundrisse* (Hamandsworth: Penguin, 1973).

— (1867), *Capital, Volume I* (New York: Random House, 1977).

— (1884), *Capital, Volume II* (New York: Random House, 1978).

— (1894), *Capital, Volume III* (New York: Random House, 1981).

Marx, Karl and Frederick Engels (1968a), *Marx–Engels Selected Correspondence* (Moscow: Progress Publishers).

— (1968b), *Marx–Engels Selected Works* (New York: International Publishers).

— (1861–63a), *Marx–Engels Collected Works*, Volume 30 (New York: International Publishers, 1988).

— (1861–63b), *Marx–Engels Collected Works*, Volume 31 (New York: International Publishers, 1989).

— (1861–63c), *Marx–Engels Collected Works*, Volume 32 (New York: International Publishers, 1989).

— (1861–63d), *Marx–Engels Collected Works*, Volume 33 (New York: International Publishers, 1991).

Mattick, Paul (1969), *Marx and Keynes: The Limits of the Mixed Economy* (Boston, Mass.: Porter Sargent).

Mattick, Jr, Paul (1981), Some aspects of the value – price problem, *Economies et Sociétés* (Cahiers de l'ISMEA Series), 15.

Morishima, Michio (1973), *Marx's Economics: A Dual Theory of Value and Growth* (New York: Cambridge University Press).

Moseley, Fred (1993), Marx's logical method and the transformation problem, in Moseley (ed.), *Marx's Method in 'Capital': A Reexamination* (Atlantic Highlands, NJ: Humanities Press).

— (1995), Marx's economic theory: true or false? A Marxian response to Blaug's appraisal, in Moseley (ed.), *Heterodox Economic Theories: True or False?* (Aldershot: Edward Elgar).

— (1997), The development of Marx's theory of the distribution of surplus-value, in F. Moseley and M. Campbell (eds), *New Perspectives on Marx's Method in 'Capital'* (Atlantic Highlands, NJ: Humanities Press).

— (1998), Marx's reproduction schemes and Smith's dogma, in C. Arthur and G. Reuten (eds), *The Circulation of Capital: Essays on Volume Two of Marx's 'Capital'* (London: Macmillan – now Palgrave Macmillan).

— (2000), The 'new solution' to the transformation problem: a sympathetic critique, *Review of Radical Political Economics*, 32.

— (2001), Marx's alleged logical error: a comment, *Science and Society*, 65/4: 515–27.

— (2002), Hostile brothers: Marx's theory of the distribution of surplus-value in Volume III of *Capital*, in M. Campbell and G. Reuten (eds), *The Culmination of Capital: Essays on Volume III of Marx's 'Capital'* (Basingstoke: Palgrave Macmillan).

Murray, Patrick (1988), *Marx's Theory of Scientific Knowledge* (Atlantic Highlands, NJ: Humanities Press).

Rosdolsky, Roman (1977), *The Making of Marx's Capital* (London: Pluto Press).

Shortall, Felton (1994), *The Incomplete Marx* (Aldershot: Avebury).

Steedman, Ian (1977), *Marx After Sraffa* (London: New Left Books).

Weeks, John (1981), *Capital and Exploitation* (Princeton, NJ: Princeton University Press).

Yaffe, David (1976), Value and price in Marx's *Capital, Revolutionary Communist*.

7
Marx and the Macro-monetary Foundation of Microeconomics

*Riccardo Bellofiore**

In many of his recent writings, and also in his chapter for this book, Fred Moseley has stressed that Marx's theory must be interpreted as a 'macro' and 'monetary' approach, which grounds the determination of prices of production.[1] Moseley recognizes that others have put forward a 'macro-monetary' reading of Marxian theory. Rather than engage in a dialogue with these other perspectives, Moseley has been content to refine his own interpretation. Open dialogue and a detailed criticism are necessary to identify similarities and differences between these positions.

I cannot but agree with the view that Marx's originality lies in his 'monetary labour theory of value' and in his 'macro-social' perspective, two defining features of my own view since the 1980s. Such statements must nevertheless be scrutinized carefully, since it is not obvious that Marx's *Capital*, Volume I, can be read according to Moseley's way of interpreting the 'macro' and 'monetary' approach. One reason is that, with few exceptions, the essential link between money and value has only recently attracted the attention of Marx's scholars, and it is still one of the most problematic areas in Marxian economics. Another is that the macro–micro divide is the heritage of the Keynesian revolution, itself a very controversial issue, so the application of these terms to Marx must be clearly spelled out.

* I thank all the members of the ISMT for their comments. I owe a special debt to Chris Arthur and Geert Reuten. Fred Moseley was kind enough to discuss with me many times the topics under discussion in this chapter. I also benefited, as usual, from thorough criticism and help by Nicola Taylor, to whom I am linked by a *concordia discors* on Marx's monetary theory of value.
1. See Moseley (1993, 1997, 2002, 2003).

Moseley's argument may be encapsulated in a few quotes from his chapter in this book. 'Volume I', he maintains 'is primarily about the determination of the total increment of money (dM), or total surplus-value, produced in the capitalist economy as a whole' (p. 146). The money magnitudes 'are *determined* by quantities of labour-time, which are taken as given' (p. 147), presupposed, a *known datum*. In this sense, the money magnitudes are the dependent variables and the quantities of labour time required to produce commodities, i.e. labour-values, are the 'givens', the independent variables. Moseley sees as integral to this 'monetary' approach a view where 'necessary labour is derived as the number of hours required for workers to produce new value (in terms of money) which is equal to the money variable capital with which their labour-power is purchased' (p. 153). This is a view where the value of labour-power is determined without taking as given the average real subsistence wage basket. Most of Volume I is framed with reference to individual capital(s) and individual worker(s), but since Marx's theory applies to each and every capital, it also applies to the *sum of all capitals*, or to the *total social capital*. In Marx, the individual capitals represent the total social capital (p. 155) and the individual workers the total working class as a whole. In this sense, the 'monetary' approach is also a 'macro' perspective.

Though Moseley's support for a 'macro-monetary' view is to be welcomed, I will argue that his reading is *neither truly monetary nor truly macroeconomic* but quite the opposite if we accept the meaning currently attributed to these terms in much of heterodox economic thought. Rather, Moseley's reading seems to be compatible with orthodox economics. Money is a *veil*: surplus-value is surplus money, and this latter is the mere, though necessary, appearance of the surplus labour determining it. 'Macro' is mere *aggregation*: with the total being nothing but the sum of these individual components, and the properties attributed to the latter the same as the properties attributed to the former. Some (redundant) references to Hegelian terminology and a few (dubious) textual quotes fail to clarify why this aggregation should give a logical priority to 'macro-monetary' magnitudes over the individual ones.

I shall argue that Moseley's attempt to reconstruct the Marxian system as if it were free from internal problems fails, and that his 'macro-monetary' interpretation is unconvincing in crucial points. I will instead suggest that a reformulation of Marx's monetary theory and a translation of his exploitation theory in contemporary 'macro' terms are needed *precisely* to overcome critical weaknesses in Marx's argument.

To begin this exercise in dialogue and criticism with Moseley I will proceed in steps, and unfortunately (because of lack of space) in a very impressionistic way, with the help of a few quotes. In the first half of the chapter (section 1, 2 and 3), I will present my own view of the macro-monetary labour theory of value, clearly distinguishing *interpretation* of Marx's original argument from my personal *reconstruction* and *development*. In the second half of the chapter (section 4 and 5) I will mix the ongoing discussion of *Capital*, Volume I, with a more direct confrontation with Moseley's approach. Thus, the present chapter will present a sketch of my own view side-by-side with a criticism of Moseley's interpretation, both evaluated against the textual evidence.

In section 1, I will present a quick general summary[2] of the main thrust of Marx's *Capital*, Volume I. Here, my aim will *not* be a too literal rendering of Marx's thought: rather, I want to clarify immediately the 'macro' and 'monetary' side of the Marxian perspective hidden in the original train of the argument. In the following sections, I will have a closer look at some key points of the development of the book, investigating more closely Marx's original formulations. In section 2, I will show in what sense Marx's 'monetary' value in its original version is inextricably connected to a theory of money as a (very special, 'excluded') commodity. It is here that we have the true foundation of the 'labour theory of value', that is, of value as expressing nothing but the peculiar sociality of labour in its capitalist form. The 'intrinsic' value (which has sometimes been called in the secondary literature and by Marx himself 'absolute' value), and the abstract labour crystallized in it, whose 'immanent' measure is labour time, is expressed in the 'external' measure, the money commodity, whose concrete labour is the necessary form of manifestation of commodities' abstract labour. In section 3, I will summarize Marx's theory of the origin of surplus-value as part of a 'counterfactual' argument (or, better, as the application of a 'method of comparison') showing it to be the outcome of a lengthening of the working day over and above the situation in which living labour is the same as necessary labour.

In section 4, I will say something about the determination of the value of labour-power in *Capital*, Volume I, reaching conclusions in contrast with Moseley's, and come closer to some of Rosa Luxemburg's sugges-tions in her chapter on wages in the *Introduction to Political Economy*. The value of labour-power is determined in Marx by reference to the 'real' subsistence basket, which regulates the money wage. In section 5, I will

2. For a more extended survey of Marxian economic thought, see Bellofiore (2001).

present some quotes from Volume I where it is quite evident that Marx's perspective is truly 'macro' as Moseley insists. Interestingly, though, these quotes show that the 'macro' perspective reaches, opposite conclusions to the 'micro' perspective, and one of the clearest examples is, exactly, the total capital's determination of the real wage for the working class as a whole, which is contrary to Moseley's interpretation of the texts.

Throughout the chapter I will have in the back of my mind what I have already argued in other writings[3]: that is, that the difficulties of Marx's monetary and value theory in its original version may be overcome only if Marx's labour theory of value is rewritten as a conflictual theory of living labour's extraction by class struggle in a sign–money system, where money enters the circuit as (bank-)finance to production. That is, if the monetary and macro elements in Marxian theory are made coherent and strengthened.

1. The main thrust of Marx's Capital, Volume I: a brief summary

According to Marx, capitalist society is a historical situation where 'objective' conditions of production (means of production, including original resources other than labour) are privately owned by one section of society, the capitalist class, to the exclusion of the other, the working class.[4] Separated from the material conditions of labour and hence unable independently to produce their own means of subsistence, workers are compelled to sell to capitalist firms the only thing they own, the 'subjective' condition of production (their labour-power), against a money wage to be spent in buying wage-goods. Labour-power is the capacity for labour: it is the mental and physical capabilities set in motion as useful work, producing use-values of any kind, and it is inseparable from the living body of human beings. The labour contract between capitalists and wage-workers presupposes that the latter are legally free subjects (unlike slaves or serfs), and hence that they put their labour-power at the disposal of capitalists only for a limited period

---

3. The most relevant are Bellofiore (1989) and Bellofiore and Finelli (1998).
4. Although the financial aspect of the picture I am giving is not spelled out in *Capital*, Volume I, and although it will be openly introduced only in Volume III, in my view it must be considered from the start as a defining feature of the capitalist social relation. The point will be clarified later in this chapter. For a more detailed presentation of this view of Marx as a forerunner of the theory of the monetary circuit, see the papers collected in Bellofiore (1997) and especially Graziani (1983a, 1983b). See also Bellofiore (2004). For a short summary of the theory of the monetary circuit, see the entry by Bellofiore and Seccareccia (1999).

of time. The owners of the means of production, the 'industrial-capitalists', need initial finance from the owners of money, 'money-capitalists', not only to buy the means of production from other capitalists (which, from the point of view of the capitalist class as a whole, amounts to a purely 'internal' transaction), but also and primarily to buy workers' labour-power (which, from the same point of view, is its only 'external' purchase). The commodity output belongs to the industrial capitalists, who sell it to 'merchant-capitalists' who, in turn, realize it on the market.

Marx assumes that industrial capitalists initially have at their disposal the money they need, and that they sell their output on the market without intermediation. The capitalist process in a given production period may be summarized in the following terms. The *first purchase* on the so-called *labour market* is the *opening act*, and it enables capitalist entrepreneurs to set *immediate production* going. Firms look forward to selling the commodity product on the output market against money. The receipts must at least cover the initial advance, thereby closing the circuit. Two kinds of monetary circulation are involved here. Wage earners sell commodities, C_{LP} (their own labour-power) against money, M, in order to obtain different commodities, C_{WB} (the commodity basket needed to reproduce the workers, arising from prior production processes and owned by capitalists). Thus, workers are trapped in what Marx calls 'simple commodity circulation', or C–M–C. On the other hand, capitalist firms buy commodities in order to sell, hence the circulation appears to be an instance of M–C–M'. Once expressed in this form, it is clear that capitalist circulation has meaning only in so far as *the amount of money at the end is expected to be higher than the money advanced at the beginning of the circuit* – that is, if M' > M and the value advanced as money has been able to earn a surplus-value, consisting in gross money profits.[5] M–C–M' is the 'general formula of capital', because capital is defined by Marx as self-expanding value. The class divide between capitalists and

---

5. Which firms will actually share with financiers, merchant-capitalists, land-owners and rentiers. I will not deal here with the issue of how the higher 'money' (as higher abstract wealth) produced by wage workers, is actually 'realised' in circulation in an amount of money (as means of exchange) higher than the one injected in the system at the opening of the circuit by monetary capitalists (nowadays banks). Marx's original framework does not seem to be correct from the point of view of the theory of the monetary circuit, which shows that firms as a whole can receive back at the end of the circuit only the same amount of finance lent out by the banking system. Interesting suggestions to provide a better answer come from Luxemburg and Kalecki, but this is an open area for research.

wage-workers may therefore be reinterpreted as separating those who have access to the advance of money as capital, 'money that begets money', from those who have access to money only as income.

The main question addressed by Marx in Volume I of *Capital* is thus the following: *how can the capitalist class get out of this economic process more than they put in*? What they put in, as a class, is money-capital, which 'represents' the abstract labour materialized in the means of production and in the means of subsistence required for the current process of production. What they get out is the money value 'representing' the abstract labour crystallized in the commodity output sold on the market at the end of the circuit. From a macroeconomic point of view, it is clear that *the 'valorization' of capital cannot have its origin in the 'internal' exchanges within the capitalist class*, i.e. between firms, because any profit one producer gains by buying cheap and selling dear would transfer a loss to other producers. As a consequence, *the source of surplus-value must be traced back to the only exchange which is 'external' to the capitalist class, namely the purchase of labour-power*.

The issue here is simply to understand *through which mechanism* this happens. I will return to this later on, but I think Marx's reasoning is, in a nutshell, the following. In the capitalist labour process, the *totality* of wage-workers are at the same time reproducing the means of production employed and producing a net product. The net product is expressed on the market as a *new* value that is *added* to the value attached to the means of production. This 'value added' is just the *monetary expression of the labour time* which has been *objectified* by wage-workers in the *current* period. The 'value of the labour-power' for the entire working class is given by the *labour contained in money wages*, which is regulated by the (commodity-producing) labour time required to reproduce the capacity for labour, and hence by *the labour time required to reproduce the means of subsistence* bought on the market. Accordingly, surplus-value arises from 'surplus labour': the positive difference between, on the one hand, the whole of *living labour* spent in producing the total (net) product of capital and, on the other, the share of living labour which it is necessary to devote to reproducing the wages, which Marx labels *necessary labour*.

2. Value as abstract labour: the monetary connection

2.1 *The monetary expression of abstract labour time*

Marx's tracing back of surplus-value to surplus labour may be better understood by looking at the special way he develops and overturns the labour theory of value originally formulated by the Classical economists

Smith and Ricardo.[6] The starting point of the reasoning is that capitalism is a *generalized commodity economy*, and, therefore, the analysis of exchange as such is given priority relative to the analysis of capitalist exchange. In *exchange as such*, individual producers are separate and in competition with each other. The labour of these individuals is immediately private and can become social *only* on the market. This happens *indirectly*: each commodity is shown to be equal to other commodities in certain quantitative ratios, to have an 'exchange-value', in as much as it is expressed through *money* as the 'universal equivalent'. Money is a *special commodity* with general purchasing power as a result of a process of selection and exclusion, sanctioned by the state. This equalization of products that takes place in the market is *also*, at the same time, an equalization of the labours producing them. Thus, *labour is not social in advance, but only in so far as its true end-product will be money*: 'generic' or 'abstract' wealth. Individual labour, which is 'concrete' labour producing an object with some utility for some other agent, a 'use-value', rather *counts* for the producer as its *opposite*, as *'abstract' labour*, as a portion of the aggregate labour whose *ex post* socialization is represented in the money value of output (and, therefore, in a portion of the concrete labour that produces the money commodity). Nevertheless, *though it is only through money that private labour becomes social labour, it is not money that renders the commodities commensurable*. On the contrary: commodities have exchange-value because, even before the final exchange on the commodity market, they have *already* acquired the *ideal* property of being universally exchangeable, so that they have the 'form of value'; this property, so to speak, *grows out* from objectified 'abstract' labour as the 'substance of value'. Money is *nothing but* 'value' made autonomous in exchange, divorced from commodities and existing alongside them: and as such it is the *outward* 'representation' of abstract, indirectly social labour.

This *qualitative* analysis of exchange as such has a *quantitative* counterpart. The 'magnitude of value' of a unit-commodity is determined by the 'socially necessary' labour time needed for its production. In a particular branch of production each commodity of a given type and quality is sold at the same money price. Hence, the magnitude of value is ruled not by the *individual* labour time actually spent by the single producer (by its 'individual value') but by the labour time that has to be expended

6. This reading is very different from the traditional one put forward by Dobb (1937) and Sweezy (1942), and is heavily influenced by Colletti (1969) and Napoleoni (1972). On this, see Bellofiore (1999).

under *normal* conditions and with the *average* degree of skill and intensity of labour (i.e. by its 'social value'). The magnitude of value is also inversely related to the productive power of the direct labour producing the commodity. Commodity values are necessarily manifested as money prices within exchange. The quantity of money that is produced by one hour of labour, in a given country and in a given period, may be defined as the 'monetary expression of labour': the socially necessary labour time multiplied by the monetary expression of labour gives what has been later called its 'simple' or 'direct' price.

Marx defines the *relative exchange-value* between two commodities as the *ratio between their simple prices*: it is therefore *proportional to the ratio between their 'intrinsic' values*. On this outlook, it is *always* possible to translate the 'external' measure of the magnitude of each commodity's value in money terms (ideally anticipated by producers before exchange) into the 'immanent' measure in units of labour time. Note, however, that value is *not* identical with price defined as any arbitrary relative ratio between commodity and money contingently fixed on the market. Value expresses a *necessary* relation with the (abstract) labour time spent in the production of commodities. To be assumed to be effective in regulating market prices even at this very abstract starting point of the inquiry, the concept of value implies a coincidence between individual supply and demand. In that case the spontaneous allocation of the private labours of the autonomous, independent producers affirms itself *a posteriori* on the market as a '*social* division of labour'. In contra distinction to this and regardless of the divergences between individual supply and demand, 'price' is the *money-name* taken by commodities: the labour it expresses may differ from the socially necessary labour contained in the commodity. The *whole* mass of the *newly* produced commodities is seen by Marx as a *homogeneous* quantity of value whose monetary expression is necessarily equal to their *total* money price. Thus, any divergence between values and prices simply *redistributes* among producers the total direct labour, the 'content' hidden behind the 'form' of value taken by the net product.

2.2 The fundamental role of money as a commodity

In the argument I have just summarized, what I want to stress, with the help of a few quotes, is how the idea that value expresses nothing but labour depends, for Marx, on the following theses: (i) that products are commodities (and thus have values) in as much as they are *sold* against money on the market; (ii) that money is a (very special) *commodity*; (iii) that this necessary monetary *ex post* validation is at the same time a *passive*, outward expression of the inner 'substance', the abstract, homogeneous labour *crystallized* in commodities, which have to assert (and measure) themselves in the sphere of circulation; (iv) that, therefore, values are a *pre-condition* of monetary circulation (with this last thesis apparently contradicting the first).

'The general form of value', writes Marx, 'can only arise as the joint contribution of the whole world of commodities' and 'the objectivity of commodities as values...can only be expressed through the whole range of their social relations' (Marx, 1867, 1890: 159).[7] Some pages before he specified that 'However, the properties of a thing do not arise from its relations to other things, they are, on the contrary, merely activated by such relations' (149). It is only within actual exchange that all commodities manifest themselves as qualitatively equal, as values in general, and as values of different quantitative magnitude. It is in the sphere of circulation, then, that private, concrete labours, show themselves as quota of social, abstract labour, through the metamorphosis with money. But Marx explicitly states that 'It is not money that renders the commodities commensurable. Quite the contrary. Because *all* commodities, as *values*, are *objectified human labour*, and therefore in themselves commensurable, their values can be communally measured in one and the same specific commodity, and this commodity can be converted into the common measure of their values, that is into money. Money as a measure of value is the *necessary form of appearance* of the measure of value which is *immanent* in commodities, namely *labour-time*' (188).

Since in general 'The body of the commodity, which serves as the equivalent, always figures as the embodiment of abstract human labour, and is always the product of some specific useful and concrete labour', and since 'This concrete labour therefore becomes the expression of abstract human labour' (150), in gold-money as the 'universal equivalent' the *concrete* labour producing gold becomes the *form of expression* of its opposite, *abstract* human labour. Although labour of 'private' producers, it acts in fact as labour in *directly* social form. The measure of value of a commodity through gold, its *money-form*, is the 'price'. Once money is considered as the 'conventional' standard of price, a quantity of metal with a fixed weight, price becomes the *money-name* of the labour

---

7. In the quotes from Marx included in this chapter the original italics, omitted in the English translation, have been retained. They are essential to understand properly Marx's train of thought. For this reason, when I would like to stress arguments I shall underline them, to let the reader distinguish my emphasis from Marx's.

objectified in the commodity. In this way the abstract labour *intrinsic* to commodities is 'represented' by the *concrete labour* producing gold as money. But the price of commodities is, 'like their form of value generally, quite distinct from their palpable and real bodily form; it is therefore a <u>purely ideal</u> or <u>notional</u> form. <u>Although invisible</u>, the value of iron, linen and coats <u>exists in these very articles</u>: it is <u>signified through their equality with gold</u>, even though this relation with gold exists <u>only in their heads</u>, so to speak' (189). While 'gold can serve as a measure of value <u>only because it is itself a product of labour</u>' (p. 192), the value of commodities is *already* expressed in their price as ideal money – that is, as a given amount of the labour producing gold – *before* they enter into circulation. Value is a *pre*-condition of circulation, not its result: and the theory of money as a commodity makes this assertion compatible with the idea that value *eventually* comes into being at the intersection of production and circulation.[8]

Indeed, the intrinsic value[9] of the commodity, as ideal money, has *yet* to be 'realized' in actual exchange, but 'In their prices, the commodities have *already* been equated with a <u>definite but imaginary</u> quantities of money ... the amount of means of circulation required is [then] determined beforehand by the *sum of the prices* of all these commodities.

8. This view is expanded in Bellofiore (1998b) and in Realfonzo-Bellofiore (2003). In the text almost always I will use the expression 'theory of *money as a commodity*', and not the more widespread 'theory of *commodity-money*'. I want to stress the difference with Ricardo. In Ricardo, money is a commodity because it is *like* and *similar* to all the other commodities, having in common the fact of being the product of labour, without any specification. In Marx, money is a commodity in as much as it is *excluded* from, and *opposed* to, the entire world of commodities. This is the reason why the *concrete* labour producing money as a commodity is the *only* means by which the *abstract* labour 'latent' in all the other commodities can eventually 'come into being'.

9. In other papers instead of the label 'intrinsic' value I used not only (following Napoleoni and some rare Marx's quotes) 'absolute' value, but also 'potential' value (see Bellofiore and Finelli 1998). It is 'potential' in the sense of being *latent* and *ideal*. But this 'potentiality', as my reasoning in this chapter tries to show (and as the paper just quoted already argued), must be seen in the wider context of the *actuality* of value at *all* phases of the capitalist circuit. Moreover, it is treating all labour as abstract in production proper, that is, in the *central* moment of the cycle of capital, that capital is produced. This outcome follows from the *'imprinting' of the value form on production from both sides*, so to speak: 'forward', from initial finance; 'backward', from final monetary exchange on the commodity market. This point will be clarified later on in this chapter through a reconstruction and development of Marx's 'macro-monetary' labour theory of value.

As a matter of fact, the money is <u>only</u> the representation in real life of the quantity of gold <u>previously expressed in the imagination</u> by the sum of prices of the commodities' (213). The monetary circulation is 'opened' by the initial barter of gold *as a commodity* against another commodity: that is, gold as money '<u>enters</u> as a *commodity with a given value*. Hence, when money begins to function as a measure of value, when it is used to determine prices, <u>its value is presupposed</u>... Henceforth <u>we shall assume the value of gold as a given factor, as in fact it is if we take it at the moment when we estimate the price of a commodity'</u> (214). Again, in Volume I, this exchange-value is accounted for by presupposing that exchange-ratios are proportional to the labour 'embodied' in them:

> Money, like every commodity, cannot *express* the magnitude of its value except relatively in *other* commodities. <u>This value is determined by the labour-time required for its production</u>, and is expressed in the *quantity* of any other commodity in which <u>the same amount of labour-time is congealed</u>. This establishing of its relative value occurs <u>at the source of its production by means of barter</u>. As soon as it enters into circulation as *money*, its value is already *given* (186).

2.3 Some criticisms to be answered

This argument, which is expressed most clearly in the opening pages of *Capital*, moves from exchange-value to value, from value to money, and from money to labour (although in the opening sections of the first chapter Marx made an unfortunate short circuit anticipating the link between value and labour before having introduced the form of value and money). His presentation may be attacked on several grounds (exactly because of it).

Böhm-Bawerk failed to notice the *essential* monetary side of Marxian value theory and looked only at what he saw as a linear deduction in the direction exchange-value/value/abstract labour. He then observed, quite reasonably, that abstracting from specific use-values does not mean abstracting from use-value 'in general'. He also countered that, to the extent that exchange-values are also attached to non-produced commodities, it follows that the common properties that allow for exchange on the market and that are hidden behind the notion of value are *utility* and *scarcity*. This *first* criticism has to be answered through a stronger argument than Marx's own, and this will be done in the next section.

A *second*, more recent and sympathetic criticism comes from within the Marxian camp. Many 'value-form' theorists (including two writers included in this volume, Geert Reuten and Nicola Taylor) stress that, while the connection of value to money as universal equivalent (but not the connection of value to money as a commodity) is in general convincing, less so is the idea of an 'intrinsic' or 'absolute' value grounded in the expenditure of labour as some homogeneous social entity that is constituted before the selling of the products on the commodity market. In fact, Marx himself shows that the social equalization among labours is *eventually* effected *only* in circulation, when the commodity is *actually* sold, and that the concrete labours in immediate production are *heterogeneous* and hence *non-additive*. There is here, as in many other interpretations, an *underestimation* of the theory of money as a commodity as the 'foundation' for the link established by Marx between value and labour: the former being *nothing but* the *materialization* of the latter, expressed in money with a *pre-given* value.[10]

Some Marxists and interpreters have also argued that values regulate prices only in a 'simple commodity economy', where workers own the means of production and where income is entirely distributed as wages. This simple commodity economy should be seen either as the *historical* precedent of capitalism or as a *fictional* economy providing a first, *imperfect* approximation to the analysis of capitalism. Since in capitalism the competitive prices that act as centres of gravity for market prices are 'prices of production' (embodying an equal rate of profit) which generally diverge from simple prices, and since the 'transformation' of the latter into the former is problematic, this has become a *third* reason to attack Marx's value theory. This position ignores the fact that for Marx commodity exchange is general *only* when the capitalist mode of production is *dominant* – that is, only when workers are compelled to sell labour-power against money as (variable) capital, which then becomes self-valorizing value. As a consequence, labour is for Marx the content of the value-form because of a *more fundamental sequence* going from money(-capital) to (living) labour to (surplus-)value. The private 'individuals' dissociated and opposed on the commodity market where they eventually become socialized through the metamorphosis of their products into

10. The internal *necessary* connection, in Marx, between value as nothing but the expression of *objectified labour*, on the one side, and money *as a commodity*, on the other, is also denied by Martha Campbell in her many writings on this topic.

money can now be interpreted as *collective workers* organized by *particular capitals* in mutual competition.

Nevertheless, as I (and others) have argued elsewhere, the theory of money as a commodity put forward by Marx analysing the sphere of commodity circulation at the beginning of *Capital* must be revised when the analysis shifts to a thorough consideration of the capitalist production process. In the end, it must be recognized that in capitalism the fundamental nature of money is *first of all* that of bank-credit financing firms' production. This is yet another reason forcing us to find a different ground – *more solid than Marx's own* – for seeing in commodity values nothing but expressions of labour. But before directly tackling this issue, we have to trace out Marx's argument about the *origin* of surplus-value: an argument where Marx still reasons by reducing monetary magnitudes to gold, then translating money prices expressing values in labour-time magnitudes.

3. The origin of surplus-value and the 'method of comparison'

3.1 *Marx on the origin of surplus-value*

The *valorization process* may be quantitatively summarized with the help of a few definitions. Marx calls the part of the money-capital advanced by firms that is used to buy the means of productions '*constant* capital' because, through the mediation of labour as concrete labour, the value of the raw materials and of the instruments of production is *merely transferred* to the value of the product. Marx calls the remaining portion of the money-capital advanced – namely, the money-form taken by the means of subsistence that buy the workers to incorporate them in the valorization process – '*variable* capital', because when living labour is pumped out from workers' capacity to labour as abstract labour, it not only replaces the value advanced by the capitalists in purchasing labour-power, but also produces value *over and above* this limit, and, so, surplus-value. The ratio of surplus-value to variable capital is Marx's 'rate of surplus-value'. It accurately expresses the 'degree of exploitation', this latter being interpreted as the appropriation by capital of surplus labour within the social working day: the higher (lower) the ratio, the higher (lower) the hours the labourers spend working for the capitalist class relative to the hours they spend producing for their own consumption. A similar division between constant capital, variable capital and surplus-value may be detected within the value of the output produced by single capitals as components of total capital.

On the other hand, as Marx will set out in *Capital*, Volume III, capitalists naturally refer the surplus-value to the total capital they advanced.

Surplus-value as related to the sum of constant and variable capital takes the new name of 'profit', and this new ratio is thereby known as the 'rate of profit'. Because it connects surplus-value not only to variable capital but also to constant capital, the rate of profit *obscures* the internal necessary relation between surplus-value as the effect and living labour as the cause. Profit increasingly comes to be seen as produced by the *whole capital as a thing* (either as money-capital or as the ensemble of means of production, including workers as things among things) rather than as a *social relation between classes*. Nevertheless, this fetishistic mystification is not mere illusion. On the contrary, it depends on the fact that, to exploit labour, capital has to be simultaneously advanced as constant capital. Thereby, wage-labour is a *part* of capital on the same footing as the instruments of labour and the raw materials, even though the living labour of the wage-earners is the *whole* from which surplus value, and then capital itself, springs. From this standpoint, the rate of profit *accurately* expresses the 'degree of valorization' of *all* the value advanced as capital.

Back to *Capital*, Volume I[11]. To understand Marx's theory of *how capital is produced*, that is, the 'genetical' explanation of gross money profits, let us initially assume, as Marx does, that capitalist firms produce to meet effective demand. The methods of production (including the intensity and the productive-power of labour), employment and the real wage are all known. Marx proceeds by what Rubin has called the *method of comparison*.[12] The labour-power bought by capital has, like any other commodity, an exchange-value and a use-value: the former expresses 'necessary labour', which is *given before production*, being nothing but the labour 'embodied' in the money variable capital advanced; the latter is 'living labour', or labour *in motion* during production. If the living labour extracted from workers were equal to necessary labour (if, that is, the economic system merely allowed for workers' consumption), there would be no surplus-value and hence no profits. Though capitalistically impossible, *this situation is meaningful and real*, since a vital capitalist production process needs to reintegrate the capital advanced to reproduce the working population at the *historically given standard of living*. In this kind of Marxian analogue of Schumpeter's 'circular flow' relative prices reduce to the ratio between simple prices.

11. Below I sometimes use the term 'profit', anticipating *Capital*, Volume III, as indicated in the previous paragraph.
12. As I explained in Bellofiore (2002, 107–8), my reading of Marx's method of comparison, summarized here, is different from Rubin's in many ways.

But the living labour of wage-workers is inherently not a constant but a variable magnitude, it is a 'fluid', and the actual quantity of its materialization is *yet to be determined*, when the labour contract is negotiated. It will 'congeal' only within production proper. The length of the working day may be extended *beyond* the limit of necessary labour, so that a surplus labour is created. Indeed, the control and the compulsion by capital of workers' effort guarantee that this *potential* extension of social working day over and above necessary labour time actually takes place. In this way what may be called 'originary profits' emerge. Marx assumes that the lengthening of the working day is the same for each worker, so that originary profits are proportional to employment. Their sum is total surplus-value. So as not to confuse the inquiry into the origin of the capitalist surplus-value with that into its distribution among competing capitals, Marx sticks to the same price rule developed in the preceding chapters, 'simple prices' proportional to the labour embodied in commodities. He can then subtract from the total quantity of living labour that has *really* been extorted in capitalist labour processes and objectified in the fresh ('social') value added the smaller quantity of labour that the workers *really* have to perform to produce the equivalent of money wages.

Note that the comparison Marx makes is *not* between a situation with petty commodity producers, whose wages exhaust income, and a situation where capitalists are present and making profits out of a proportional reduction in wages. It is rather between two *actually capitalist* situations, where the determining factor is the 'continuation' of the social working day (holding constant the given price rule). Note also that an implication of the price rule adopted by Marx[13] is that the labour time *represented* through the value of the money wage bill *is the same* as the labour time

13. One of the arguments showing why and how Marx *implicitly* adopted *this* preliminary 'price rule' – which implies average social and technical conditions (but *not* equality in the organic compositions of capital) – has been clearly spelled out by the present writer in Bellofiore and Finelli (1998) and Bellofiore (2002). In fact, a price rule of the kind 'prices' = 'values' naturally springs from Marx's *explicit* method of comparison, and it is the *necessary logical prerequisite* for Marx's way of explaining the origin of surplus-value. As will be clear later a price rule of this kind is also implied in Marx's macroeconomic theory of the wage, and thereby in his theory of distribution. In any case, it corresponds to one of Marx's major assumptions in Volume I expressed in a crucial footnote: 'the formation of capital must be possible though the price and the value of a commodity be the same, for it cannot be explained by referring to any divergence between price and value. If prices actually differ from values, we must first reduce the former to the latter,

necessary to *produce* the means of subsistence bought on the market. If the *real consumption* that the wage-earners can buy with the money wages they get on the labour market is set as a 'given' at the *subsistence* level, and if *firms' expectations about sales* are taken to be *confirmed* on the commodity market, then the process of capital's self-expansion is *transparently* determined by the *exploitation* of the working class *in production*, and this is simply *reflected* in circulation as the place where money gnoss profits are earned. Of course, the possibility of surplus labour is there from the start, after the productivity of labour has reached a certain level. However, Marx's key point is that, because the special feature of the commodity labour-power is that it is inextricably bound to the bodies of the workers, they may *resist* capital's compulsion. In capitalism there is creation of value only in so far as there is creation of surplus-value, valorization; and the potential valorization expected in the purchase of labour-power on the labour market is realized *only in so far as the capitalist class wins the class struggle in production* and *succeeds in making workers work* (provided, of course, firms are then able to sell the output).

In my opinion, this is the *most basic and sound* justification for (*living*) *labour being the sole source of (new) value*. And it is the only strong answer to Böhm-Bawerk's criticism to which I referred in Section 2.3. Value exhibits nothing but 'dead', objectified labour (expressed through money) because surplus-value – namely, in the end, the only real capitalist wealth – depends *causally* on the 'objectification', or 'materialization', of the living labour of the wage-workers *pumped out* and *prolonged* over and above necessary labour in the capitalist labour process, the latter being a *contested terrain* where workers are potentially recalcitrant, and where capital *needs to secure labour in order to get surplus labour*. In capitalism, therefore, the 'generativity' of surplus is an *endogenous* variable influenced by the *form-determination* of production as production for a surplus-value to be realized on the market.

---

i.e. disregard this situation as an accidental one in order to observe the phenomenon of the formation of capital on the basis of the exchange of commodities in its purity, and to prevent our observations from being interfered with by disturbing incidental circumstances which are irrelevant to the actual course of the process'. (p. 269) Marx adds that to all those interested in 'disinterested' thinking the problem of the formation of capital *must* be formulated as follows: 'How can we account for the origin of capital on the assumption that prices are regulated by the average price, i.e. ultimately by the value of commodities? I say 'ultimately' because average prices do not *directly* coincide with the values of commodities, as Adam Smith, Ricardo, and others believe'. (ivi) *Hic Rhodus, hic salta!*

With given technology and assuming that competition on the labour market establishes a uniform real wage, 'necessary labour' is a *given*. Surplus-value is then extracted, at first, by *lengthening* the working day. Marx calls this method of raising surplus-value the production of *'absolute surplus-value'*. When the length of the working day is limited legally and/or by social conflict, capital can enlarge surplus-value only by the extraction of *'relative* surplus-value' that is, either by *speeding up* the pace of production with a greater *intensity* of labour or by introducing *technological innovations*. Technical change, which increases the productive-power of labour, lowers the unit-values of commodities. To the extent that the changing organization of production directly or indirectly affects the conditions of production of wage-goods, necessary labour *decreases* because there is a fall in the labour-values of the goods making up the real subsistence wage, and thus there is a lowering of the value of labour-power. This makes room for a higher surplus labour and thus a higher surplus-value. Changing production techniques to increase relative surplus-value is a much more powerful way of controlling worker performance than is the simple personal control needed to obtain absolute surplus-value or even the mere speeding up of the pace of production (if divorced from the introduction of technological innovations).

Moving from 'cooperation' to the 'manufacturing division of labour' to 'the machine and big industry' stage, a *specifically* capitalist mode of production evolves. In this latter, labour is no longer subsumed 'formally' to capital – with surplus-value extraction going on within the technological framework historically inherited by capital – but 'really', through a capitalistically-designed system of production.[14] Workers become mere attendants and 'appendages' of means of production that act as means of absorption of labour-power *in motion*. They are mere bearers of the value-creating substance. The concrete qualities and skills possessed by workers spring from a structure of production incessantly revolutionized from within and designed to command living labour within the valorization process. Now labour not only counts but *is* purely abstract, indifferent to its particular form (which is dictated by capital) *in the very moment of activity*, where capitalists in their incessant search for (extra) profits try to manipulate workers as passive objects, rather than as active subjects.[15] This stripping away from labour of all its qualitative determinateness and its reduction to mere quantity encompass both the

---

14. The real subsumption of labour to capital is the key point in Patrick Murray's writing, including chapter 9 in this book.
15. See below section 3.3 for some notes on competition in Marx.

historically dominant tendency towards deskilling and the periodically recurring phases of partial reskilling.

3.2 A new view of exploitation

A moment of reflection is needed to appreciate the special features of this *unique* social reality. Profit-making springs from an 'exploitation' of workers in a *double sense*. There is exploitation because of the *division of the social working day*, with labourers giving more (living) labour in exchange for less (necessary) labour. The perspective here is that of the traditional, 'distributive' notion of exploitation, which considers the sharing out of the quantity of social labour embodied in the new value added within the period. Its 'immanent' measure is *surplus labour* over and above necessary labour. This, however, is the outcome of a *more basic* exploitation of workers. Capitalist wealth arises from the *use of workers' capacity to work*: this use perverts the nature of labour, which is rendered abstract – namely, 'pure and simple' because it is 'other-directed' – *already* in immediate production. The quantitative measure of this 'productive' notion of exploitation – a notion referring to the formation rather than to the distribution of *all* the new value added – is the *entire* social working day. From this second perspective, exploitation is to be identified with the abstraction of living labour within production – namely, with the *whole* of the labour time pumped out from workers.

Marx shows in *Capital*, Volume I, and more so in the *Results*, that abstract labour reflects an 'inversion of subject and object' (or, more precisely, a *'real hypostatization'*), which is deepened in the theoretical journey from the commodity-output market to the labour market to the production process. Within exchange on the commodity-output market, 'objectified' labour is 'abstract' because, when represented in value, the products of human working activity appear as an *independent* and *estranged* reality divorced from their origin in living labour. The consequent 'alienation' of individuals is coupled by 'reification' and 'fetishism': reification because production relations among people necessarily take the *material* shape of an exchange among *things* in a market (capitalist) economy; and fetishism because, as a consequence, the products of labour now appear endowed with social properties *as if* these latter were bestowed upon them *by nature*.

These characteristics reappear emphatically in the other two moments of the capitalist circuit. On the labour market, even human beings become the 'personifications' of the commodity they sell, labour-power or 'potential' labour. Within production, labour 'in becoming' is organized and shaped by capital as 'value-in-process', and embedded in a definite material organization which is specifically designed to enforce the extraction of surplus-value. To grow, dead labour must incorporate living labour: and dead labour 'sucking' living labour in the process of abstraction is the *true subject* for which the single concrete workers performing it are the predicates. In this way, Marx's capital as self-valorizing value is akin to Hegel's Absolute Idea seeking to actualize itself and reproduce in their entirety its own conditions of existence: but it is faced by the limit that workers may resist their incorporation as internal moments of capital.[16]

3.3 'Dynamic' competition in Volume I

Before going on, it is also necessary to underline the crucial role of competition in Marx. Competition is, for him, an essential feature of capitalist reality. *What all capitals have in common*, the inner tendency of 'capital in general', is their systematic ability to make money grow. We have seen how it is accounted for by the exploitation of the working class by capital as a whole. The nature of capital, however, is realized *only* through the inter-relationship of the many capitals in *opposition* to each other. This was already clear in the very definition of abstract labour and value. 'Socially necessary labour' comes to be established through the ex post socialization in exchange of dissociated capitalist-commodity producers. Therefore, the determination of 'social values' as regulators of production leading to some 'equilibrium' allocation of social labour – the 'law of value' – affirms itself at the level of individual capitals only through the mediation of the reciprocal interaction on the market.

The Marxian notion of competition is novel relative to the Classicals because it is of *two* kinds. The Ricardian notion of competition, which is also in Marx, is what may be labelled *inter-branch* (or 'static') competition, and it expresses the tendency to *equalize* the rate of profit *across* sectors. This will be the focus of the analysis in Volume III, especially Part Two. But in Marx, already in Volume I (Part Four, Chapter 12), there is also *intra-branch* (or 'dynamic') competition, and it was this side of Marx's legacy which acted as a powerful source of inspiration for Schumpeter.[17] The struggle to secure, if only temporarily, an extra surplus-value expresses a tendency to *diversify* the rate of profit *within* a given sector.

16. On this Chris Arthur (1993, 1999) is very good.
17. Henryk Grossmann (1941) has the merit of having stressed this point, recently revived by Tony Smith in many of his writings. See also Bellofiore (1985a, 1985b).

Within a given sector, there is a stratification of conditions of production, and firms may be ranked according to their high, average or low productivity. The *social value* of a unit of output tends towards the individual value of the firms producing the dominant mass of the commodities sold within the sector (this, of course, implies that a sufficiently strong shift in demand may indirectly affect social value). Those firms whose individual value is lower (higher) than social value earn a surplus-value that is higher (lower) than the normal. There is, therefore, a permanent incentive for single capitals to *innovate* in search of extra surplus-value, whatever the industry involved. This provides the *micro*-mechanism leading to the systematic production of relative surplus-value, independently of the conscious motivations of the individual capitalists. The new, more advanced methods of production increasing the productive-power of labour are embodied in more mechanized labour processes. Thus, the 'technical composition of capital', that is, the number of means of production relative to the number of workers employed, rises. This is represented by a growth in the ratio of constant capital to variable capital, both measured at the values ruling before innovation, what Marx calls the 'organic composition of capital'. But the 'devaluation' (the reduction in unit-values) of commodities resulting from innovation permeates also the capital-goods sector and may well result in a fall of the 'value composition of capital', that is, of the value-index of the composition of capital measured at the values prevailing after the change.

3.4 Towards a non-commodity theory of money: finance as monetary ante-validation of abstract labour

At this point, it is possible to understand that behind the *anarchic* 'social division of labour', carried out independently by each private producer, and effected *a posteriori* via the market, a different *'technical* division of labour' within production is going on. In the latter, inasmuch as it is subjected to the drive of valorization, an *a priori despotic* planning by capitalist firms leads to a *technological equalization* and *social precommensuration* of the expenditure of human labour-power, tentatively anticipating the final validation on the commodity market.[18] This process imposes on labour – *already* within direct production and *before*

---

18. The point about 'precommensuration', which was already hinted at by Napoleoni (1973), is at the heart of Reuten and Williams (1989), especially ch. 1. In chapters 2 and 5 they also expand towards some kind of notion of 'prevalidation', what I call 'antevalidation'. My source of inspiration here were however authors as different as de Brunhoff (from whom the term is borrowed) and Graziani (for his notion of initial finance).

'final' exchange – the quantitative and qualitative properties of being abstract labour which has been spent in the socially necessary measure. In a non-commodity theory of money – where justification of values being nothing but materializations of labour (contained in gold as the measure of value) no longer holds – the problematic dichotomy between the heterogeneity of concrete labours in production and the homogeneity of abstract labour eventually achieved in circulation through realization of values into money may be overcome. Indeed, bank finance to firms is nothing but a *monetary ante-validation* allowing industrial capitalists to perform a *precommensuration* of labour *within production*: so that, even more than in Marx's original approach, the capitalist process must be seen as 'money in motion', a *sequential* monetary process which hides behind it 'labour in motion'. The capitalist monetary circuit and the abstraction of labour are two sides of the same coin.

Once capitalism has reached its full maturity in large-scale industry, *the subjection of wage-workers' living labour to capital* and the consequent *preliminary abstraction of labour in production* must be seen as the *true, inner foundation of the abstraction of labour in the final exchange on the commodity-market*. And this abstraction of labour going on in production could not be effected *without a prior advance of bank money as money-capital*, expressing a preliminary agreement between bankers and entrepreneurs about the expected outcome of production not as a generic labour process but as the *central* moment of capitalist valorization.

Value and surplus-value have an 'ideal' *pre-existence*, that is prior to the actual circulation. These consequent notional values already have definite monetary *and* labour-time quantitative dimensions, as in Marx. But their *condition of possibility* is now a *prior monetary* ante-validation *bank-financing of production*: that is, a monetary *pre*condition, the advance of (non-commodity) money needed to begin production. The monetary nature of Marxian theory comes out *reinforced* and not weakened from this perspective, without impairing the labour theory of value as a theory of the origin of surplus-value, that is, as a theory of exploitation.

4. Non commodity money and the value of labour power

4.1 Capitalist valorization as a monetary sequence

There is, however, a further problem abandoning Marx's theory of money as a commodity. It is the following. If gold is assumed as the money-commodity, as it is in *Capital*, Volume I, three consequences follow: (i) the *purchasing power of money* (which later on will sometimes be labelled for short as the 'value of money', though the term is ambiguous) may be taken as given *prior* to the production process; (ii) variable capital, as a money magnitude may then be translated in an amount of labour-time *before* production begins; (iii) further assuming there is no problem of realising *commodity-output*, this latter may be computed as 'embodiment' of labour time *before* actual exchange. Exploitation – both as the extension of the social working day, objectified by living labour, and as the surplus labour hidden behind surplus-value – is here accurately defined. But once we leave the world of money as a commodity this seems not to be true any more. However, this conundrum may be resolved by a closer inspection of the quantitative meaning of the 'value of labour-power' in Volume I.

We have seen that Marx adopted a *dual* determination of this magnitude. It is, at one and the same time, (a) the amount of (concrete) labour time spent to *produce* the money-commodity (with a given value) and which, as money, is advanced as variable capital, and (b) the amount of (abstract) labour time *materialized* in the subsistence bundle. That is: the concrete labour time 'contained' in the money commodity is the (necessary) form of manifestation of the abstract labour time contained in the wage goods. There is *no tension* between the two definitions as long as we stick to the price rule according to which relative prices are proportional to the (socially necessary) labour embodied in commodities. Things change when the price rule changes. If, as in Volume I, wages are the *known datum* at some subsistence benchmark driven by an historical and moral element and then by social conflict, when, as in Volume III, prices of production diverge from labour-values the money variable capital must now be thought of as the *given* subsistence wage-goods *at these prices of production*. On the contrary, if wages are taken to be the 'given' as a *monetary* amount *which has no link with the 'historical and moral' subsistence*, then there will be a change in the use-values workers can buy at these new prices. In the last two decades it has become fashionable to take the second route. This is also what Moseley does. In the following, I will discuss the meaning of the cycle of money-capital as the 'general formula of capital' in *Capital* and present textual evidence showing that Marx took the *real* subsistence wage as the 'given', as the *known datum*, in Volume I.

The first point is to provide a better understanding of Marx's argument about capitalist valorization as production of (more) money by means of money. Moseley reads this argument as if value should be identified *only* with the monetary form, so that the commodity-form cannot be a form of existence of value – hence, as if production goods and wage-goods as such are not themselves modes of existence of value. But Marx explicitly states the opposite: 'in the circulation M–C–M both *the money and the commodity* function only as *different modes of existence of value itself*, the money as its *general* mode of existence, the commodity as its *particular* or, so to speak, *disguised* mode' (255). Thus, capital cannot be reduced to money as such – still less, of course, to commodities as such. It is the *movement of changing these forms one into the other to produce more abstract wealth*, surplus-value to be reinvested and then growing in a *spiral*:

> It is constantly <u>changing from one form into the other</u>, without becoming lost in this movement; it thus becomes transformed into <u>an automatic subject</u>. If we pin down the specific forms of appearance assumed in turn by self-valorizing value in the course of its life, we reach the following elucidation: *capital is money, capital is commodities*. In truth, however, *value* is here *the subject of a process* in which, while <u>constantly assuming the form in turn of money and commodities</u>, it changes its own magnitude, throws off surplus-value from itself considered as original value, and thus *valorizes itself independently*...As the dominant *subject* of this process, in which it <u>alternately</u> assumes and loses the form of money and the form of commodities, but preserves and expands itself through all these changes, value requires above all an independent form by means of which its identity may be asserted. Only in the shape of *money* does it possess this form. Money therefore forms the starting-point and the conclusion of every valorization process. It was £100 and now it is £110. But the money itself is only *one* of the *two forms* of value ... The capitalist knows that *all commodities*, however tattered they may look, or however badly they may smell, are in faith and in truth *money*, are by nature circumcised Jews, and, what is more, a wonderful means for making still more money out of money... *Value therefore now becomes value in process, money in process, and, as such, capital* (255–6).

How can the production process be seen as an instance of money producing money *even when capital has abandoned the immediate shape of money and taken the disguised shape of commodities*? The answer is as follows. For the analysis of the origin of surplus value, constant capital, which buys means of production, may be assumed as having zero value: even though, in fact, production goods act as bearers of dead labour 'sucking' living labour from workers. Thus, the metamorphosis from the money form to the commodity form is *irrelevant* for constant capital. Variable capital, in its turn, does *not* intervene in the capitalist labour process either in its money- or in its commodity-form, because the buying of means of subsistence through the expenditure of money wages falls outside production as such. What enter production are the *workers in flesh and blood* that the money wage bill is able to buy, and what matters is the *living* labour extracted from them. The value of the commodities they produce is determined by the quantity of labour *materialized* in them, by the *labour-time socially necessary to produce* use-values. This value is *calculated* before actual exchange as a *monetary* magnitude through its *price*, which *directly* expresses as *average social labour*, as *immediately* social labour, the *indirectly* social labour embodied in commodities. Thus we have the 'objectification' of living labour expressed as a monetary quantity *before* final exchange on the commodity market. Since money as a commodity has a given purchasing power, this nominal quantity *expresses only that which labour in its 'fluid' dynamics has 'congealed' in the commodities* produced: something which can be 'ideally' reduced to a certain amount of labour time *before* actual circulation has taken place. For the same reason workers' *money wages are known as an expression of a given amount of labour time*, both because for Marx (as we already know) money is a commodity and because (as I will show) for him the level of the wages is determined by the labour materialized in the *real* subsistence basket.

It is clear then that *in any of its forms* capital is money 'in faith and in truth'. It is such because, *in any of its forms*, it is 'abstract wealth' producing more 'abstract wealth'. Abstract wealth must necessarily take the form of money, of course: but this 'nominal' monetary shape is *nothing but the outward expression of the 'latent' abstract labour* lying dormant within the 'real' form of existence of the commodities created by living labour, and struggling to 'come into being' as actual money in circulation (again, a Rubinian theme[19]). *Capital is neither money nor commodities, it is a self-moving substance for which both money and commodities are mere forms.* This self-moving substance is value creating more value. In the last instance value exhibits nothing but a quantity of objectified social labour. Money in circulation 'represents' this value, *already* given *before* final exchange as a 'latent' magnitude within commodities.

The 'general formula of capital', contrary to Moseley's reading, does not give any reason to privilege the accounting of values starting from

19. See Rubin (1928), throughout, and especially chapter 13.

the money shape of capital rather than the commodity shape as 'disguised' money in motion. The more so since in *Capital*, Volume I, the change of form does not entail any change in the magnitude of value. The two, given the assumption on relative prices, *mirror* each other. In fact, Marx is constructing a theoretical object of knowledge, which *definitely* has a quantitative dimension, but this quantitative dimension is *not yet* fully specified.

4.2 *Marx on the value of labour-power*

To resolve the issue of the determination of the wage we have to look for *explicit* statements by Marx on the value of labour-power. Marx is crystal clear in Volume I that he takes the *subsistence* wage as a 'given': and he never lets the reader think that taking the money wage as presupposed, as Marx also does, contradicts the *real* wage taken as a *known datum*. Though, in contrast with other commodities, the value of labour-power embodies an historical and moral element, Marx writes without any ambiguity that 'in a given country and at a given period, the *average* amount of *means of subsistence necessary* for the worker is a known datum' (275). On the previous page, Marx clarified that 'the production of labour-power consists in his reproduction and his maintenance. For his maintenance he requires a certain quantity of the means of subsistence. Therefore the labour-time necessary for the production of labour-power is the same as that necessary for the pro-duction of the means of subsistence', and it is in *this* sense that 'the *value of labour-power* is the *value of the means of subsistence necessary* for the maintenance of its owner' (274).

The issue comes up again on p. 340: the value of labour-power, 'like that of all other commodities, is determined by the labour-time necessary to produce it. If it takes 6 hours to produce the average daily means of subsistence of the worker, he must work an average of 6 hours a day to produce this daily labour-power, or to produce the *value* received as a result of this sale.' It is here evident that money wages have to 'reflect' the labour-values of the commodities going into the subsistence. The argument reappears again on p. 655: 'The value of labour-power is determined by the value of the means of subsistence habitually required by the average worker. [Though the *form* may change,] the *quantity* of the means of subsistence required is given at any particular epoch in a particular society, and can therefore be treated as a constant magnitude. What changes is *the value of this quantity*' (the words in brackets are omitted from the English translation). On p. 659 the point is a little obscured in the English translation: 'The value of labour-power is determined by the value of a <u>certain</u> [read: determinate] quantity of means of subsistence. It is the *value* and not *the mass* of these means of subsistence that varies with the productivity of labour'.[20] In sum: what is given is the *real* subsistence wage whose value may change, because of a change in the socially necessary labour needed to produce it. Its value may also change, I would add, if there is a change in the price rule and, therefore, in the 'representation' through money of the labour materialized in commodities, which compels to evaluate the subsistence consumption basket at the ongoing prices.

Marx knows very well that capitalists have to advance wages *in money* before the production process begins, though in reality money acts here not as means of purchase but as means of payment, with wages being paid to the workers only *after* work is done

> The price of the labour-power is fixed by the contract, although it is not realized till later, like the rent of a house. The labour-power is sold, although it is paid for only at a later period. It will therefore be useful, if we want to conceive the relation in its *pure* form, to pre-suppose for the moment that the possessor of labour-power, on the occasion of each sale, <u>immediately</u> receives the price stipulated in the contract (279).

He also knows very well that capitalists in practice try to force the price of labour-power *below* the value of labour-power. Thus, the amount of wage-goods received by workers may fall *under* the subsistence level as he defined it. This notwithstanding, he wants to analyse the capitalist generation of surplus-value again in its 'purity', and therefore he assumes that there is no cheating against workers. Indeed, Marx in the Part III chapter on 'The working day', as well as in the Part IV chapters on 'Co-operation', 'Division of labour' and 'Machinery and modern industry', shows how working-class struggles again and again *impose* – 'from below', so to speak, and *against* the individual capitalists' will – the subsistence basket needed by wage-earners to reproduce themselves. This subsistence wage is moreover taken by him only as the (minimum) ruling real wage, and the same workers' struggles may

20. In the first sentence 'determinate' should be substituted for 'certain' – the repetition occurs also in the German text, which reads: 'Der Wert der Arbeitskraft ist bestimmt durch den Wert eines *bestimmten* Quantums von Lebensmitteln' MEW 23, 545 (the italics are mine).

succeed in pushing it up.[21] This 'conventional' and 'conflictual' view of the subsistence wage justifies the hypothesis running throughout *Capital* that the amount of the money wage bill is *no less* than that which is needed to buy the given subsistence real wage.

4.3 A Luxemburghian perspective on the value of labour-power

Rosa Luxemburg, in her chapter on the wage in her *Introduction to Political Economy*, was probably the most lucid interpreter of Marx's theory on this point.[22] To understand Marx's position in its full force, the starting point is the qualitative difference, the *differentia specifica*, of wage-labour versus feudal labour; and it is necessary to show how this latter casts a new light on the consequences of the real subsumption of labour to capital and the related relative surplus-value extraction. Rosa Luxemburg underlines that in feudalism what is given is not the amount of output going to serfs but the one going to landlords, so that in principle the share of direct producers may rise along with their 'effort'. In capitalism, on the contrary, *the real subsistence is given*, and the share going to wage-workers is determined mainly and 'automatically' by the incessant technical change. The consequent rise of the productive-power of labour pushes *down* the value of wage-goods, 'necessary labour', and the relative position of the working class vis-à-vis the capitalist class. For Luxemburg this means that we may have a rise in the real wage together with a rise of the productive-power of labour, but that the former inevitably tends to *lag behind* the latter. Hence, a *fall in the 'relative' wage*, and therefore in the *share of living labour going to workers*. This is indeed the distributive 'law' in capitalism, according to Luxemburg.

The full thrust in Rosa Luxemburg's reading of Marx on the wage lies in the contrast between the workers' standard of living as a constant, *predetermined* magnitude, and capital's never-ending drive to increase *to the greatest possible extent* surplus-value, and thus surplus labour. To quote Marx again:

> The working day is thus not a constant, but a *variable quantity*. One of its parts, certainly, is determined by the labour-time required for the

---

21. For developments of this view of wage and distribution within the tradition of the theory of the monetary circuit, see Bellofiore and Realfonzo (1997) and Bellofiore *et al.* (2000).
22. See Luxemburg (1925). The absence of a full English translation of the book I hope will be remedied in the near future (only the first chapter is available). Rosdolsky (1968) in his Appendix to chapter XX, on Marx's wage theory, gives some excerpts from Luxemburg's book.

reproduction of the labour-power of the worker himself. But its total amount varies with the duration of surplus labour. The working day is therefore <u>capable of being determined</u>, but in and for itself is <u>indeterminate</u> (341).

When workers' struggles are able to win legal limits to the 'extensive' working day, blocking *mere prolongation* of the total amount of hours worked, capital's offensive takes the dual form of either an increase of the 'intensive' working day (through *higher intensity* of labour everywhere) or of making surplus labour a variable entity (through competition within the branches of production which, as we have seen, leads to a progressive lowering of social value everywhere, and thereby also to the ensuing devaluation of the value of labour-power).

It is important to understand that this tendency of the relative wage to fall, as the converse of relative surplus-value extraction, is an essential feature to understand Marx on income distribution. First of all, this reading allows us to reject the widespread idea that the labour theory of value as a theory of exploitation implies a worsening in capitalism of workers' well-being from the *use-value* point of view. This is clearly untenable, *since the relative wage may fall while the real wage rises.* Even with a fall in the money wage,

> it is possible, given increasing productive-power of labour, for the price of labour-power to fall constantly and for this fall to be accompanied by a constant growth in the mass of workers' means of subsistence. But in *relative* terms, i.e. in comparison with surplus-value, the value of labour-power would keep falling, and thus the abyss between the life-situation of the worker and that of the capitalist would keep widening (659)[23].

When and if this relative impoverishment has been countered, this has been the result of working-class struggles, not of an automatic, built-in tendency of capitalist mechanics.

This reading is also essential to see the original way Marx connects not only surplus-value extraction and distribution but also capitalist *accumulation* and income distribution: 'the rate of accumulation is the

---

23. I have substituted 'productive-power' for 'productivity' in the quote.

independent, not the dependent variable; the rate of wages is the dependent, not the independent variable' (770). The truth behind this assertion is twofold. First, though in each period the *real* wage is taken to be a *known datum*, capitalist accumulation puts forward an evolutionary dynamics which, on the one hand, pushes *down* the *relative* wage and, on the other, may accomodate an *increase* in time in the *real* wage through social conflict: that is, a rise in real wage which is *compatible* with a higher profitability and with further accumulation. Second, capitalist accumulation – as long as it implies a *qualitative* change in methods of production, and as long as it is not merely producing an extensive growth – is acting on *two* sides at once: on the demand for labour *and* on the supply of labour. It increases the demand at the same time that it makes some of the supply redundant, creating again and again an *industrial reserve army*, so that the pressure on wages is inhibited.

It must be noted, however, that this 'absolute' dependence of workers upon the capitalist class may be reversed in certain historical circumstances. The determination of the supply from demand – that is, the specific capitalist 'law of population' – may be turned upside down when the *potential* 'counter-productivity' of workers becomes *actual*: that is, when their struggles are powerful enough to interrupt the tendency of the relative wage to fall, and to limit capital's command in the labour process. This is what happened during the 1960s and 1970s, according to some 'productivist' versions of the profit-squeeze crisis theory: I am thinking here more of the early Aglietta than the Glyn-Sutcliffe version.[24] This view is quite consistent with the Marx I am presenting. That conflict within the capitalist labour process is the *core* of valorization and is *exactly* what much of *Capital*, Volume I, is about. Length of the social working day, intensity of labour, the ability of capital to 'exploit' the potential increase in the productive-power of labour: *all* these aspects are indeed 'capable of being determined', but are in and for themselves 'indeterminate'. To determine *them* capital needs to win workers' antagonism at the point of production, and this is indeed the *main* topic of the book (qualitatively *and* quantitatively).

We may conclude that Moseley's insistence that in Volume I 'values' are the 'givens', at least in the sense of being a *known datum*, cannot be accepted. In Marx's inquiry about (absolute or relative) surplus-value extraction, either the total (extensive or intensive) labour time spent or the unit-values of the commodities going into the subsistence bundle must be *variable*. Volume I explains the process of their 'formation' through

24. See Aglietta (1976) and Glyn and Sutcliffe (1972).

the intertwined processes of class struggle and 'dynamic' competition. If instead 'values' are taken to be the 'givens' in the weaker meaning that labour quantities are the 'independent variables' – allowed to vary, so to speak, 'from outside' in the inquiry included in Volume I – Moseley's position is again problematic. I have already shown in the previous section that the necessary reformulation of Marx's 'macro-monetary' perspective needed today makes money, as bank finance to production, enter *into the same constitution* of those same values even before immediate production begins, so that the existence of some (socially homogeneous) 'substance' of value is dependent on a monetary ante-validation.

4.4 The purchasing power of money capital and the value of labour-power in a non-commodity money view

Let me draw some implications from the argument above in a more reconstructive tone. If the real wage can be assumed as given and constant for *the subsistence* at the beginning of the capitalist circuit, then *the value of money-capital can be taken as given as an amount of labour time, even when money is not a commodity*. The purchasing power of variable money capital – the value of money *as capital* – at the opening of the Marxian monetary circuit is regulated by the labour time 'embodied' in the means of subsistence. *Given the average daily real wage*, the purchasing power of variable capital is then expressed by the *number of workers* bought by that monetary magnitude, and this latter magnitude depends from the subsistence bundle. *Given the expected 'degree of exploitation'*, these workers' labour-power can be ideally 'transformed' into *living labour*, and therefore into the *new value* produced in the period.

Two points need to be stressed. First, the abstraction of labour is, as Marx says in the *Grundrisse*, 'in becoming' in immediate production. It is an abstraction which is 'latent' in the objectified labour materialized in the commodity-output, and which awaits confirmation on the 'final' commodity market. In the view I am proposing, this abstraction decisively rests on bank finance *ante*validating the expected value and surplus-value production. It is this *monetary* process which *grants* that concrete labours transmit *a homogeneous social quality*, 'becoming' bearers of abstract labour. But this view compels us to abandon the theory of money as a commodity. Second, since abstract labour *eventually* 'comes into being' *only* in circulation, the monetary *ex post* validation is given only when (monetary) effective demand fixes money income and actual prices, irrespective of whether or not they gravitate around production prices. As a consequence, in a non-commodity monetary framework the purchasing power of money spent at the 'closing' of the

Marxian monetary circuit – the value of money *as income* – is known *only in final* exchange.

This means, of course, that Moseley's assertion that the 'value of money' must be assumed as given and constant cannot be taken for granted *once we abandon Marx's original conception of money as a commodity*. This is *not* meant as a criticism but simply as an implication. In order to be coherent Moseley has to openly embrace the view of money as a commodity as integral to the labour theory of value. In the different perspective I am putting forward here, the value of money ex post may be taken as known ex ante – *as long as the short-run expectations of firms about their ability to sell their output at 'ideal' money prices are assumed to be confirmed in commodity exchange at 'actual' money prices*. This is for the most part what Marx does over the three volumes of *Capital*, with very few exceptions.

If this is accepted, then Marx's sequence fully holds in my reconstruction: 'ideal' money prices represent only abstract labour 'congealed' in commodities – namely objectified labour whose preliminary, expected sociality must find an eventual validation through money as a universal equivalent, as general purchasing power. However, the sequence is a monetary sequence in a *stronger* sense than in Marx's original presentation, because living labour now acquires this *preliminary* social quality *only* because of an *ex ante*, and not merely thanks to an *ex post*, monetary confirmation through money universal equivalent.

5. 'Macro' versus 'micro' in Volume I and in the *Results*: a preliminary assessment

Things being this way, it is clear that at least two of the pillars of Moseley's interpretative line cannot be accepted. First, I have provided unambiguous textual evidence that Marx takes the value of labour-power as 'given' in *real* terms in the first volume of *Capital*. Second, I have clarified that, even though the value of money is 'given' before the analysis of valorization and pricing, as Moseley rightly stresses, this holds true *only* if Marx's original theory of money as a commodity is retained: a point which this author has never clearly stated. I take the theory of money as a commodity to be *insufficient* in the analysis of capitalism as a monetary production economy: it may be provisionally accepted only as the starting point of the systematic construction of *Capital*, when the capital/labour social relation and the production of capitalist commodities have not yet been the focus of the analysis, and the inquiry is limited to circulation on the commodity market. But when we come to a view of money as a 'sign', the value of money is determined *ex post* when the commodity output has been actually sold on the market. It can be taken as given *ex ante*, at the beginning of the monetary circuit, only under very precise assumptions about the expected outcome of class struggle in production and about the eventual realization of the (potential, ideal) surplus-value.

We must now confront Moseley's statement about the 'macroeconomic' nature of Marx's argument in Volume I. As I stated in the Introduction, I share with Moseley the plea for a 'macro-monetary' reading of Marx's theory. Yet, as before when commenting on the 'monetary' aspect of his perspective, I disagree with Moseley: in this case, again, what divides us is both the meaning to be given to the term 'macroeconomic' and the textual evidence. Moseley has to confront the fact that the 'macro' nature of the Volume I is, as he repeatedly writes, *not obvious*. His strategy is to interpret the indisputable fact that Marx very often analyses the valorization process at the level of *individual* capital as if this reference may be methodically extended to total capital – that is, as if individual capital could be seen as some kind of 'representative' of the aggregate. But this is, of course, 'macro' in the usual, mainstream economics meaning: where the macro system is nothing but the mere sum of the micro elements constituting it.

I rather see 'macro' as more than the sum of its constituent parts: a meaning where the 'macroeconomic' foundation and results are not only *prior* but also *opposed* to the micro logic: in a sense, the 'micro' is upside down relative to the 'macro'. In my view, the *priority* and *autonomy* of the 'macroeconomic' logic means that the inquiry has *first* to discover the laws of survival and growth of the system, and *afterwards* to show how individuals' behaviour obeys or contradicts those 'laws' of reproduction. The originality of Marx's position, if it is 'translated' into the later terminology, is not only in his macro-social foundation of microeconomics, but also in his careful analysis of the micro-competitive mechanism realising the systemic tendency, that is, in his *circular* journey from 'macro' to 'micro', and from 'micro' to 'macro'. The two movements are cancelled in a view which reduces the 'total' to the sum of individual capitals, and then arbitrarily makes this supposed 'macro' dimension a 'given' for the 'micro' behaviour of agents. The point cannot be treated adequately in the remaining space. What I will do is to give some *preliminary* assessment of how Marx treats the macroeconomic dimension in Volume I. The justification of this procedure will be that very few of Marx's quotes enable us to understand why and how the 'macro' logic is sometimes opposed and inverted relative to the 'micro' one: interestingly enough, this happens in connection with the determination of the wage for the working class.

When discussing the production of absolute surplus-value, Marx *explicitly* set his argument in a macro way, and this time it appears *as if* his approach can be read as mere *aggregation*. Marx writes: 'The labour which is set in motion by the total capital of a society, day in, day out, may be regarded as *a single working day*. If for example the number of workers is a million, and the average working day is 10 hours, *the social working day* will consist of 10 million hours' (422). In this direction go Moseley's quotes. This outlook may be confirmed when looking at how the surplus-value produced by a given capital is later defined: it is 'the surplus-value produced by each worker multiplied by the number of workers simultaneously employed... it is clear that the collective working day of a large number of workers employed simultaneously, divided by the number of these workers, gives one day of average social labour' (439–40). As long as we assume the macro social division between the capitalist class and the working class, and as long as the capitalist labour process is going on 'smoothly' as expected, and there is no dynamic competition and no structural change, Marx constructs the social working day as nothing but the sum of the socially necessary labour time spent in the different branches of production. From this point of view, the analysis of the extraction of the living labour from individual workers by individual capitalists may be safely extended to the total (but always keeping in mind the fact that what we are adding together are amounts of *socially* necessary labour time, and what this 'socially' means has still to be investigated).

Things change, however, in later chapters – and, as anticipated, it is significant that this happens in consideration of the *monetary* nature of the capitalist process and of the hidden nature of the *wage*. Look, for example, at the following quote:

The illusion created by the money-form vanishes immediately if, instead of taking a single capitalist and a single worker, we take the whole capitalist class and the whole working class. The capitalist class is constantly giving to the working class drafts, in the form of money, on a portion of the product produced by the latter and appropriated by the former. The workers give these drafts back just as constantly to the capitalists, and thereby withdraw from the latter their alloted share of their own product. The transaction is veiled by the commodity-form of the product and the money-form of the commodity. *Variable capital* is therefore only a *particular historical form of appearance* of the fund for providing the means of subsistence, or the *labour fund*, which the worker requires for his own maintenance and reproduction, and which in *all* systems of social production, he must himself produce and reproduce (713).

Here it is obvious that variable capital as a monetary advance is *hiding* the essential class process of income distribution, which can be understood only once the real wage – not of the individual worker, but *of the whole working class* – is taken as *given*. As in other pre-capitalist modes of production, the 'fund for providing the means of subsistence' must be taken as the *known datum*, the 'allotted share' for the workers – the *differentia specifica* of capitalism is relative to the dynamics of the (extensive and/or intensive) length of labour time and of the productive-power of workers. It is also clear that this truth may be grasped *only if*, to paraphrase Marx two pages later, 'we contemplate <u>not</u> the single capitalist and the single worker, <u>but</u> the capitalist class and the working class, *not* an isolated process of production, <u>but</u> capitalist production in its full swing, and on its actual social scale' (717). Because the macro and micro logics are *opposed*, and the latter *distorts* the former, a standard foreign to what seems at first appropriate to commodity production must be adopted: '<u>in place of</u> the individual capitalist and of the individual worker, we view them in their <u>totality</u>, as the capitalist <u>class</u> and the working <u>class</u>' (732). This way, to use Marx's phrase on the same page, 'To be sure, *the matter looks quite different*' than from the micro perspective. In fact, translated into contemporary jargon, Marx's journey in Volume I has been from (what appeared at first as) an inquiry about 'micro' and 'individual' valorization processes to the theoretical construction of the 'macro-social' production and reproduction of surplus-value *as a whole*, and then of the *constitution and reproduction* of the same class relation which was assumed at an earlier stage of the argument in the book. In fact, we have here an instance of Marx's (and Hegel's) method of the *positing of the presuppositions*.

Indeed, once the *entire* theoretical structure of Volume I of *Capital* is considered, it emerges that the conflictual extraction of living labour within production as contested terrain, rather than being a 'micro' process, is a 'macro' one incorporated in a larger complex capital/labour social relationship. This fundamental social relation – whose analysis is at the centre of *Capital*, Volume I – includes the bargaining on the so-called 'labour market', which in its turn is dependent on the intra-capitalist relationship between money-capital and industrial capital. The ground of the thesis according to which money income represents *nothing but* abstract labour follows from the argument that the capitalist class as *a whole* can gain abstract wealth *only if* it is able to control the extraction of living labour from the *whole* working class. Once this point is firmly grasped, then it can also be understood that it is this 'macro' process of class division that, through class struggle, determines either a higher intensity of labour or a lengthing of the social working day or an increase of its productive-power. Note, however, that the latter is obtained through the permanent hunt for extra profit – a competition not among but within industries which tends to differentiate the rate of profits. This *dynamic* competition here works in fact as the 'micro' process *defining* the productive configuration and the state of the techniques, and thereby what in the end determines the same *values* of commodities.

As a consequence, 'values' are not only *monetarily* constituted, through banks' *ante*-validation: as I stressed in prior sections of this chapter they are also the outcome of a *social* process, the intra-branch competition defining the *socially* necessary labour time, and can then be taken 'as given' only temporarily. The resulting structural change realizes the *systemic* tendency which, according to Marx, is implicit in the capital/labour social relationship itself: *but this latter would not become real without that kind of competition. Capital*, then, amounts to nothing less than a macro-foundation of micro-behaviour, *in a spiral*: a macro-foundation which, at the same time, is built upon a notion of competition very different from both the Classical and the Neoclassical 'free' and 'perfect' competition, in all their differences and disputes.

This mutual integration of the macro-social perspective and the micro-mechanism that realizes it is another reason why quantities of labour cannot too simply be taken as 'givens' in Volume I, and why the 'macro' system cannot be reduced to the sum of the 'micro' valorization processes. That in Marx the macro perspective is in a sense opposite to the micro one is crystal-clear on the issue of the wage in the *Results*. When analysing the origin of surplus-value at the 'individual' level, the theorist is compelled to look at the wage merely as a money magnitude, whose real counterpart depends on the price of commodities and on individual consumption choices by workers. But when the capitalist process is described in 'macro' terms things dramatically change. For the 'free' worker, according to Marx, the wage is received 'in the shape of *money, exchange-value*, the abstract social form of wealth . . . nothing more than the *silver* or *gold* or *copper* or *paper* form of the necessary means of subsistence into which it must constantly be dissolved' (1033). It is the worker who converts the money into the use-values he or she desires: and 'as the *owner of money*, as the buyer of goods, he stands in precisely the same relationship to the seller of goods as any other buyer' (p. 1033). This is the 'micro' perspective.

However, Marx had written before (pp. 1003–4), in a passage from which Moseley himself presents a quote, but so abridged that he loses the gist of the reasoning: 'if we think of the whole of capital as standing on one side, i.e. the totality of the purchasers of labour-power, and if we think of the totality of the vendors of labour-power, the totality of workers on the other', then 'all *material wealth* confronts the worker as *the property of the commodity possessors*', the capitalist firms. 'The fact that Capitalist No. 1 owns the money and that he buys the means of production from Capitalist No. 2, who owns them, while the worker buys the means of subsistence from Capitalist No. 3 with the money he has obtained from Capitalist No. 2 <u>does not alter the fundamental situation</u> that Capitalists No. 1, 2 and 3 are <u>together</u> the exclusive possessors of money, means of production and means of subsistence.' Thus, even in the initial circulation act, when money-capital confronts workers as labour-power on the labour market, and therefore *before* the real production process, 'what stamps money or commodities as *capital* from the outset . . . is neither their money nature nor their commodity nature, nor the material use-value of these commodities as means of production or subsistence, but the circumstance that this money and this commodity, these means of production and these means of subsistence confront *labour-power*, stripped of all material wealth, as autonomous powers, personified in their owners'. And he concludes:

> *Commodities*, in short, appear as the purchasers of *persons*. The buyer of labour-power is nothing but the personification of *objectified* labour which cedes a part of itself to the worker in the form of the means of subsistence in order to annex the living labour-power for the benefit of the remaining portion, so as to keep itself intact and even to grow beyond its original size by virtue of this annexation. <u>It is not the worker who buys the means of production and subsistence, but the means of subsistence that buy the worker to incorporate him into the means of production.</u>[25]

Marx could not have been clearer.

25. Unfortunately, the Penguin translation is here completely wrong, since 'the means of subsistence' in the last phrase is translated as 'the means of production'. But in the *Collected Works* the point is translated correctly: 'It is

6. Instead of a conclusion

Let me draw very quickly to a close. The present chapter has shown that Fred Moseley is quite right in stressing the 'macro-monetary' aspects of Marxian theory. It is true that for Marx value and money are inextricably linked. It is also true that important points in his argument nowadays sound definitely macroeconomic in their structure.

Unfortunately, Moseley fails to stress adequately how the original Marxian formulation of the monetary labour theory of value is built upon a view of money *as a commodity*, which also grounds the assertion that the value of money is a 'given' at the beginning of the cycle of money capital. Moseley also has not until now confronted the various unambiguous quotes where it is clear that Marx's wage theory is based on the idea that the *real* subsistence wage has to be taken as the *known datum*. More generally, Moseley sees 'money' aggregate quantities (constant and variable capital plus surplus-value) as a mere *veil* of the amounts of labour they represent; and interprets 'macro' as the mere *sum* of individual capitals and workers.

I have tried to present an alternative account of Marx as a *macro-monetary foundation of microeconomics* within a *non-commodity theory of money*.

I have argued that banks' *ante*validation of valorization is a *necessary* precondition for the *social homogeneity* of the various *living* labours spent in different capitalist labour processes. Thanks to this, each of them is part of the same (latent) abstract labour *prior* to commodity circulation (to be eventually validated ex post by the universal equivalent). This has allowed me to *maintain* Marx's clear sequence going *from* ideal value (or ideal money) *to* actual value (or actual money) as a 'necessary form of manifestation' of *nothing but* quantities of labour time. We have here a *new* view of capitalist 'exploitation' as affecting the *whole* social working day, a view which better than Marx's succeeds in grounding the thesis that the (new) value produced is the objectification and materialization of *nothing but* the (living) labour *conflictually* extracted in

not a case of the worker buying means of subsistence and means of production, but of the means of subsistence buying the worker, in order to incorporate him into the means of production'. See Marx (1867, 1990) in the translation from Collected Economic Writings of Marx and Engels, vol 34, page 411. The original German is: 'Es ist nicht der Arbeiter, der Lebensmittel und Produktionsmittel kauft, sondern die Lebensmittel kaufen den Arbeiter, um ihn den Produktionsmitteln einzuverleiben' (quoted from the MEGA^2, II/4.1: 78, 16–18, the italics are mine).

immediate production within the *whole* economy. Moreover, I have shown how this 'macro' perspective is necessary to fully understand Marx's theory of the determination of the wage and the dependence of distribution on accumulation. Following this lead, I have presented evidence according to which the *real* consumption of *all* workers as decided in fact (though unconsciously) by the capitalist class is *strictly* Marxian, though this appears to contradict what the 'micro' perspective suggests.

It is interesting that in this different perspective the 'monetary' aspects of Marxian theory are a major example of what Schumpeter (1954: 276–278) defined as *monetary analysis* in his *History of Economic Analysis*. We have here an analysis where money is not secondary, but introduced *on the very ground floor* of the analytic structure. It cannot be reduced to an "expression' of quantities of commodities, because it has a life and an importance *of its own*, and affects *all* the essential features of the capitalist process: even in the same *constitution* and *quantitative determination* of real magnitudes. It is also interesting that in Marx we already find Keynes's idea that the 'macro' logic is not only prior but *opposed* and *inverted* in many respects to the 'micro' logic.

But how, then, to interpret the fact that in *Capital* we have *both* the money wage-bill *and* the real subsistence as givens? Does this signal an implicit contradiction in the Marxian system, which Marx himself didn't fully grasped? I don't think so; and even if an interpretative line of this kind is taken, this supposed contradiction could be overcome staying within the macro-monetary labour theory of value as I have sketched it. Once Volume I of *Capital* is interpreted and reconstructed along the lines of this chapter, and once the outcome of the transformation of values into prices of production is taken into account,[26] we may look to the capitalist process in a different way than usual. The circuit of money capital 'opens' and 'closes' with money magnitudes. The quantity of labour 'represented' by constant and variable capital (as *given* amounts of *money*) must now be determined by evaluating the means of production and the means of subsistence at prices of production. At the same time the value produced in the *whole* economy is nothing but the labour 'represented' by constant capital plus the living labour extracted by the capitalist *class* from *all* workers, the new value, represented by *money* income. Subtracting from this latter magnitude the labour represented by the *money* wage bill, we have surplus-value as an amount of labour 'represented' in gross *money* profits. But *hidden behind* this there is the

26. See Bellofiore (2002).

real division of the output accomplished by the unconscious but powerful behaviour driving the capitalist class, which fixes a *given* real wage for the working *class* whose minimum level is the 'subsistence'. In other words, behind the labour 'represented' in money wages and in money gross profits we have a division of commodity output *resulting* from class struggle in production, which corresponds to a division of the social working day between the 'necessary labour' *congealed* in the means of subsistence (the labour time needed to *produce* them) and the residual 'surplus labour' once the former is subtracted from the living labour of workers.

The appearance – namely, given *money* wages and gross *money* profits, *even* 'translated' in the amount of labour they are able to 'command' on the market at the prevailing price rule – *disguises* the essential process, the given real 'macro' and 'class' division of real output between classes. The 'essential' process of exploitation is quite clearly the one we got from *Capital*, Volume I, an essential process *fully* captured by the argument in 'values', that is, holding strictly to Marx's major assumption about the 'price rule' needed for the inquiry about the 'formation of capital' in its purity. And this essential process stays the same, as the *core* of capitalist valorization, throughout the whole systemic construction.

References

Aglietta, Michel (1976), *A Theory of Capitalist Regulation: The US Experience* (Eng. trans. 1979) (London: New Left Books).

Arthur, Chris (1993), Hegel's *Logic* and Marx's *Capital*, in Fred Moseley (ed.) (1993): 63–87.

— (1999), Napoleoni on labour and exploitation, in Riccardo Bellofiore and Mario Baldassarri (eds) (1999): 141–63.

Bellofiore, Riccardo (1985a), Marx after Schumpeter. *Capital and Class*, 24: 60–74.

— (1985b), Money and development in Schumpeter, *Review of Radical Political Economics*, 1–2: 21–40. Also in John Cunningham Wood (ed.) *Joseph Alois Schumpeter: Critical Assessments*, Vol. IV (London: Routledge, 1991): 371–94.

— (1989), A monetary labour theory of value, *Review of Radical Political Economics*, 21, 1–2: 1–25.

— (ed.) (1997), *Marxian Theory: The Italian Debate*, special issue of *International Journal of Political Economy*, XXVII 2 (Summer).

— (ed.) (1998), *Marxian Economics: A Centenary Appraisal*, 2 vols (London/New York: Macmillan/St. Martin's Press).

— (1998), Marx's theory of money and credit: a comment on the chapters by Suzanne de Brunhoff and Ferdinando Meacci, in Bellofiore (ed.) (1998): 205–15.

— (1999), The value of labour value. the debate on Marx in Italy: 1968–1976, in Riccardo Bellofiore and Mario Baldassarri, (eds) (1999): 31–69.

— (2001), Marxian economic thought, in N.J. Smelser and Paul B. Baltes (eds), *International Encyclopedia of the Social & Behavioral Sciences* (Oxford: Pergamon): 9286–92.

— (2002), 'Transformation' and the monetary circuit: Marx as a monetary theorist of production, in Martha Campbell and Geert Reuten (eds), *The Culmination of Capital: Essays on Volume III of Marx's 'Capital'*. (London/New York: Macmillan/St Martin's Press): 102–27.

— (2004), As if its body were by love possessed. Abstract labour and the monetary circuit: a macro-social reading of Marx's labour theory of value, in Richard Arena and Neri Salvadori (eds), *Money, credit and the role of the state. Essays in honour of Augusto Graziani* (Aldershot: Ashgate), forthcoming.

— and Mario Baldassari (eds) (1999), *Classical and Marxian Political Economy: A Debate on Claudio Napoleoni's views*, special issue of *Rivista di Politica Economica* (April–May).

— and Roberto Finelli (1998), Capital, labour and time. the Marxian monetary labour theory of value as a theory of exploitation, in Riccardo Bellofiore (ed.), (1998): 48–74.

— Forges Davanzati, Guglielmo and Riccardo Realfonzo (2000), Marx inside the circuit. Discipline device, wage bargaining and unemployment in a sequential monetary economy, *Review of Political Economy*, XII 4 (December): 403–17.

— and Riccardo Realfonzo (1997), Finance and the labor theory of value. Toward a macroeconomic theory of distribution from a monetary perspective, in Riccardo Bellofiore (ed.) (1997): 97–118.

— and Mario Seccareccia (1999), Monetary circuit, in Philip Anthony O'Hara (ed.) (1998) *Encyclopedia of Political Economy* (London, Routledge): 753–756.

Colletti, Lucio (1969), *From Rousseau to Lenin. Studies in Ideology and Society* (Eng. trans. 1972) (London: New Left Books).

Dobb, Maurice (1937), *Political Economy and Capitalism. Some Essays in Economic Tradition* (London: Routledge).

Glyn, Andrew and Bob Sutcliffe, (1972), *British Capitalism, Workers, and the Profit Squeeze*. (London: Penguin).

Graziani, Augusto (1983a), Let's rehabilitate the labour theory of value, in Riccardo Bellofiore (ed.) (1997): 21–5 .

— (1983b), The Marxist theory of money, in Riccardo Bellofiore (ed.) (1997): 26–50.

Grossmann, Henryk (1941), Marx, classical political economy and the problem of dynamics. English translation in *Capital and Class*, 2 (1977): 32–55 and 3 (1977): 67–99.

Luxemburg, Rosa (1925) *Einführung in die Nationalökonomie*. Collected in *Ausgewählte Reden und Schriften*, II.

Marx, Karl (1863–1866), *Results of the Immediate Production Process*, Appendix in Marx (1867, 1890).

— (1867, 1890), *Capital*, Volume I (Harmondsworth: Penguin, 1976). Another translation in English is from the third edition (1884), in vol. 34 of Collected Economic Writings of Marx and Engels: *Capital, A Critical Analysis of Capitalist Production, Volume I* (1974) (London, Lawrence and Wishart). See, for the original German edition, MEW. (Marx-Engels-Werke), vol. 23: *Das Kapital. Kritik der Politischen Ökonomie Erster Band*, (Berlin: Dietz Verlag). For the German original of the *Results of the Immediate Production Process*, included in the Penguin edition, see MEGA2, II/4.1: *Ökonomische Manuskripte 1863–1867* (1988–1992) (Berlin: Dietz Verlag).

Moseley, Fred (1993), Marx's logical method and the transformation problem, in Fred Moseley (ed.), *Marx's Method in 'Capital': A Reexamination* (Atlantic Highlands, NJ: Humanities Press).

— (1997), The development of Marx's theory of the distribution of surplus-value in Fred Moseley and Martha. Campbell (eds), *New Perspectives on Marx's Method in 'Capital'* (Atlantic Highlands, NJ: Humanities Press).

— (2002), Hostile brothers: Marx's theory of the distribution of surplus-value in Volume III of *Capital*, in Martha Campbell and Geert Reuten (eds), *The Culmination of Capital: Essays on Volume III of Marx's 'Capital'* (Basingshoke: Palgrave Macmillan).

— (2003), Money and totality: Marx's logic in Volume I of *Capital*, Chapter 6 in this volume.

Napoleoni Claudio (1973), *Smith Ricardo Marx* (Eng. Trans. 1975) (Oxford: Blackwell).

— (1972), *Lezioni sul Capitolo sesto inedito* Torino: Boringhieri.

Realfonzo, Riccardo and Riccardo Bellofiore (2003), Money as finance and money as general equivalent: re-reading Marxian monetary theory, in Sergio Rossi and Louis-Philippe Rochon (eds), *Modern Theories of Money: The Nature and Role of Money in Capitalist Economies* (Cheltenham/Northampton: Edward Elgar): 198–218.

Reuten, Geert and Michael Williams (1989), *Value-Form and the State. The Tendencies of Accumulation and the Determination of Economic Policy in Capitalist Society*. (London: Routledge).

Rosdolsky, Roman (1968), *The Making of Marx's Capital* (Eng. trans. 1977) (London: Pluto Press).

Rubin, Isaak I. (1928), *Essays on Marx's Theory of Value* (Eng. trans. 1973) (Montreal: Black Rose Books).

Schumpeter, Joseph Alois (1954), *History of Economic Analysis* (London: Allen and Unwin).

Sweezy, Paul (1942), *The Theory of Capitalist Development. Principles of Marxian Political Economy* (Eng. Trans. 1970) (New York: Monthly Review Press).

Reply to Bellofiore by Fred Moseley

I appreciate Riccardo Bellofiore's critical attention to my interpretation of Marx's theory in his chapter, and I am happy to note that Bellofiore seems to agree with the two main points of my chapter in this volume. Although we have some disagreements about what exactly is meant by 'macro' and 'monetary', Bellofiore seems to agree that Volume I is about the determination of monetary variables, especially the increment of money or surplus-value that is the main purpose of capitalist production, and that Volume I is about the determination of the total surplus-value produced in the capitalist economy as a whole. These are important agreements that should not be forgotten.

One important point in my 'macroeconomic' interpretation of Marx's theory, that Bellofiore does not discuss, is that the total surplus-value that is determined in Volume I is then taken as given in Volume III, and *does not change* as a result of the distribution of surplus-value that is analysed in Volume III. The textual evidence to support this interpretation is very strong, as I have presented in two papers (Moseley 1997 and 2002; please see the references in Chapter 6 in this volume). This assumption is repeated in every part of Volume III and in the earlier drafts of Volume III. I will return to this point below.

Our main disagreement is over the determination of variable capital (we would probably have a similar disagreement over the determination of constant capital, but Bellofiore's emphasis is on variable capital). I argue (along with the 'new solution' of Foley and Duménil, etc.) that variable capital is *taken as given*, as the actual money-capital advanced by capitalists to purchase labour-power, and that this given money variable capital remains the same in both Volume I and Volume III. Bellofiore argues, on the other hand (along with most other Marxists and interpreters of Marx), that variable capital is *derived from a given quantity of means of subsistence*, and that therefore variable capital changes from Volume I to Volume III. In Volume I, variable capital is equal to the value of the given means of subsistence, and in Volume III variable capital is equal to the price of production of the same given means of subsistence.

I argue that there is considerable textual evidence, which I have presented in several papers (Moseley, 1993, 2000 and 2001), to support my interpretation that variable capital is taken as given. Bellofiore argues, and I agree, that there is also textual evidence to support his interpretation that the quantity of means of subsistence is taken as given. However, what Bellofiore seems to overlook is that it does not necessarily follow that this given quantity of means of subsistence is used to determine the magnitude of variable capital in Marx's theory of surplus-value in Volume I.

According to my interpretation of Marx's logical method, variable capital cannot be determined in Volume I, because variable capital refers to the *actual* quantity of money-capital advanced to purchase labour-power, which is equal to the *price of production* of the given means of subsistence, and the price of production of means of subsistence cannot be determined in Volume I. The determination of the price of production has to do with the division of the surplus-value into individual parts, and this division of surplus-value can be explained only in Volume III, after the total amount of surplus-value has been determined in Volume I. Therefore, the actual money wage cannot be determined in Volume I, and is instead taken as given. The given actual variable capital is then used in Volume I to explain the actual total surplus-value produced.

So what role does the given quantity of means of subsistence play in Marx's theory?

First of all, it provides in Volume I a *partial explanation* of the given actual variable capital in Volume I – that it depends *in part* on the value of the given means of subsistence. Then in Volume III, it provides a *more complete explanation* of the given actual variable capital – that it also depends on the equalization of profit rates across industries, which determines the price of production of the given wage goods. But the given means of subsistence cannot be used in Volume I to determine the actual variable capital (as explained above), and therefore plays no role in the determination of the actual surplus-value in Volume I. Instead, the actual variable capital is taken as given, and used to determine the actual surplus-value.

Bellofiore's interpretation of the determination of variable capital in Volume I from given means of subsistence implies that the magnitude of the variable capital changes as a result of the determination of prices of production. Therefore the total surplus-value also changes inversely in Volume III, thereby contradicting Marx's basic assumption in Volume III of a given, unchanging total surplus-value. My interpretation, on the other hand, of a given and unchanging variable capital, is consistent with the basic assumption of Volume III of a given and unchanging total surplus-value. Since variable capital does not change in Volume III, the total surplus-value also remains unchanged in Volume III.

Therefore, taking variable capital as given, as the actual variable capital advanced, seems to be the most reasonable interpretation of Marx's method of determination of variable capital, because only this assumption is consistent with Marx's basic assumption in Volume III of a given, unchanging total surplus-value. If, instead, one takes the real wage as given, this contradicts the basic assumption of Volume III, and the whole logic of Volume III falls apart. Why choose an interpretation of Marx's determination of variable capital that contradicts his basic assumption regarding the determination of the total surplus-value and leads to further 'logical errors' allegedly committed by Marx (failing to transform the inputs in the determination of prices of production), when there is an alternative interpretation with at least as much supporting textual evidence and that makes Marx's theory a logically consistent whole?

References

Duménil Gérard (1980), *De la valeur aux prix de production* (Paris: Economica).

Foley Duncan (1982), The Value of Money, the Value of Labor Power, and the Marxian Transformation Problem, *Review of Radical Political Economics*, XIV, 2: 37–47.

Rejoinder to Moseley by Riccardo Bellofiore

I am happy to engage in a dialogue with Fred Moseley; the reciprocal criticism helps to locate (some of) our disagreements. I see that Moseley, on his side, is happy to note that I 'seem to agree' that Volume I is 'macro' and 'monetary'. Unfortunately, I fear that behind the similarity of this label the differences are too many.

First, there is in *Capital* no 'fixed' unchanging quantity running throughout the three volumes. The quantitative incarnation of value depends on the development of the theoretical argument at different layers of abstraction. To give an example, in the first part of Volume I Marx shows that to see how value 'comes into being' we have to *integrate* production proper *and* circulation, so that the commodity must affirm itself in *final* commodity exchange as use-value *for others*. From Part Two of Volume I up until the middle of Part Two of Volume III, he *assumes* that all the commodity output is *sold*, so that supply equals demand. In Chapter 10 of Volume III he begins to remove this major assumption: changes in ordinary demand *may* now affect the magnitude of value produced at the sectoral level.

Second, Volume I is *also*, but *not only*, about monetary quantities (and I would add that even this does not imply that the latter remains fixed in the three volumes). Indeed, a large part of the book explains how the *whole* new value produced in the year follows from the 'exploitation' of living labour-power, and then from the variability of extensive and intensive length of the working day and of productive-power, with labour-values as variable entities. This will have further quantitative (also monetary) determinations in the other volumes, and as I have said even the magnitude of value *may change* in the course of *Capital*. As long as capitalist firms have produced in accord with sectoral demand (and only with this caveat), however, it is true that the outcome of class struggle within production – that is, the amount of socially necessary labour time and the new monetary value exhibiting it – *remains the same* in the three volumes. In this sense, the 'value' dimension is perfectly adequate in itself, and there is no need of further approximations or concretions. When demand changes, we have to modify the quantitative determination, but this is *not* a cancellation of 'ideal' money expressing the new value produced by workers.

Third, Moseley's attempt to define Volume I as 'macro' in its entirety is pure 'reconstruction', not 'interpretation'. Marx's method for more than two-thirds of *Capital I* is very different, and definitely not 'macro'. In most of Volume I, individual capitals are the subject of the inquiry, and they are treated not as aliquot parts of the aggregate but as *typical* case. I have tried to show, however, that especially in Part Seven Marx resorts, here and there, to what today appears as an openly 'macro' argument, and that this is especially amazing in a quote from the *Results*: here Marx is talking about accumulation and the reproduction of *social total capital*, and about real wage determination for the *working class*. The agreement with Moseley here is simply that I think that a *reconstruction* of *Capital* as a 'macro-monetary foundation of microeconomics' is a reasonable enterprise *in itself*, and that it captures what today appears to me as *most relevant* in his legacy.

About the determination of variable capital, I find Moseley's argument very awkward. He (now) agrees that there is *overwhelming textual evidence* that Marx took the quantity of *means of subsistence* as *given*. He then writes. 'Variable capital refers to the *actual* quantity of money-capital advanced to purchase labour-power, which is equal to the *price of production* of the given means of subsistence, and the price *of* production of means of production cannot be determined in Volume I ... therefore, the actual money wage cannot be determined in Volume I' (p. 212). It is *exactly* my position. But then Moseley says: since Marx cannot determine variable capital in Volume I, he takes the money wage bill as *given*, and *derives from it* total surplus-value. I find very strange the idea that something which *cannot be determined* is then *assumed* as a *given quantity*. I fear that what sustains this procedure is the idea that this has something to do with Hegel's logic (which I doubt) and that it is good as long as the empirical predictions are corroborated by the historical evidence. This would appear to me as a mixture of idealism and empiricism.

Moseley says that for me the magnitude of capital changes as a result of the determination of prices of production. But the only reason this does not happen in his approach is because he *superimposes* on Volume I the *same* quantity of money capital as that which would be determined in Volume III as *the real wage bill at prices of production*. Since there cannot be *any* price of production notion in Volume I, Moseley then takes this quantity *as a stipulation*. Indeed, in his reply Moseley advances the suggestion that his interpretation of Volume I should be preferred because it makes this volume coherent with Volume III.[1]

---

1. Moseley points out that he agrees with Foley's and Duménil's definition of the 'value of labour power'. *So do I*. As the two authors have stressed many times, theirs are definitional *ex post* accounting identities. They are compatible with the idea that, though the value of labour-power in Volume I is temporarily assumed as the given real subsistence wage at labour-values, in Volume III it may be given by the real subsistence wage at prices of production.

Moseley and I now agree that Marx assumed the real wage as given in Volume I; and that variable capital in money can be accurately defined only when prices of production are determined. If this opens up a tension within Marx's argument, this is not a good reason to cancel it.[2]

2. Moseley says I have *not* commented on his interpretation of Volume III. The reader finds in Bellofiore (2002: 120–1) some critical remarks on his approach to the transformation problem.

8
Technology and History in Capitalism: Marxian and Neo-Schumpeterian Perspectives

Tony Smith[1]

The equilibrium models of neoclassical economics fail to account adequately for one of the most striking facts of capitalism, its unprecedented technological dynamism. Extrapolating from Schumpeter's notion of 'creative destruction', contemporary neo-Schumpeterian economists have formulated a devastating critique of the neoclassical theory of technological change.[2] Their position can be provisionally defined in terms of the following six theses:

- technological change is endogenous to capitalism;
- science tends to become increasingly central to production;
- 'learning by doing' is of fundamental importance in the innovation process;
- technological change cannot be adequately comprehended in abstraction from the institutional context in which it occurs, including the organizational structures of firms and the technology policies of states;

1. I would like to thank Chris Arthur, Riccardo Bellofiore, Fred Moseley, Patrick Murray, Geert Reuten, Nicola Taylor and, especially, Martha Campbell for their many helpful comments and criticisms on earlier drafts of this paper.
2. See Coombs *et al*. (1987) Chapter 2 and Coricelli and Dosi (1988). For the purposes of this chapter the terms 'neo-Schumpeterianism' and 'evolutionary economics' will be used interchangeably. Readers interested in the contrast between Marx and Schumpeter himself should consult Bellofiore (1985a, 1985b).

- capitalism is characterized by radical uncertainty and disequilibrium tendencies due to technological change; and
- different technologies and forms of social organization play leading roles in different periods of capitalist development.[3]

It is noteworthy that these six theses are all defended in the first volume of *Capital* as well.[4] Neo-Schumpeterians acknowledge Marx as an important predecessor. Nonetheless, they clearly hold that whatever Marx had to say of continuing validity regarding technology in capitalism can be easily incorporated within their perspective. If this were true, there would be little reason to consider the theory of technology in Volume I besides historical curiosity. But it is not true. In this chapter I shall discuss three crucial issues for which the claim does not hold: the subsumption of technological change under the valorization imperative, the connection between technological change and the capital/wage labour

---

3. Formal models and extensive empirical evidence in support of these theses are found in the following representative neo-Schumpeterian works: Dosi *et al.*, 1988; Saviotti and Metcalfe, 1991; Freeman, 1992, Part II; Nelson, 1995; Metcalfe, 1997; Freeman and Soete, 1999; Ziman, 2000; and Freeman and Louçã, 2001.
4. A few citations must suffice here (see Smith, 1997 for a fuller account). 'Modern industry never views or treats the existing form of production process as the definitive one. Its technical basis is therefore revolutionary, whereas all earlier modes of production were essentially conservative' (Marx, 1867: 617; unless otherwise noted, all page references are to this text). Marx recognizes that this endogenous process of innovation becomes more science-intensive over time: '(l)arge-scale industry ... makes science a potentiality for production which is distinct from labour and presses it into the service of capital' (482). Nonetheless, even science-based innovation requires on-going 'learning by doing' at the point of production: 'The problem of how to execute each particular process, and to bind the different partial processes together into a whole, is solved by the aid of machines, chemistry, etc. But of course, in this case too, *the theoretical conception must be perfected by accumulated experience on a large scale*' (502, italics added). Chapter 15, Section 4 of Marx, 1867 ('The factory') presents an exemplary account of the relationship between the command structure of production within capitalist firms and technological change. Regarding the state, legislation limiting the length of the working day plays a crucial role in Marx's account of the emergence of systems of machinery, to cite only one example (see 533–4, 607). Taken together, these factors ensure that the 'tendency on the part of the various spheres of production towards equilibrium comes into play only as a reaction against the constant upsetting of this equilibrium' (476). Finally, in Volume I Marx describes in great detail the role of technology in the evolution from the epoch of manufacturing to that of big industry.

relation, and the role of technological change in assessments of the world historical significance of capitalism.

1. Technological change and the self-valorization of value

For neo-Schumpeterians the conceptual apparatus of evolutionary biology provides helpful tools for theorizing technological change in capitalism. The flavour of this approach is captured in the following passage from Richard Nelson:

> The general concept of evolution that I propose...involves the following elements. The focus of attention is on a variable or set of them that is changing over time and the theoretical quest is for an understanding of the dynamic process behind the observed change; a special case would be a quest for understanding the current state of a variable or a system in terms of how it got there. The theory proposes that the variable or system in question is subject to somewhat random variation or perturbation, and also that there are mechanisms that systematically winnow that variation. Much of the predictive or explanatory power of that theory rests with its specification of the systematic selection forces. It is presumed that there are strong inertial tendencies preserving what has survived the selection process. However in many cases there are also forces that continue to introduce new variety, which is further grist for the selection mill (Nelson, 1995: 54).

Evolutionary accounts of technology in capitalism, then, must address three main questions: What are the basic units of evolution? What mechanisms generate technological variations? And what mechanisms are responsible for selecting the subset of those variations that are evolutionarily successful? A wide range of answers has been given to each question.

Possible units of technological evolution in capitalist markets mentioned by neo-Schumpeterians include technological artefacts, the technological knowledge embodied in those artefacts, the organizational routines of firms, the firms themselves, interfirm networks, geographical regions and national innovation systems.[5] Evolutionary economists

---

5. 'Whereas the gene has come to be recognized as the fundamental unit of selection in biology, it is still unclear at what level evolutionary selection and innovation operate in socio-economic systems. In terms of the Schumpeterian model of creative destruction, for example, it is not obvious whether the basic

have explored various mechanisms generating technological variations in these units, including the cognitive processes of individual researchers (Carlson, 2000), the risk-taking disposition of entrepreneurs (Schumpeter, 1934), the organized searches of research and development labs (Schumpeter, 1947), the formal and informal interactions occurring within networks of firms and geographical regions where particular industries are clustered (Schrader, 1991), communication between technologists and users of the technology (Lundvall, 1988), various technology policies of states and interstate regulatory bodies (Dosi *et al.*, 1988: Part V; Nelson, 1993; Freeman, 1997), the cultural values that generate dispositions to engage in scientific research and to innovate (Landes, 1999), and so on. Finally, a plurality of mechanisms responsible for selecting certain technological variations and rejecting others have been proposed as well. These include success in responding to natural constraints discovered through Bayesian learning processes (David, 2000; Constant, 2000), compatibility with established technological paradigms (Dosi, 1988), compatibility with cultural practices and political interests (Nelson, 1993), and, most of all, suitability to human needs as revealed through market success.[6]

It should go without saying that these sorts of factors must be part of any rich and plausible account of technological evolution. Marxists have a great deal to learn from the insights of neo-Schumpeterians on these matters. The problem from a Marxian standpoint is not so much what the above list includes, but rather what it omits. We may begin with a discussion of the relevant unit(s) of economic evolution. In neo-Schumpeterian writings we find technological artefacts, technological knowledge, the routines of firms, interfirm networks, regions and states all considered as possible units of technological evolution in capitalism. But we do not find a discussion of *capital*. And this, as they say, is like staging *Hamlet* without the prince. For Marx the

---

    unit should be the firm, or the innovation or technology itself. In addition, one may attempt to model behavioural strategies, rules of thumb, etc., as subject to an evolutionary process. All of these approaches are represented in the literature. It remains to be seen to what extent they can be reconciled' (Silverberg, 1988: 538).
6. '[T]echniques exist for an unequivocal, deeper purpose – namely to increase the utility of human agents. Each technique, when it is applied, serves an "ultimate" purpose, which, while obviously intertwined and correlated with its fitness, can be treated separately ... Ultimately a selector will have to be judged by its success in satisfying human needs, and the survival of each entity is correlated with that criterion' (Mokyr, 2000: 62–3).

various factors discussed by neo-Schumpeterians are all incorporated within a higher-order complex totality, a 'self-moving substance which passes through a process of its own, and for which commodities and money are both mere forms' (256; see Campbell, Chapter 3 in this volume). Whatever other aspects of Marx's account have been assimilated within the neo-Schumpeterian framework, this notion of capital is absent.

Marx is certainly aware of how bizarre it is to assert that capital is a 'self-moving substance' undergoing evolution in the course of technological development. Isn't this way of speaking blatantly guilty of reifying an abstraction, that is, treating it as if it were a thing? But for Marx 'capital' is not merely a formal abstraction, a mere name referring to features common to investment money (M), commodities purchased as inputs to production (C), the production process (P), the inventories of commodities that emerge from production (C'), and the money accumulated after final sale (M'). 'Capital' is the principle of unity underlying the entire M–C–P–C'–M' circuit, forming it into a single dynamic whole. More complexly, 'capital' is a higher-order unity that maintains its identity within countless dispersed chains of particular capital circuits, a unity expressed quantitatively in accumulation on the level of total social capital (Moseley, 2002).

In capitalist societies artefacts, individuals, firms, networks, markets and states are subsumed under capital. They all take on qualitatively distinct and historically specific shapes when subsumed under the capital form, and they can only be adequately comprehended in terms of their contributions to capital's self-reproduction (Murray, 1998). Specifically, they are subjected to certain systematic mechanisms ensuring that they tend to function in a manner fulfilling the immanent goal of the capital form, capital accumulation. Among the most important of these mechanisms are those underlying the processes of variation and selection in technological evolution.

From a Marxian standpoint the myriad factors introduced by neo-Schumpeterians to account for technological variations are all necessary conditions for the possibility of technological change in capitalism. But there is nothing specifically capitalist about individual cognitive processes, risk-taking, interactions within organizations, informal communications across organizations, market transactions, or state formations. The items on this list have all been present in a wide variety of historical contexts. Even the most comprehensive list of this sort is thus unable to account for the unprecedented rate of technological variation in the capitalist mode of production. We need to comprehend how these factors are essentially transformed once they have been subsumed under the capital form.

Technological variations can be grouped under the heading of product innovations and process innovations. Use-values are the bearers of exchange-values, and so the self-valorization of value demands the production of commodities with some sort of use to those who purchase them (179–80, 201). If a particular unit of capital successfully introduces new products useful to those with disposable income, it can steal market share from the existing product lines of competitors or open entirely new markets. Units of capital that do not engage in this form of innovation lose market share or are shut out of new markets entirely. As a result individual units necessarily tend to act in a manner furthering the accumulation of total social capital. This necessity cannot be comprehended through reference to technological artefacts themselves, or the dispositions, capacities and needs of individuals, or the mere presence of firms, networks, markets and states. The systematic imperative to product innovation arises only when these phenomena are incorporated within the higher-order unity of the self-valorization of value. It is this that accounts for the unprecedented rate of new product variations in the system as a whole.

The necessary tendency for process innovations follows immediately from the thesis that surplus-value, the difference between the money-capital initially invested in a given period and the money-capital accumulated at the conclusion of that period, represents surplus labour. If we assume sufficient demand for the produced commodities, any increase in the self-valorization of value requires an increase of surplus labour. This can be accomplished through extending the workday, a strategy that sooner or later reaches its limits. The other manner of furthering valorization is to reduce the time spent in necessary labour. When technological change increases productivity in sectors producing means of consumption for workers (or in sectors producing the means of production used in wage-goods sectors), the price of these consumption goods tends to decline. Less of the working day now needs to be devoted to producing the economic value equivalent to the wages workers must receive to maintain their given standard of living. This leaves more of the working day for the production of surplus-value on the level of total social capital (432).

While Volume I is mostly written from the standpoint of capital in general, Marx explicitly notes that all of the determinations discussed on this level of abstraction concretely require the interaction of many capitals (Arthur, 2002). The individual capitals that introduce product and process innovations do so because they face the imperative to 'grow or die'. Growth comes from attaining the power to set prices, and not from passively accepting the prices dictated in the perfectly competitive markets fantasized by neoclassical economists. Successful technological innovation provides this power. Successful process innovations allow firms to produce a given good or service cheaper than their competitors, thereby winning both market share (from lower prices) and 'surplus profits', that is, profits above the average holding in both the economy as a whole and the particular sector (434–6, 436–7, 530; see also Mandel, 1975; Storper and Walker, 1989; Smith, 2002). Successful product innovations enable firms to divert effective demand away from other units of capital. They too allow firms to charge prices sufficiently high to generate surplus profits until competitors are able to imitate or surpass the innovations.

Once the capital form is in place, the 'personifications' of capital (individual entrepreneurs, the managers of joint stock companies, boards of directors, mutual fund mangers, etc.) will necessarily tend to use the immense power granted to them by ownership and control of capital to shape individual cognitive processes, formal and informal communication within and across organizations, the material effects of cultural traditions, and so on, in order to harness these energies to the discovery of technological variations. The proximate end of this arrangement is the surplus profit of a particular unit of capital; the ultimate end is capital accumulation on the level of total social capital. In their drive to appropriate surplus profits for the units of capital with which they are associated the owners and controllers of capital are typically quite indifferent to their role in furthering the accumulation of total social capital, just as individual neurons are indifferent to their role in fulfilling the tasks of the brain. But in both cases a macro-level self-reproducing system (the brain in the one case, capital as a 'self-moving substance' in the other) is present that possesses emergent properties irreducible to the properties of more micro-level entities (neurons and individual capitalists, respectively).

Technological evolution in capitalism is not simply a matter of the proliferation of variations of technological artefacts, technical knowledge, corporate routines, industrial districts and national innovation systems. Mechanisms must be in place to select certain of these variations over others. As noted above, neo-Schumpeterians propose a number of considerations to explain why some innovations are successful while others are not: certain variations exhibit a superior response to challenges set by nature, greater compatibility with the given capacities of organizations and networks of organizations, greater compatibility with established cultural practices and, most of all, greater ability to meet human needs as measured by market success. The problem, once again, is not so much what the list includes, but rather what is absent: the category of capital.

When the self-valorization of value is the organizing principle of social life, the ultimate purpose of technological change is not to respond to the challenges of nature, develop the capacities of firms, meet human needs, or even successfully engage in market transactions. The ultimate end is the accumulation of capital. No adequate account of why certain technological variations are selected over others can abstract from this essential consideration. Here too the sorts of factors discussed by evolutionary economists are certainly relevant. But these other goals are realized only to the extent that their realization furthers the goal of capital; they are not goals in their own right. And there is nothing historically specific about natural constraints, organizational routines, or the other selection mechanisms they examine. To account for technological change in capitalism we need to comprehend how these factors are essentially transformed once they have been subsumed under the capital form. These transformations follow along the same general lines as those introduced in the discussion of the technological variations. Two further considerations can be emphasized here.

First, variations in technologies (technological practices and so on) that fulfil other relevant criteria for selection discussed by neo-Schumpeterians will nonetheless tend to fail to be selected if they do not take the commodity-form. Evolutionary economists recognize the significance of market success, of course. But they do not explicitly acknowledge how the drive to capital accumulation trumps all other considerations. Consider the contrast between variations in agricultural technologies promising to further the production of feed grains for animals consumed in wealthy regions and variations emerging from research on local subsistence crops for poor regions. Or consider the contrast between variations in medical technologies addressing the life-style concerns of the affluent and those directed at deadly afflictions of the poor. In both cases the former sort of technological variations necessarily tend to be selected over the latter under the capital form.[7]

---

7. 'Every year, more than $70 billion is spent on global health research and development by the public and private sectors. Only about 10 percent of this money is used for research on 90% of the world's health problems' (Singer, 2002: 77).

This dynamic has nothing to do with relative success at resolving challenges posed by natural constraints, or the organizational forms of corporations and states. Nor does it have to do with relative success at meeting human needs. The explanation lies in the fact that the commodity-form is a moment in the self-valorization of value. Capital is accumulated only through the production and sale of commodities, and so technologies will necessarily tend to be selected promising to result in commodities for which effective demand is higher than alternative variations.

It is also worth noting in passing that technological variations will sometimes fail to be selected even when they promise to result in commodifiable products. If a significant portion of the foreseeable profits from selecting the variations in question are likely to 'leak' to units of capital different from the one considering the selection, that unit will necessarily tend to bypass those variations. This illustrates a point widely acknowledged among non-Marxian theorists: capital rationality and social rationality tend to diverge systematically whenever privately appropriable returns on investment in R&D are significantly less than social returns (Mansfield *et al.*, 1967).

Another manner in which the self-valorization of value serves as a mechanism of section in technological evolution concerns time. Three general cases can be noted here, all of which stem from Marx's thesis that the basic drive of capital is to accumulate as much surplus-value as possible as rapidly as possible (449). Given this drive, it follows that investments in technological change promising returns in a short- to medium-term time-frame are superior from the standpoint of capital to those requiring a medium- to long-term time-frame. This general tendency holds even if from the use-value standpoint of the selection mechanisms discussed by neo-Schumpeterians the latter are equal or superior to the former. Second, this temporal framework of capital is quite different from what David Harvey terms 'ecological time' (Harvey, 1996: 229–31). There is thus a necessary tendency in capital for variations in technologies to be selected that involve higher levels of environmental risks than feasible alternatives.[8] Finally, this compressed rhythm of capital time conflicts with the temporal rhythm of community life as well. This implies that innovations will necessarily tend to be selected that impose

---

8. 'Capitalist production, therefore, only develops the techniques and degree of combination of the social process of production by simultaneously undermining the original sources of all wealth – the soil and the worker' (638).

immense social disruptions whenever this furthers the self-valorization of value more than feasible alternatives.[9]

The discussion thus far has abstracted from perhaps the most significant manner in which the self-valorization of value operates as a selection mechanism in technological evolution. When the capital form has been institutionalized paths of technological change necessarily tend to be selected that systematically reproduce the capital/wage labour relation.

2. Technological change and the capital/wage labour relation

In the above discussion of product innovations we have already noted the systematic tendency for technologies increasing the intensity of the labour process to be introduced in capitalism. The capital/wage labour relation affects the selection of specific paths of technological evolution in three other respects as well. First, in Volume I Marx notes a number of instances in which technical advances leading to higher levels of labour productivity were available and yet *not* selected over other technological options. If wages are so low that the projected cost savings from introducing labour-saving technologies are not likely to compensate for the costs of machinery within a relevant time-frame, these technologies tend to not be selected (516–17).

Second, in circumstances where wage levels are considered high by the 'personifications of capital', technologies will tend to be selected that promise to lower those levels. It may be possible to replace expensive workers with machinery (791). New technologies will also be selected if they promise to allow production to continue for extended periods in the face of labour strikes.[10] A further consideration stems from the fact that when different sectors of the workforce are set against each other the balance of power in the capital/wage labour relation generally shifts

9. Neo-Schumpeterians categorize these three tendencies as 'market failures' that can be reversed through the technology policies of states and international agencies. But capitalist states and interstate agencies are themselves intrinsically tied to the self-valorization of value. And so their technology policies will also tend to exhibit a bias towards selecting technological paths that are most likely to result in commodifiable products in the short to medium term, even when they impose higher environmental risks and greater social disruptions than feasible alternatives. Theories of the state and the interstate system fall on a much more concrete theoretical level than Volume I, and so this point will not be pursued here.

10. 'It would be possible to write a whole history of the inventions made since 1830 for the sole purpose of providing capital with weapons against working-class revolt' (563).

in favour of capital, at least for a period of time. If technologies can be introduced that allow production chains to extend across vast geographical distances, there is a systematic tendency for those who control investment capital to make use of them as part of such a 'divide and conquer' strategy (578–80, 591). The same holds for technologies that allow capital to take advantage of gender differences in the workforce (526).[11]

Finally, technologies will tend to be selected that systematically reproduce authority relations in the production process. In principle the self-valorization of value may be furthered by increasing skill levels in order to raise the level of labour productivity. Or valorization may be furthered by objectifying skills, since lower-skilled – cheaper – workers can be hired when previously necessary skills are embedded in fixed capital. In some contexts the former path may appear more promising for capital; in others the latter may appear the better bet.[12] But necessary skills monopolized by a sector of the workforce threaten capital's control of the labour process. And so the two options just mentioned are not quite equivalent from the standpoint of capital. There is considerable evidence that technologies that mobilize the intelligence and creativity of the workforce in contexts where job security is guaranteed do in fact encourage productivity improvements measured in use-value terms (Freeman, 1988; Schweickart, 1993: Chapter 3; Appelbaum and Batt, 1994). Despite this, industry on a global scale has by and large continued to select technologies and forms of social organization where most labour remains routinized, worker involvement in decision-making is kept within extremely narrow bounds and job security is systematically eroded over time (Parker and Slaughter, 1994; Bellofiore, 1999; Smith, 2000a). The problem is that the alternative path of socio-technological development threatens capital/wage labour relations in the labour process, and thus eventually threatens 'productivity' gains to capital measured in value terms (monetary returns on capital invested). This crucial dimension of technology cannot be comprehended without a theory that acknowledges the self-valorization of value as the overriding

---

11. There are, of course, no guarantees that the sorts of technologies mentioned in this paragraph will always be available. But if they are available in the short term, they tend to be selected over alternatives that are equally feasible from a technical standpoint. And if they are not available, private (and public) funds will tend to be devoted to making them available in the medium to long term.
12. For two contrasting samples of the vast literature devoted to this topic, see Braverman (1974) and Adler (1990).

variation and selection mechanism for technological evolution in capitalism. This far-reaching point slips through the conceptual grid of neo-Schumpeterianism.

Two additional points need to be made before concluding this discussion. First, it would be quite mistaken to believe that Marx's theory of technological change can be entirely reduced to the role of technology in class struggle. He was well aware that product innovations and innovations reducing circulation time and constant capital costs cannot all be adequately understood solely in terms of capital's drive to exploit wage labour. The need to produce commodities with use-values, that is, commodities that actually meet the wants and needs of consumers with purchasing power, cannot be reduced to class struggle. Neither can the logic of intra-capital competition, or the manner in which techno-logical change in one sector calls forth technological adjustments in another. These considerations are as necessary for the comprehension of technological change in capitalism as the logic of class conflict.[13] But not all equally necessary factors are equally essential. The capital/wage labour relation is the essential social relation of the capitalist mode of production, defining its most basic differences from other modes of production. Sales to final consumers, inter-capital competition, and the

---

13. Marx's account of technological change in the Industrial Revolution is hardly devoted exclusively to the capital/wage labour relation. He traces, for example, the way in which technological change in one sector encourages development in another:

> The transformation of the mode of production in one sphere of industry necessitates a similar transformation in other spheres. This happens at first in branches of industry which are connected together by being separate phases of a process, and yet isolated by the social division of labour, in such a way that each of them produces an independent com-modity. Thus machine spinning made machine weaving necessary, and both together made a mechanical and chemical revolution compulsory in bleaching, printing and dyeing. So too, on the other hand, the revolution in cotton-spinning called forth the invention of the gin, for separating the seeds from the cotton fibre; it was only by means of this invention that the production of cotton became possible on the enormous scale at present required. But as well as this, the revolution in the modes of production of industry and agriculture made necessary a revolution in the general condi-tions of the social process of production, i.e. in the means of communication and transportation. (505–6)

In passages such as this the crucial neo-Schumpeterian categories of 'technology systems' and 'technological trajectories' are fully anticipated.

cascading effects of technological evolution must thus ultimately be comprehended as moments in the systematic reproduction of the capital/wage labour relation. The Marxian account of technological change in capitalism stands alone in giving this relation the weight it warrants.

Second, in the dialectic of class struggle presented in Volume I of *Capital* wage-labourers are not simply passive victims of technological change. The very communication technologies that allow capital to play different sectors of the workforce against each other may also enable dispersed workers to articulate common concerns. Technologies designed to increase the pace of the labour process may also make the production chain more vulnerable to disruption. Technologies associated with the deskilling of certain sectors of the workforce may require enhanced capacities in other sectors. And attempts by capital to use technology as a weapon in class struggle necessarily tend to provoke counter-struggles by wage-labourers.[14]

Our presentation of Marx's theory has focused on the self-valorization of value as a principle of variation and selection in technological evolution. As important as this topic is, it does not bring us to the heart of his account of technology in capitalism. The single most significant thesis of Volume I of *Capital* is that the self-valorization of value simply *is* the class exploitation of wage-labour by capital.[15] But the social relation between capital and wage-labour does not appear directly as what it is; it is mediated through the impersonal value-form, money. The reign of capital as an alien subject standing above the social world rests entirely

14. There are passages scattered throughout Volume I referring to tendencies for workers to become mere 'appendages' in the course of capitalist development. Some refer to the erosion of the social conditions enabling individuals to act as independent producers apart from capital (482). Others concern the manner in which systems of machinery force workers to submit to the pace of machines (614). A third group has to do with the fact that workers' activities to secure their own reproduction are simultaneously moments in the self-reproduction of capital (719). These considerations establish that 'the dice are loaded'; the rules of the game systematically favour capital (793). But they do not establish that the disposition of wage-labourers to engage capital in struggles necessarily tends to dissipate over time: 'By maturing the material conditions and the social combination of the process of production, it [capital] matures the contradictions and antagonisms of the capitalist form of that process, and thereby ripens both the elements for forming a new society and the force tending towards the overthrow of the old one' (635).

15. 'In every case, the working class creates by the surplus labour of one year the capital destined to employ additional labour in the following year. And this is what is called creating capital out of capital' (729).

on the manner in which the essential social relations of capitalism appear in a fetishized form.[16]

While neo-Schumpeterians break with the neoclassical perspective in many respects, they have not broken from the neoclassical account of the 'fundamental ontology' of the technological artefacts employed in production and distribution. These artefacts continue to be categorized as 'capital inputs'. Marx, in contrast, categorized them as forms of 'dead labour', objectifications of social labour that appear in the alien form of capital. To think otherwise is to fall into capital fetishism. This is not merely a terminological difference: the use of different categories results in different understandings of the world and different orientations to practical activity. In so far as neo-Schumpeterians persist in treating technological artefacts as capital they simultaneously reflect and reinforce the objective alienation rooted in the capital/wage labour relation. It may appear natural to regard technological artefacts as the results of the creative powers of capital. But there is nothing 'natural' about this mode of appearance; it rests on historically specific social forms.[17]

As the productive forces necessarily tend to expand under the capital form, the alienation of wage-labourers from the productive forces necessarily tends to intensify as well. This alienation emerges from, and is reproduced by, the alienation of the individual worker from social collective labour, including especially the growing sector of the

16. 'This natural power of labour [the power to maintain the established value of means of production when producing new value] appears as a power incorporated into capital for the latter's own self-preservation, just as the productive forces of social labour appear as inherent characteristics of capital, and just as the constant appropriation of surplus labour by the capitalists appears as the constant self-valorization of capital. All the powers of labour project themselves as powers of capital, just as all the value-forms of the commodity do as forms of money' (755–6).

17. 'Since past labour always disguises itself as capital, i.e. since the debts owed to the labour of A, B, C etc. are disguised as the assets of the non-worker X, bourgeois citizens and political economists are full of praise for the services performed by past labour, which according to that Scottish genius MacCulloch, ought indeed to receive a special remuneration in the shape of interest, profit, etc. The ever-growing weight of the assistance given by past labour to the living labour process in the form of means of production is therefore attributed to that form of past labour in which it is alienated, as unpaid labour, from the worker himself, i.e. it is attributed to its form as capital. The practical agents of capitalist production and their ideological word-spinners are as incapable of thinking of the means of production separately from the antagonistic social mask they wear at present as a slave-owner is of thinking of the worker himself as distinct from his character as slave' (757).

workforce devoted to scientific–technical labour. From the standpoint of individual labourers, the contributions to innovation made by social collective labour in general, and scientific–technical labour in particular, appear to be the contributions of capital (482, 799). Neo-Schumpeterian accounts do not call these appearances into question. In many respects they even further 'capital fetishism', for instance, when they posit 'the firm' (a reified legal fiction) as the repository of the capacities required for successful innovation, rather than the collective workforce.[18]

Overcoming this alienation from the technological artefacts of production theoretically requires more than a mere acknowledgement of the creative contribution of workers in the 'learning by doing' process, whose importance to innovation neo-Schumpeterians rightfully stress. It requires the category of 'collective social labour' and an understanding that this category refers to real material ties connecting subjects backwards and forwards in time, as well as across vast geographical spaces. The practical overcoming of this alienation, of course, requires far more than this.

3. Technological change and the world historical significance of capitalism

Neo-Schumpeterians and Marx have both developed future-oriented theories. But the time horizons of the two frameworks are quite different, as are the social agents to whom they are addressed.

The temporal horizon of neo-Schumpeterians extends to a possible future long wave of capitalist expansion. This involves a consideration of incipient technology trajectories with a potential to generate high levels of investment and growth for an extended epoch, combined with a concern for the socio-political frameworks most likely to further the transition to these new paths. Computer technologies, biotechnologies and technologies that significantly reduce environmental risks have been examined at length in this context, along with the forms of corporate organization, financial institutions, and governmental and inter-governmental technology agencies best suited to their development (Freeman, 1992; Archibugi and Michie, 1997; Dosi *et al.*, 1998; Freeman and Louçã, 2001: Chapter 9). These investigations provide immensely valuable assessments of the technologies and technology policies of our day. Nonetheless, from a Marxian standpoint this literature suffers from a drastic constriction of theoretical and political imagination. In Volume I of *Capital* Marx sought to uncover world historical possibilities beyond

18. This criticism was proposed in Perelman (1998).

capitalism, possibilities opened up by capitalism's own technological advances.

Of course the restricted focus of neo-Schumpeterians would count as a defect only if limits to the reign of capital can in fact be discerned in the technologies and forms of social organization of contemporary capitalism. In Volume I Marx points to a number of such limits, all of which remain of immense contemporary significance.

3.1 Technology and uneven development

The heart of inter-capital competition is the drive to appropriate surplus profits through temporary monopolies from product or process innovations. Research and development is obviously a crucial element in these innovations. Units of capital with access to advanced (publicly or privately funded) R&D are best positioned to win this form of surplus profits. They are thus also best positioned to establish a virtuous circle in which surplus profits enable a high level of future R&D funding, which provides important preconditions for the appropriation of future surplus profits, and so on. In contrast, units of capital without initial access to advanced R&D tend to be trapped in a vicious circle. The resulting inability to introduce significant innovations prevents the appropriation of surplus profits, which in turn tends to limit participation in advanced R&D in the succeeding period. This then limits future innovations and future profit opportunities.

This fundamental dynamic of capitalist property relations has profound implications. Units of capital with the greatest access to advanced R&D almost by definition tend to be clustered in wealthy regions of the global economy. Units without such access tend to be clustered in poorer regions. The former are in a far better position to establish and maintain the virtuous circle described above, while the latter have immense difficulty avoiding the vicious circle.[19] When units of capital in poorer regions engage in economic transactions with units of capital enjoying temporary monopolies on process and product innovations, they thus necessarily tend to suffer disadvantageous terms of trade

19. 'The worldwide distribution of R&D performance is concentrated in relatively few industrialized countries. Of the $500 billion in estimated 1997 R&D expenditures for the 28 OECD [Organization for Economic Cooperation and Development] countries, 85 percent is expended in just 7 countries' (National Science Board, 2000: 2–40). Ninety-seven per cent of all patents are held by nationals of OECD countries; at least 90 per cent of all technology and product patents are held by global corporations (UNDP, 2000: 84).

(579–80). In other words, there is a redistribution of the value produced in the production and distribution chain from the periphery of the global economy to the centre. The drive to appropriate surplus profits through technological innovation – an inherent feature of capitalist property relations – thus tends to systematically reproduce and exacerbate tremendous economic disparities in the world market over time.[20] In this manner capitalism systematically limits both the satisfaction of wants and needs essential to human happiness and the opportunities to develop essential human capacities far below what the present state of technological development enables.

3.2 Technology and the politics of information

In Volume I Marx discusses how the contribution of scientific and technological knowledge to capital accumulation falls into a special category. Units of capitals with access to this knowledge treat it as a free gift of nature, increasing productive power without requiring further capital investment (508, 754). He argues that the intensification of the real subsumption of scientific and technological knowledge under the capital form results in this 'free gift' becoming ever more central to social life over time. We should note that scientific–technological knowledge counts as a type of public good in three respects (Perelman, 1998). First, knowledge is a *non-rivalrous* good. A piece of knowledge fully possessed by one person can simultaneously be fully possessed by another, unlike rivalrous goods such as cars or sandwiches. Second, once a piece of scientific–technological knowledge has been formulated, the marginal cost of distributing it approaches zero, in sharp contrast to the cost of producing additional cars or sandwiches. Finally, excluding others from this knowledge is costly. The extension and enforcement of intellectual property rights, the private ownership of scientific–technological journals, and so on, can prevent scientific–technological knowledge from possessing the 'non-excludability' that is a feature of most public goods. But such measures require extensive private expenditures and significantly raise the social costs of diffusing the technology.

Neo-Schumpeterian theorists assume that the market system is the most efficient mechanism for the production and distribution of scarce goods imaginable. They also note that the dynamic of capitalist development is bringing about an ever more information-intensive economy.

20. This is but one of the many social mechanisms underlying the tendency to uneven development. More complete accounts are found in Toussaint (1999) and Went (2000).

But knowledge is not a scarce good. Once it has been formulated it can be endlessly reproduced and more or less costlessly distributed.[21] This implies that over time the very heart of the capitalist system itself points beyond the logic of this system, based as it is on the private ownership and exchange of scarce products.

3.3 Technology and overaccumulation crises

Neo-Schumpeterians have explicitly acknowledged that extended periods of economic decline regularly occur in capitalism; they have made major contributions to the study of long waves of expansion and decline (Freeman and Louçã, 2000: *passim*). In these accounts the blame for the loss of human happiness and the waste of human potential associated with extended economic downturns ultimately lies with an exhaustion of dominant technological trajectories and the institutional inertia that prevents a rapid shift to new socio-technical systems. But all social systems must confront the exhaustion of reigning technological paradigms and the challenge of adjusting institutions in response. In the Marxian framework the cause of downturns in capitalism is rooted in its historically specific social forms.

Building upon scattered remarks in Volume I and elsewhere, Geert Reuten has connected Marx's account of technological change in capitalism with a systematic tendency to crises (580, 785–7; Reuten, 1991). First, the logic of inter-capital competition necessarily tends to lead to the introduction of new firms and plants into an industry that are more technologically advanced than those already established. These firms win surplus profits due to their superior productivity. But established firms and plants do not all automatically withdraw when this occurs. Given that their fixed capital costs are already 'sunk', they may be happy with receiving the average rate of profit on their circulating capital. They also may have established relations with suppliers and customers that would be impossible (or prohibitively expensive) to duplicate elsewhere in any relevant time-frame. Further, their management and labour force may have industry-specific skills. Or they may have access

21. The tremendous successes of publicly funded R&D (the ultimate source of all significant contemporary technological trajectories) suggests that ever more extensive private intellectual property rights are not required for the initial production of scientific–technical knowledge. In fact, *The Economist*, a far from radical publication, has recently argued that the intellectual property rights regime now profoundly hampers innovation (*Economist*, 2002). An extended argument for the technological dynamism of a democratic form of socialism is found in Smith (2000a: Chapter Seven).

to state subsidies for training, infrastructure, or R&D that they would not be able to replace if they shifted investment to other sectors. If enough firms fail to withdraw an overaccumulation of capital crisis erupts, manifested in excess capacity and declining rates of profit. Insufficient surplus-value is now produced to valorize the investments that had been made in fixed capital, leading to a fall in profit rates for an extended historical period (Smith, 2000b).

When overaccumulation crises break out, previous investments in fixed capital must be devalued. At this point the entire system becomes convulsed in endeavours to shift the costs of devaluation elsewhere. Each unit, network and region of capital attempts to shift the costs of devaluation onto other units, networks and regions. And capital as a whole attempts to shift as much of the cost as possible onto labour by increasing unemployment, lowering wages and worsening work conditions.[22] As the concentration and centralization of capital proceed, the overaccumulation and devaluation of capital necessarily tend to occur on an ever more massive scale. Global turbulence and generalized economic insecurity increasingly become the normal state of affairs (Brenner, 2002; Smith, 2000a: Chapter 5).

The neo-Schumpeterian response to long waves of capitalist decline is to seek new technological paradigms promising a new wave of growth, and to call for whatever institutional adjustments appear to be required to set those paradigms in place. Once again we find that the absolutely essential questions from a Marxian viewpoint cannot even be formulated within the perspective of evolutionary economics. Will there not come a point at which the social costs of overaccumulation crises force increasing numbers of people to consider alternative social forms? Isn't it just possible that there are feasible forms within which technological evolution can occur without the immense human suffering that follows in the wake of overaccumulation crises?

3.4 Technology and the politics of time

Advances in labour productivity present a fundamental choice. Either the same output can be produced in less time, or a greater output can be produced in the same period of time. The most basic drive of capital is to increase the accumulation of capital, and the accumulation of additional capital generally requires the production and sale of additional

---

22. The on-going human catastrophes in East Asia in response to the crisis of 1997–98 provide only the most recent example. See Burkett and Hart-Landsberg (2001).

commodities. And so capitalism necessarily tends to proceed down the path of using technology to increase output rather than to reduce labour time.[23]

It must be granted that this dynamic has brought about an unprecedented increase in living standards for vast numbers of people. As output expands, unit costs and prices tend to decline. Many products that were initially luxury commodities eventually become more widely affordable. Marxists, of course, are quick to point out that uneven development, overaccumulation crises and other structural tendencies of capitalism profoundly distort the manner in which the increased output due to technological change is socially distributed. Two other considerations are relevant as well. First, technological changes advancing labour productivity in principle allow greater amounts of 'time for education, for intellectual development, for the fulfilment of social functions, for social intercourse, for the free play of the vital forces of [the worker's] body and mind' (375). These are immensely important matters, and are widely regarded as such. Must there not be *some* point beyond which the promise of more commodities fails to compensate for their loss?

A second issue concerns the world historical pattern of evolution from agricultural to heavy industrial and then knowledge-based economies. Neo-Schumpeterians correctly discern that leading sectors of the economy today are characterized less and less by labour intensity or 'capital intensity' in the sense of investment in raw materials and machinery, and more and more by intensity in the use of knowledge resources (Freeman and Louca, 2001). It is also correct to assert that the forms of labour best suited to knowledge-based economies are likely to be quite different from those associated with earlier periods. In this sense the rhetoric of 'knowledge workers' contains an element of truth. Nonetheless, this rhetoric ideologically distorts analysis of the contemporary capitalist workplace. Most factory and office workers simply lack the time to become knowledge workers in any meaningful sense of the

23. When we take into account forced overtime, increased commuting distances and an intensification of labour that leaves workers exhausted when the workday is over, we may even say that there is a tendency for a *greater* appropriation of workers' time as labour productivity advances in capitalism. In Volume I Marx refers to 'the economic paradox that the most powerful instrument for reducing labour-time suffers a dialectical inversion and becomes the most unfailing means for turning the whole lifetime of the worker and his family into labour-time at capital's disposal for its own valorization' (532), a paradox that continues to hold today (Fraser, 2001).

term.[24] From a world historical standpoint, then, capitalism systematically limits the evolution of the very knowledge-based economy it has itself generated (Richta, 1968). This limit to social evolution cannot even be articulated within the confines of mainstream evolutionary economics.

3.5 Technology and environmental risks

As we have seen, the tension between 'capital time' and 'ecological time' in the course of technological development necessarily tends to generate an excessive level of environmental risk. The manner in which technological change in capitalism necessarily tends to result in increased output rather than reduced labour time exacerbates environmental risks as well. As a result, the need to subject technological change to some version of the 'precautionary principle' can be expected to intensify in the course of capitalist development. This need conflicts in principle with the forms of technical change imposed by the valorization imperative (Burkett, 1999: 226–7).

4. Conclusion

Neo-Schumpeterian theories are addressed to groups charged with the task of developing new socio-technological paradigms, capable of setting off an extended historical epoch of capitalist growth. But overcoming uneven development, overaccumulation crises and the other limitations connected to the development and use of technology in capitalism demands a break from capitalist production and property relations. The social agents to whom neo-Schumpeterian theories are addressed (scientists, technologists, investors, managers, political elites, and so on)

---

24. See Fraser (2001) for a discussion of office and professional workers. For a discussion of contemporary factory work see Parker (1999), who examines the manner in which time constraints prevent the emergence of knowledge workers in any substantive sense. One contemporary trend is to eliminate electricians and quality control workers, transferring their duties to line workers. Line workers may then enjoy more variety in their workday. But this sort of 'multitasking' does not leave them with the time required to acquire the level of knowledge attained by specialists workers in the past. When demand increases for a firm's commodities, there is also a tendency to increase output through forced overtime. This too denies workers the time required to become 'knowledge workers' in any meaningful sense of the term. Parker further notes the manner in which the lack of work time devoted to training gives the lie to the talk of 'knowledge workers' in contemporary manufacturing (Parker, 1999).

are unlikely to initiate this world historical project, let alone complete it successfully.

Marx's theory, in contrast, is addressed to working men and women and their communities. Are they capable of undertaking and completing the historical task in question? No definitive answer to such a question can be expected here. But two preliminary points can be proposed. First, if the account of technological change developed in Volume I of *Capital* is accurate, the vast majority of humanity has reason to resist the idea that capitalism is the final stage of social evolution. Second, any effective movement towards a post-capitalist society must occur on a global level, for capitalism is a global system. This latter point brings us to one final social implication of technological change discussed in Volume I. Marx argues that the technological changes enabling interconnections in the capitalist world market simultaneously bring about the material conditions for an effective internationalist movement of workers and their allies. For instance, he discusses how workers in different regions of the global economy are connected in a common learning process. Transportation and communication technologies enable positive and negative lessons from social struggles to be transmitted across borders (Chapter 10). The immense social disruptions associated with technological change in capitalism also set off flows of immigrant labourers (Chapter 25). These flows create the material conditions for extensive and intensive community ties across borders (Sassen, 1998).

Neo-Schumpeterians have not focused on this sort of 'globalization from below'. Evolutionary economists have generally taken the nation as the basic social unit, with contrasts between different 'national innovation systems' one of their central research topics (Nelson, 1993; Freeman, 1997). International issues have been considered only in so far as technological developments create a need for global regulatory institutions, capable of addressing externalities beyond the reach of individual states (Freeman and Soete, 1999: Chapter 18). The manner in which technological developments in capitalism necessarily tend to further the material preconditions for the formation of a world community of wage-labourers and their allies is thoroughly occluded. In contrast, this world historical possibility is a central theme of *Capital*.

The most fundamental practical implication of Marx's theory is that the self-organization of working men and women as a transnational class in-and-for-itself is the major project of the present epoch of world history (Robinson and Harris, 2000). Only such self-organization holds the promise of overcoming the various limitations on technological development described in this chapter. When all is said and done, this is by far the most profound distinction between Marxian and non-Marxian accounts of technological change in capitalism. In Volume I Marx wrote,

It took both time and experience before the workers learnt to distinguish between machinery and its employment by capital, and therefore to transfer their attacks from the material instruments of production to the form of society which utilizes those instruments (554–5).

This process remains to be completed.

References

Adler, Paul (1990), 'Marx, machines, and skill', *Technology and Culture*, 31/4: 780–812.

Appelbaum, Eileen and Rosemary Batt (1994), *The New American Workplace: Transforming Work Systems in the United States* (Ithaca, NY: ILR Press).

Archibugi, Daniele and Jonathan Michie (eds) (1997) *Technology, Globalisation and Economic Performance* (Cambridge: Cambridge University Press).

Arthur Christopher (2002), Capital, competition and many capitals, in M. Campbell and G. Reuten (eds): 128–48.

— and Geert Reuten (eds) (1998), *The Circulation of Capital: Essays on Volume II of Marx's 'Capital'* (New York: St Martin's Press).

Bellofiore, Riccardo (ed.) (1999), *Global Money, Capital Restructuring and the Changing Patterns of Labour* (Northampton, MA: Edward Elgar).

— (1985a) 'Marx after Schumpeter', *Capital and Class*, 24: 60–74.

— (1985 b) 'Money and development in Schumpeter', *Review of Radical Political Economy*, 17/1–2: 21–40.

Braverman, Harry (1974), *Labor and Monopoly Capital* (New York: Monthly Review Press).

Brenner, Robert (2002), *The Boom and the Bubble: The US in the World Economy* (New York: Verso).

Burkett, Paul (1999), *Marx and Nature: A Red and Green Perspective* (New York: Palgrave).

— and Martin Hart-Landsberg (2001), Crisis and recovery in East Asia: the limits of capitalist development, *Historical Materialism*, 8: 3–47.

Campbell, Martha and Geert Reuten (2002), *The Culmination of Capital: Essays on Volume III of Marx's Capital* (Basingstoke/New York: Palgrave).

Carlson, W. Bernard (2000), Invention and evolution: the case of Edison's sketches of the telephone, in J. Ziman (ed.): 137–58.

Constant, Edward (2000), Recursive practice and the evolution of technological knowledge, in J. Ziman (ed.): 219–33

Coombs, Rod, Saviotti, Paolo and Vivien Walsh (1987), *Economics and Technological Change*, (London: Macmillan).

Coricelli, Fabrizio and Giovanni Dosi, (1988), Coordination and order in economic change and the interpretative power of economic theory, in G. Dosi *et al.* (eds): 124–47.

David, Paul (2000), Path dependence and varieties of learning in the evolution of technological practices, in J. Ziman (ed.): 118–34.

Dosi, Giovanni (1988), The nature of the innovative process, in Dosi *et al.* (eds): 221–38.

— Freedman, Christopher, Nelson, Richard, Silverberg, Gerald and Luc Soete (eds) (1988), *Technical Change and Economic Theory* (New York: Pinter Publishers).

— Teece, David and Josef Chytry (1998), *Technology, Organisation, and Competitiveness: Perspectives on Industrial and Corporate Change* (New York: Oxford University Press).

The Economist (2002), Patently absurd, 23 June: 40–2.

Fraser, Jill (2001), *White-Collar Sweatshop: The Deterioration of Work and Its Rewards in Corporate America* (New York: W.W. Norton).

Freeman, Christopher (1988), Japan: a new National System of Innovation?, in G. Dosi *et al.* (eds): 330–49.

— (1992), *The Economics of Hope* (London: Pinter).

— (1997), The 'National System of Innovation' in historical perspective, in D. Archibugi and J. Michie (eds): 24–49.

Freeman, Chris and Francisco Louçã (2001), *As Time Goes By: From the Industrial Revolutions to the Information Revolution* (New York: Oxford University Press).

Freeman, Christopher and Luc Soete (1999), *The Economics of Industrial Innovation* (Cambridge, Mass.: MIT Press).

Harvey, David (1996), *Justice, Nature and the Geography of Difference* (Malden: Blackwell).

Landes, David (1999), *The Wealth and Poverty of Nations* (New York: W.W. Norton).

Lundvall, Bengt-Ake (1988), Innovation as an interactive process: from user–producer interaction to the National System of Innovation', in G. Dosi *et al.* (eds): 349–69.

Mandel, Ernest (1975), *Late Capitalism* (London: New Left Books).

Mansfield, Edward, John Rapoport, Anthony Romeo, Samuel Wagner and George Beardsley (1967), Social and private rates of return from industrial innovations, *Quarterly Journal of Economics*, 41: 221–40.

Marx, Karl (1867), *Capital: Volume I* (trans. Ben Fowkes) (New York: Penguin, 1976).

Metcalfe, Stan (1997), Technology systems and technology policy in an evolutionary framework, in D. Archibugi and J. Michie (eds): 268–96.

Mokyr, Joel (2000), Evolutionary phenomena in technological change, in J. Ziman (ed.): 52–65.

Moseley, Fred (2002), Hostile brothers: Marx's theory of the distribution of surplus-value in Volume III of *Capital*, in M. Campbell and G. Reuten (eds): 65–101.

Murray, Patrick (1998), Beyond the 'commerce and industry' picture of capital, in C. Arthur and G. Reuten (eds): 33–66.

National Science Board (2000), *Science and Engineering Indicators, 1996*, NSB 96–21, (Washington, DC: U.S. Government Printing Office).

Nelson, Richard (ed.) (1993), *National Innovation Systems* (New York: Oxford University Press).
— (1995), Recent evolutionary theorising about economic change, *Journal of Economic Literature*, 32/1: 48–90.
Parker, Mike (1999), Management-by-stress and skilled work: the US case, in Riccardo Bellofiore (ed.): 125–40.
— and Jane Slaughter (1994), *Working Smart: A Union Guide to Participation Programs and Reengineering* (Detroit: Labor Notes).
Perelman, Michael (1998), *Class Warfare in the Information Age* (New York: St Martin's Press).
Reuten, Geert (1991), Accumulation of capital and the foundation of the tendency of the rate of profit to fall, *Cambridge Journal of Economics*, 15/1: 79–93.
Richta, Radovan (1968), *Civilization at the Crossroads: Social and Human Implications of the Scientific and Technological Revolution* (Prague: International Arts and Sciences Press).
Robinson, William and Jerry Harris (2000), Towards a global ruling class: globalization and the transnational capitalist class', *Science and Society*, 64/1: 11–54.
Sassen, Saskia (1998), *Globalization and Its Discontents: Essays on the New Mobility of People and Money* (New York: The New Press).
Saviotti, P. Paolo and Stan Metcalfe (eds) (1991), *Evolutionary Theories of Economic and Technological Change* (London: Harwood).
Schrader, Steven (1991), Informal transfer between firms: cooperation through information trading, *Research Policy*, 20: 153–70.
Schumpeter, Joseph (1934), *The Theory of Economic Development* (Cambridge, Mass.: Harvard University Press).
— (1947), *Capitalism, Socialism, and Democracy* (London: George Allen & Unwin).
Schweickart, David (1993), *Against Capitalism* (New York: Cambridge University Press).
Silverberg, Gerald (1988), 'Modeling economic dynamics and technical change, in G. Dosi *et al.* (eds): 531–60.
Singer, Peter (2002), Rx for reform, *Foreign Policy*, May/June, 76–7.
Smith, Tony (1997), A critical comparison of the Neo-classical and Marxian theories of technical change, *Historical Materialism*, 1: 113–33.
— (1998), The capital/consumer relation in lean production: the continued relevance of Volume Two of *Capital*, in C. Arthur and G. Reuten (eds): 149–73.
— (2000a), *Technology and Capital in the Age of Lean Production: A Marxian Critique of the 'New Economy'* (Albany, NY: State University of New York Press).
— (2000b), Brenner and crisis theory: issues in systematic and historical dialectics, *Historical Materialism*, 5: 145–78.
— (2002), Surplus profits from innovation: a missing level in *Capital III*?, in M. Campbell and G. Reuten (eds): 67–94.
Storper, Michael and R. Walker 1989), *The Capitalist Imperative: Territory, Technology, and Industrial Growth* (New York: Basil Blackwell).
Toussaint, Eric (1999), *Your Money or Your Life! The Tyranny of Global Finance* (London: Pluto).
UNDP (United Nations Development Program) (2000), *Human Rights and Human Development* (New York: UNDP).

Went, Robert (2000), *Globalization: Neoliberal Challenge, Radical Responses* (London: Pluto).

Wresch, William (1996), *Disconnected: Haves and Have-nots in the Information Age* (New Brunswick, NJ: Rutgers University Press).

Ziman, John (ed.) (2000), *Technological Innovation as an Evolutionary Process* (Cambridge: Cambridge University Press).

9
The Social and Material Transformation of Production by Capital: Formal and Real Subsumption in *Capital, Volume I*

Patrick Murray

1. Why wealth is a poor concept: on the purpose of production

What is the *purpose* of production in those societies where wealth is generally produced in the form of commodities, that is, in those societies where the capitalist mode of production predominates? Marx's answer to this simple, but commonly neglected, question enables him to begin the huge Chapter 15, 'Machinery and large-scale industry', by one-upping John Stuart Mill:

> John Stuart Mill says in his *Principles of Political Economy*: 'It is questionable if all the mechanical inventions yet made have lightened the day's toil of any human being'. *That is, however, by no means the aim of the application of machinery under capitalism*. Like every other instrument for increasing the productivity of labour, machinery is intended to cheapen commodities and, by shortening the part of the working day in which the worker works for himself, to lengthen the other part, the part he gives to the capitalist for nothing. *The machine is a means for producing surplus-value* (492; my emphases[1]).

Mill's surprise only reveals his thoughtlessness regarding the specific purpose of capitalist production. Stocking up (unpaid surplus) labour, not saving labour, is the point of a system whose goal is the accumulation

---

1. Page numbers with no further attribution refer to *Capital, Volume I*, which contains the *Results of the Immediate Production Process* (*Results*), beginning on p. 948.

of capital. *The cruel irony of capitalist development is that it is constantly driven to increase productivity for the purpose of appropriating more and more surplus labour.*

Like economists generally, Mill is oblivious to the question that animates Marx's inquiry: What is the specific social form and purpose of wealth?[2] Two questions about material wealth are well understood and widely asked. How much wealth is there? How is wealth distributed? While Marx is interested in these two, he focuses on the elusive, though more fundamental, question: *What is the specific social form and purpose of wealth?* Answering this third question, to which so many inquirers are oblivious, also provides the answer to the question: What is the specific *measure* of wealth? For capitalism, the purpose and measure is *surplus-value*, the increment in value beyond the value invested by a capitalist. The capitalist's 'aim is to produce not only a use-value, but a commodity; not only use-value, but value; and not just value, but also surplus-value' (293). By pressing this third question, Marx reveals that the everyday concept of wealth is impoverished.

In the *Grundrisse* Marx observes, 'all production is appropriation of nature on the part of an individual within and through a specific form of society' (Marx, 1939: 87). When we abstract from the specific social form and purpose of *wealth* (and from the specific social character of *needs* and *labour*), we lose our grip on actuality. That's what happens with wealth. Beginning with the first sentence of *Capital*, Marx announces that his topic is not wealth but rather a specific social form of wealth, wealth in the (generalized) commodity-form. With that opening, Marx establishes the theme of the *double character* of wealth and production under capitalism – use-value and value. The genius of *Capital* is that it maintains the theme of the double character of capitalism from start to finish; it never loses track of the powers of the peculiar social forms and purposes that animate the capitalist mode of production. By contrast, the concept of wealth is poor because it bleaches out social form.

The same difficulty arises when we come to capital. Oblivious to the topic of the specific social form and purpose of wealth, everyday thought and economics attempt to define capital on the basis of *natural*

---

2. By 'economics' I mean any investigation into the production and distribution of wealth that does not incorporate specific social forms of needs, labour and wealth as ingredients of the theory. Classical and neoclassical economics both fit this description; 'institutional economics' does not. (On the latter point, see Martha Campbell's Chapter 3 in the present work.)

(socially non-specific) characteristics. This leads to the common definition: capital is wealth capable of being used to produce more wealth.[3] It should be easy to see that this generally applicable definition of capital provides no bridge to the understanding of the capitalist mode of production as historically specific. If the concept of capital is generally applicable, then what makes the capitalist mode of production distinctive has nothing to do with capital. So the everyday conception of capital, the one we find also in economics, is a non-starter for understanding the capitalist mode of production.

The ordinary conception of capital is at once too broad and too narrow. It is too broad because it encompasses all human societies, but how is it too narrow? Marx's answer comes out most clearly in the *Results* and in Part One of Volume II of *Capital*. Marx observes that, under capitalism, wealth is produced not simply in the commodity-form but in the form of *commodity capital*, that is, commodities whose sale realizes surplus-value. Since goods for individual consumption, including luxury items, are produced in the social form of commodity capital, not all commodity capital is suitable as a means for new production. According to the commonplace definition of capital, then, such goods and services must not be capital. Because of the role they play in the realization of surplus-value, however, they do function as capital. Here the commonplace definition is too narrow. Were economics and everyday discourse to include commodity capital as capital, their concept of capital would collapse into that of wealth, since there are no distinctive natural characteristics of wealth in the form of commodity capital. The effort to define capital in abstraction from specific social forms and purposes, then, breaks down in a twofold failure.

Recognizing Marx's profound break with the discourse of economics opens the conceptual space needed to grasp what Marx means in talking of various forms of *subsumption under capital*. Talk of any sort of subsumption under capital is unintelligible on the basis of the commonplace conception of capital, which is silent on the question of the determinate social form and purpose of wealth. The whole point of Marx's discourse of different forms of subsumption is to reveal the diverse ways in which capital, as a specific social form of wealth, exercises its epoch-making power. Marx's discourse of subsumption drives home the point that *Capital* is fundamentally a study of the nature, inseparability, powers and consequences of the specific social forms belonging to the capitalist mode of production. The several subsumption concepts point to the

3. See Marx, 1939: 85–6, for Marx's direct criticism of this conception of capital.

diverse ways that capital, understood as a specific – and explosive – social form of wealth, revolutionizes society, its goods and services, and the ways they are produced.

2. Absolute surplus-value and relative surplus-value

The middle third of the first volume of *Capital*, on which this chapter focuses, is devoted to two topics, *absolute surplus-value* and *relative surplus-value*. The present chapter relates these two, respectively, to the concepts of the *formal subsumption* and *real subsumption* of labour under capital. While mentioned in *Capital*, the terms 'formal subsumption' and 'real subsumption' are treated at greater length in Marx's manuscript of 1861–3 and in the intended, but unfinished, conclusion to Volume I, *Results of the Immediate Production Process (Results)*.[4] In those manuscripts Marx also develops the concepts of *ideal subsumption* and *hybrid subsumption*, which we will examine. I argue that the changes to the production process that Marx identifies with increasing *absolute* surplus-value involve simply *formal* subsumption, while those transformations required for *relative* surplus-value involve *real* subsumption. Between them, formal subsumption and real subsumption under capital bring about a continual hubbub of social and material revolution, yet in the same stroke, they enforce social stasis because they strengthen and expand the hold of the law of value and capital's web of value-forms. The middle third of *Capital I* works out a surplus-value theory that provides a powerful theoretical explanation for the endless transformation of the globe by the bourgeoisie that Marx and Engels announced in *The Communist Manifesto*.

In 'The labour process and the valorization process', the first of the chapters that compose this middle third of Volume I, Marx shows how the capitalist is able to turn the trick of making money from money (valorization). He begins by noting two fundamental characteristics of the capitalist form of production. First, simply by being the purchaser of labour-power and of the means of production, the capitalist commands the production process. Second, the workers' entire product, including any surplus-value realized by its sale, belongs to the capitalist (291–2). The solution to the riddle of surplus-value's source is this: the capitalist purchases labour-power at its value but then commands its seller, the wage-labourer, to keep producing value beyond the amount necessary to match the worker's wage. Remarkably, capital turns the trick of valorization without putting a dent in simple commodity circulation's rules

---

4. See 645; Marx, 1861–3: 83–4 and 2130–59; and *Results*: 1019–38.

of fairness.[5] In this way Marx discloses the irony of bourgeois justice: the whole sphere of commutative justice, that is, the exchange of equivalent values, which is the norm for simple commodity circulation, rests on the exploitation of those who sell their labour-power by those who own the means of production. Bourgeois fairness is counterfeit.

In explaining absolute surplus-value and relative surplus-value, Marx uses a divided line (ABC) to represent the working day. The first part of the line, AB, represents *necessary labour*, that is, the amount of labour required to produce enough value to match the value of the worker's labour-power, the monetary expression of which is, by assumption, the wage. The second part of the line, BC, represents *surplus labour*, which creates surplus-value for the capitalist. To increase surplus-value the capitalist has three options.

1. Keep AB constant but increase BC by lengthening the working day; this is the strategy of absolute surplus-value.
2. Keep AC constant but increase BC by decreasing AB. On the assumption that workers' wages cover the value of their labour-power, only lowering the value of labour-power can decrease AB.[6] That requires decreasing the value of the commodities that go into sustaining labour-power.[7] The strategy of relative surplus-value pumps out more surplus-value by increasing the productivity of labour so as to cheapen labour-power. For increasing the productivity of labour, the

5. 'Every condition of the problem has been satisfied, while the laws governing the exchange of commodities have not been violated in any way. Equivalent has been exchanged for equivalent' (301).
6. As Marx well knows, this assumption need not be respected in reality.
7. Actually, there are other ways to lower the value of labour-power. Capitalists can deskill workers for the purpose of lowering the value of their labour-power. But this has its problems. First, deskilled labour does not produce as much value as skilled labour (304–5). Second, introducing more productive techniques may well require introducing new skilled labourers. Marx does not argue that deskilling is a necessary strategy of relative surplus-value. By contrast, he states unequivocally, 'Capital therefore has an immanent drive, and a constant tendency, towards increasing the productivity of labour' (436–7).

   Another possibility, a bloody one, is implicit in Marx's inclusion of a historical ingredient in the determination of the value of labour-power (275). Capital could try to turn back the hands of time and lower the minimal expectations of wage-labourers. Or, more likely, in a world where workers of different sexes, ages, races, regions, or nations have various minimal standards, capitalists can reduce the value of labour-power by employing more workers with lower standards.

worker is 'rewarded' with a lower wage (in value terms). Wages that are lower in value terms need not be lower in use-value terms – indeed the assumption here is that, though the commodities consumed by workers contain less value, they will *not* be lower in use-value terms. With increased productivity, wages can simultaneously go down in value terms and up in use-value terms: capitalists and workers can split the relative surplus-value.

3. Lengthen AC and shorten AB.

Absolute and relative surplus-value are 'flow' concepts; they discriminate, *at any level of the development of productive power*, whether an increase in surplus-value is due to extending the working day (absolute surplus-value) or increasing the productivity of labour (relative surplus-value).[8] Thus, highly productive firms can follow an absolute-value strategy by expanding the workday while holding productivity (and wages) constant. Marx thought it common for advances in productivity to be accomplished by lengthening of the working day (646).

The chief way to decrease the value of labour-power that Marx studies in the middle third of Volume I is to increase the productivity of labour. Cooperation, division of labour, manufacture, machinery and large-scale industry are all ways of increasing productivity. But why, according to Marx, does increasing productivity reduce the value of commodities to begin with? Because abstract, not concrete, labour produces value. Productivity is a concrete, use-value consideration, so 'the productivity of labour does not affect the value' (Marx, 1904/1910, 1956/66, Part I: 393). Consequently, productivity increases across a given branch of production, more commodities are turned out yet no more value is added per hour. It is only because of this 'value treadmill' that the values of the commodities that enter into determining the value of labour-power decrease, opening the door to relative surplus-value (436–7).[9]

Lowering the value of labour-power, however, is not what motivates a firm to introduce a more productive labour process and thereby cheapen their goods. Capitalist firms that produce at higher than the average levels of productivity in their branch appropriate extra surplus-value, because an hour worked in such firms counts as more than an

8. See Marx, 1861–3: 2126.
9. Marx triumphantly observes, 'we have here the solution of the following riddle: Why does the capitalist, whose sole concern is to produce exchange-value, continually strive to bring down the exchange-value of commodities?' (437).

hour of socially necessary abstract labour.[10] Notice that this mechanism gives even firms whose products do not enter into the determination of the value of labour-power a good reason to keep looking for ways to increase productivity (434–5). The 'value treadmill' and the logic of relative surplus-value show that this drive to increase the productivity of labour is a powerful *immanent tendency* of the capitalist mode of production. Since Marx reaches this result solely by tracking the consequences of capital conceived of as a distinctive social form of wealth, we glimpse the power of his social form approach.

Marx's use of a divided line to illustrate absolute surplus-value in terms of extending the line and relative surplus-value in terms of shortening its first division (necessary labour) is a neat pedagogical stroke. However, it has its risks. It could suggest that Marx's inquiry into surplus-value addresses solely *quantitative* considerations: What portion of the working day is devoted to 'necessary labour'? What portion to 'surplus labour'? What is the rate of surplus-value (surplus labour over necessary labour)? Concentrating on the lengths and proportions of the line segments can deflect attention from a prior question: What is the *dimension* of the line? Then it is easy for the bad habits of economics and everyday talk to slip in this answer: the divided line takes the measure of *wealth* and surplus *wealth* – instead of *value* and surplus-*value*.

In this way, the divided line can play into the Ricardian socialist misreading of *Capital*, for which the all-consuming issue is the exploitative, class division of *wealth*. Because it is oblivious to the fundamental issue of the specific social form and purpose of wealth, Ricardian theory – including Ricardian socialism – fails to register the difference between wealth and *value*. If you overlook the fact that *value* is not wealth but *a specific social form of wealth*, then absolute surplus-value looks applicable to any class society. Wherever one class lives off the labour of another, the labour of the servile class must be divided into necessary and surplus, and, holding the necessary constant, any lengthening of the working day will increase the surplus wealth appropriated by the dominant class (344). The division between necessary and surplus labour forms the basis of any system of exploitation, but not just any social sort of labour

10. In Chapter 12, 'The concept of relative surplus-value', Marx explains this by invoking a distinction between 'individual' and 'social' values. 'The individual value of these articles is now below their social value . . . The real value of a commodity, however, is not its individual, but its social value; that is to say, its value is not measured by the labour-time that the article costs the producer in each individual case, but by the labour-time socially required for its production' (434).

produces *value* and surplus-*value* (976–7). Marx's divided line measures not 'wealth' but a definite social form of wealth, namely value, which is bound up with special social relations and purposes.

Exploitation and class divisions are nothing new. Capitalism is unique in presenting itself as a universalistic and egalitarian society in which exchanges are governed by the law of commutative justice: equal value for equal value. In other words, capitalism presents itself precisely as the fair society that has rid itself of class and exploitation. One of *Capital*'s prime accomplishments is to place capitalist society among the ranks of exploitative, class societies. Ricardian socialism gets this right, but by collapsing *value* into wealth, surplus-*value* into surplus wealth, it turns a blind eye to Marx's brilliant explorations of the effects of capital's web of distinctive social forms and purposes. Consequently, like many critics of *Capital*, Ricardian socialists squander what I.I. Rubin, calls the 'qualitative sociological side of Marx's theory of value' (Rubin 1972: 73–4).

Connecting the concepts of absolute and relative surplus-value with those of formal and real subsumption under capital helps us avoid the pitfall of a Ricardian socialist misreading of *Capital*. Why? Because the subsumption concepts force us to ask, *subsumption under what?* To that question the only plausible answer is *specific social forms*, notably, *capital*.

3. Marx's four subsumption concepts: formal, real, hybrid and ideal

Marx discusses four different types of subsumption under capital: *formal, real, hybrid* and *ideal*.[11] Formal subsumption and real subsumption are central to the present chapter, but we will briefly consider hybrid and ideal subsumption. First, how are absolute and relative surplus-value related to formal and real subsumption? Marx writes,

> The production of absolute surplus-value turns exclusively on the length of the working day, whereas the production of relative surplus-value completely revolutionizes the technical processes of labour and the groupings into which society is divided.

11. To these four a fifth might be added. It might be called the subsumption of pre-capitalist commercial *forms* under capital. Merchant's capital and usurer's capital are ancient commercial forms that are subordinated to industrial capital under modern capitalist conditions. 'We see here how even economic categories appropriate to earlier modes of production acquire a new and specific historical character under the impact of capitalist production' (950).

It therefore requires a specifically capitalist mode of production, a mode of production which, along with its methods, means and conditions, arises and develops spontaneously on the basis of formal subsumption of labour under capital. This formal subsumption is then replaced by a real subsumption (645).

While 'a merely formal subsumption of labour under capital suffices for the production of absolute surplus-value' (645), the production of relative surplus-value involves the real subsumption of labour under capital.[12] In other words, *the middle third of Capital I is all about formal and real subsumption.* More specifically, Part Three, 'The production of absolute surplus-value', treats of the formal subsumption of labour under capital, while Part Four, 'The production of relative surplus-value', deals with real subsumption of labour under capital. This second correlation implies that, since the three chapters devoted to cooperation, the division of labour and manufacture, and machinery and large-scale industry (Chapters 13–15) all fall within Part Four, all three are forms of real subsumption.

Several of those authors who were among the first to write on formal and real subsumption reject this conclusion. Étienne Balibar and Derek Sayer identify 'simple' cooperation and manufacture with formal subsumption and large-scale industry with real subsumption.[13] Balibar claims, 'The "formal subsumption" which begins with the form of out-work on behalf of a merchant capitalist and ends with the industrial revolution includes the whole history of what Marx calls "manufacture"' (Balibar, 1968: 302–3). Sayer writes along the same lines, 'Marx distinguishes what he calls manufacture and machine industry as successive historical stages... in the development of a specifically capitalist production process. These stages rest upon different historical forms of the labour/capital relation, which Marx refers to as formal and real subordination, subjection or subsumption of labour to capital respectively' (Sayer, 1987: 30–1). Sayer does not recognize that Marx's phrase 'specifically capitalist production' is equivalent to production that has undergone real subsumption. Consequently, if manufacture is a specific historical stage in the development of 'a specifically capitalist production process', then it

12. For similar statements see *Results*: 1025 and 1035, and Marx, 1861–3: 2130.
13. Ernest Mandel, in his introduction to *Results* (1976), concurs: 'Formal subsumption is characteristic of the period of manufacture; real subsumption is characteristic of the modern factory' (944).

must be a form of real subsumption. Sayer also fails to see that the terms 'formal subsumption' and 'real subsumption' refer first to *concepts of subsumption* and only secondarily – if at all – to *historical stages of subsumption*. Marx considers the possibility of a distinct historical stage of *merely* formal subsumption but finds no evidence of one. Neither does Marx think that there is any historical period of 'simple co-operation' (454). Manufacture and large-scale industry are the only two historical periods of real subsumption that Marx acknowledges. Because they conceive of formal and real subsumption as historical stages rather than as concepts of subsumption, Sayer and Balibar lose sight of the fact that a production process must be formally subsumed under capital in order to be really subsumed.

With a thinker like Marx, the architectonic considerations alone make a strong case against Balibar and Sayer. But here are a couple of passages that directly undercut their view. Marx describes cooperation as 'the first change experienced by the actual labour process when subjected to capital' (453). He goes on to remark that not only is cooperation the first form of real subsumption but that 'Co-operation remains the fundamental form of the capitalist mode of production, although in its simple shape it continues to appear as one particular form alongside the more developed ones' (454). Though there is no *period* of 'simple' cooperation, *cases* of 'simple' cooperation occur. All forms of real subsumption are forms of cooperation; 'simple' cooperation is a type of cooperation, but so are manufacture and large-scale industry.

Where division of labour and manufacture are concerned, consider two passages. 'The division of labour in the workshop, as practised by manufacture, is an entirely specific creation of the capitalist mode of production' (480). 'While simple co-operation leaves the mode of the individual's labour for the most part unchanged, manufacture thoroughly revolutionizes it, and seizes labour-power by its roots' (481). These statements should remove any doubt: *division of labour and manufacture are forms of real subsumption*.

3.1 Formal subsumption

Marx writes that the formal subsumption of labour under capital 'is the general form of every capitalist process of production' (1019); real subsumption, then, always presupposes formal subsumption. To begin to grasp capital's transformative power, we need to answer the following question: If formal subsumption of labour under capital is the 'general form', what social and material transformations does it bring about? The *social* transformations involved in formal subsumption are epochal;

the *material* transformations are slight – until *merely* formal subsumption gives way to real subsumption. Formal subsumption assumes that labour takes the specific social form of 'free' wage-labour and that wealth is generally in the commodity-form. These conditions enable the capitalist both to monopolize the means of subsistence of wage-labourers and to purchase all three factors of the production process: objects of production, means of production and labour-power (1026). With formal subsumption,

> the process of production has become the process of capital itself. It is a process involving the *factors of the labour process* into which the capitalist's money has been converted and which proceeds under his direction with the sole purpose of using money to make more money (1020).

Marx dwells on the exact social character of the relation between capitalist and 'free' wage-labourer.

> The pure money relationship between the man who appropriates the surplus labour and the man who yields it up: subordination in this case arises from the *specific content* of the sale – there is not a subordination underlying it in which the producer stands in a relation to the exploiter of his labour which is determined not just by money (the relationship of one commodity owner to another), but, let us say, by political restraints. What brings the seller into a relationship of dependency is solely the fact that the buyer is the owner of the conditions of labour. There is no fixed political and social relationship of supremacy and subordination (1025–6[14]).

This means that capitalism announces the end of social classes *as we knew them*, where class membership was fixed by birth and received explicit political or social recognition. With the rise of capitalism, then, not only does class structure assume a new form, *the very idea of class is radically transformed*.

14. On the other hand, not only do various forms of dependency based on religion, sex, race, ethnicity and 'birth' persist in actual capitalist societies, but they can serve various capitalist interests. Notably, they put downward pressure on wages and disrupt organized resistance to capital by workers.

In Chapter 6, 'The sale and purchase of labour-power', Marx had already emphasized the wage-labourer's freedom to dispose of his labour-power. In the marketplace, that 'Eden of the innate rights of man' (280), the wage-labourer and the capitalist meet as equals, one in the role of *seller*, the other *buyer*. The perfect liberty and egalitarianism of that sphere are, of course, dealt a blow by the shift into the sphere of production, where the wage-labourer is subordinate to the capitalist. But Marx's insistence that nothing other than the '*specific content* of the sale' enters into this unique type of subordination reveals how the characteristic social forms of simple commodity circulation condition the sphere of production.

Marx highlights the peculiar features of this social form of labour by contrasting the wage-labourer with slaves, serfs and vassals; the independent peasant; and the medieval guild labourer. He points up several distinctive, and mostly libratory, aspects of wage-labour.

1. Because of the voluntary and egalitarian aspects of the wage contract, wage-labourers *feel free*.
2. The wage-worker's livelihood and the livelihood of any dependants are the worker's own *responsibility*. Carrying the burden of this responsibility promotes a kind of *self-reliance* with the attendant ideologies and sensibilities. *Positive social recognition* and *self-esteem* also generally accompany these factors.[15]
3. The wage-worker is working *for herself* (as well as for her employer); her wages are hers to spend. While this increases self-esteem, it is also conducive to *selfishness*.[16]
4. Because wages are paid in *money*, it is up to the wage-labourer to choose what to buy: 'It is the worker himself who converts the money into whatever use-values he desires; it is he who buys commodities as he wishes' (1033). Marx observes that this requires workers to

15. Simone de Beauvoir writes in *The Second Sex*, 'It is through gainful employment that woman has traversed most of the distance that separated her from the male; and nothing else can guarantee her liberty in practice... with the money and the rights she takes possession of, she makes a trial of and senses her responsibility... I heard a charwoman declare, while scrubbing the stone floor of a hotel lobby: "I never asked anybody for anything; I succeeded all by myself". She was as proud of her self-sufficiency as a Rockefeller' (1949: 679–80).
16. Recall what Marx wrote of the participants in simple commodity circulation: 'each looks only to his own advantage. The only force bringing them together, and putting them into relation with each other, is the selfishness, the gain and the private interest of each. Each pays heed to himself only, and no one worries about the others' (280).

develop *self-control*, while making it possible for them to *break with a parochialism of needs*.

5. In making his purchases, the worker reenters that egalitarian sphere of commodity circulation: 'as the *owner of money*, as the buyer of goods, he stands in precisely the same relationship to the sellers of goods as any other buyer' (1033). We all call ourselves 'consumers'.

6. The variability of wages adds to the worker's perception that he is master of his fate: 'the size of his wage packet appears to vary in keeping with the results of his own work and its individual quality' (1032). The wage-labourer's own talents can benefit him.

7. Marx points out a chilly side of the wage: 'Since the sole purpose of work in the eyes of the wage-labourer is his wage, money, a specific quantity of exchange-value from which every particular mark of use-value has been expunged, he is wholly indifferent towards the content of his labour and hence his own particular form of activity' (1033). Even this indifference has its positive side, greater *versatility* on the part of workers.

8. As wealth increasingly takes on the commodity-form, everyone needs money, so that '*money-making* appears as the ultimate purpose of activity of every kind' (1041). This leads to slurring the differences among the forms of revenue: wages, profits, interest and rent: everyone's a money-maker. This obscures crucial differences while promoting egalitarian ideologies and sensibilities among wage-labourers.

Even though, as a consequence of the formal subsumption of labour under capital, 'the process of exploitation is stripped of every patriarchal, political or even religious cloak' (1027), Marx insists that 'a new relation of *supremacy and subordination*' (1027) takes the place of the outmoded ones. A production process that has been formally subsumed under capital is one that is under the command of the capitalist and is so for no other reason than that the capitalist owns the factors of the production process. To what end does the capitalist command the production process? To the only end that capital knows, surplus-value. The concrete production process and all the factors of production are simply *instruments* for the valorization of capital (1019). In this respect, capital holds particular use-values and wage-labourers in a calculated disregard. All the same, since the valorization process requires concrete production processes, the capitalist does not have the luxury of ignoring the specifics of the products, the process of their production or the people who produce them.

The final social implication of formal subsumption to be mentioned is the *mystification* inherent in it. At the beginning of the fetishism section of Chapter 1, Marx wrote of the commodity, 'it is a very strange thing, abounding in metaphysical subtleties and theological niceties' (163). He went on to argue that 'the mystical character of the commodity' stems from the peculiarity of the commodity form as a specific social form of wealth. The peculiarly asocial social form of commodity-producing labour results in commodities being fetishes possessed, in addition to their sensible properties, with the occult power to provide their owners a share in the wealth of the commodity-producing 'community'. Commodities are use-values that pack a social clout that, strangely, appears to be an inherent property. In the *Results*, Marx echoes the language of the fetishism section, writing, 'capital becomes a highly mysterious thing' (1056). The peculiar social forms and purposes involved in formal subsumption under capital result in capital becoming a more imposing fetish than the commodity.[17]

> Since – within the process of production – living labour has already been absorbed into capital, all the *social productive forces of labour* appear as the *productive forces* of capital, as intrinsic attributes of capital, just as in the case of money, the creative power of labour had seemed to possess the qualities of a thing. What was true of money is even truer of capital (1052).

Capital possesses the occult power not simply of command over some portion of social wealth but rather of *command over living labour*, an uncanny consequence latent in the phrase 'subsumption of labour under capital'.[18] As a consequence, all the socially developed productive powers appear to inhere in capital.

How, then, does formal subsumption transform the production process *materially*? Not much, says Marx. For all the social transformation involved, 'this change does not in itself imply a fundamental modification in the real nature of the labour process' (1021).[19] What changes do occur are more of a *quantitative* than qualitative sort: the process becomes more *continuous* and *orderly, less wasteful* in the use of means of production.

---

17. For a reading of the three volumes of *Capital* as organized around the commodity fetish and the capital fetish, see Murray (2002).
18. See 651.
19. See also 1026.

And, of course, there are those hallmarks of absolute surplus-value, *lengthening* and *intensifying* the workday. Such slight changes characterize *merely* formal subsumption, that is, formal subsumption where real subsumption does not occur. This reminds us that we must be cautious with the terminology of 'formal subsumption', as it has two meanings.[20] 'It is the general form of every capitalist process of production; at the same time, however, it can be found as a *particular* form alongside the *specifically capitalist mode of production* [that is, production that has undergone real subsumption]' (1019). The first, and original, sense of 'formal subsumption' applies to all processes of production organized along capitalist lines; the second, *merely* formal subsumption, refers only to those where real subsumption has not taken place.

3.2 Real subsumption

The social transformation of production involved in the formal subsumption of labour under capital lays the groundwork for the endless material (and social) transformation of production processes through their real subsumption under capital (1035).[21] What is real subsumption of labour under capital, and what social and material transformations does it bring about? Real subsumption transforms, and keeps transforming, production processes materially (and socially) into forms that are more adequate to capital for the simple reason that they press out more surplus-value (1037). This is why 'real subsumption' is matched with the phrases 'specifically capitalist mode of production' and 'capitalist production' (for short).[22] The term 'real subsumption' can apply (1) to the concept of materially transforming a formally subsumed production process for the purpose of increasing surplus-value, (2) to a particular production process that has undergone real subsumption – McDonald's

20. A third sense of 'formal subsumption' would identify a historical period in which *merely* formal subsumption (the second sense) was the dominant mode of production. Marx finds no such period.
21. Marx's concepts of formal and real subsumption challenge 'technological' versions of historical materialism such G.A. Cohen's. 'Technological' historical materialism misses the basic point of Marx's historical materialism when it falsely *separates* technology from specific social forms and purposes. Neither the conceptual point that specific social forms and purposes *co-determine* what the forces of production *are*, nor the specific historical point that *merely* formal subsumption precedes real subsumption fits 'technological' historical materialism. Cohen sees the latter problem and appeals to functional explanations to try to get around it. For a criticism of his attempt, see Sayer (1987).
22. See *Results*: 1024 and 1034–6.

fast food 'restaurants' are so prominent a case that 'Mc' has become, so to speak, the prefix of real subsumption (hence *USA Today* is 'Mcpaper') – and (3) to a historical period characterized by real subsumption.[23]

Marx has a great deal to say about particular types of real subsumption. The three chapters devoted to cooperation, division of labour and manufacture, and machinery and large-scale industry come to two hundred pages (439–639). Marx defines cooperation as follows: 'When numerous workers work together side by side in accordance with a plan, whether in the same process, or in different but connected processes, this form of labour is called cooperation' (443). While *simple* cooperation is a particular type of real subsumption, cooperation 'remains the fundamental form of the capitalist mode of production' (454). The concept of cooperation, then, belongs to the *systematic dialectical* argument of *Capital*, while simple cooperation, manufacture and large-scale industry all pertain to *historical dialectics*.[24] Here, our focus will be on what we can say in general about real subsumption.

First, since real subsumption presupposes formal subsumption, everything that was said about the transformations it brings about applies to production processes that undergo real subsumption (1035).

Second, 'a definite and constantly *growing minimum amount of capital* is both the necessary precondition and the constant result of the *specifically* capitalist mode of production' (1035). It is the enlargement of merely formally subsumed production processes that leads to the simplest, and the basic, form of real subsumption, cooperation (1022).

Third, in cooperation, the mere quantitative increase in the scale of production shifts into qualitative changes.

> A large number of workers working together, at the same time, in one place...in order to produce the same sort of commodity under the command of the same capitalist, constitutes the starting-point of capitalist production. This is true both historically and conceptually (437).

---

23. Since Marx judges that there is no historical period of merely formal subsumption, the historical period of real subsumption largely coincides with modern capitalism.
24. On systematic dialectics and historical dialectics see Smith (1990, 2003) and Murray (2003).

By 'capitalist production' here Marx means the 'specifically capitalist mode of production': 'capitalist production' begins historically *and conceptually* with cooperation. *All real subsumption involves cooperation.* What qualitative changes does cooperation bring about?

1. Only with an expanded scale of production do the different proficiencies of individual workers begin to balance out enough so as to resemble the socially average character of labour for that branch of production. Only then does the law of valorization come 'fully into its own for the individual producer' (441).
2. 'Even without an alteration in the method of work, the simultaneous employment of a large number of workers produces a revolution in the objective conditions of the labour process' (441). Here Marx has economies of scale in mind (442). The savings on means of production involved here cheapen commodities and thereby increase surplus-value by lowering the value of labour-power. *Cooperation is a relative surplus-value strategy.* At the same time, these savings on means of production (constant capital) raise the rate of profit by reducing constant capital.
3. Certain tasks can be undertaken only cooperatively; in such cases we have 'the creation of a new productive power, which is intrinsically a collective one' (443).
4. Emending Aristotle's observation that the human is a *political* animal, Marx calls humans *social* animals, for whom 'mere social contact begets in most industries a rivalry and a stimulation of the "animal spirits", which heighten the efficiency of each individual worker' (443).
5. Cooperation makes possible the accomplishment of huge tasks that must be completed quickly and at a particular moment, such as harvesting crops.
6. Other projects, building a large dam, for example, are so vast as to require the power of cooperative labour.
7. Cooperation can also allow for a spatial concentration of efforts that reduces incidental expenses.

Marx pulls all of these advantages together in a long paragraph culminating in the observation that whatever the source of cooperation's special productive power, it is 'under all circumstances, the social productive power of labour, or the productive power of social labour. This power arises from cooperation itself' (447). This social productive power of cooperation costs the capitalist nothing. It is these new productive powers of social labour that make cooperation a strategy of relative surplus-value. Real subsumption of labour under capital, then, is all about the development of the productive powers of *social labour* – on capital's terms and to serve capital's end. The mystification of social productive powers as inherent in capital increases with the progress of real subsumption.

Fourth, there is a (continual) transformation in the capitalist's command of the production process.

> We also saw that, at first, the subjection of labour to capital was only a formal result of the fact that the worker, instead of working for himself, works for, and consequently under, the capitalist. Through the co-operation of numerous wage-labourers, the command of capital develops into a requirement of carrying on the labour process itself, into a real condition of production (448).

With real subsumption the workers' dependence on capitalists takes a *material* form; capitalists, not workers, take charge of the coherence and plan of operations in the workplace.

Leadership of the 'cooperative' production process falls to the capitalist because he is the capitalist – this much follows from formal subsumption. But the capitalist is not a generic leader, 'As a specific function of capital, the directing function acquires its own special characteristics' (449). These special characteristics stem from the specific social form and purpose of the capitalist mode of production. The goal of the capitalist's 'industrial' leadership is 'the greatest possible production of surplus-value' (449). A further important factor conditioning the capitalist's 'industrial' leadership is the antagonistic relationship between capital and wage-labour. Here, Marx once again draws our attention to the *double character* of capitalist production.

> If capitalist direction is thus twofold in content, owing to the twofold nature of the process of production which has to be directed – on the one hand a social labour process for the creation of a product, and on the other hand capital's process of valorization – in form it is purely despotic (450).

Due to the material changes to the production process, this despotism, which is capital's despotism personified, settles into the physical make-up of production processes.[25]

With his conception of the real subsumption of production under capital, Marx thinks of modern 'industry' in a profoundly new way. A common, everyday way to imagine modern capitalism is to picture it in terms of 'commerce and industry'.[26] Industry is thought of in generic terms as the process by which wealth with no particular social form or purpose gets produced. Commerce is treated simply as an efficient technique for distributing the 'wealth' that industry produces. Commerce and industry, then, are not internally related beyond the banal point that, without the wealth that industry produces, there would be nothing for commerce to distribute. Marx's claim that simple cooperation, manufacture and large-scale industry are all 'specifically capitalist' kinds of production has no place in this picture. For the 'commerce and industry' picture, there is no 'specifically capitalist' kind of production: industry is industry. The fact that Marx adopts the ordinary terminology of simple cooperation, division of labour and manufacture, and machinery and large-scale industry may lull his reader. But once we appreciate the significance of formal subsumption and real subsumption and grasp what Marx means by 'the specifically capitalist mode of production', there can be no mistaking Marx's radical break with the 'commerce and industry' picture. Still, two deep conceptual mistakes interfere with our understanding of real subsumption.

One is the error of thinking that use-value and value categories are mutually irrelevant. In fact, use-value considerations enter into Marx's critique of political economy at many points, whether because the use-value considerations affect the value considerations, as in the case of the use-value of the commodity labour-power, or because the value considerations shape use-value ones.[27] Productivity is an interesting and pertinent case. Precisely because productivity is a use-value consideration and because the social kind of labour that produces value is

25. The opening factory scene of Charlie Chaplin's film *Modern Times* brings home the despotism of the assembly line, the time clock, and electronic surveillance of workers. The fanciful 'Billows Feeding Machine', designed to prolong capital's despotism through the lunch break, turned out not to be 'practical'.
26. See Murray (1998). The present chapter reinforces that critique of the 'commerce and industry' picture by pointing out its incompatibility with subsumption concepts.
27. See Marx, 1939: 852–3. See also Arthur (2003) and Murray (1998).

abstract labour, changes in productivity across a branch of production do not affect the amount of value added per hour. As we saw, this is the 'value treadmill' effect. But that does not prove that changes in productivity have no effect on value considerations: the whole strategy of relative surplus-value is to increase productivity in order to drive down the value of labour-power. Increased productivity, a use-value consideration, allows capital to extract more surplus-value from the same sum of new value added.

With real subsumption, production processes are transformed in use-value terms, *materially*, in order to satisfy capital's appetite for surplus-value. I call the failure to recognize this phenomenon 'technological *naïveté*'. I pair that notion with 'use-value romanticism', the idea that socialism reduces to 'expropriating the expropriators', that is, eliminating surplus-value by ending the monopoly of capitalists and landowners on the means of production. Once that is accomplished, the idea is that the means of production can be redirected to the production of use-values ('wealth') instead of surplus-value. This romantic conception fails to recognize that, if production for the sake of surplus-value were overthrown, it would have to be replaced with some new and definite social form of production with a definite social purpose. That new purpose would have to be thicker than just producing use-values. 'Use-value romanticism' misses the significance of real subsumption. With real subsumption, the distinctive social forms and purposes of the capitalist mode permeate and mould the material, technological make-up of the production process. A socialist society, then, would face the formidable challenge of undoing much of what real subsumption has brought about.[28]

Understanding real subsumption can also be blocked if we fail to see the *inseparability of production and exchange*. The false 'commerce and industry' picture of capitalism exemplifies that failure. One simple example of the inseparability of production and circulation is that the whole point of capitalist production, namely, the endless accumulation of surplus-value, makes no sense without money and simple commodity circulation. Marx's criticism of economics on this point is original and profound.[29] It fits with his seminal contribution – to recognize the

28. Chris Arthur makes this point: 'a considerable reworking of the use-value sphere would be necessary before a socialist mode of production could take root' (Arthur, 2003: 149, n. 26).
29. See Marx, 1939: 94–100, and also Chapter 51, 'Relations of distribution and relations of production', in Marx, 1894.

fundamental significance of the specific social forms and purposes of all actual production processes. Acknowledging the inseparability of production and exchange pressures us to drop the 'commerce and industry' picture and adopt the Marxian concepts of formal subsumption and real subsumption.

3.3 Hybrid subsumption

Marx devotes one paragraph of *Capital I* to what he calls the 'hybrid' (*Zwitter*) form of subsumption under capital (645). Marx also discusses this form, though he does not use the term 'hybrid', in his manuscript of 1861–3 and in the *Results*.[30] In hybrid subsumption, capital appropriates surplus-value without formal subsumption under capital occurring; indeed, Marx employs the concept of hybrid subsumption as one foil in his discussion of formal subsumption. Marx makes clear, both in the 1861–3 manuscript and in *Capital*, that capital's extraction of surplus-value through hybrid subsumption, while it may well be more exploitative than under the conditions of formal subsumption, cannot be a form of direct, personal domination.

> It will be sufficient if we merely refer to certain hybrid forms, in which neither is surplus labour extorted *by direct compulsion from the producer* nor has the producer been formally subsumed under capital. In these forms, capital has not yet acquired a direct control over the labour process (645; my emphasis and amended translation).

This condition on hybrid subsumption directs us to two related points.

1. For Marx, it is one of the most decisive historic features of capitalism that it is not based on personal forms of domination. We saw that Marx makes a great deal of this in his discussion of the social effects of formal subsumption, in particular, of 'free' wage-labour.
2. As Marx observes in the *Results*, with the spread of capitalism, the commodity and wage-labour forms become 'absolute'; they predominate even where the commodity is not commodity capital and wage-labour is not directly surplus-value-producing labour (1041).

30. The heading used in the 1861–3 manuscript (2152–9 and 2182) is 'transitional forms' (*Uebergangsformen*). That term as well as the term 'accompanying forms' (*Nebensformen*) come up in the *Results* (1023, 1044 and 1048).

With the spread of the commodity and wage-labour forms, money tends to become the universal mediator in human exchanges. With the pre-eminence of money comes the erosion of personal domination: commercial exchanges presuppose formally free and equal persons, buyer and seller or borrower or lender. Money is the great leveller (179). And in this passage from the 1861–3 manuscript, Marx insists that in hybrid subsumption the power of capital is mediated – as it always is – by money and the social roles of buyer and seller:

> We can speak of such transitional forms only where *formally* the *relationship of buyer or seller* (or, a modification, borrower or lender) between the actual producer and the exploiter predominates, where it is generally the case that the content of the transaction between the two parties is not conditioned by relationships of domination and submission [*Knechtschaft und Herrschaft*] but that they face one another as formally free (Marx, 1861–3: 2152[31]).

Marx recognizes two types of hybrid subsumption: one he calls *transitional* (*Uebergangsform*), the other, *accompanying* (*Nebensform*). The *transitional* form refers to a kind of hybrid subsumption that is a bridge to modern capitalist social relations. Historically, two sub-types of transitional hybrid subsumption stand out: both involve ancient forms of capital, *interest-bearing capital* and *merchant capital*. In the former case, the usurer takes interest payments from producers who are not formally subsumed under capital; in the latter, the merchant capitalist profits by mediating between producers and consumers. As transitional hybrid subsumption moves labour processes toward formal subsumption under capital, it pulls them away from pre-capitalist forms of personal domination. Transitional hybrid subsumption's historic significance and scope of application are great even though the concept is marginal to *Capital*'s systematic dialectic. The *accompanying* type of hybrid subsumption refers to forms that keep appearing alongside established capitalist firms, as previously unsubsumed sectors of

31. This requirement explains why, when Marx takes up examples of transitional subsumption, he does not mention the case of the apprentice–master relationship. Instead, he uses it to explain, by way of contrast, formal subsumption under capital. Because the relationship between apprentice and master does not reduce to a simple cash nexus, it fails to qualify as either formal or hybrid subsumption.

production come actually, though indirectly, under the power of capital. Hybrid subsumption endures, then, as a subordinate feature of life in a capitalist society.

3.4 Ideal subsumption

The types of ideal subsumption under capital involve treating labour that is not *actually* subsumed under capital (whether formally or in a hybrid manner) as if it were. Ideal subsumption may be sorted as follows.

1. *Ideal subsumption of precapitalist economic formations under capital.* Because of their lack of attention to specific social form, which capitalism encourages by camouflaging itself, economists confuse the capitalist mode of production with production in general. Marx observes,

> The *determinate social character* of the means of production in capitalist production – expressing a particular *production relation* – has so grown together with, and in the mode of thought of bourgeois society is so inseparable from, the material existence of these means of production as means of production, that the same determinateness (categorical determinateness) is assumed even where the relation is in direct contradiction to it (Marx, 1904/10, 1956/66: 408).

Consequently, economists are prone to subsume precapitalist forms of production under the capital form. Marx catches J.S. Mill in a striking example of this, where Mill goes on about *profit* where there is no buying or selling (652).

2. *Ideal subsumption of non-capitalist processes of production that exist side by side with capitalist ones.*

> Within capitalist production there are always certain parts of the productive process that are carried out in a way typical of earlier modes of production, in which the relations of capital and wage-labour did not yet exist ... But in line with the dominant mode of production, even those kinds of labour which have not been subjugated by capitalism in reality are so in thought (1042).

The term 'self-employed' worker points to a type of ideal subsumption where a single person comes to regard herself as her own wage-labourer and her own means of production as her capital (1042). This sort of ideal subsumption reveals the unseen power that specific social forms have over the imaginations of participants in capitalist societies.

3. *Ideal subsumption within capitalist firms.*

One curiosity of a capitalist production process is that, *within it*, goods and services no longer actually function even as commodities. However, goods and services functioning within a particular department within a capitalist firm may be ideally subsumed under the capital form and calculations made *as if* the department were its own capitalist firm, in order to locate the firm's profit centres. Because it is typical for industrial capitalists to rely on external financing, those who are self-financing may ideally subsume a portion of their own profits under the form of interest (Marx, 1861–3: 2180).

4. Results and peculiarities of the specifically capitalist drive to increase productivity

In the *Results* and in the 1861–3 manuscript, Marx identifies two chief consequences of relative surplus-value (real subsumption) as (1) 'the development of the *social productive forces of labour*' (1037) and (2) 'to *raise the quantity of production* and *multiply* and *diversify the spheres of production* and their sub-spheres' (1037).[32] Actually, Marx calls attention to this second development already in connection with formal subsumption's '*compulsion to perform surplus labour*', which increases production (not productivity) and pushes the mass of products beyond the traditional needs of workers (1026).

At this point, one may want to respond to Marx, 'So you are saying that it is capitalism's nature constantly to increase the quantity of production, raise productivity, and diversify products. Aren't these strong recommendations of capitalism?' There is an important truth expressed in this reaction, and Marx does find something deeply hopeful in these and other tendencies of capitalism. But the matter is not simple. The concept of 'the' drive to increase productivity – *What could possibly be wrong with increasing productivity?* – is problematic in just the same way as are the ordinary concept of wealth and the commonplace concept of capital. It shuns specific social form and purpose. There is something peculiar to the *capitalist* drive to increase productivity that makes it unexpectedly

32. See also Marx, 1861–3: 2142–3.

and elusively conflicted. We need to expose the troubling aspects of *this* drive to increase productivity and its tendency to camouflage itself as general and benign. Our purpose, once again, is to reveal that what may easily be taken as universal or natural, that is, not socially specific, in this case, 'the' drive for increased productivity, is specific. We want to see the capitalist colours of this drive to increase productivity.

4.1 Production for the sake of production? Productivism and wealthism

Increasing productivity seems so unassailable a goal in a capitalist society precisely because, apparently devoid of any definite social purpose, capitalist production appears to be 'production for the sake of production' (1037). Because money is necessarily, if bizarrely, the way that the specific social form of the products of labour gets expressed in the capitalist mode of production, and, because money appears as a separable thing, the capitalist production process and its products appear to lack specific social form. They appear to be 'production in general' and 'wealth in general'. Consequently, 'production' and 'wealth' appear as society's goals. Capitalism's specific social forms seem to be written in invisible ink.

I call 'production for the sake of production' *productivism*. By the same token, I call productivism's counterpart, 'wealth for the sake of wealth', or 'wealth as end in itself' (1037), *wealthism*. As ways to represent the capitalist mode of production, both reveal and conceal truth. Marx notes that the ideologies of productivism and wealthism arise naturally as participants in a capitalist society represent their society to themselves (742). Productivism and wealthism are what I call *shadow forms* of capital: they mimic the abstractness, quantitative focus and indifference of the value-forms that cast them.

Productivism and wealthism in no way express universal truths. Quite the opposite, they are exclusively appearance forms of the peculiar purpose of *capitalist* production. Marx states,

'Production for the sake of production' – production as end in itself – enters in certainly already with the formal subsumption of labour under capital, as soon as it generally becomes the case that the immediate purpose of production is the production of the greatest possible amount of surplus-value (1037).

Marx conceives of 'production for the sake of production' as a necessary manifestation of the drive for surplus-value, 'that the individual product contain *as much surplus-value as possible*, is achieved only through production for the sake of production' (1038).

By the phrase 'production for the sake of production', Marx means production that is driven not by existing needs but rather by capital's imperative, 'Accumulate, accumulate'. As Marx puts it in the *Results*, 'instead of the scale of production being determined by existing needs, the quantity of products made is determined by the constantly increasing scale of production dictated by the mode of production itself' (1037–8). Capital's need to accumulate, not human needs, is its mainspring. Marx's disaffection with productivism and wealthism echoes Aristotle and Aquinas: humans are not made for wealth; wealth is made for humans.

Marx nevertheless commends the transcendence of preexisting limits on need; this is the *positive* side of capitalism, 'This is the one side, in distinction from earlier modes of production; if you like, the positive side' (1037). Here Marx sides with the moderns against the ancients. But the universality of capitalist needing, while a progressive development, is, for Marx, an inadequate *kind* of universality. To be about human needs is not necessarily to be *wealthist*. Marx contrasts the modern, capitalist universality of needing, which is in thrall to the demands of surplus-value accumulation, with a new type of universality.

When the limited bourgeois form is stripped away, what is wealth other than the universality of individual needs, capacities, pleasure, productive forces etc., created through universal exchange? The full development of human mastery over the forces of nature, those of so-called nature as well as of humanity's own nature? The absolute working-out of his creative potentialities, with no presupposition other than the previous historic development, which makes this totality of development, i.e. the development of all human powers as such the end in itself, not as measured on a predetermined yardstick?... In bourgeois economics – and in the epoch of production to which it corresponds – this complete working-out of the human content appears as a complete emptying-out, this universal objectification as total alienation, and the tearing-down of all limited, one-sided aims as sacrifice of the human end-in-itself to an entirely external end (Marx, 1939: 488).

The capitalist brand of universality inescapably subjects human beings to the imperious demands of their own creation, capital, and conceals barriers imposed by the demands of capital accumulation. Surplus-value is its measure of success. Marx has a very different universal measure of wealth in mind, one that synthesizes the Aristotelian emphasis on the development of human capabilities with the modern emphasis on universality and the openness of human nature.

4.2 The drive's selectivity

In capitalism, production is not actually for the sake of production. The very idea of 'production for the sake of production' is false, the counterpart to the imaginary 'production in general'. So-called 'production for the sake of production' is actually undertaken for the sake of accumulating surplus-value. Consequently, the capitalist drive to increase productivity is *selective*; it is directed where it conforms to the goal of increasing surplus-value. If building Mcmansions for the comfortably housed is more lucrative than constructing homes for the homeless, 'production for the sake for production' will build Mcmansions.

4.3 The drive's contradictory character

Because 'production for the sake of production' is actually production for the sake of surplus-value, *capital becomes a barrier to itself* and proves *contradictory* (1037). Surprisingly, increased productivity can result in a reduction in the rate of profit, despite the strategy of relative surplus-value.[33] *Crises* and *overproduction* manifest this contradictory nature; these phenomena bring home the stark reality that the capitalist mode of production imposes limits on itself. If production were simply for the sake of production, the very idea of overproduction would be a joke. In capitalism, of course, overproduction is no laughing matter. In crises, production declines *because of* its actual purpose (surplus-value), *not in violation of* its purported purpose (production as an end in itself).

4.4 The drive's exclusivity

Because the purpose of the capitalist drive for increased productivity is singular, it gives the cold shoulder to other social objectives, for example, leisure time or time for domestic responsibilities; safe and attractive working conditions; preservation of natural beauty or historically significant sites. When accumulating surplus-value is all that matters, workers get squeezed:

---

33. Marx relished his demonstration (in *Capital, Volume III*) that a falling rate of profit can be a consequence not of diminishing productivity, as in Ricardo's theory, but of increasing productivity.

On the other hand, the negative, or the contradictory character [of the drive]: production in contradiction to, and unconcerned for the producer. The actual producer as mere means of production, material wealth as end in itself. And the development of this material wealth, therefore, in contradiction to and at the cost of the human individual (1037).

Here Marx expresses just the idea we are after. What appears universal, 'the' drive to increase the productivity of labour, is – *precisely in that abstractness* – a manifestation of a specific mode of production, the mode of production organized around surplus-value – not the illusory 'production in general'. By contrast, Marx points out how in the ancient world, 'where the worker counted as an end in himself' (1050), inventions were banned where they would break up the old social order. Protectionism and labour laws ensuring job security echo those ancient practices. As Marx coldly remarks, however, 'all of that is for the developed capitalist mode of production outdated and untrue, false perceptions' (1050).

4.5 The drive's domineering character

There is something driven, something *domineering*, about the push to increase productivity within capitalism. Thus Marx writes, 'Productivity of labour in general [*ueberhaupt*] = maximum of product with minimum of labour, and therefore the greatest possible cheapening of commodities. This becomes the law, *independent of the wills* of individual capitalists' (1037). The heedless drive to increase productivity is *imposed* on participants in a capitalist society – capitalists included – by the impersonal demands of capital accumulation.

4.6 The drive's false generality

There are several features of the specific social forms of capitalism that ensure that the methods of increasing productivity of social labour brought about by real subsumption will be *general*, rather than parochial, but *general in a particular way*. Unlike other modes of production, capitalism necessarily posits a form of universalism. The social fetish of value itself is the consequence of the abstract way in which the universal equivalence of labour is recognized in capitalist society. Wage-labour erodes patriarchal, political and religious forms of domination. Capitalist competition in the world market presses toward a cosmopolitan outlook:

'The intellectual creations of individual nations become common property. National one-sidedness and narrow-mindedness become more and more impossible' (Marx and Engels, 1848: 84). We have already noted how the wage form and capitalism's push for product innovation burst the parochialism of needs.

Moishe Postone directs us to a tension between two sorts of generality that develop with capitalism, one that is radically indifferent to the particularities of use-value and one that 'does not necessarily exist in opposition to particularity' (Postone, 1993: 367). The tension between these two sorts of generality may be the most hopeful product of real subsumption under capital. It creates what Postone calls 'shearing pressures' in capitalism that may yet, as Marx anticipated, open space for fundamental alternatives to capital.[34]

Appendix: On relative surplus-value and inflation

In a recent essay (Reuten, 2003), Geert Reuten proposes that a steady, low rate of inflation has become a systematic tendency of capitalism. I would like to sketch an argument that may provide further support for his conclusion. Consider what the strategy of relative surplus-value implies if there is no inflation. The strategy is to drive down the value of labour-power, while continuing to pay wage-labourers full value. But, where the value of money is constant, this requires lowering the nominal wage. Instead of being paid $100 per day, workers are now to be paid, say, $90. If we make the reasonable assumption that the price of labour-power, the wage, is 'sticky', that is, workers balk at any lowering of their nominal wages, then the strategy of relative surplus-value constantly runs into an obstacle.

The resistance of workers to a lowering of their wages in value terms is lessened by the ruse of a steady, low rate of inflation, which avoids 'sticker shock'. Inflation allows employers to cut wages in value terms while keeping the nominal wage steady or even rising. Thus, a 0 per cent raise will be presented as a 'wage freeze', not as the wage cut that it actually amounts to under even mildly inflationary conditions. As the inflation rate goes higher, however, the discrepancies involved in this deception become more noticeable and, let's assume, less effective. In fact, the ruse may turn counterproductive: if workers come to anticipate

34. For their valuable comments on earlier versions of this paper I would like to thank Chris Arthur, Ricardo Bellofiore, Martha Campbell, Mino Carchedi, Paul Mattick Jr, Fred Moseley, Geert Reuten, Jeanne Schuler, Tony Smith and Nicky Taylor.

ever-higher rates of inflation, they will want to hedge against that pro-spect by demanding pay rises that shoot past the going rate of inflation. That is a recipe for a disruptive inflationary spiral.

References

Albritton, Robert and John Simoulidis (eds) (2003), *New Dialectics and Political Economy* (Basingstoke: Palgrave Macmillan).
Arthur, Christopher J. (2003), The problem of use-value for a dialectic of capital, in Albritton and Simoulidis (eds) (2003).
— and Geert Reuten (eds) (1998), *The Circulation of Capital: Essays on Volume II of Marx's 'Capital'* (London: Macmillan – now Palgrave Macmillan).
Balibar, Étienne (1968), The basic concepts of historical materialism, in Louis Althusser and Etienne Balibar, *Reading 'Capital'* (trans. Ben Brewster) (New York: Pantheon Books, 1970).
Campbell, Martha and Geert Reuten (eds) (2002), *The Culmination of Capital: Essays on Volume III of Marx's 'Capital'* (Basingstoke: Palgrave Macmillan).
Cohen, G.A. (1978), *Karl Marx's Theory of History: A Defense* (Princeton, NJ: Princeton University Press).
de Beauvoir, Simone (1949), *The Second Sex* (trans. and ed. by H.M. Parshley) (New York: Vintage Books, 1989).
Mandel, Ernest (1976), Introduction to *Results of the Immediate Production Process*, in *Capital, Volume I*.
Marx, Karl (1867), *Capital, Volume I*. (trans. Ben Fowkes) (New York: Vintage, 1977).
— (1894), *Capital, Volume III* (1st German edn 1894, 1st English edn 1909) (trans. David Fernbach) (Harmondsworth: Penguin/NLB, 1981).
— (1939), *Grundrisse* (trans. Martin Nicolaus) (Harmondsworth, England: Penguin, 1973).
— (1933), *Resultate des unmittelbaren Produktionsprozesses*. Archiv sozialistischer Literatur 17 (Frankfurt: Verlag Neue Kritik, 1969).
— (1933), *Results of the Immediate Production Process*, in *Capital, Volume I*.
— (1904/10 and 1956/66), *Theories of Surplus-Value*, Part I (ed. S. Ryazanskaya; trans. E. Burns). (London: Lawrence & Wishart, 1963).
— (1861–3), *Zur Kritik der Politischen Oekonomie (Manuskripte 1861–1863)*, in *Karl Marx, Friedrich Engels, Gesamtausgabe* (MEGA), Zweite Abteilung, Band 3, Teil 1 (Berlin: Dietz Verlag, 1976).
— and Frederick Engels (1848), *The Communist Manifesto* (trans. Samuel Moore). (Harmondsworth: Penguin, 1967).
Murray, Patrick (1998), Beyond the 'commerce and industry' picture of capital, in Arthur and Reuten (eds) (1998).
— (2002), The illusion of the economic: the Trinity Formula and the 'religion of everyday life', in Campbell and Reuten (eds) (2002).
— (2003), Things fall apart: historical and systematic dialectics and the critique of political economy, in Albritton and Simoulidis (eds) (2003).
Postone, Moishe (1993), *Time, Labour, and Social Domination: A Reinterpretation of Marx's Critical Theory* (Cambridge: Cambridge University Press).
Reuten, Geert (2003), On 'becoming necessary' in an organic systematic dialectic: the case of creeping inflation, in Albritton and Simoulidis (eds) (2003).

Rubin, I.I. (1972), *Essays on Marx's Theory of Value* (trans. Milos Samardzija and Fredy Perlman). (Detroit: Black & Red).

Sayer, Derek (1987), *The Violence of Abstraction* (Oxford: Basil Blackwell).

Smith, Tony (1990), *The Logic of Marx's 'Capital': Replies to Hegelian Criticisms* (Albany, NY: State University of New York Press)

— (2003), Systematic and historical dialectics: towards a Marxian theory of globalization, in Albritton and Simoulidis (eds) (2003).

10
The Inner Mechanism of the Accumulation of Capital: The Acceleration Triple – A Methodological Appraisal of Part Seven of Marx's *Capital I*

Geert Reuten

In this chapter I discuss Marx's theory of the accumulation of capital in Part Seven of Volume I of *Capital*, especially in reference to its methodological status. The accumulation of capital – or the conversion of surplus-value into capital – is one of the two aspects of 'The production process of capital' (the subtitle of the book), the other aspect being the production of surplus-value, treated in the middle part of the book.

Starting from simplified notions of accumulation, Marx gradually explicates the complex dynamics of an interconnected triple accelerator of: increasing accumulation of capital, increasing productive forces of labour, and an increasing composition of capital. All along, however, his focus is methodologically restricted to the 'inner mechanism' of capital accumulation (as explained in section 1 below); I will indicate that this is important for understanding what Marx can achieve here.

We will see – in section 3 – that Marx introduces an idea of cyclical accumulation of capital. The character of this cyclical accumulation has been an issue of debate within the Marxian tradition and amongst historians of thought. It is shown that Marx does not introduce a 'labour-shortage' theory of the cycle. In fact he does not present a theory of the cycle at all: in *Capital I* cyclical accumulation is introduced by way of an empirical reference. (I do not argue that the later Marxian theory of cyclical labour-shortage makes no sense; I argue that Marx does not introduce it in this book – the same applies for a theory of cyclical under-consumption; in fact, he never introduces these theories in any of the volumes of *Capital*.)

In this chapter my concern is the methodological status of the final text of the book and not its genesis. Where required I compare the *Capital I* text with the text of *Das Kapital I*.[1] For reasons of space I abstain from specific comments on interpretations in the secondary literature.

1. Part Seven within the systematic of *Capital*, Volume I

1.1 Part Seven in the German and English editions

The most general theoretical conclusions that Marx draws in *Capital I* on the process of accumulation of capital can be found in Chapter 24, Section 4 (the factors determining the extent of accumulation of capital) and the first four sections of Chapter 25 ('The general law of capitalist accumulation'). These will be discussed in sections 2–3 below. The corresponding chapters in the German edition are 22 and 23 – the difference is due to a reordering by Friedrich Engels for the English edition (1887) of the book. With some reluctance I follow this English convention for my chapter references – with apologies to those who read *Das Kapital* or its other language translations.

Engels also broke up the German Part Seven into two parts: Part Seven encompassing the systematic chapters (German chapters 21–3) and Part Eight the historical chapters (German chapters 24–5). When I refer to 'Part Seven' I mean the three systematic chapters – with the same apologies.

1.2 A cursory survey of Part Seven

'Earlier we considered how surplus-value arises from capital; now we have to see how capital arises from surplus-value. The employment of surplus-value as capital, or its reconversion into capital, is called accumulation of capital' (725).[2] In Part Seven of *Capital I*, from which this quote is taken, Marx first sets out the elementary shape of accumulation: extension or growth of capital. Next he shows how this growth accelerates

---

1. I have great respect for the translators. Translators have to rely on contemporary text interpretations. When interpretations shift, earlier translations will inevitably become defective. Here lies a fundamental difference between an original text and a translation (of course a translation itself may be reinterpreted).
2. All unspecified numbers, like this one, are page references to the English edition of *Capital I* in the Fowkes translation (Marx, 1867F). Where the context requires it I specify with a prefix 'F', e.g. F: 725. Page references to the German edition of the work are always prefixed by a 'G', e.g. G: 668 (Marx, 1867G).

in combination with the development of the productive forces of labour (section 2 below). And finally he introduces another accelerator: the technical composition of capital (section 3 below). All along his focus is on the dynamic consequences of this triple interaction on the capital–labour relation, and particularly on their propagation of a reserve army of unemployed labour which is a necessary condition for continuous accumulation of capital.

1.3 The assumptions delineating the level of abstraction

Since around 1990, Marx scholars have increasingly come to appraise Marx's *Capital* as a systematic dialectical work (to be distinguished from historical dialectics – both of these different types of dialectics find their modern roots in Hegel).[3] Relevant for this chapter is not so much the dialectic (I will not stress that) but the systematic, which is a systematic of, in principle, rigorous levels of abstraction running both in terms of the terrain analysed and synthesized (see below) and in terms of the movement from simple determinations to complex ones (both within and across these terrains).

In considering the meaning of Marx's statements about the effects of the accumulation of capital – including cyclical aspects – it is of preeminent importance to list the assumptions on which these statements are based, assumptions that delineate Marx's level of abstraction. Here I list the assumptions relevant for these chapters.[4]

1. Earlier (Part Four) Marx explicitly considers an average capital (thus abstracting from intra- and inter-branch differences, including differing production periods and compositions of capital – dealt with in Volume III, Parts One and Two). In Part Seven, however, he deals with average *changes* in the composition of capital. Although much of Part Seven can still be read in terms of the average capital the

---

3. See Reuten (2003a) for a brief history of the methodological appraisal of *Capital*, as well as for references to the literature. A problem in this appraisal is, first, that Marx experimented with the method so as to find his own way with it – but was hardly explicit about this; second, that he did not complete *Capital* (even less its planned continuations). Another problem is the status of 'Part Eight' of *Capital I*, which does not fit the systematic (see Tony Smith, 1990: 133–5 for a scholarly account; see Murray, 2000–2 for qualifications of the appraisal).
4. Others are listed in my Chapter 5 n. 3 in the present collection. In comparison to those, Marx now considers average changes in the composition of capital. He also states explicitly: that some share of surplus-value is accumulated (or consumed); that, generally and on average, there is some reserve army of labour; that wages are variable (within limits).

analysis *leans*, and sometimes explicitly, towards a macroeconomic treatment.[5]

2. In the introduction to Part Seven Marx indicates that he assumes capital to pass 'through its process of circulation in the normal way'.[6] The 'normal way' implies that commodities produced are sold 'at their value' (709–10). (This again implies that production and sales are carried out at the normal profit, or the normal surplus-value.) 'Normal' also implies, as Marx states, abstraction from any supply/demand discrepancies of the commodities produced. (He will explicitly introduce changes in the reserve of labour though, without considering their effect on the demand for commodities.)

3. Marx also abstracts from differentiations of capital into industrial capital, commercial capital, finance and banking and from landed property. Hence the 'various mutually independent forms' into which surplus-value is fragmented, 'such as profit, interest . . . rent' are abstracted from (709–10).[7]

Immediately following this, Marx makes a formal methodological statement:

> Hence we initiate the accumulation abstractly, that is, merely as moment of the immediate process of production.
>
> (Translation of Marx, 1867G: 590[8])

Both of the main English translations miss the term 'moment' and (therefore) its reference to the subject matter of Volume I; that is, *its* level of abstraction.[9] A 'moment' is a 'systematic-dialectical' notion, referring to a type of analysis. First, it is the analysis of a constituent (in this case accumulation) that is not yet fully constituted (indeed, in the abstract perspective posited by, and extending through Volume I,

5. Though it is not macroeconomic – see my Chapter 5 n. 3, and Bellofiore's Chapter 7, section 5, both in this volume.
6. He refers to Volume II for its analysis. Discrepancies especially are dealt with in Part Three of that volume.
7. For the analysis of 'these modified forms of surplus-value' he refers to Volume III.
8. 'Wir betrachten also zunächst die Akkumulation abstrakt, d. h. als bloßes Moment des unmittelbaren Produktionsprozesses.' As emphasized in the *Results* (published in 1933 – Appendix in Marx 1867F) the 'immediate' refers to the *Capital I* level of abstraction.
9. Cf. Marx, 1867MA: 530 and 1867F: 710.

we cannot yet grasp accumulation concretely). Second, a moment can have no isolated existence (it obviously cannot be isolated from everything presented so far in Volume I but, more importantly in the current context, it also has no existence in isolation from the presentation still to come in the following volumes). Indeed it is the analysis of something abstract.[10]

Next, Marx makes a second methodological remark, this time relating to the content of his particular abstractions. He says that we can nevertheless consider accumulation merely as moment of the current level of abstraction; in other words, it is adequate to do this provisionally (*vorläufig*), since dropping the assumptions 2 and 3 would hinder a pure (*reine*) analysis of accumulation:

> A pure analysis of the process, therefore, demands that we should, provisionally, disregard all phenomena that conceal the workings of its inner mechanism (F: 710 amended; G: 590).

Fowkes has 'exact' instead of 'pure' for *reine*; and he has 'for a time' instead of 'provisionally' for *vorläufig* (and Moore has the same). The 'inner' here refers, in my view, to the 'immediate process of production', that is, the capital–labour relation in general. In reference back to the first methodological remark, this does *not* mean that the 'inner mechanism' can have an isolated existence, *nor* that 'the inner working' would be unaffected (qualitatively or quantitatively) by the successive introduction into the presentation of additional phenomena (cf. the inner–outer pair in Hegel's *Logic*).[11]

In other (non-dialectical) words, Marx's assumptions here are not negligibility assumptions, but heuristic assumptions.

10. On the notion of 'moment' see also Reuten and Williams, 1989: 22.
11. To stay close to the metaphor, we could analyse the inner working of the heart and the blood circulation; but each of these 'inner' parts of the body stands in a physical and social relation to its external surroundings; the body's interaction affects the actual blood circulation and we may, for example, lose blood. Thus the body and its surroundings affect the blood circulation qualitatively and quantitatively. What is more, the heart and the blood circulation have no meaningful existence without the 'outer' body. That is to say, concretely commodities are not produced 'at their value' (et cetera) and this fact affects 'their' production and the accumulation of capital. (This is also a contribution to the discussion between Bellofiore and Moseley at the end of Chapter 7.)

2. Transformation of surplus-value into capital

2.1 The drive for and the force for accumulation

Accumulation of capital is the reconversion of surplus-value into capital. Its degree thus depends, *ceteris paribus*, on the part of surplus-value accumulated as capital. On the one hand this is the capitalist's 'act of will' and 'drive towards self-enrichment' (738–9). On the other hand, Marx indicates (739), with

> the development of capitalist production ... competition subordinates every individual capitalist to the immanent laws of capitalist production, as external and coercive laws. It compels him to keep extending his capital, so as to preserve it, and he can only extend it by means of progressive accumulation.

Nevertheless, 'with the growth of accumulation and wealth, the capitalist ceases to be merely the incarnation of capital'; 'there develops in the breast of the capitalist a Faustian conflict between the passion for accumulation and the desire for enjoyment' (740–1).

2.2 The dynamics of accumulation introduced: productive forces and accelerated accumulation

In this and the following section I summarize a number of Marx's statements in a formal way. At the same time I try to stay as close as possible to Marx's text; of course, any reading and summarizing are necessarily interpretative. Although I use a mathematical form (equations), what I do is not mathematics; rather I adopt a shorthand notation for purposes of precision and logical consistency checking.

I keep the equations as simple as possible, that is, in so far as Marx's text allows. Marx is not always explicit about whether the relations he posits are linear or non-linear. Whenever that is unclear I just phrase the relation as a function ($A = f(B)$). Determination should be read from right to left; if no determination is posited I use a $\equiv$ sign. An unspecified change in a variable is indicated by the prefix Δ. Thus $\Delta A = A_t - A_{t-1}$. Rates of growth are indicated by a circumflex. Thus $\hat{A} = \Delta A / A_{t-1}$.

In this chapter all capitalized symbols refer to values in monetary terms (thus calculated in a monetary dimension, e.g. £). All time indices have been suppressed; thus, for A read A_t (unless otherwise indicated). Time refers to a calender period (t), for example a year.

Marx introduces the dynamics of accumulation of capital in the fourth section of Chapter 24. Without always being very explicit about this, he now introduces fixed capital (i.e. capital that is only in part 'consumed' within the production period). I use the symbol K for capital. In order to keep transparent the connection with Marx's concepts and symbols as used in the middle part of *Capital I* (see my Chapter 5), I adopt as simplification the total constant capital (K_c) to be a multitude (μ) of the circulating constant capital C.[12] Note that μ may be taken as a temporary constant, but it is in fact variable and part of Marx's dynamics.

$$K \equiv \mu C + V \qquad\qquad [\mu > 1] \qquad\qquad \text{[definition] (1)}$$

Marx starts (747) by taking the accumulation of capital (ΔK) to be a given fraction ($\mathring{a}$) out of surplus-value (S):

$$\Delta K = \mathring{a}S \qquad\qquad [0 < \mathring{a} \leq 1] \qquad\qquad \text{[determination] (2)}$$

The magnitude of surplus-value depends on the rate of surplus-value (e) and on the magnitude of the initial capital:[13]

$$S = f(e; K) \qquad\qquad [f' > 0]^{14} \qquad\qquad \text{[determination] (3)}$$

Or also:

$$S = f(\Delta e) \qquad\qquad [f' > 0] \qquad\qquad \text{[determination] (3')}$$

(Marx is not explicit about time – the focus of Volume II. Nevertheless it should be noticed that if we consider a production period, S is an 'end of period' result, K a 'begin of period' stock and e a *process variable*, conditioned by the value of labour-power *and the labour process*. Having analysed the latter we may, for the sake of heuristic simplicity, take e each time again as a given. Being a process variable, there is nevertheless also a result for e (in the magnitude of surplus-value S). A difficulty

---

12. $K \equiv K_c + K_v$. More precisely we should have $K \equiv (\mu C_f + \tau C_c) + \upsilon V$, where: C_f is the component of instruments of labour; C_c the component of circulating constant capital; and τ and υ turn-over coefficients (Marx introduces turnover time only in *Capital II*, Part Two).

13. In the middle part of *Capital* the rate of surplus-value (e) has been explained by e^*, the rate of surplus labour to necessary labour (see my Chapter 5). On pages 751–2 Marx sets out why $\Delta K = f(K)$ is false (or perhaps we should say a false start – see the next section).

14. $f' > 0$ means that there is a positive relation between S and each of e and K.

in Marx's text is that he sometimes switches between these two notions of e without notification.[15])

Next, in refocusing his conclusions from Parts Three to Five towards the accumulation of capital, Marx considers the effect of changes in the productive forces of labour (pfl)[16] that press down commodity prices:[17]

$$\Delta\Pi = f(\Delta pfl) \qquad\qquad [f' < 0] \qquad\qquad \text{[determination] (4a)}$$

Increasing productive forces have a twofold effect on accumulation. First, because the physical surplus product increases, capitalists 'may' buy the same consumption basket with a smaller 'consumption-fund', hence the 'accumulation-fund' may increase. Thus the fraction å in equation (2) is turned into a variable depending on the development of the productive forces ('may' depending on the 'drive' and force for accumulation, which I abbreviate as dfa):[18]

$$å = f_1(dfa) + f_2(\Delta\Pi) \qquad\qquad [f_1' > 0; \ f_2' < 0] \qquad\qquad \text{[determination] (5)}$$

Thus:

$$å = f(dfa; \ \Delta pfl) \qquad\qquad [f' > 0] \qquad\qquad \text{[reduced form of 4–5] (A)}$$

15. The reconstruction in my Chapter 5 tried to take account of this. In terms of that chapter, we each time take *beta* as given.
16. The *effect* of rising 'productive forces' is a *potential* rise in productivity of labour (see also my Chapter 5). If Marx had lived a hundred years later he would perhaps have cast this in terms of techniques of production. Note that in this section he abstracts from the value composition of capital (or perhaps, he considers such changes in 'technique' that leave unaffected the *value* of means of production).
17. I take Π to be some composite indicator for prices (at the level of *Capital I*, i.e. on the basis of its assumptions, and particularly in abstraction from strictly monetary determinations of the price level). Today it might perhaps be interpreted as a particular price index.
    Equations with a number plus letter, e.g. (4a), will be amended in the course of the argument – into e.g. (4b). Capitalized equation indicators – e.g. (A) – are derived from other ones.
18. Pages 752–3. Note again the assumptions. It is only in *Capital II*, Part Three, that Marx considers the problems of sectoral adaptation of such switches from consumption to accumulation. In fact Marx's labour theory of value allows him to stylize all kinds of complications into a tractable shape.

The second effect is on the rate of exploitation. Let us first simply translate the value of labour-power per day (*VLP*) into the wage rate per hour (*W*) given some length of the working day (*h*).

$$W \equiv VLP/h \qquad \text{[definition] (6)}$$

Thus to the extent that the working day is a constant, we can use the wage rate and the *VLP* interchangeably.[19] Marx posits:

$$\Delta e = f(\Delta W) \qquad [f' < 0] \qquad \text{[determination] (7)}$$

Of course we know that this determination is defective and represents *merely one factor* (Marx 'freezes' changes in the labour process, including the intensity of labour). The value of labour-power (and the wage rate) is made up of a given 'real' component (some basket of commodities *w*) and a price component.

$$W \equiv w\Pi \qquad \text{[definition] (8)}$$

Thus:

$$\Delta W = f(\Delta pfl) \qquad [f' < 0] \qquad \text{[reduced form of 4 and 8] (B)}$$

Therefore the change in productive forces similarly affects the value of labour-power (or *W*) – the production of relative surplus-value, treated in Parts Four and Five. Hence the nominal wage is pressed down, and the rate of surplus-value up. All this *ceteris paribus*, we should add (see the next sections).

Taking (1)–(8) together we see how, *ceteris paribus*, the accumulation of capital (ΔK) depends on, first, K and the initial C/V division (eqn 1) – to which we will return in section 3 – and second on the development of the productive forces (Δpfl). Or, more precise, starting from an initial rate of growth of accumulation ($\hat{K}$), a change in that rate depends on changes in the productive forces:[20]

19. I expanded on this in section 2.5 of Chapter 5 above
20. For the productive forces I have used, in Chapter 5, the shorthand «*C/L*», or «*K/L*» if we include fixed capital. Although I believe that representation to be close to Marx, also for the current part (e.g. 'the value and mass of the means of production set in motion by a given quantity of labour increase as the labour becomes more productive' – 754; cf. 759), I refrain from adopting it here.

$$\Delta \hat{K} = f(\Delta pfl) \qquad\qquad [f' > 0] \qquad\qquad \text{[reduced form of 2–8] (C)}$$

Marx calls this 'accelerated accumulation' (e.g. 753; this terminology became fashionable in mainstream economics around 1935). Therefore:

> science and technology are formative [*bilden*] to a potential expansion of capital, independent of the prevailing magnitude of the functioning capital (F: 754; translation amended, cf. G: 632)[21].

In the next pages Marx clarifies that changes in the productive forces also impact on the replacement investment (and that it has depreciative effects); thus the change in *pfl* spreads gradually over the existing capital (753–4).

3. 'The general law of capitalist accumulation'

3.1 Interdependency of wage rate and rate of exploitation – 'the law of capitalist production'

I now turn to Chapter 25 of *Capital I*, 'The general law of capitalist accumulation': the investigation of 'the influence of the growth of capital on the fate of the working class'. Its 'most important factor', Marx writes, 'is the composition of capital, and the changes it undergoes in the course of the process of accumulation' (762). Since Marx, for the purposes of his first section, takes the 'composition of capital' as constant, I just present two definitions and postpone their discussion until later (section 3.2). The 'value composition of capital' (*vcc*) is the ratio of constant capital (*C*) to variable capital (*V*).

$$vcc \equiv C/V \qquad\qquad \text{[definition] (9)}$$

(In terms of equation (1): $vcc = \{(K/V) - 1\}\{1/\mu\}$.)

The 'organic composition of capital' (*occ*) is the ratio of the value of the means of production (*C*) to the labour working up those means of production (*l*) – the latter measured in hours.

$$occ_l \equiv C/l \qquad\qquad \text{[definition] (10)}$$

(In terms of equation (1): $occ_l = \{(K - V)/l\}\{1/\mu\}$.)

---

21. The translation misses both the 'formative' (*bilden*, rendered as 'give') and the 'potential' (*Potenz*). Of course they have to be *applied* for valorization. (See also the chapters of Smith and Murray in this volume.)

When the term 'composition of capital' is used without further specification, Marx writes (762), the organic composition is meant. As indicated, in this section he sets these constant – the same applies for the productive forces.

$$v\hat{c}c = 0 \qquad\qquad \text{[heuristic assumption] (11a)}$$

$$o\hat{c}c = 0 \qquad\qquad \text{[heuristic assumption] (12a)}$$

$$\Delta\Pi = f(\Delta pfl) = 0 \qquad\qquad \text{[heuristic assumption] (4b)}$$

Marx notices (763):

> If we assume that, while all other circumstances remain the same, the composition of capital also remains constant... then the demand for labour, and the fund for the subsistence of the workers, both clearly increase in the same proportion as the capital, and with the same rapidity.

Hence $\hat{L} = \hat{V} = \hat{K}$. Next he sets out how this, and especially the proportional growth of the middle term, is unlikely. Marx takes the 'value of labour-power' to be a historical datum around which the actual price of labour-power fluctuates. $w^*\Pi$ stands for this datum and $w'\Pi$ for the negative or positive fluctuation around it.[22]

$$W \equiv w\Pi \equiv (w^* + w')\Pi \qquad\qquad \text{[definition] (13)}$$

Therefore:

$$\hat{W} = \hat{w} \qquad\qquad \text{[reduced form of 4b and 13] (D)}$$

Wages may fluctuate because the growth in K may outrun the growth of labour-power (i.e. the supply), so inducing rising wages (763, 769). Accumulation then still goes on but at a lower rate (since the wage rise affects the rate of surplus-value and hence S). With the decreased rate of growth of accumulation, wages will decrease (770). Thus we have the relations (14) and (15a).

---

22. See also Bellofiore's Chapter 7. Marx began the text discussed in section 2.2 above by addressing wage reduction, thus dropping his previous assumption 'that wages were at least equal to the value of labour-power' (747–8).

$$\hat{w} = f(\hat{l}) \qquad\qquad [f' > 0] \qquad\qquad \text{[determination]} \ (14)$$

where $\hat{l}$ is the growth in the 'demand for workers' (763). This relation, including its 'right to left' determination, is of *key* importance to *all* of Marx's further reasoning in this chapter, including his critique of 'Malthusian' doctrines (section 3.3 below). This cannot be stressed too much. Marx expands on it at the beginning of the next section, where he refers approvingly to Adam Smith (not only is he usually 'moderate' in tributes to Smith, it is also one of the scarce 'in text' references – i.e. instead of in a footnote):[23] it is not the absolute magnitude but 'the degree of rapidity of that growth' in accumulation which is relevant for a rise of wages (772).

Marx posits *in this section* (763, indeed it is conditioned by 12a – cf. 772):

$$\hat{l} = \hat{K} \qquad\qquad\qquad\qquad \text{[determination]} \ (15a)$$

And hence:

$$\hat{w} = f(\hat{K}) \qquad\qquad [f' > 0] \qquad \text{[reduced form of 14–15a]} \ (E)$$

Marx lays particular stress on this relation by his formulation: 'To put it mathematically: the rate of accumulation is the independent, not the dependent variable; the rate of wages is the dependent, not the independent variable' (770).

Thus whereas the nominal wage is affected by the productive forces (equation B), the real wage is affected by the rate of accumulation (therefore also the nominal wage, *ceteris paribus*, the productive forces).

Hence we have what Marx calls *the law of capitalist production* (771), that is, the rate of growth of the real wage ($\hat{w}$) depends via the rate of growth in accumulation (eqn D) and the ratio of accumulation ($\hat{a}$ in eqn 2) on the rate of surplus-value (eqn 3):

$$\hat{w} = f(\Delta e) \qquad\qquad [f' > 0] \qquad \text{[reduced form of 2–3, 4b, 9–15a]} \ (F)$$

This is very interesting. We have the apparent paradox that an increase in the rate of exploitation generates an increase in the real wage rate.

---

23. That is, in the theoretical sections of *Capital*.

In fact it would seem (on the basis of the current conditions and *ceteris paribus* qualifications, especially 12a and 4b) that given some rate of exploitation, the real wage rate stabilizes at some level at which its rate of growth has become zero (or oscillates around that point). 'The rise of wages is therefore confined within limits that not only leave intact the foundations of the capitalist system, but also secure its reproduction on an increasing scale' (771); that is, most briefly, a positive rate of exploitation.

3.2 Increasing capital composition – the acceleration triple

In Section 2 of Chapter 25 Marx introduces the variation in the composition of capital, notably its increase.

Marx's definitions of his three variants of the capital composition (we have talked about two of them) are not crystal-clear. Their interpretation is of some importance to the interpretation of *Capital III*, Part Three – where the composition of capital reappears. However, for the general interpretation of the current Chapter 25, Marx's specific definitions are not very important. He knows that each concept has its limitation and he just shifts terms according to the state of his analysis (even if not always consistently).

Non-controversial is the value composition of capital (*vcc*), which is defined as (762):

$$vcc \equiv C/V \qquad\qquad \text{[definition] (9)}$$

Marx writes about the 'technical composition of capital' (*tcc*): 'As material, as it functions in the process of production, all capital is divided into means of production and living labour-power. This latter composition is determined by the relation between the mass of the means of production [*mp*] employed on the one hand, and the mass of labour necessary for their employment on the other [*l*]' (762). Thus we can safely render:

$$tcc \equiv mp/l$$

Of course this is no more than an intuitive notion, as especially *mp* cannot be measured without prices. Controversial is the term 'organic composition of capital' (*occ*). Marx writes a bit cryptically: 'There is a close correlation between the two [i.e. *vcc* and *tcc*]. To express this, I call the value composition of capital, in so far as it is determined by its technical composition and mirrors the changes in the latter, the organic composition of capital' (762). It seems to me that two interpretations square with Marx's text:

$$occ_y \equiv C/(V+S) \qquad \text{[definition] (16)}$$

$$occ_l \equiv C/l \qquad \text{[definition] (10)}$$

Note that over time this occ_l does not reflect change in the *tcc* to the extent that productivity rise is translated in price decrease (of means of production). The *vcc* and the occ_y bear similar problems in different ways.[24]

The differences are relevant in so far that each concept has its limitations. First, the *vcc* is not independent of wage changes (wage changes affect the ratio; and a wage change – as we will see – may be the effect of an initial change in the *vcc*). Thus it is no purely socio-technical ratio. Hence Marx evidently also needs another concept, which he reaches via the (intuitive) *tcc*. The occ_y seems useful to the extent that wage changes (and hence V) are directly translated into changes in surplus-value (S). However, Marx is concerned about another variable, namely the intensity of labour, and the occ_y is not independent of intensity changes, whereas the occ_l is (at least if l is measured in constant intertemporal clock hours – that is how I take it). Each of the concepts is relevant depending on the particular analysis.

Marx, throughout this chapter, is concerned with 'the average... composition of the total social capital' (762–3).

Now that these terminological issues have been addressed, I return to Marx's Section 2 where he introduces increase in the composition of capital. Thus:

$$\hat{vcc} > 0 \qquad \text{[thesis] (11b)}$$

$$\hat{occ} > 0 \qquad \text{[thesis] (12b)}$$

the development of the productivity of social labour becomes the most powerful lever of accumulation... Apart from natural conditions... the level of the social productivity of labour is expressed in the relative extent of the means of production that one worker, during a given

---

24. Marx was well aware of this and points at it several times (e.g. 774). See Fine and Harris (1979: 58–61) for a different interpretation/reconstruction building on this problematic.

time, with the same degree of intensity of labour-power, turns into products (F: 772–3; G: 650).

However, and as we will see in the next section in some more detail, this is not a linear process (774):

> The relative magnitude of the part of the price which represents the value of the means of production, or the constant part of the capital, is in direct proportion to the progress of accumulation, whereas the relative magnitude of the other part of the price, which represents the variable part of the capital, or the payment made for labour, is in inverse proportion to the progress of accumulation.

From the remainder of the section (and the next) it is obvious that Marx takes these proportions as variable, thus:

$$\hat{C} = \phi'\hat{K} \qquad [\phi' \text{ variable and } \phi' > 1] \qquad \text{[determination]}^{25} \text{ (11c)}$$

$$\hat{V} = \phi\hat{K} \qquad [\phi \text{ variable and } \phi < 1] \qquad \text{[determination] (11c')}$$

(The implication is a modified version of equation (E).) On the same page Marx writes about 'the variable part of capital ... that this by no means thereby excludes the possibility of a rise in its absolute magnitude' (thus $\phi > 0$). He also writes that these changes 'provide only an approximate indication of the change in the composition of its material constituents' (i.e. the *tcc*) because of the price changes that go along with 'the increasing productivity of labour' (774). (Thus implicitly he says that these price changes may unevenly affect the two components.)

This increasing productivity along with increasing productive forces and the changing composition of capital is the main theme of the rest of this section. Without deriving further conclusions, Marx connects the changing capital composition with the production of relative surplus-value (Part Four) and price decrease (Chapter 24, discussed in my section 2.2). Recall the synthetical equation:

$$\Delta\hat{K} = f(\Delta pf l) \qquad [f' > 0] \qquad \text{[reduced form of 2–8] (C)}$$

---

25. The determination here or in the next equation lies in the variable ϕ' which represents the result of capitalist behaviour directed at accelerating accumulation.

First Marx posits the mutual dependency of these two factors, in fact already anticipated by the end of Chapter 24, Section 4. Because of this mutual dependency 'it appears' [*erscheint*] – this is no delusion – that 'All the forces of labour project themselves as forces of capital' (F: 756 – amended; cf. G: 634). Here he writes:

> all methods of raising the social productive forces that grow up on this basis [capitalist production] are at the same time methods for the increased production of surplus-value, or surplus product, which is in its turn the formative element of accumulation. They are, therefore, also methods for the production of capital by capital, or methods for its accelerated accumulation (F: 775 – amended; G: 653).

Next he connects these methods for accelerating the accumulation of capital with the composition of capital (776):

> These two economic factors [eqn C] bring about, in the compound ratio of the impulses they give to each other, that change in the technical composition of capital by which the variable component becomes smaller and smaller as compared with the constant component.

Thus we have the triple accelerating growth of:

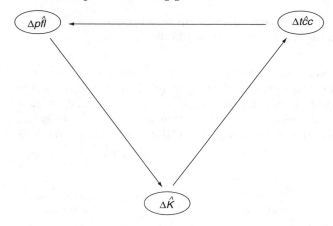

The working out of this schema is postponed until Marx's (and my) next section.

The remainder of the current section is devoted to the 'tendency to centralization of capital'. In the face of Marx's method it is rather surprising to find that, here, it is a phenomenon related to the competition *between* capitals, which should have been dealt with in or after Part Two of *Capital III*. Marx is aware of the limitations of his analysis (777): 'The laws of this centralization of capitals...cannot be developed here. A few brief factual indications must suffice' (these are provided in about three pages).[26] I merely note that Marx (here) does not treat centralization in reference to the cycle.

3.3 Progressive growth – a dialogue on limitations of the theory so far

It is obvious from the text of Chapter 25, and especially Section 3, that Marx struggles with the dynamics consequent on the rising composition of capital. In a dialogue-like fashion he moves from argument to counter-argument (though in the sub-headings below I have made this process more explicit than it is in Marx's presentation).

Before reporting on this 'dialogue' I should make a terminological point. Readers of *Capital* may wonder why Marx when addressing 'unemployment' apparently uses such bombastic terminology: 'reserve army of labour', 'surplus population', or 'redundant working population'. He may have had his reasons for the particular choice, but the simple point is that in his day the term 'unemployment' (or its German equivalent) just did not exist.[27]

(A) *Progressive growth.* Marx begins by setting out the (general?) effect of a rising capital composition on labour:

> the demand for labour...falls progressively with the growth of the total capital, instead of rising in proportion to it, as was previously assumed [Section 1]...and at an accelerated rate...With the growth of the total capital, its variable constituent...does admittedly increase, but in a constantly [*beständig*] diminishing proportion (781–2; G: 658)[28].

---

26. I am not suggesting that anything introduced should be grounded at that same level of abstraction. I question the systematic need for introducing it at all here. There is no need. (In fact it plays a role in the rhetoric of the brief Chapter 32 – a chapter loaded with assertions instead of arguments.)
27. Rodenburg (forthcoming) provides further details.
28. Here and elsewhere I insert the German term *beständig*. For 'constant' in the mathematical sense of unchanging the German would likely be *konstant* (or perhaps *gleichbleibend* or *unveränderlich*).

Hence the *ceteris paribus* relation of Section 1

$$\hat{I} = \hat{K} \qquad\qquad \text{[determination] (15a)}$$

is modified into an exponential relation: I increases with K, but at a decreasing rate:

$$\hat{I} = \hat{K}^{\phi} \qquad [\phi \text{ variable and } 0 < \phi < 1] \quad \text{[determination] (15b)}$$

Similarly:

$$\hat{V} = \hat{K}^{\phi''} \qquad [\phi'' \text{ variable and } 0 < \phi'' < 1] \quad \text{[determination] (11d)}$$

(B) Continuous accelerated accumulation with pauses. It is, however, more complicated, as the acceleration seems to occur with intervals: 'The intermediate pauses in which accumulation works as simple extension of production on a given technical basis are shortened' (782). Apart from this, the 'accelerated relative diminution of the variable component [of capital] ... produces ... a relatively redundant working population' (782). (Thus he implicitly assumes something near to constant population growth, or at least one that does not decelerate to the extent that accumulation accelerates.)

(C) Periodic changes. Next he qualifies this (782–3, italics added):

If we consider the total social capital ... the movement of its accumulation sometimes causes periodic changes ...; in all spheres, the *increase* of the variable part of the capital, and therefore of the number of workers employed by it, is always connected with violent fluctuations and the *temporary production of a surplus population*, whether this takes the more striking form of the extrusion of workers already employed or the less evident, but not less real, form of a greater difficulty in absorbing the additional working population through its customary outlets.

This sentence contains some cryptic elements, but the idea seems clear. In a half-page footnote he shows census figures of employment for 1851 and 1861, diverging branch-wise. Note that the periodic changes or fluctuations are not theorized, but implanted into the presentation.[29]

Thus under *A* (and next *B*) Marx posits a specified recapitulation of his theory of Section 2. The fluctuations (*C*), however, do not fit the theory developed so far.

(*D*) *Once again progressive growth.* Then again he redresses (783–4, italics added):

> The working population ... produces both the accumulation of capital and the means by which it is itself made relatively superfluous; and it does this *to an extent which is always increasing.* This is a law of population peculiar to the capitalist mode of production.

(*E*) *Cyclical path as characteristic.* But once more he shifts perspective (785–6, italics added; cf. G: 661–2):

> The path characteristically described by modern industry, which takes the form of a decennial cycle (interrupted by smaller oscillations) of periods of average activity, production at high pressure, crisis, and stagnation, *depends* on the constant [*beständigen*] formation, the greater or less absorption, and the reformation of the industrial reserve army ... Just as the heavenly bodies always repeat a certain movement, once they have been flung into it, so also does social production, once it has been flung into this movement of alternate expansion and contraction. Effects become causes in their turn, and the various vicissitudes of the whole process ... take on the form of periodicity.

This is interesting, but in fact Marx appends an empirical phenomenon to the theory without explaining it, i.e. without theory (the metaphor is a phenomenal analogy, no analogous explanation). In particular, Marx does not tell how the phases of this 'path' relate to the development of capital composition or all of – what I have called – the 'acceleration triple'. It is interesting because he posits the obvious limitations (empirically) of the theory so far (good scientific practice).

29. Not only would an 'increase ... in the rapidity of the change in the organic composition of capital' (783) itself require explanation, more important is that it does not explain cyclical turning points, nor why 'pauses' would be associated (if so) with downturns and increasing surplus population (if so). A theory can be constructed on the basis of these elements (and others – see *Capital III*, Part Three), but Marx does not do it here.

(F) *Wages.* A final issue enters the dialogue, namely wage increase.[30] Marx denies any relation between population growth and the decennial cycle (he cites Malthus: 'From the nature of a population, an increase of labourers cannot be brought into market in consequence of a particular demand till after the lapse of 16 or 18 years' – 787). He also rejects the doctrine that 'restraint' on the part of the working population should be the remedy for the diminution of the 'surplus population' and so the impulse to (real) wage increase (798). Instead Marx posits: (1) the dynamic of capitalist production – with its main element of a rising composition of capital – creates a 'relative surplus population' (the 'progressive growth' thesis – A and D in the dialogue); (2) wage changes do *not* depend on the absolute level of the surplus population, *nor* on the absolute level, or state, of the accumulation of capital: they depend (Adam Smith's insight) on the *change* in the demand for labour. Thus (790):

Taking them as a whole, the general movements of wages are exclusively regulated by the expansion and contraction of the industrial reserve army, and this in turn corresponds to the periodic alternations of the industrial cycle. They are not therefore determined by the variations of the absolute numbers of the working population, but by . . . the extent to which it is alternately absorbed and set free.

It may be tempting to read into this quote (and the following) – as many have done – a 'labour shortage' theory of the cycle (in which case, to begin with, the first sentence would have to be a tautology). No, the first part of the first sentence makes Adam Smith's point, and the second part *refers* to the periodic cycle. Marx does not posit the wage rate mechanism to *explain* the cycle; the wage movements *correspond* to it (and if, instead, he believed wage movements to be causative he would certainly have said so). The second sentence combats the Malthusian doctrine.

The next quote (equally from page 790) follows the same pattern – ending with a reference to the generational (16-or 18-year lapse) versus the decennial issue.

30. All along Marx is aware that wage changes affect the value composition of capital (788–9). Aside from the general line of the argument – but important in itself – Marx indicates that 'with the progress of accumulation' wages may increase along with increasing intensity of labour. This is not particularly related to the cycle, moreover intensity increase generally reinforces the 'production of a relative surplus population' – i.e. relatively less labour working at higher intensity.

The appropriate law for modern industry, with its decennial cycles and periodic phases... is the law of the regulation of the demand and supply of labour by the alternate expansion and contraction of capital...It would be utterly absurd, in place of this, to lay down a law according to which the movement of capital depended simply on the movement of the population.

Thus, wages are not determining for they are determined by the growth of accumulation of capital.

3.4 The final two sections

The final two sections of Chapter 25 contain no new theoretical analysis. Section 5 (some 70 pages) provides empirical illustrations for the theses advanced in the chapter. Section 4 begins with a number of 'surplus population' distinctions (floating, latent and stagnant). Then Marx summarizes the 'general law' – the cycle, though, does not appear in this summary. We have the one moment of the acceleration triple and their effect on the working population.

Marx sets out that, on the one hand (for those employed), the worker is degraded to 'an appendage of a machine' and alienated from 'the intellectual potentialities of the labour process in the same proportion as science is incorporated in it as an independent power' (a conclusion from the middle part of the book). Therefore, 'in proportion as capital accumulates, the situation of the worker, be his payment high or low, must grow worse'. On the other hand (for those not employed), we have 'an accumulation of misery' for the surplus population (799).

Why does Marx, in this section, posit 'the general law' apparently unqualified? In the concluding section I expand on theory-systematic aspects; here I address but one theory-empirical aspect.

On the basis of the triple acceleration theory developed through into Section 3, the demand for labour should fall progressively with the growth of capital. However, Marx knows that empirically the development is cyclical. Thus his theory is incomplete (it might be wrong of course). This theoretical problem might have been overcome by combining his theory with what was later called a 'labour-shortage' theory of the cycle.[31] He seems to have the material before him to posit such

---

31. A major proponent is Itoh (1988: ch. 9). For references see Clarke (1994), who – to be sure – does not take this view.

a theory, but he does not do it.[32] Instead he makes an empirical reference to the cycle.

But this empirical attitude seems to work in two ways. On the one hand Marx is aware of 'a ten-year cycle' (in fact, Marx was one of the first to put it on the economists' research agenda). On the other hand the empirical facts of his day all pointed in the direction of increasing degradation and increasing misery of the working population. Faced with this, the triple accelerator of increasing accumulation and increasing composition of capital together with increasing labour productivity (the reverse of Ricardo) seemed of great explanatory power.

Still, in Section 4 Marx inserts a seemingly fairly weak warning about the generality of the law: 'Like all other laws, it is modified in its working [*Verwirklichung*] by many circumstances, the analysis of which does not concern us here [*nicht hierher gehört*]' (798; G: 674). Note that the warning in the German text is much stronger. In the latter it is not, say, the 'precise working' that gets modified, but its 'reality' – its 'actualization' (*Verwirklichung*).[33]

4. Summary and methodological conclusions

Throughout the three volumes of *Capital* Marx presents the dynamics of the accumulation of capital in a number of steps. These represent, first, a movement from 'inner determinations' to outer determinations (no less important). The inner determinations are discussed in *Capital I* and in section 1.3 I set out the delineation of the latter's terrain. Second, both between and within the terrains, these steps also represent a movement from simple accounts to more complex ones.

In sections 2 and 3 we have seen how Marx proceeds in this respect. He first discusses the effect of changing productive forces of labour on the acceleration of accumulation (keeping real wages and the composition of capital constant and neglecting any problems of the growth of labour) (section 2.2). Next he discusses the effect of accumulation of capital on the growth of labour employment and the possible real wage changes along with it – resulting in an oscillating growth in real

---

32. Cf. the relations posited in Section 1, my 3.1. Recall what Marx said about equation (E): 'the rate of wages is the dependent, not the independent variable'. As we know from *Capital III*, Part Three – drafted before the publication of *Capital I* – his theory of the acceleration triple can be developed into a theory of the cycle (see Reuten, 2004, for the textual evidence based on Marx's manuscripts).

33. With Hegel's *Logic* in mind the qualification is even heavier. (Aveling's translation – Marx, 1867MA: 603 – is the same: 'working'.)

wage rate determined by an oscillating growth rate of exploitation (here keeping constant the productive forces, prices and the composition of capital) (section 3.1). Finally he drops all the assumptions just mentioned (keeping intact those set out in 1.3) and so arrives at what I have called the acceleration triple of capital accumulation, productive forces of labour and composition of capital (section 3.2). Taking their multiple interaction together at first seems to result in a continuously growing 'surplus population' (unemployment is the later term). As Marx sets out, however, this is contrary to the empirical observation of a fairly regular cyclical movement. Thus the theory is incomplete, because, in Marx's view, a theory of the cycle cannot be developed at this level of abstraction (more is needed: the terrains and concepts developed in Volumes II and III of *Capital*); instead he just appends empirical observations to the theory developed so far and postpones explanation (and synthesis).

All this is theoretically and historically (1867) most exciting. From the point of view of a systematic-dialectical methodology (and many other methodologies) all this is fine. We reach a point at which the presentation so far is insufficient, so we must go on (in this case to the analysis to be covered in other volumes of *Capital*). It is also acceptable, at this point, to *blend out* (or bracket) the insufficiency, on the condition that it is made crystal-clear that this 'blending out' is procedural. Marx is reluctant to do this (the blending out) in his Section 3 of Chapter 25 (section 3.3 above); but he does do it in his summarizing Section 4. In the latter section Marx also gives a procedural warning, but in the English text this warning is greatly deemphasized (section 3.4 above). However, to fully understand the warning (in both languages) the reader must remember that about ninety pages earlier Marx signals that he is presenting a '*pure* analysis of the process' which 'demands that we should, provisionally, disregard all phenomena that conceal the workings of its inner mechanism' (710). (English readers were not much helped by the translator's rendering of *reine Analyse* into 'exact analysis'.) What is more, to understand that 'inner' and 'outer' mechanisms are necessarily *inseparably* connected, the reader has to have at least 'leafed' through Hegel's *Logic*.[34]

This must give rise (and has given rise) to misunderstandings about Marx's 'general law of capitalist accumulation'. The neglect that Marx's general law is merely posited as a 'moment' has been fostered by the

---

34. This is a paraphrase of Marx in a letter to Engels at the time (1858) when he drafted *Capital*.

view Engels expressed in his Preface to the English edition of *Capital I* (1887): namely, that Volume I is 'in a great measure a whole in itself, and has for twenty years ranked as an independent work'. Although, strictly speaking, the indication 'whole *in itself'* is correct, Engels's statement carries the impression that a missing of Volumes II and III is no big deal.

As indicated, in Volume I Marx does not present – and methodologically could not present – a theory of capital centralization or a theory of the cycle. *A fortiori* he presents no labour-shortage theory of the cycle. In section 3.3 (especially its heading F) I have provided textual evidence for my interpretation. What is more, only a little reconstruction of the relationships that Marx posits might generate a cyclical *pattern*. It would be a grave underestimation of Marx (and all of his insights on dynamics point against it) to believe that he was not aware of this. He just did not want to posit this theory, at the level of the 'pure' 'inner mechanism' of the production process of capital.

References

Superscripts indicate first and other relevant editions; the last mentioned year in the bibliography is the edition cited.

Bellofiore, Riccardo (2003), Marx and the macro-monetary foundation of micro-economics, Chapter 5 in this volume.

Clarke, Simon (1994), *Marx's Theory of Crisis* (London/New York: Macmillan/St Martin's Press).

Fine, Ben and Laurence Harris (1979), *Rereading Capital* (London: Macmillan).

Itoh, Makoto (1988), *The Basic Theory of Capitalism* (London: Macmillan).

Marx, Karl (1867^1G, 1890^4), *Das Kapital, Kritik der politischen ökonomie, Band I, Der Produktionsprozeß des Kapitals* (MEW 23) (Berlin: Dietz Verlag, 1973).

— (1867^1MA, 1883^3), *Capital, A Critical Analysis of Capitalist Production, Volume I* (trans. of the 3rd German edn by Samuel Moore and Edward Aveling (1887^1)) (London: Lawrence & Wishart, 1974).

— (1867^1F, 1890^4), *Capital, A Critique of Political Economy, Volume I* (trans. of the 4th German edn by Ben Fowkes (1976^1)) (Harmondsworth: Penguin, 1976).

Murray, Patrick (2000–2), Marx's 'truly social' labour theory of value: Part I, Abstract labour in Marxian value theory, *Historical Materialism*, 6: 27–66; Reply to Geert Reuten, *Historical Materialism* 10/1: 155–76.

— (2003), The social and material transformation of production by capital: formal and real subsumption in *Capital*, Volume I, Chapter 9 in this volume.

Reuten, Geert (2003a), Karl Marx: his work and the major changes in its interpretation, in Warren Samuels, Jeff Biddle and John Davis (eds), *The Blackwell Companion to the History of Economic Thought* (Oxford: Blackwell, 148–66).

— (2003b), Productive force and the degree of intensity of labour, Chapter 5 in this volume.

— (2004), 'Zirkel vicieux' or trend fall?; the course of the profit rate in Marx's 'Capital III', *History of Political Economy*, Spring issue (forthcoming).

298   *The Constitution of Capital*

Reuten, Geert and Michael Williams (1989), *Value-Form and the State: The Tendencies of Accumulation and the Determination of Economic Policy in Capitalist Society* (London/New York: Routledge).

Rodenburg, Peter (forthcoming), PhD thesis in preparation, University of Amsterdam, Department of Economics.

Smith, Tony (1990), *The Logic of Marx's Capital* (Albany, NY: State University of New York Press).

— (2003), Technology and history in capitalism: Marxian and neo-Schumpeterian perspectives, Chapter 8 in this volume.

Name Index

Key: f = figure; n = footnote [number of footnote given only when there is more than one footnote on the same page] 16n = footnote on page sixteen (only one footnote on that page) 17(n23) = note 23 on page 17 (to distinguish it from note 22 on the same page); t = table; **bold** extended discussion or heading emphasized in main text.

Subject Index